Y0-BCF-183

ILLNESS AND HEALTH CARE IN THE ANCIENT NEAR EAST

The Role of the Temple in Greece, Mesopotamia, and Israel

HARVARD SEMITIC MUSEUM PUBLICATIONS

Lawrence E. Stager, General Editor

HARVARD SEMITIC MONOGRAPHS

edited by
Peter Machinist

Number 54
ILLNESS AND HEALTH CARE
IN THE ANCIENT NEAR EAST
The Role of the Temple in
Greece, Mesopotamia, and Israel

by
Hector Avalos

Hector Avalos

ILLNESS AND HEALTH CARE IN THE ANCIENT NEAR EAST

The Role of the Temple in Greece, Mesopotamia, and Israel

Scholars Press
Atlanta, Georgia

ILLNESS AND HEALTH CARE IN THE ANCIENT NEAR EAST
The Role of the Temple in Greece, Mesopotamia, and Israel

by
Hector Avalos

Library of Congress Cataloging in Publication Data

Avalos, Hector.
    Illness and health care in the ancient Near East : the role of the temple in Greece, Mesopotamia, and Israel / Hector Avalos.
        p.   cm. — (Harvard Semitic museum publications. Harvard Semitic monographs ; no. 54)
    Includes bibliographical references and index.
    ISBN 0-7885-0098-8 (alk. paper)
    1. Healing—Religious aspects—Comparative studies. 2. Healing in the Bible. 3. Temples—Greece. 4. Temples—Iraq. 5. Temples—Palestine. 6. Greece—Religion. 7. Iraq—Religion. 8. Israel—Religion. I. Title. II. Series: Harvard Semitic museum publications. III. Series: Harvard Semitic monographs ; no. 54.
BL65.M4A83   1995
306.4'61—dc20   95-190
                                CIP

Printed in the United States of America
on acid-free paper

ILLNESS AND HEALTH CARE IN THE ANCIENT NEAR EAST
The Role of the Temple in Greece, Mesopotamia, and Israel

xiv

Preface

The present work is a revised and expanded version of a dissertation that I completed at Harvard in 1991. It is a study of the health care systems of Greece, Mesopotamia, and Israel. On a more general level, this volume represents an attempt to combine the fields in which I was formally trained, anthropology and biblical and Near Eastern studies. I hope that I have done justice to them. A planned companion study will treat the health care systems of Anatolia, and perhaps Phoenicia.

I wish to thank my thesis director, F. M. Cross, who provided invaluable comments for which I shall always be grateful. Professors Paul D. Hanson, P. Steinkeller, Larry Stager, and D. Mitten are responsible for many improvements, and none of the deficiencies of this work. Prof. Piotr Michalowski (U. of Michigan) also provided many useful comments on the second chapter. Professors R. D. Biggs (U. of Chicago), Byron Good (Harvard), Patricia Smith (Hebrew University), Gary Beckman (U. of Michigan), and H. Remus (Wilfrid Laurier University) provided many useful bibliographic references and comments. As always, I am grateful to Peter Machinist for his friendship and advice throughout my academic career.

Some of the newer material and reformulations in my thought on illness and health care were added while I was at the U. of North Carolina at Chapel Hill as a Carolina Minority Postdoctoral Fellow, a program that owes its vitality to Dr. Mary Sue Coleman, Vice Chancellor for Graduate Studies and Research. I thank Dr. Coleman, and Professors Jack Sasson (Religious Studies) and James Peacock (Anthropology) for being gracious hosts and discussing various aspects of my topic with me. Prof.

Wilbert Gesler, a specialist in medical geography at UNC-CH read the chapter on Asclepius, and provided some useful comments.

I am grateful for the permission granted by Andromeda, Oxford Limited to reproduce Figure 1. Prof. Barthel Hrouda of the Institut für Vorderasiatische Archäologie at the Universität München kindly provided permission to reproduce Figures 2-5 from his wonderful volumes on Isin.

Amy Richter, Mark LaRocca-Pitts, Carey Walsh, Fook Kong Wong, Josh Friedman, and Becky Schmitz formed a band of trusty assistants who helped to collect the library materials needed for my research, and they proofread various versions of it.

I am extremely grateful for the financial support provided by a grant from the Ford Foundation. In addition, the preparation of this research was made possible by a grant from the Memorial Foundation for Jewish Culture, and by a grant from the Dorothy Danforth Compton Foundation. A computer and other support provided by my colleagues (Gary Comstock, Bill Robinson, and Mary Sawyer) at Iowa State University were indispensable in finishing the final draft of my manuscript. Most of all, I would like to thank my wife Lisa for her patience and support during the preparation of this book.

Pain is a phenomenon whose appearance exhausts its reality.
Inspired by R. Rorty, *The Mirror of Nature*
(Princeton, 1979) 30.

ABBREVIATIONS

A. Bibliographical

AA	*American Anthropologist.*
AB	*Anchor Bible.*
ABD	D. N. Freedman et al. *The Anchor Bible Dictionary.* New York: Doubleday, 1992.
ABL	R. F. Harper. *Assyrian and Babylonian Letters I-XIV.* London and Chicago, 1892-1914.
AfO	*Archiv für Orientforschung.*
AHw	W. von Soden. *Akkadisches Handwörterbuch.* Wiesbaden, 1959-1981.
AIPHOS	*Annuaire de l'Institut de Philologie et d'Histoire Orientale et Slaves.*
AJPA	*American Journal of Physical Anthropology.*
AMT	R. C. Thompson. *Assyrian Medical Texts.* Oxford, 1923.
ANETS 8	*Ancient Near Eastern Texts and Studies 8 =* W. W. Hallo, B. W. Jones and G. L. Mattingly, eds. *The Bible in the Light of Cuneiform Literature; Scripture in Context III;* Lewiston, New York, 1990.
AOAT	*Alter Orient und Altes Testament.* Kevelaer, Neukirchen-Vluyn.
AOS	American Oriental Society.
ArOr	*Archiv Orientalni.*
AS	*Assyriological Studies.* Chicago, 1931-.
BaM	*Baghdader Mitteilungen.*
BAM	F. Köcher. *Die babylonisch-assyrische Medizin in Texten und Untersuchungen.* 4 volumes; Berlin, 1963-80.

BARev	*Biblical Archaeology Review.*
BASOR	*Bulletin of the American Schools of Oriental Research.*
BBR	H. Zimmern. *Beiträge zur Kenntnis der babylonischen Religion.* Leipzig, 1901.
BTB	*Biblical Theology Bulletin.*
BWL	W. Lambert. *Babylonian Wisdom Literature.* Oxford, 1959.
BZAW	Beihefte zur *ZAW.*
CAD	*The Assyrian Dictionary of the Oriental Institute of Chicago.* Chicago, 1956-.
CBQ	*Catholic Biblical Quarterly.*
CH	Code of Hammurabi. Citations follow the edition of G. R. Driver and J. C. Miles. *The Babylonian Laws.* Oxford, 1955.
CMHE	F. M. Cross, *Canaanite Myth and Hebrew Epic.* Cambridge, Mass., 1973.
CT	*Cuneiform Tablets from the Babylonian Tablets in the British Museum.* London, 1896-.
DB	F. Vigoroux, ed. *Dictionaaire de la Bible.* 5 volumes; Paris, 1895-1912.
EA	J. A. Knudtzon. *Die El Amarna Tafeln.* Leipzig, 1915.
ExpTim	*Expository Times.*
HSM	Harvard Semitic Monographs.
HTR	*Harvard Theological Review.*
HUCA	*Hebrew Union College Annual,* Cincinnati.
IB I, II, III	B. Hrouda et al., eds., *Isin-Išān Baḥrīyāt I: Die Ergebnisse der Ausgrabungen 1973-1974.* München: Bayerische Akademie der Wissenschaften, 1977; B. Hrouda, et al., eds., *Isin-Išān Baḥrīyāt II: Die Ergebnisse*

der Ausgrabungen 1975-1978. München: Bayerische Akademie der Wissenschaften, 1981; B. Hrouda, et al., *Isin-Išān Baḥrīyāt III: Die Ergebnisse der Ausgrabungen 1983-1984.* München: Bayerische Akademie der Wissenschaften, 1987.

IDB   G. A. Buttrick, ed. *The Interpreter's Dictonary of the Bible.* 4 Volumes; Nashville, 1962.

IDBSup   K. Crim, ed. *The Interpreter's Dictonary of the Bible Supplementary Volume.* Nashville, 1976.

IEJ   *Israel Exploration Journal.*

ILOT   S.R. Driver, *Introduction to the Literature of the Old Testament.* 13th ed.; Edinburgh, 1913.

JANES   *Journal of the Ancient Near Eastern Society of Columbia University.*

JAOS   *Journal of the Americal Oriental Society.*

JBL   *Journal of Biblical Literature.*

JCS   *Journal of Cuneiform Studies.*

JJS   *Journal of Jewish Studies.*

JNES   *Journal of Near Eastern Studies.*

JRAS   *Journal of the Royal Asiatic Society.*

JSOT   *Journal for the Study of the Old Testament.*

K   Texts from Kuyunjik; Cf. C. J. Mullo-Weir, "Four Hymns to Gula," *JRAS* (1929) 8-15.

KAR   E. Ebeling. *Keilschrifttexte aus Assur religiösen Inhalts.*

KTS   J. Lewy. *Keilschrifttexte in den Antiken-Museen zu Stambul. Die Altassyrischen Texte vom Kültepe.* Constantinople, 1926.

KTU	M. Dietrich, O. Loretz, and J. Sanmartín. *Die keilalphabetische Texte aus Ugarit.*
LABS	S. Parpola, *Letters from Assyrian and Babylonian Scholars* (State Archives of Assyria 10; Helsinki: Helsinki University Press, 1993).
LAS	S. Parpola, *Letters from Assyrian Scholars to the Kings Esarhaddon and Assurbanipal* I, II, AOAT 5/1, 5/2, Kevelaer, Neukirchen-Vluyn, 1970, 1983.
LKA	E. Ebeling. *Literarische Keilschrifttexte aus Assur.* Berlin:Akademie Verlag, 1953.
LKU	A. Falkenstein. *Literarische Texte aus Uruk.* Berlin, 1931.
Maqlû	G. Meier. *Die assyrische Beschwörungs-sammlung Maqlû. AfO* 2; Berlin, 1937.
MSL	*Materialen zum sumerischen Lexicon.* Rome, 1937-.
NCBC	*The New Century Bible Commentary.* Grand Rapids, Mich.
OECT	*Oxford Editions of Cuneiform Texts.*
OIAR	*Oriental Institute Annual Report.* U. of Chicago.
OIP	*Oriental Institute Publications.* Chicago.
Or	*Orientalia.*
PBS	*Publications of the Babylonian Section, University Museum, University of Pennsylvania.* Philadelphia.
PEQ	*Palestine Exploration Quarterly.*
PKTA	E. Ebeling. *Parfümrezepte und kultische Texte aus Assur.* Rome, 1950.
RA	*Revue d'assyriologie et de archéologie orientale.*

RB	*Revue biblique.*
RevQ	*Revue de Qumran.*
RIME	*The Royal Inscriptions of Mesopotamia.* Toronto.
RLA	*Reallexicon der Assyriologie.* Leipzig, Berlin and New York, 1932- .
RMA	R. C. Thompson. *The Reports of the Magicians and Astrologers of Niniveh and Babylon.* London, 1900.
RSO	*Rivista degli studi orientali.*
RTA	E. Ebeling, "*Religiose Texte aus Assur,*" *ZDMG* 74-75 (1920-21) 175-177.
SEL	*Studi epigrafici e linguistici sul Vicino Oriente antico.* Verona.
SJLA	*Studies in Judaism in Late Antiquity.*
SLT	E. Chiera, *Sumerian Temple Texts from the Temple School of Nippur; OIP 11*; Chicago, 1929.
SRT	E. Chiera, *Sumerian Religious Texts.* Upland, 1924.
StBoT	*Studien zu den Bogazköy-Texten.* Wiesbaden, 1965- .
STT	O. R. Gurney, J. J. Finkelstein, P. Hulin. *The Sultantepe Tablets* I, II. London, 1957, 1964.
TA	*Tel Aviv.*
TCL	*Tablettes cunéiformes. Museé du Louvre* Paris, 1910- .
TCS	*Texts from Cuneiform Sources.* Locust Valley, New York.
TDOT	J. Botterweck and H. Ringgren, eds., *Theological Dictionary of the Old Testament* . Grand Rapids, Mich., 1974- .

TDP	R. Labat, *Traité akkadien de diagnostics et pronostics médicaux.* Leiden, 1951.
ThLZ	*Theologische Literaturzeitung.*
TWAT	J. Botterweck and H. Ringgren, eds., *Theologisches Wörterbuch Zum Alten Testaments.* Berlin. 1971- .
UF	*Ugarit-Forschungen.* Kevelaer, Neukirchen-Vluyn.
VAT	*Tablets in the collections of the Staatliche Museen, Berlin.*
VS	*Vorderasiatische Schriftdenkmäler der Königlichen Museen zu Berlin.*
VT	*Vetus Testamentum.*
W	Texts from Warka as numbered in E. von Weiher, *Spätbabylonischer Texte aus Uruk* Berlin: G. Mann, 1983.
WzM	*Wege zum Menschen.*
YOS	*Yale Oriental Series, Babylonian Texts.* New Haven, 1915- .
ZDMG	*Zeitschrift für die Deutschen Morgendländischen Gesellschaft.*
ZKT	*Zeitschrift für Katholische Theologie.*

B. Other

ANE	Ancient Near East
Chr	the Chronicler (or Chronicles when preceded by 1 or 2)
cons.	consultant
DN	divine name
DtrH	Deuteronomistic History
ED	Early Dynastic (period)

G/N	Gula/Ninisina
H	Holiness Code
LXX	Septuagint
MT	Masoretic Text
OB	Old Babylonian
obv.	obverse
P	Priestly source
r.	reverse
rec.	recommendation
Suppl.	Supplement
s. v.	*sub verbo*, under the word in question

INTRODUCTION

A. JUSTIFICATION AND PURPOSE OF THIS STUDY

Among all of the features of the human experience, illness has been one of the most constant. The earliest known written languages evolved in the ancient Near East, and it was also there that human beings first began to write about illness and health care. Mesopotamia, Greece, and Egypt all produced an extensive corpus of medical literature which has been studied intensively in the last century.

The literature of Israel, and particularly the Bible, also has a variety of ideas about illness and health care which have proved influential in Western civilization. But while some scholars praise the supposed lack of "magical" healing procedures used in ancient Israel, others would argue that the ancient Hebrews had no real physicians or that their ideas were not as "scientific" as those of other Near Eastern cultures. Such discussions show that the nature and complexity of health care in ancient Israel have not received the proper attention. One reason for this misjudgment of the nature and complexity of the Israelite health care system is that most scholars who focus on ancient Israel remain unaware of, or uninterested in, medical anthropology.[1]

---

[1]Even many scholars who focus on the sociology of ancient Israel focus on the political, not the medical, aspects of the society. Recent examples include: R. E. Clement, ed., *The World of Ancient Israel: Sociological, Anthropological and Political Perspectives* (New York:

For example, Klaus Seybold and Ulrich B. Mueller[2] have provided one of the most recent and comprehensive surveys on health care in the biblical traditions, but they have given only cursory attention to various sociological aspects of illness and health care in ancient Israel. In contrast to modern medical anthropologists, Seybold and Mueller do not approach health care as a system at all. Moreover, much of the work on Israelite health care has focused on the identification of diseases rather than on the sociological implications of their incidence.[3]

1. Previous Scholarship

The history of the study of biblical health care has yet to be written, and it is not within our scope to do so.[4] As indicated by the texts collected by Julius Preuss, there is

---

Cambridge, 1991); A. H. Mayes, *The Old Testament in Sociological Perspective* (London: Marshall Pickering, 1989).

[2]*Sickness and Healing* (Nashville: Abingdon, 1978).

[3]In Second Temple and New Testament studies the focus on medical anthropology is in a nascent stage and in the hands of scholars with little formal training in anthropology. Some of the best known works include: Larry P. Hogan, *Healing in the Second Temple Period* (Göttingen: Vandenhoeck and Ruprecht, 1992); Howard Clark Kee *Medicine, Miracle, and Magic in the New Testament* (Cambridge: Cambridge University Press, 1986); and John J. Pilch, Healing in Mark: A Social Science Analysis," *BTB* 15 (4, 1985) 142-150; *idem,* "The Health Care System in Matthew: A Social Science Analysis," *BTB* 16 (3, 1986) 102-106. John Dominic Crossan (*The Historial Jesus: The Life of a Mediterranean Jewish Peasant* [San Francisco: Harper and Row, 1991] 313-321) adopts much of Douglas' Grid/Group schema far too uncritically. See below pp. 303-05.

[4]Our general impression is that there are sufficient materials to write such a history, but they have yet to be catalogued systematically.

already an abundance of speculation on biblical illnesses in Mishnaic and medieval Hebrew literature.[5] The enumeration of 248 bones in the Mishnaic tractate *Oholot* 1:8 demonstrates that there was some serious interest in empirical anatomy in the Mishnaic period.[6]

For our purposes, we shall first review some of the major developments in medicine and the history of medicine. We shall then relate these developments to the work of scholars who exemplify the types of approaches that have been applied to the study of biblical illnesses within the last century and a half.[7]

Among the most important developments was the discovery of the microbiological causes of disease ("germ theory"). Although various scientists had theorized before the middle of the nineteenth century that microscopic organisms could cause disease, it was only after the dramatic discoveries of Louis Pasteur (1822-1895) and Robert Koch (1843-1910) that the microbiological basis of many diseases became firmly established.[8] Germ theory provided scholars

---

[5]J. Preuss, *Biblical and Talmudic Medicine* (Trans. of *Biblisch-talmudische Medizin* [Berlin, 1911] by F. Rosner; Brooklyn, N.Y.: Hebrew Publishing Co., 1977) especially 339ff.

[6]See comments by J. Preuss *(Biblical and Talmudic Medicine*, 61) on the comparison between Mishnaic and modern bone counts.

[7]See F. Schiller ("The Earliest Western Account of Talmudic Medicine," *Koroth* 9 [1988] 255-261) and J. L. Fuchs and M. Plaut ("Jewish Medicine and Renaissance Epistemology:Ethical and Scientific Encounters," *Koroth* 9 [1988] 218-225) for comments on the medical interaction between Judaism and Christendom.

[8]See E. H. Ackerknecht, *A Short History of Medicine* (Baltimore:The Johns Hopkins Press, 1982) 175-85. Earlier theories of contagious disease were propounded by scholars such as Girolamo Fracastorius (1484-1553) of Verona, but they lacked the confirmation that could

of Israelite health care with whole new avenues of inquiry regarding biblical illnesses. Scholars who were apologists for the Bible could even regard some of the dietary and purity laws in Leviticus as examples of scientific precocity. [9]

An important development that predated germ theory, and that began with great vigour in the eighteenth century, was an emphasis on hygiene (public and private).[10] It is within this framework that many works on biblical illnesses pointed to the Priestly Code as an example of the best hygienic code in antiquity.[11] Another major development was the birth of the clinic and the hospital as places to care for the ill.[12] As M. Foucault has argued, various socio-economic factors prompted the development of hospitals, and these factors involved a new way of "seeing" illness.[13] The development of clinical examination and the care of the ill at special places also led to comparisons between modern and biblical health care by various scholars.[14]

It should be noted that other features of medicine prior to the nineteenth century continued in force, and chief among them was the anatomical tradition in medicine that was renewed in the Renaissance by scientists such as

---

only be provided after the invention of the microscope by Anton van Leeuwenhoek (1632-1723).

[9]See, for example, the comments of R. K. Harrison, *Introduction to the Old Testament* (Grand Rapids, Michigan:Eerdmans, 1969) 605.

[10]E. H. Ackerknecht, *A Short History of Medicine*, 140ff.

[11]For example, J. P. Trusen's *Die Sitten, Gebräuche und Krankheiten der alten Hebräer* (1853) discussed below.

[12]For comments on how hospitals of the nineteenth century differed from earlier versions, see E. H. Ackerknecht, *A Short History of Medicine*, 145ff.

[13]M. Foucault, *The Birth of The Clinic* (New York:Vintage, 1973).

[14]See, for example, J. Preuss, *Biblical and Talmudic Medicine*, 444.

Andreas Vesalius (1514-1564)[15] and Giovanni Battista Morgagni (1682-1771).[16] The influence of the "head-to-toe" progression used in the textbooks by Morgagni and other "pathological anatomists" may be seen in many works on biblical "medicine."[17]

Equally important for the study of Israelite health care are the discoveries of medical texts from various areas of the ancient Near East in the late nineteenth century and in the twentieth century. For example, the Egyptian Papyrus Ebers, which contains a collection of remedies, was published in 1875; the Edwin Smith Surgical Papyrus, which is a systematic treatise of great importance, was published in 1930.[18] Some of the most important Mesopotamian medical texts were not published until this century by scholars such as F. Küchler and R. Campbell Thompson.[19] These discoveries became a source of new data that could be used to compare the health care systems of various cultures

---

[15]Ackerknecht (*A Short History of Medicine*, 103) notes that Vesalius reversed an earlier trend which divorced surgery from medicine.

[16]As Ackerknecht notes (*A Short History of Medicine*, 134), Morgagni based his work on about 700 dissections, a colossal figure for the time.

[17]Thus, Julius Preuss (*Biblical and Talmudic Medicine*, 45) begins his description of the body with the head. Morgagni's "head-to-toe" descriptions are actually a revival of the organization of some Egyptian treatises on medicine. Mesopotamian treatises (e.g., SA.GIG discussed more fully in chapter 2), were less systematic in their discussion of bodily regions.

[18]For the chronology of discoveries of Egyptian medical papyri, see J. V. Kinnier Wilson, "Medicine in the Land and Times of the Old Testament," in T. Ishida, ed., *Studies in the Period of David and Solomon* (Winona Lake, Indiana:Eisenbrauns, 1982) 337-347.

[19]For a study of these publications on Mesopotamian medicine, see J. V. Kinnier Wilson, "Medicine in the Land and Times of the Old Testament," 347-358.

of the ancient Near East. In light of the developments mentioned above, we shall study briefly some of the major scholars and approaches that precede our comparative study of illness and health care in ancient Israel.

a) Comprehensive Treatments

(1) J. P. Trusen

J. P. Trusen exemplifies a scholar who wrote about "biblical medicine" from a non-critical stance, and prior to the widespread establishment of the Germ Theory of diseases. In 1853 J. P. Trusen published his *Die Sitten, Gebräuche und Krankheiten der alten Hebräer.*[20] He divided his work into four sections: 1) The customs and practices of the ancient Hebrews; 2) Midwifery; 3) The Mosaic law code; and 4) and analysis of specific biblical passages that refer to illnesses. The biblical passages were not critically examined, and different traditions within the Bible were not acknowledged. The attention paid to midwifery is a reflection of the importance of that institution. Despite the advent of medical obstetrics in the seventeenth century, midwifery continues as a visible and important type of health care in many areas of the world.[21]

During Trusen's lifetime diseases were still often categorized into large classes of general symptoms and areas of affliction. For example diseases often were classified as

---

[20]J. P. Trusen, *Die Sitten, Gebräuche und Krankheiten der alten Hebräer* (Breslau: Wilh. Gott. Korn., 1853).

[21]On the rise of modern obstetrics, see Ackerknecht, *A Short History of Medicine*, 125ff. On midwifery, see Carol Shepherd McClain, *Women as Healers: Cross Cultural Perspectives* (New Brunswick, NJ: Rutgers, 1989).

"fevers" and "eye ailments."   Trusen sought to apply the comparative method by alluding to illnesses found in classical sources. Such sources classify diseases by symptoms, geographical areas of presumed origin,[22] and areas of the body that are afflicted. However, the purpose of such comparisons was often apologetic. Trusen wished to show that biblical health care (which for him included the New Testament writings) was superior to that found in any other corpus. He sought to show the eternal wisdom (*"ewige Weisheit"*)[23] of biblical health practices. However, on a rare occasion Trusen could also show himself to be a keen observer of social institutions. In view of the descriptions of Levites as hygienic inspectors of persons, Trusen called the Levites "Polizeiärtze,"[24] a term which, as we shall show below, may have some validity.

(2) Wilhelm Ebstein

Wilhelm Ebstein of Göttingen published *Die Medizin im Alten Testament* in 1901. He wrote at a time when the microbial causes of many diseases had been determined. Much of his work is devoted to hygiene, and this reflects the importance of the topic during Ebstein's lifetime. The new knowledge of microbes led Ebstein to apply some of these new discoveries to the descriptions of illnesses found in the Bible. For example, he could explain many biblical

---

[22]For example, Trusen (*Krankheiten der alten Hebräer*, 166-169) speaks of different classifications of "leprosy" by geographical or ethnic origin. Hence, *lepra graecorum, lepra aegyptiaca, lepra occidentalis.*

[23]*Krankheiten der alten Hebräer*, x.

[24]*Krankheiten der alten Hebräer*, 8.

epidemics in terms of "natural events" (*Naturerreignissen*)[25] more confidently after the discovery in 1894 of the cause of bubonic plague, and the discovery in 1897 of the role of fleas in its transmission.[26] Ebstein also typifies the anatomical approach in his treatment of biblical health care. For example, he devotes separate sections to diseases of the nervous system and the muscles. In contrast to Trusen, Ebstein applied some of the findings of the historical-critical schools that had developed in Germany in the latter half of the nineteenth century.[27]

(3) Julius Preuss

Julius Preuss (1861-1913) probably has been the foremost student of biblical health care in the last one hundred years. His writings on health care commenced in 1894 with an article entitled: "Der Arzt in Bibel und Talmud" in *Virchow's Archiv,* one of the most prestigious medical journals of the era. In 1911 he published his principal compendium on biblical health care, *Biblisch-talmudische Medizin,* which is still unsurpassed in many aspects.[28] The

---

[25]Ebstein, *Die Medizin,* 100. Ebstein (*Die Medizin,* 101) also sees another infectious disease," influenza," as perhaps a better explanation than bubonic plague for some ancient epidemics.

[26]On these discoveries, see Ackerknecht, *A Short History of Medicine,* 180 and 183.

[27]For example, Ebstein (*Die Medizin,* 98) accepts E. Kautzsch's theory that 2 Sam 24:15-16 derives from a translator (*andern Uebersetzer*) other than the one responsible for the discrepancies found in the parallel version (1 Chr 21:14-16) of the plague after David's census.

[28]J. Preuss, *Biblical and Talmudic Medicine* (Trans. of *Biblisch-talmudische Medizin* [Berlin, 1911] by F. Rosner; Brooklyn, N.Y.:

organization of his work reflects an anatomical approach to the study of biblical health care. He was principally a pathologist examining the human body of ancient Israelites. He attempted to collect systematically all the references to illness in the Bible and in the Talmud, and this is perhaps his most important contribution.

As a careful scientist, Preuss also provided a mild corrective to those who made facile diagnoses of biblical illnesses. Although he was not above diagnosing some biblical illnesses, he would sometimes add a cautionary note regarding the tentative nature of the diagnosis. For example, on "leprosy" he comments:

> The interpretation that *tzaraath* is leprosy is at best a diagnosis of probability. Indeed it shares this lot with a large number of names of illnesses in antiquity.[29]

The disadvantage of Preuss' work is a function of the times in which he wrote. Although he was very familiar with Hebrew literature, he had no extensive training in Assyriology, and so the material from Mesopotamia was considered only briefly and unsystematically. Preuss did not cite much of the critical literature regarding the Bible, but he was not a fundamentalist or a zealous apologist for the superiority of biblical health care. For example, he says: "Among readers, only a small minority has the inclination and the ability to verify the original sources, and therefore

---

Hebrew Publishing Co., 1977). See also F. Rosner, "Julius Preuss and his classic '*Biblisch-talmudische Medizin*,'" *Koroth* 9 (1-2, 1985) 58-59.

[29]*Biblical and Talmudic Medicine*, 325-26.

accepts as historical tradition what is in reality only the fantasy of the author." [30] He also stated: The Bible is "not a handbook of medicine or hygiene."[31]

(4) Klaus Seybold

Klaus Seybold exemplifies the interest of modern critical biblical scholars (as opposed to those with extensive medical training) in Israelite health care. Along with U. B. Mueller, Seybold has produced the one of the most recent comprehensive treatises of biblical health care, *Sickness and Healing*.[32] Although only about half of the work is devoted to the Hebrew Bible (the other half is on the New Testament), Seybold, who is responsible for the section on the Hebrew Bible and ancient Israel, attempts to draw on information from Mesopotamia and Egypt in the discussion of Israelite health care.

There is a noticeable difference with past treatments on biblical health care insofar as Seybold has abandoned the strict anatomical format. Instead, he concentrates on "case studies" and on other features of illness and health care in ancient Israel which had not received much sustained

---

[30]*Biblical and Talmudic Medicine*, 153.

[31]*ibid.*

[32]K. Seybold and U. B. Mueller, *Sickness and Healing* (Nashville: Abingdon, 1978). Despite the book's popular style, the intentions of the authors (or publishers) to provide a comprehensive treatise are expressed on the back cover of the English paperback edition: "Klaus Seybold thoroughly reviews the Old Testament literature and the concepts of sickness and healing held by Israel's neighbors." We shall sometimes refer only to Seybold when the book discusses the Hebrew Bible because he is primarily responsible for that section of the book.

attention in the past. In particular, Seybold has focused on the use of the psalms in illness.[33] He has made useful contributions in the identification of the form and structure of psalms that were probably used in cases of illness. We are indebted to his work for our own identification of psalms that are useful in the study of the health care system of ancient Israel.

Another important contribution of Seybold is his attempt to reconstruct a "restoration" process for patients after an illness, particularly in the Hebrew Bible.[34] His work on restoration involved discussion of the temple, but he never provided a coherent account of the functions of the temple in the health care system. Nonetheless, his discussion of the patient's restoration process has provided many insights into what we call the thanksgiving function of the temple. Finally, Seybold has also contributed numerous philological studies on the biblical terminology regarding illness and health.[35]

Although Seybold is more interested in some social aspects of Israelite health care than previous scholars, he overlooks and is largely unfamiliar with advances in medical anthropology. Seybold does not treat health care as a system, nor does he discuss how different socio-economic strata used the health care system in ancient Israel. He provides little discussion of the dynamics of the selection of health care consultants, and he regards Israel as largely

---

[33]Seybold's most important contribution in the study of illness in the Psalms is *Das Gebet des Kranken im Alten Testament* (Stuttgart: W. Kohlhammer, 1973).

[34]K. Seybold, *Das Gebet des Kranken*, especially 169ff.

[35]We shall cite these studies in our third chapter on Israel.

devoid of "physicians." The main conclusions of Seybold are worth quoting in full:[36]

> According to the Old Testament documents, the situation of the sick person in Israel differentiated itself from that in cultures surrounding Israel in four points, which in conclusion we can summarize as follows:
>
> (1) In general a sick person had virtually no *aids* at his disposal worth mentioning, no physicians in the real sense, and no knowledge of medicine.
>
> (2) In general he had access to *no* really recognized or tolerated healing procedures or *practices*, including no ritualistic incantations or exorcism-related manipulations.
>
> (3) Well into the later period, a sick person in ancient Israel was limited in both directions, and these limitations reduced his possibilities both in general and in principle. That sick person in ancient Israel did not have access to that which was so readily available to the blind father from Amarna, the mayor of Nippur, the carpenter from Syracuse, or the unknown person with the amulet from Chadattu. Here he met with limitations and hindrances.
>
> (4) The sick person in Israel had undisturbed, unconditional access to only one path--at least according to the Old Testament--if he wanted to comprehend his illness religiously; namely to turn to his God in supplication and prayer.

---

[36]*Sickness and Healing*, 35. All italics are those of Seybold and Mueller.

In our Conclusion, we shall re-examine the conclusions of Seybold in light of our intensive comparative study of the Israelite health care system. Such a re-examination hopefully will demonstrate the value of the medical anthropological approach in the study of ancient health care systems. For the moment, we may say that the conclusions of Seybold do not reflect the complexities that can occur in ancient health care systems. Seybold, furthermore, does not base any of his conclusions on an intensive study of the health care systems that he uses for comparison.[37]

b) Comparative approaches

J. V. Kinnier Wilson exemplifies a current comparative approach to medicine. Kinnier Wilson has taken great advantage of the data from Egypt and Mesopotamia which have been discovered in the last century. His orientation is still within the tradition that focuses on the identification of diseases, but which is also interested in philological analysis.[38]

K. van der Toorn has engaged in a sustained comparison between Israelite and Mesopotamian concepts of sin and punishment. In the process he often speaks of illness and health care. K. van der Toorn has documented the overlap between Mesopotamia and Israel insofar as ideas

[37]Mesopotamia, for instance, is alloted five pages (27-32) in *Sickness and Healing*.

[38]See, for example, J. V. Kinnier Wilson, "Medicine in the Land and Times of the Old Testament," in T. Ishida, ed., *Studies in the Period of David and Solomon* (Winona Lake, Indiana:Eisenbrauns, 1982) 354-357; "Leprosy in Ancient Mesopotamia," *RA* 60 (1966) 57-58; and "An Introduction to Babylonian Psychiatry," *AS* 16 (1965) 289-298.

concerning hygiene, illness, sin, and punishment are concerned.[39] Although van der Toorn provides many insightful discussions of illness, he did not intend to provide a systematic study of the health care system of Israel or Mesopotamia. K. van der Toorn represents the triumph of the approach which sees biblical concepts of illness, hygiene, and punishment as part of a larger Near Eastern context.

c) Osteo-archaeological approaches

Osteological remains uncovered by archaeologists have the potential to contribute to our knowledge of ancient health care systems. Joseph Zias, for example, has focused on osteo-archaeological remains to discuss the disease(s) called צרעת, and usually translated as *leprosy* by modern scholars.[40] He has investigated the use of trephination,[41] and the identification of instruments that might have been used to rid the body of ecto-parasites such as lice.[42] B. Arensburg and Y. Rak have focused on a wide variety of scientific analyses of osteo-archaeological materials in the

---

[39]K. van der Toorn, *Sin and Sanction in Israel and Mesopotamia* (Aasen/Maasricht:Van Gorcum, 1985).

[40]For example, J. Zias, "Lust and Leprosy:Confusion or Correlation?" *BASOR* 275 (1989) 27-31; *idem*, "Leprosy in the Byzantine Monasteries of the Judean Desert," *Koroth* 9 (1-2, 1985) 242.

[41]J. Zias, "Three Trephinated Skulls from Jericho," *BASOR* 246 (1982) 55-58.

[42]K. Y. Mumcuoglu and J. Zias, "How the Ancients Deloused Themselves," *BARev* 15 (6, 1989) 66ff.

first millennium B.C.E.[43] J. Angel has published a noted study of health in the eastern Mediterranean region.[44] Other researchers such as Patricia Smith[45] and Theya Molleson[46] have focused on a wide variety of studies of osteo-archeological materials from Syria-Palestine, some of which pre-date the biblical periods considerably. Their studies have helped to analyze long-term evolutionary trends in the health of populations in the Near East.

Also important are studies of groups which have been relatively isolated from Westernization. M. L. Alcorn and A. H. Goodman, for example, have studied the dental health of sedentary and nomadic groups in modern Jordan.[47]

---

[43] See B. Arensburg, M. S. Goldstein and Y. Rak, "Observations on the Pathology of the Jewish Population in Israel (100 B.C. to 600 C.E.)," *Koroth* 9 (1-2, 1985) 73-83; and B. Arensburg and Y. Rak, "Jewish Skeletal Remains from the Perod of the Kings of Judea," *PEQ* 117 (Jan.-June, 1985) 30-34.

[44] J. Angel, "Ecology and Population in the Eastern Mediterranean," *World Archaeology* 4 (1972) 88-105.

[45] P. Smith, "The Physical Characteristics and Biological Affinities of the MB I Skeletal Remains from Jebel Qa aqir," *BASOR* 245 (1982) 65-73; "Evolutionary Trends in Pre-Agricultural Populations," *Rivista di Antropologia* LXVI Suppl. (1988) 281-94; P. Smith and B. Peretz,"Hypoplasia and Health Status: A Comparison of two Lifestyles,"*Human Evolution* 1 (6, 1986) 535-544; P. Smith, R. A. Bloom, and J. Berkowitz, "Diachronic Trends in Humeral Cortical Thickness of Near Eastern Populations," *Journal of Human Evolution* 13 (1984) 603-611; A. Sillen and P. Smith, "Weaning Patterns are Reflected in Strontium-Calcium Ratios of Juvenile Skeletons," *Journal of Archaeological Science* 11 (1984) 237-45.

[46] Theya Molleson, "The Eloquent Bones of Abu Hureyra," *Scientific American* 271 (August, 1994) 70-75.

[47] M. L. Alcorn and A. H. Goodman, "Dental Enamel Defects Among Contemporary Nomadic and Sedentary Jordanians," *AJPA* 66 (1985) 139-140. See also M. Goldstein, B. Arensburg, and H. Natan,

J. V. Kinnier Wilson has surveyed Iraqi medical journals for studies of illnesses in modern Iraq that might be broadly similar to those of ancient times.[48] F. L. Black has recently analyzed the extent to which we can use information from such non-Westernized groups to make inferences about ancient illnesses.[49]

These types of studies have produced some insights into illness and health care in ancient Israel, but there are not yet sufficient data to form precise profiles of the incidence of diseases and other important information. Perhaps the best result of these inquiries is that they have illustrated the difficulty involved in making facile diagnoses of biblical illnesses.

d) Theological approaches

A number of scholars have focused on the theological issues posed by biblical references to illness and healing. Among the scholars who have contributed studies in

---

139-140.   See also M. Goldstein, B. Arensburg, and H. Natan, ""Pathology of Bedouin Skeletal Remains from Two Sites in Israel," *AJPA* 45 (1976) 621-640.

[48]J. V. Kinnier Wilson, "Gleanings from the Iraq Medical Journals," *JNES* 27 (1968) 243-247.

[49]F. L. Black, "Modern Isolated Pre-Agricultural Populations as a Source of Information on Prehistoric Epidemic Patterns," in N. F. Stanely and R. A. Joske, eds., *Changing Disease Patterns and Human Behavior* (London: Academic Press, 1980) 37-54.

this regard are G. Hasel,[50] P. Humbert,[51] A. Lods,[52] and C. Westermann.[53] Usually such studies appear in brief essays in which conclusions are not preceded by sustained argumentation. Although there is an effort to deal seriously with some historical and philological issues, the purposes of such studies are usually apologetic and religio-centric insofar as they assume the validity of the theological presuppositions of the scholar's tradition but not those of the non-biblical ones. For example, in the article on "medicine" in the respected *Interpreter's Dictionary of the Bible*, R. K. Harrison states:

> The medical principles of the early Hebrews, as enshrined in the Pentateuch, represented a notable advance upon contemporary theories of disease in that they repudiated magic completely, and sought to consider disease either from an empirical standpoint or else in terms of the personal spiritual relationship which exists between the sufferer and his God.[54]

As we shall demonstrate, however, the Israelite health care system was very indebted to its ancient Near Eastern neighbors in a number of aspects. Harrison's definition of the word "magic" is not outlined, and words such as

---

[50]G. Hasel,"Health and Healing in the Old Testament," *Andrews University Seminary Studies* 21 (1983) 191-202.

[51] P. Humbert "Maladie et médecine dans l'Ancien Testament," *Revue d'histoire et de philosophie reliegieuses* 44 (1964) 1-29.

[52]A. Lods, "Les idées des Israélites sur la maladie, ses causes et ses rémedes," *BZAW* 41 (1925) 181-93.

[53]C. Westermann,"Heilung und Heil in der Gemeinde aus der Sicht des Alten Testament," *WzM* 27 (1975)1-12.

[54]R. K. Harrison, "Medicine," IDB, 331-332.

"spiritual relationship" are either too ambiguous, or may also be found in Mesopotamian concepts. H. Eilberg-Schwartz, among others, has warned us that the search for uniqueness in the Bible is misguided in many respects.[55] Evaluations such as "better" and "more advanced" are too relative and superficial to do justice to reality. A new approach must study the health care system of ancient Israel in a critical and non-apologetic vein.

e) "Hyper-diagnostic" approaches

   The diagnosis of ancient diseases is a goal that should always be sought, but it is usually unreachable. Although most scholars discussed above attempt in some instances to provide modern diagnoses, there is a strain of scholarship that persistently strives for diagnoses that reach far beyond the available textual and scientific evidence. We may term such attempts as "hyper-diagnostic."
   Diagnosis is a precarious enterprise in a modern setting, but it is even more so when attempting to provide long-range diagnoses. To illustrate this misguided type of diagnosis that still forms a significant component of research into biblical illnesses, we refer to an article by Eli Davis, "The Illness of Miriam, Sister of Moses," published in one of the most significant journals devoted to the study of

---

[55]Eilberg-Schwartz (*The Savage in Judaism:An Anthropology of Israelite Religion and Judaism* [Bloomington:Indiana University, 1990] 87ff) calls the aversion to ancient Near Eastern parallels "parallel-anoia"; See also Peter Machinist, "The Question of Distinctiveness in Ancient Israel," in F. E Greenspahn, ed., *Essential Papers on Israel and the Ancient Near East* (New York:NYU Press, 1991) 420-442.

Israelite health care.[56] On the basis of the fact that the text states that Miriam became "as white as snow," Davis makes the following diagnosis:

> I suggest that Miriam's symptoms were caused by hyperventilation, when she was in a panic situation when scolded by the Lord. The hyperventilation syndrome usually attacks women in a panic or fright and results in bizarre physical signs which include agitation, profound weakness and pallor, and sometimes a feeling of impending death and collapse...
>
> The loss of CO_2 in the expired air in hyperventilation leads in some sufferers to extreme vasoconstriction. Indeed the whole skin can appear as white as snow. Miriam was put in isolation for a week. This would take her away from an audience and inhibit further hyperventilation.

Davis is clearly motivated by an attempt to provide a modern scientific explanation for what the Bible calls miraculous. He says: "Some of the miracles in the Bible are natural phenomena. It is the timing which is miraculous." This is followed by the reference to his personal clinical experience for an analogy:

> I have had patients who exhibited a hyperventilation syndrome in circumstances not dissimilar to the quarrel between sister and brother, Miriam and Moses.

---

[56]*Koroth* 9 [1-2, 1985] 99-100.

But Davis apparently ignores the fact that, for the biblical author, Miriam's symptoms were most unusual and unexpected in states of emotional agitation. Yet, for Davis, "The hyperventilation syndrome usually attacks anxious tense women in panic or fright..." As far as can be determined, the biblical author is attempting to link Miriam's condition with the illness known in Leviticus 13-14, and nowhere in Leviticus or in other parts of the Bible is this illness associated with breathing difficulties, which should have been obvious even in biblical times. Moreover, seven days of isolation would probably not have been required to recover from hyperventilation. The author of Numbers 12 is simply depicting another case of a miraculous infliction of an illness that is never linked with breathing difficulties in women or men (e.g., Exod 4:6-7).

Davis' poor exegesis and unguarded diagnosis is an extreme case, but it is not very unusual.[57] Even the latest reference works continue to disseminate diagnoses that reach far beyond the textual evidence. For example, in a recent article in *The Anchor Bible Dictionary* Max Sussman claims that there are persuasive arguments for identifying the fiery serpents in Numbers 21:6-9 with guinea worms (*Dranunculus medinensis*).[58] Such a diagnosis ignores the plain meaning of the text as well as the archaeological evidence that indicates that bronze serpents (not guinea worms) were known therapeutic devices in the ancient Near East.

---

[57]"The Illness of Miriam," 99.

[58] "Sickness and Disease," *The Anchor Bible Dictionary* (New York: Doubleday, 1992) 6:10.

2. Summary of past approaches

There has been some progress in the study of biblical health care from a scientific viewpoint. The final overthrow of the equation between Hansen's disease and biblical צרעת, for example, is a significant scientific advance that we shall discuss in more detail in chapter 3. The interest in osteo-archeology is a relatively recent phenomenon in Syro-Palestinian archaeology, and new techniques should increase the amount of information one can extract from bones in the future. As exemplified in the work of E. Neufeld,[59] there is still interest in the study of hygiene in ancient Israel.

Although one must continue efforts to diagnose ancient diseases, such endeavours are too limited to produce significant advances in the study of illness and health care in ancient Israel. One must accept that many, if not most, of the illnesses mentioned in the Bible will never be diagnosed or translated into a modern medical classification. One must, therefore, concentrate on other aspects in the study of ancient illnesses without abandoning efforts to gather information which might lead to a better identification of ancient illnesses in modern terms.

---

[59]E. Neufeld, "Hygiene Conditions in Ancient Israel (Iron Age)," *BA* 34 (2, 1971) 42-66.

B. A NEW APPROACH TO THE STUDY OF
ILLNESS AND HEALTH CARE

1. General comments

As Thomas Kuhn argued, advances in a field are rarely the products of new data.[60] Rather, advances are most often the product of new questions and paradigms applied to data that already exist. At its most fundamental level, our study is guided by a new primary question posed to data that already exist: **How does a socio-religious conceptual framework affect and interact with the type of health care that a society devises for its members?**

We may describe our approach as one which combines the best insights of medical anthropology with the best of critical biblical studies. We view the data relevant to illness and health care from the perspectives suggested by various medical anthropologists. We aim to study health care as a system which includes theological, social, historical, and other relevant components. We shall propose new typologies and paradigms to study ancient health care systems and to place them in comparative perspective. Although we shall discuss the modern classification of an ancient disease whenever that is possible, we shall concern ourselves primarily with the social consequences of illnesses.

The field of illness and health care is so vast that a productive study must be selective. The ancient Near East has many examples of temples which have a role in the

---

[60]T. Kuhn, *The Structure of Scientific Revolutions* (Chicago:U. of Chicago, 1970).

health care system. These temples provide excellent focal points around which one may explore the varying socio-religious ideas that shaped health care in particular societies. Accordingly, this study shall focus on the role of the temple in illness and health care in ancient Israel and in other neighboring societies in order to illustrate how different socio-religious frameworks affected the particular forms of health care that a society devised for its members. In particular, a comparative study of the role of the temple in illness and health care shall elucidate the approach to illness and health care in Israel in the first millennium B.C.E.

2. The medical anthropological approach

The distinct aspect of our approach is drawn from recent advances in medical anthropology. In its most general sense, an anthropological approach to biblical studies seeks to apply the insights and theories that develop from the observation of actual societies.[61] Such insights may help place an ancient culture in comparative perspective.

Foremost among the advances in medical anthropology is the exploration of health care as a system. A system is a set of elements whose links and interactions bear discernible functions. A health care system may be defined as a set of interacting resources, institutions, and strategies that are intended to prevent or cure illness in a particular community. A health care system usually includes, but is not limited to, the presuppositions regarding the causes and

---

[61]For further comments on the anthropological approach and biblical studies, see B. Lang, ed., *Anthropological Approaches to the Old Testament* (Philadelphia: Fortress, 1985).

diagnosis of illness, the options available to the patient, and the modes of therapy administered. Other dimensions include any social or geographic differences in accessibility to what is perceived to be the best care available in the society, and the attitudes toward the patient in the society and toward the health care expert. Most health care systems, modern or not, offer a plurality of options for patients.

Of course, what a system intends is not always what it yields. In our case, many systems aimed at preventing and curing illness may have actually unintentionally promoted illness. For example, Asclepieia, which were meant to cure the sick, may have unintentionally caused the spread of illness in the larger community by concentrating large numbers of sick people in small places. Thus, visitors who came to be cured of Illness A at the Asclepieion may have contracted Illness B from other patients at the temple. Illness B may have then been transported back to their home.

In any event, since health care is treated as a system, one must explore a number of data from areas that might be relevant. These areas includes ecology, demography, and paleopathology. Changes in the components or their relationships in a health care system may cause significant changes in the delivery of health care in a society.

Among the medical anthropologists to whom we are most indebted is Arthur Kleinman. In a series of articles, monographs, and extensive fieldwork, he has advanced the theoretical and practical aspects of medical anthropology.[62] We cannot claim that Kleinman's is the only approach that may be used in the study of health in the ancient Near East.

---

[62]A. Kleinman, *Patients and Healers* (Berkeley: U. of California, 1980); Arthur Kleinman and B. Good, eds., *Culture and Depression* (Berkeley: U. of California Press, 1985).

Nor can we claim that all aspects of his theories can be applied in the ancient Near East. For our purposes, one of the most important aspects of his approach is the focus on the strategies used to seek health care by a patient. Among the important questions posed by Kleinman's approach are: What options are available to the patient? Is there a hierarchy of options?

Among other medical anthropologists to whom we are indebted are M. N. Cohen, M. Foucault, G. M. Foster, W. M. Gesler, T. M. Johnson, and C. E. Sargent.[63] We are also indebted to historians of ancient medicine such as M. Grmek,[64] H. Sigerist,[65] and W. H. McNeill.[66] Even if all of his conclusions are not acceptable, McNeill has integrated the study of history, demography and health crises in a provocative manner. Finally, we acknowledge our debt to scholars who are approaching the study of illness and pain from literary and psychological perspectives.[67]

---

[63]George M. Foster,"Disease Etiologies in Non-Western Medical Systems,"*AA* 78 (1976) 773-782; George M. Foster and B.G. Anderson, *Medical Anthropology* (New York: John Wiley & Sons, 1978); M. N. Cohen, *Health and the Rise of Civilization* (New Haven: Yale, 1989); M. Foucault, *The Birth of The Clinic* (New York:Vintage, 1973); W. M. Gesler, *The Cultural Geography of Health Care* (Pittsburgh: U. of Pittsburgh, 1991); T. M. Johnson and C. E. Sargent, *Medical Anthropology* (New York: Praeger, 1990).

[64]M. Grmek, *Diseases in the Ancient Greek World* (Baltimore: The Johns Hopkins University Press, 1989).

[65]H. E. Sigerist, *A History of Medicine* (2 volumes; New York: Oxford, 1961).

[66]See especially, W. H. McNeill, *Plagues and People* (New York: Doubleday, 1976).

[67]For an example of the depiction of pain in literature, see E. Scarry, *The Body in Pain: The Making and Unmaking of the World* (Oxford:Clarendon, 1985); and D. Aberbach, *Surviving Trauma: Loss*

3. Terminology

Many advances in a field of inquiry necessitate an increasing precision and consensus in the use of terminology. All studies of ancient societies are in essence a *translation* of ancient categories into modern ones. One has to balance between representational accuracy and the selection of those modern categories that would render the ancient ones most understandable for the modern audience.[68] A persistent problem in previous studies of ancient illnesses is the belief that every ancient category has a precise modern equivalent whose representation is most often sought in a single word. This problem has been particularly acute in the study of Hebrew term usually translated as "leprosy" (צרעת). As we shall demonstrate, the Hebrew term does not have a precise equivalent which may be expressed by one word or term in modern English or in any modern language because our paradigm and classification of diseases are very different from what they were in biblical times. Similar problems attend the study of "purity," "biblical medicine" and other aspects of ancient health care systems. We are aware that terms such as "health care system" are modern categories meant to help render ancient categories more understandable to a modern audience. The following are some terminological and conceptual distinctions that shall be used in our new approach to the study of ancient health care systems.

---

and Literature (New Haven: Yale, 1989). A psychological study of illness from the Freudian perspective may be found in David Bakan, *Disease, Pain and Suffering: Toward a Psychology of Suffering* (Boston: Beacon, 1968).

[68]On the anthropologist as translator and author, see C. Geertz, *Works and Lives: The Anthropologist as Author* (Stanford, 1988).

a) Illness and disease

A. Kleinman, among other medical anthropologists, has advanced a useful distinction between illness and disease. A. Kleinman states:

> *Disease* refers to a malfunctioning of biological and/or psychological processes, while the term *illness* refers to the psychosocial experience and meaning of perceived disease.[69]

This distinction allows one to study non-Western definitions of illness with a minimum of modern Western biases. We allow the society in question to outline its own definitions of illness regardless of whether we regard the same conditions as an illness in our society. We shall use the term *disease* to speak of a modern Western classification that is applied to an ancient or modern condition (e.g., *lupus erythematosus*). *Biomedicine* is the usual term used to describe modern Western scientific medicine.

The identification of diseases is important, but we treat as highly suspect any specific diagnosis made on the basis of descriptions of symptoms in the Bible. It is often more important to understand what an ancient culture defined as an "illness" than what the actual cause might have been from a modern scientific standpoint.

---

[69]A. Kleinman, *Patients and Healers* (Berkeley: U. of California, 1980) 72.

b) Professional designations

Another term that we shall use is *consultant*. This term attempts to avoid specific terms that may be misleading when speaking of an ancient culture. For example, in Mesopotamia the term *physician* has been applied to the *asû* in order to emphasize his alleged use of a strictly non-magical approach to illness. However, as we shall demonstrate, such a characterization is flawed, and the term *physician* in this sense is to be avoided. The term *health care consultant,* on the other hand, is more neutral and yet retains a useful measure of correspondence with an actual role--namely, someone who is consulted, usually as a normal option, in any health care system. Some terms cannot be translated adequately by a single English word, and so it is best to preserve the ancient word (e.g., *āšipu* and *asû*). We have also attempted to diminish our use of the term "medicine" when speaking of ancient institutions that specialized in healing because it may induce misleading comparisons with modern Western medicine. We prefer the more neutral term "health care."

4. New typology for temple functions

Any application of the ideas of medical anthropology to ancient health care systems is confronted with a significant reduction in the data base on health care. Unlike the study of health care in modern societies, a student of ancient health care does not have ready access to a census, or even to very precise measures of the incidence of disease in a particular community. However, this lack of abundant data does not mean that the study of ancient health care systems is hopeless. It simply means that we must be content to work with broader parameters and measures that do not require precise quantification.

For example, in order to investigate the role of temples in health care, we shall, for heuristic purposes, devise a typology of possible functions for the temple of a healing deity. A healing deity is one that specializes in healing or that has healing as an important part of his or her repertory. By examining the interplay of these temple functions, one may illuminate some of the distinctive developments in the temples of a particular society. In our paradigm, a temple of a healing deity in the ancient Near East may have one or more of the following functions. [70]

a) Petitionary

A temple may be said to have a petitionary function if it provides the patient or a proxy a place to petition for healing. This function is linked with, among other things, ideas about the efficacy of the healing locus itself and the geographical range of efficacy of the god. The petitionary function may include the request for oracles concerning the prognosis, and not simply the petition for healing itself.

b) Therapeutic

If, in addition to simple petitions, a temple locus provides services designed to restore the ill, then the temple may be said to have a therapeutic function. The temple, for example, may be a place for the application of *materia*

---

[70]For other typologies applied to temples, see Harold W. Turner, *From Temple to Meeting House* (The Hague: Mouton, 1979).

medica, surgery, exorcism, incubation, and the performance of other rituals and procedures which are part of the therapy.

c) Thanksgiving

The thanksgiving function is defined here as one that provides a place for the suppliant to thank the deity which s/he believes is responsible for the healing. This may be something enjoined by the cult, or an optional practice.

d) Other functions

We shall keep this category open for functions that are unexpected or that are related to those above in a manner which had not been anticipated.[71] By examining the interplay of these functions, one may begin to understand some of the distinctive developments in the healing temples of a particular society.

5. Socio-religious typologies

Another set of typologies is necessary to explore the socio-religious conceptual framework of the medical theology of the relevant temples. Following the methods that sociologically oriented biblical scholars such as P. D.

---

[71]For studies which treat various theoretical and mythological aspects of the temple which we shall not discuss in detail, see M. V. Fox, *Temple in Society* (Winona Lake: Eisenbrauns, 1988); J. Levenson, "The Temple and the World," *Journal of Religion* 64 (1984) 275-298; *idem, Sinai and Zion* (New York: Harper and Row, 1985); T. G. Madsen, ed., *The Temple in Antiquity* (Provo, Utah: Brigham Young University, 1984).

Hanson and H. Eilberg-Schwartz have applied to various aspects of Israelite society,[72] we shall describe some contrasting views (polarities) of health care that are never fully realized, but which provide an idea of the tendencies found in some of the societies that we shall study.

One of the most important polarities is between what we shall term utopian and realist views of illness etiology and prognosis. We shall characterize as utopian the view that the cause of illness follows a regular and systematic cause and effect that can be fully understood by the patient. A realist view regards the causes of illness as ones which cannot always be understood. We also shall characterize as utopian a view of the prognosis of an illness which regards all illnesses as curable if the patient follows the appropriate prescription which is available for every illness. In contrast, a realist approach acknowledges that not all illnesses are curable, and that prescriptions are not available for every illness.

A related question explores the extent to which divine beings use illness as an instrument. The utopian position is characterized by the belief that the deity uses illness as an instrument whose mechanisms are not only fully understood by the patient, but also are regarded as just. The realist position believes the a deity may use illness for purposes which are not always disclosed to the patient. A divine being (e.g., a demon) may use illness for seemingly arbitrary or malevolent purposes.

---

[72]P. D. Hanson, *The People Called: The Growth of Community in the Bible* (San Francisco: Harper and Row, 1986); *idem, The Dawn of Apocalyptic: The Historical and Sociological Roots of Jewish Apocalyptic Eschatology* (2nd ed.; Philadelphia: Fortress, 1979); H. Eilberg-Schwartz, *The Savage in Judaism* (Bloomington: Indiana U. Press, 1990).

Our polarities assume that medical theologies are explanatory models that have socio-political components. In contrast to scholars who rightly emphasize the "cosmic" aspects of the temple, we seek to emphasize the forces and problems of everyday life that affected the role of the temple. Medical theologies sometimes produce a conflict between what the patient actually observes or experiences and what the dominant theology leads the patient to expect. Ancient medical theologies may seek to explain and to provide hope when the situation is hopeless from a modern medical standpoint. As we shall explain in more detail below, these theologies also may serve to exclude unwanted individuals from the community, and to express status relationships in the society.

Another question that we shall pose is the extent of the role of the state in the care of the ill. We shall describe as maximalist an ideology which sees the state as fully responsible for the care of the ill. This might involve providing consultants, a therapeutic locus, and economic support. A minimalist position would view the state as having no responsibility in the care of the ill, and, indeed, regarding the ill as such a great burden (socio-economic, contamination etc.) that it seeks to exclude them from the "healthy" community altogether. We may summarize these polarities as follows:

MODELS OF ILLNESS ETIOLOGY AND PROGNOSIS

	Utopian	Realist
Etiology	Illness has a systematic etiology that can always be understood by the patient.	Illness has a large variety of causes that cannot always be understood by the patient.
Prognosis	All illnesses are curable if the patient follows the proper prescriptions, and there is a prescription available for each illness.	All illnesses are not curable, and there is not always a prescription available for each illness.

MODELS OF DIVINE INSTRUMENTALITY IN ILLNESS

Utopian	Realist
Divine beings use illness for purposes that are fully disclosed to the patient, and which are regarded as "just."	Divine beings use illness for purposes that are not always disclosed to the patient, or which may be malevolent or arbitrary.

STATE RESPONSIBILITY IN THE HEALTH CARE SYSTEM

Maximalist	Minimalist
The state provides a	The state provides no
full range of benefits	benefits and views the
for the ill, including	ill as, among other things,
therapy, therapeutic loci,	a burden (e.g., pollution,
and perhaps economic	socio-economic) which
relief.	must be excluded from
	the "normal" community.

We shall explain the particulars of these polarities, and their relevance to the role of the temple, as our examination progresses. We also shall discuss other anthropological typologies applied to the study of illness, particularly "leprosy," by some New Testament scholars when they are relevant to the study of ancient Israel.

C. THE BASIC STRATEGY OF OUR STUDY

In order to explore the role of the Israelite temple in illness and health care, it is worthwhile to compare it with temples which are known to have had a role in their respective health care systems. The intention of this study is to provide some illustrative case studies that shall place Israel's temple in a comparative perspective. In particular, we shall study the temples of Asclepius in Greece, and the temples of Gula/Ninisina in Mesopotamia. It is not within our scope to provide a comprehensive study of the association of temples with healing in all of these areas. We shall discuss only those aspects that provide sufficient data for a productive comparison, especially insofar as the polarities discussed above are concerned. In any event, the comparison shall attempt to explain those socio-religious features that led Israel to develop its own ideas about the role of the temple in health care in view of the developments in the other areas that we shall study.

CHAPTER I

GREECE
The Temples of Asclepius

A. GENERAL COMMENTS

1. Sources

Asclepius is perhaps the most celebrated of the ancient deities who heal, and his temples are an obvious attraction for our comparative study of the role of the temple in ancient health care systems. Textual and archaeological evidence is rich. We shall discuss the archaeological evidence when we speak of specific sites.

The most important collection of the textual materials about Asclepius and his temples remains that of Emma J. Edelstein and Ludwig Edelstein.[1] A number of votive inscriptions (especially those in the *Corpus inscriptionum atticarum*) and other materials not included among the

---

[1] L. Edelstein and E. Edelstein, *Asclepius* (Baltimore: The Johns Hopkins University Press, 1945) = the Edelsteins. We shall use the following abbreviations for the sources reproduced by the Edelsteins: T. = Testimonia as numbered in the Edelsteins. Unless there is a significant disagreement in translation (which we shall note), English translations of the testimonia are those of the Edelsteins.

sources compiled by the Edelsteins have been collected and studied by, among others, W. H. D. Rouse,[2] H. E. Sigerist,[3] and Sara B. Aleshire.[4] These and other convenient collections of sources and studies have been re-examined from the perspective of our analysis. This re-examination focuses on the various socio-religious concepts regarding the efficacy of the temple locus, and the issue of competition between the temple priests and non-temple healers.[5]

2. Brief history of the origin of Asclepius

    The earliest mention of Asclepius is in Homer (*Iliad*, iv:194), and there he was a highly skilled human physician. One view of the origin of Asclepius holds that he was a pre-Homeric chthonic deity from Thessaly who was demoted to the status of a hero (in Homer), then restored to full divinity by the classical period.[6] The most prevalent view is that of

---

[2]Relevant Asclepius inscriptions of the *CIA* = *Corpus inscriptionum atticarum* (Berlin: Reimer, 1873-) have been collected by W. H. D. Rouse, *Greek Votive Offerings* (Cambridge: Cambridge University Press, 1902).

[3]H. E. Sigerist, *A History of Medicine* (2 volumes; New York: Oxford, 1961) II:44-83.

[4]Sara B. Aleshire, *The Athenian Asklepieion: The People, their Dedications, and the Inventories* (Amsterdam: J. C. Gieben, 1989).

[5]For an example of the study of the methodology of Greek naology see J. C. van Leuven, "Problems and Methods of Prehellenic Naology," in R. Hägg and Nanno Marinatos, ed., *Sanctuaries and Cults in the Aegean Bronze Age* (Svenska Institutet I Athen: Stockholm, 1981) 11-25.

[6]So Henri Grégoire avec la collaboration de R. Goossens et de M. Mathieu, *Asklèpios, Apollon Smintheus et Rudra; Etudes sur le dieu à*

the Edelsteins who argue that Asclepius was originally a
patron hero of the physicians. If he was originally a human
being, his origins are not much earlier than Homer. As
fictive sons of the hero, physicians were called Asclepiads,
although one should not assume that this epithet always
implies contiguity between the temple priests and the
"secular" physicians. According to the Edelsteins, it was not
until the 6th century B.C.E. that Asclepius became deified.[7]
At first he was simply an adjunct divinity to Apollo
Maleatas, a healing god who was himself of diverse
ancestry, but by the fourth century B.C.E. Asclepius had
become an independent healing god who eclipsed Apollo as
a healing deity. Nonetheless, Asclepius continued to be
regarded as a son of Apollo.

Also disputed is the etymology of Asclepius, a
dispute related to the uncertainty about the proper division
of the etymological elements in the name. As the Edelsteins
note, some classical sources connected the Greek ἤπιος (=
gentle) with the latter part of the name *Asclepius*, but the first
part of the name still puzzles most scholars.[8] Another, and
now largely discredited, attempt by Henri Gregoire
connected the name with *skalops, aspalax,* or *spalax,* and
these words describe a mole rat. Gregoire sought to explain
Asclepius as a chthonic deity by connecting him with an
earth dwelling rodent.[9] In a relatively recent article, O.
Szemerényi argues that the name derived from the Hittite
assul(a) (= "well being") + *piya-* (= "to give"), and so

---

la taupe et le dieu au rat dans la Gréce et dans l'Inde (Brussels: Ac.
Roy. Belgique, 1950)

[7]*Asclepius*, II, 91-101.

[8]*Asclepius*, II, 80-83.

[9]See, Henri Grégoire *Asklèpios, Apollon Smintheus et Rudra*. Cited
in Sigerist (II, 76 n. 62).

"health-giver."[10] But this proposal still lacks an explanation for the unvoiced stop (c or k) in the name. Nonetheless, if Szemerényi is correct, then Asclepius' origins should be sought in Anatolia or farther to the east. Further archaeological research in Anatolia is needed to test Szemerényi's proposal.[11]

We should not exclude the possibility that Asclepius may have had his origin in the Levant, and Damascius (5th-6th centuries C.E.) may have preserved an ancient tradition:[12]

> ῞Οτι ἐν Βηρυτῷ...᾽Ασκληπιὸs ουκ ἔστιν
> Ελλην, οὐδε Αἰγύπτιος, ἀλλά τις ἐπιχώριος
> Φοῖνιξ. Σαδύκω γὰρ ἐγένοντο παῖδες, οὕς
> Διοσκούρους ἑρμηνεύουσι καὶ Καβείρους.
> ὄγδοος δὲ ἐγένετο ἐπὶ τούτοις ὁ ῎Εσμουνος,
> ὅν᾽Ασκληπιὸν ἑρμηνεύουσιν.

> For the Asclepius in Berytus... is neither Greek nor
> Egyptian, but rather a native Phoenician. For to
> Sadycus were born the children whom they interpret
> as the Dioscuri, and the Cabiri. Eighth, after these,

---

[10]O. Szemerényi, "The Origins of the Greek Lexicon: Ex Oriente Lux," *Journal of Hellenic Studies* 94 (1974) 154.

[11] Szemerényi does not discuss the fact that Anatolia apparently had cults in which dogs played a prominent role. One such cult at Sardis involved eating dogs, and it may have involved the god Kandaulas who is called *skyllopniktes* (puppy-choker) by some ancient glosses. For a treatment of this cult at Sardis, see Crawford H. Greenewalt, *Ritual Dinners in Early Historic Sardis* (Berkeley: University of California Press, 1976). The possible connections of this cult (and the word *skyllop*) with Asclepius, however, are not discussed by Greenewalt.

[12]*Vita Isidori*, 302 = T. 826.

[was born] Esmounos, whom they interpret as
Asclepius.

Eshmun, was a noted Phoenician god of healing.[13] Yet such
an origin cannot help us decipher Asclepius' name very well.
For the moment, any etymology can only cite possibilities,
and not certainties.

3. The social context of the first temples

The reasons for the rise of the Asclepius healing
cult are not entirely clear, and are undoubtedly complex.
According to the Edelsteins, the physicians' guilds which
Asclepius patronized grew in power and prestige in the
middle of the first millennium B.C.E., and, consequently,
the association of Asclepius with healing eclipsed that of
Apollo. Perhaps one could also suggest that the initial
impulses for the proliferation of Asclepieia may have been
due to an increased incidence of disease during the fifth-
fourth centuries B.C.E. It is well known that many diseases
need a particular population density in order to thrive.[14]

---

[13]See P. Xella, "Sulla più antica storia di alcune divinità fenicie," *Atti
del I Congresso Internazionale di Studi Fenici e Punici, Roma, 5-10
Novembre 1979* (2 vols.; Roma: Consiglio Nazionale delle Ricerche,
1983) 2:401-408.

[14]For example, F. L. Black ("Measles Endemicity in Insular
Populations: Critical Community Size and Its Evolutionary
Implications," *Journal of Theoretical Biology* 11 [1966] 207-11)
estimates that 7,000 susceptible individuals are needed perpetually in a
population to maintain measles in certain areas. For another discussion
of the relationship between population density and disease in ancient

Increases in population densities, especially in the sixth-fourth centuries B.C.E., are noted by various paleodemographers such as M. Grmek:

> The total number of inhabitants of Greece was not much more than 3 million, 2 million of whom lived on continental Greece (surface area 56,000 km.^{2}), with another 800,000 on the Peloponnesus (surface area 21,500 km.^{2}) and some 400,000 on the islands. So the demographic density, excluding the islands, amounts to 36 inhabitants per square kilometer. [15]

As Grmek notes, urbanization caused the density of certain areas to be higher than others.[16] Attica, which had 160 inhabitants per square kilometer, and Corinth, which had 110 inhabitants/km.^{2} in the fifth century B.C.E., were some of the most densely populated areas in Greece. Athens and the Peiraeus had approximately 200,000 people at the time of Thucydides. [17] The population of Greece remained stable during the fifth and fourth centuries, but there was a large decline by the 2nd century B.C.E.

---

times, see T. Aidan Cockburn, "Infectious Diseases in Ancient Populations," *Current Anthropology* 12 (1971) 51-56. The most comprehensive recent study of disease in ancient Greece is that of M. Grmek, *Diseases in the Ancient Greek World* (Baltimore: The Johns Hopkins University Press, 1989).

[15]Grmek, *Diseases*, 97.

[16]Grmek, *Diseases*, ibid.

[17]Grmek, *Diseases*, 98. An earlier estimate of 155,000-200,000 for Athens is provided by A. W. Gomme (*The Population of Athens in the Fifth and Fourth Centuries B.C.E.* [Oxford: Clarendon, 1933]).

The highly tentative and selective paleodemo-graphical data studied by, among others, Angel,[18] Richardson,[19] and Grmek indicate that there was a decrease in life expectancy at the beginning of the fourth century B.C.E. Grmek says: "The decline in average lifespan probably began in the fifth century B.C.E. and became apparent in the fourth century."[20] The decline may have been due to combination of war, famine[21] and disease. A plague at Athens occurred in 429 B.C.E. that may have killed a quarter of the Athenian land army, and it was a few years after this plague that the cult of Asclepius was introduced into Athens.[22] The cult of Asclepius was also introduced into Rome after a plague in 293/2 B.C.E.[23]

However, a rise in disease need not be the only factor in explaining why certain places became central shrines for healing deities. The rise of Epidauros may have benefited from its relative neutrality as well as a decrease in the general health status of Greece.

---

[18]See J. L. Angel, "Health and the Course of Civilization as Seen in Ancient Greece," *The Intern* (1948) 15-48; *idem* "The Bases of Paleodemography," *American Journal of Physical Anthropology* 30 (1969) 427-38; *idem*, "Ecology and Population in the Eastern Mediterranean," *World Archaeology* 4 (1972) 88-105.

[19]B. E. Richardson, *Old Age among the Ancient Greeks* (Baltimore Johns Hopkins, 1933).

[20]Grmek, *Diseases*, 104.

[21]For a study of the effects of the food supply on the health of ancient Greece, see Robert Sallares, *The Ecology of the Ancient Greek World* (Ithaca: Cornell, 1991).

[22]The plague is described by Thucydides, II, 47-55. A modern study may be found in J. F. D. Shrewsbury, "The Plague of Athens," *Bulletin of the History of Medicine* 24 (1950) 1-25.

[23]*Asclepius* I, 431.

The fourth century B.C.E. seems to have witnessed a general socio-economic upheaval according to the Marxist analysis of Fuks.[24] The latter's analysis points to a social imbalance caused by the rise of a rural "proletariat" that resulted from the loss of land among numerous small farmers. These farmers swelled the population of cities. Fuks also argues that the change to slave labor by large wealthy landowners caused rural unemployment among small farmers. At Argos, a few miles west of Epidauros, a revolt broke out in 370 B.C.E., that resulted in the confiscation of land of the wealthy, and the redistribution of that land to the poor.[25] One should note the proximity of Argos to Epidauros, and that the Asclepius temple was built about 370 B.C.E. Some of Epidauros' clients were from Argos in the fourth century B.C.E. (e.g., T. 423, 37).

Although critical of Marxist analyses of ancient Greek society, A. Lintott agrees that the fourth century witnessed a higher than normal incidence of civil strife.[26] According to Lintott, such strife was not always caused by a class struggle.[27] Instead, the important factors were inter-city rivalry, political maneuvering within the ruling classes (e.g., who among the aristocrats would rule), and the changing loyalties of significant pools of mercenary

---

[24] *Social Conflict in Ancient Greece*, (Brill: Leiden, 1984) [14]. See also, G. E. M. de Ste. Croix, *The Class Struggle in the Ancient Greek World* (Ithaca: Cornell, 1981).

[25] Sources for the history of this revolt include Diodorus XV 57:-3-58 and Isokrates, *Philippus*, 52.

[26] Andrew Lintott, *Violence, Civil Strife, and Revolution in the Classical City* (London: Croom Helm, 1982). See also E. Ruschenbusch, *Untersuchungen zu Staat und Politik in Griechenland vom 7.-4. Jr. v. Chr.* (Bamberg: Aku, 1978).

[27] Lintott, *Violence, Civil Strife, and Revolution*, 251-262.

manpower. According to Isokrates (*Panegyrikos,* 167-170) there were significant numbers of homeless people who wandered around Greece with their families because of poverty (δι ἔνδειαν). Many of the homeless men may have become mercenaries. Lintott, however, argues that inter-city strife, not so much poverty, resulted in the exile of a large population of men who became mercenaries.[28] Regardless of the exact causes of the strife, the fourth century seems to have had a high incidence of civil unrest.

In any event, the famous Asclepius temple at Epidauros in the fourth century B.C.E. came into prominence amidst rapid urbanization, civil strife, and some tensions between the rich and the poor in the nearby city of Argos. Epidauros was involved in a number of hostilities between 425 and 362 B.C.E., and Alison Burford argues that the building of the temple around 375-370 was the result of a respite that provided some needed laborers for temple construction.[29] The significant question regarding the social context of the Asclepius temple at Epidauros is why the civil strife so apparent in a number of sources in the fourth century was not explicit in contemporary testimonia of Asclepius. Rich and poor seem to mingle at the Asclepieion at Epidauros. As we have mentioned, nearby Argos had suffered a significant revolt at the time of the building of the Asclepius temple at Epidauros, and yet hostilities seem not to have affected the willingness of sometime enemies (Athens and Argos) to support the cult of Asclepius at Epidauros.

One possible reason is that, with few exceptions, Asclepius was not a politically oriented deity. The specialization of Asclepius in healing was undoubtedly one

---

[28]Lintott, *ibid.,* 257.
[29]Burford, *The Greek Temple Builders,* 25-34.

factor in evading political conflict. In general, the Asclepius temple at Epidauros may have been a place where patients, no matter their politics or social origins, could be seen as equals in illness. The rich and the poor, the Argive and the Athenian, were welcome in the Asclepieion (See Excursus for further details).

Gratitude from the patient was expected but it was generally proportional to the economic ability of the patient. In effect, the Asclepius temple at Epidauros may have provided an excellent place where differences that caused civil strife elsewhere were subordinated to the needs of a person as a sick individual. The Asclepius temple at Epidauros may have functioned as a haven and as a retreat from the strife that afflicted other places in Greece in the fourth century B.C.E. Epidauros was attacked and invaded at times (See Excursus), but for the most part it retained its independence. As we shall see, however, one cannot claim that such egalitarianism obtained in all periods and in all places.

In sum, while we cannot always argue for an absolute causal link between socio-economic circumstances and the rise of some of the temples of Asclepius, we can at least illuminate some of the more plausible reasons for the success of these shrines. Thus, while a catastrophic health crisis may have been primarily responsible for the rise of the temple of Asclepius at Athens, more complex socio-economic factors may explain the rise of the shrine at Epidauros. Future investigations may paint a more complex picture that may explain both the local and regional factors that affected the Asclepius shrines at Cos, Pergamum, and at lesser known places.

4. Description of the temples

It is still uncertain where the earliest Asclepius temple was located. The oldest shrine, according to Strabo,[30] was in Tricca (Thessaly), but it has not been found. Asclepius seems active in Thessaly and the Peloponnese, but he is rarer in inland sites. In Boeotia another healing god, Trophonius, was prominent.[31]

The main centers of the Asclepius cult were at Epidauros in the Peloponnese, Cos,[32] Pergamum[33], Athens,[34] and Corinth,[35] and it is these sites that have provided much of the archaeological information on Asclepieia. Shrines can also be found at Syracuse, Thasos,

---

[30]*Geographica*, IX, 5, 17 = T. 714.

[31]Edelstein and Edelstein, *Asclepius*, II, 248.

[32]For an archaeological report see, R. Herzog, *Kos, Ergebnisse der Deutschen Ausgrabungen und Forschungen* (Berlin, 1932).

[33]O. Ziegenaus and G. de Luca, *Das Asklepieion 1-2* (*Altertümer von Pergamon* XI; Berlin: De Gruyter, 1968-75). Wolfgang Radt, *Pergamon: Geschichte und Bauten, funde und Erforschung einer antiken Metropole* (Cologne: Du Mont, 1988); O. Deubner, *Das Asclepieion von Pergamon* (Berlin, 1938). Ziegenaus and de Luca (*Das Asklepieion, XI*, 1, pp. 10-21) date the initial phases of construction in the late 5th and in the 4th centuries B.C.E.

[34]See Sara B. Aleshire, *The Athenian Asklepieion: The People, their Dedications, and the Inventories* (Amsterdam: J. C. Gieben, 1989). For an earlier archaeological report, see P. Gérard, *L'Asclépieion d'Athènes, d'apres de récentes découvertes* (Paris, 1881).

[35]Carl Roebuck, *Corinth XIV: The Asklepieion and Lerna* (Princeton: The American School of Classical Studies at Athens, 1951); R. Struckmann, *Important Medical Centers in Antiquity: Epidaurus and Corinth* (Athens: Editions Kansas, 1979). According to Roebuck (*Corinth XIV*: 154), the cult was introduced in the late 5th century B.C.E., and it rose to a grand scale, even if only locally, in the late 4th century B.C.E.

Delos, and Paros, and all of these flourished after the fourth century B.C.E.[36] Newer material has been published from the cult of Asclepius at Fregellae (Italy), a site that was apparently destroyed by 125 B.C.E.[37] Although we shall comment on a variety of Asclepius temples, our main focus shall be the temple at Epidauros. Aside from healing rites, the cult of Asclepius had a daily and yearly liturgical calendar that included sacrifices, processions and games.[38]

a) Site and plan

It appears that the earliest known shrines of Asclepius were in caves or in open air sites near springs. Some Asclepius shrines remained in caves and open air sites even after the establishment of the most famous temples. For example, during the lifetime (2nd c. C.E.) of Pausanias there was a cave of Asclepius (σπήλαιον ἱερον ᾿Ασκληπιοῦ) in the ruins of Cyphanta in Laconia.[39]   As the following passage shows, Vitruvius notes that Asclepius shrines were established in places deemed to be healthy.[40]

> *Naturalis autem decor sic erit, si primum omnibus templis saluberrimae regiones aquarumque fontes in his locis idonei eligentur, in quibis fana constituantur, deinde maxime Aesculapio, Saluti, et eorum deorum, quorum plurimi medicinis aegri curari*

---

[36] Edelstein and Edelstein, *Asclepius*, II, 249.

[37] See Filippo Coarelli et al., *Fregellae 2. Il Santuario di Esculapio* (Rome: Tognon, 1986).

[38] Edelstein and Edelstein, *Asclepius*, II, 208.

[39] *Descriptio Graeciae*, III, 24, 2 = T. 755.

[40] *De Architectura*, I, 2, 7 = T. 707.

videntur. Cum enim ex pestilenti in salubrem locum
corpora aegra translata fuerint et e fontibus salubribus
aquarum usus subministrabuntur, celerius
convalescent. ita efficietur, uti ex natura loci
maiores auctasque cum dignitate divinitas excipiat
opiniones.

Therefore, it shall be much more naturally suitable if,
for all temples in the first place, the most healthy
sites be chosen and suitable springs of water in those
places in which shrines are to be set up, and for
Asclepius in particular and for Salus and for those
gods by whose medical power a great many of the
sick seem to be healed. For when sick persons are
moved from a pestilent to a healthy place and the
water supply is from salubrious fountains, they will
recover with more speed. So will it happen that the
divinity from the nature of the site will gain a greater
and higher reputation and authority.

Likewise Plutarch discusses the question of why the
sanctuary of Asclepius was outside the city. He states that
these shrines are "in places that are both clean and high" (ἐν
τόποις καθαροῖς καὶ ὑψηλοῖς).[41] Vitruvius' explanation is
debated by the Edelsteins and by Sigerist.[42] They note that
the climate of Epidauros was not more healthy than that of
the city, and that other Asclepieia were established in cities.
Nonetheless, one need not fault Vitruvius for being
scientifically incorrect. If there was a perception that distant

---

[41]*Aetia Romanae*, 94, 286 D = T. 708.
[42]Edelstein and Edelstein, *Asclepius*, II, 233; and Sigerist (1961: II,
64).

sites were healthy, then the reality may not have mattered as much as the perception. In fact, an entire Hippocratic treatise called *On Airs, Waters, Places* (ΠΕΡΙ ΑΕΡΩΝ ΥΔΑΤΩΝ ΤΟΠΩΝ) reflects the existence of the idea that environment was a significant factor in health at least by Hellenistic times.

The comments of Vitruvius and Plutarch also indicate that urban areas were not deemed, at least by some, as healthy as the countryside. The major Asclepieia of Epidauros, Cos, and Pergamum were located outside the city. One of the constant features in Asclepieia seems to be the presence of springs in (e.g., at Athens) or near the temple.[43] Asclepieia were also established in valleys,[44] outside towns (T. 759) and within the walls of cities.[45]

The temple of Asclepius at Epidauros was located about 6 miles from the town of Epidauros in a broad open valley between Mounts Kynortion and Tittheion. Excavations were conducted by P. Cavvadias from 1881 to 1928.[46] A recent and detailed analysis of the history and economics of the building of the Asclepius temple at Epidauros is provided by A. Burford.[47] Another recent treatment is that of R. Tomlinson.[48] The Asclepieion was built about 370 B.C.E., although Asclepius was probably worshipped there as early as the sixth century alongside Apollo. The worship of Asclepius at Epidauros cannot be

---

[43]Edelstein and Edelstein, *Asclepius*, II, 237 n. 15.

[44]Pausanias, *Descriptio Graeciae*, II, 27, 1-7 = T. 739.

[45]Pausanias, *Descriptio Graeciae*, I, 21, 4-5 = T. 725.

[46]See P. Cavvadias, το ἱερον τοῦ ᾽Ασκληπιοῦ ἐν ᾽Επιδαύροι (Athens: Perry, 1900).

[47]Alison Burford, *The Greek Temple Builders at Epidaurus* (Liverpool: Liverpool University Press, 1969).

[48]R. Tomlinson, *Epidauros* (Austin: University of Texas Press, 1983).

traced before the 6th century B.C.E.[49] The Asclepieion at Epidauros had a predecessor on the heights of Kynortion dedicated to Apollon Maleatas, and this shrine was excavated by J. Papadimitriou between 1948-1951.[50] The worship of Asclepius at Epidauros lasted for about 800 years.

The temple complex at Epidauros in the fourth century B.C.E. was not very large (See Figure 1), and the main temple was built in about 4 years and 8 months (between 375 and 370 B.C.E.) according to the pertinent records.[51] The temple was about 79 feet long x 42 feet wide x 40 feet high, and it consisted of a single cella. The temple was approached by a ramp. A number of sources indicate that its construction was financed by an international effort.[52]

The interior of the temple had many of the objects that one expects to see in other Greek temples. It had a statue of the god, who was seated on a throne with a staff in one hand and a serpent under the other hand. A dog lay at his feet. Murals decorated the temple at Athens and Epidauros. A table for the food offerings was also part of

---

[49]See Tomlinson, *Epidauros*, 23; Burford, *The Greek Temple Builders at Epidaurus*, 47-48.

[50]J. Papadimitriou in *Praktika* 1948 (published, 1949) 90-111; and *Praktika* 1951 (published 1952) 204-212. See also V. Lambrinudakis, "Remains of the Mycenean period in the Sanctuary of Apollon Maleatas," in R. Hägg and Nanno Marinatos, ed., *Sanctuaries and Cults in the Aegean Bronze Age* (Svenska Institutet I Athen: Stockholm, 1981) 59-65.

[51]R. A. Tomlinson, *Greek Sanctuaries* (New York: St. Martin's Press, 1976) 100.

[52]Tomlinson, *Epidauros*, 25-27; and Tomlinson, *Greek Sanctuaries*, 97.

the furniture. What may have been different is the provision of furniture for the patients to rest or to spend the night.

Located about 5 meters to the north of the temple at Epidauros was a building called the Abaton, and this was the main site for incubation by the patient. The Abaton was about 118 feet long and 31 feet wide in the fourth century B.C.E., and it included a well in one corner.[53] The Abaton adjoined a bath-house located to the east. Near the Abaton was a labyrinthine structure known as the Tholos, whose foundation consisted of six concentric rings with a pit in the center. Its function is still unclear, but it may have housed the famous serpents of Asclepius.[54] The Epidauros temple precinct also had a magnificent theater, and a grove.[55] Whoever took refuge in the temple was protected by the right of asylum from persecution.[56] Some temples were locked at night.

Insofar as the distinctive aspects of Asclepieia are concerned, the Edelsteins note:

> The Asclepieia did not differ much from the temples
> of other divinities with the exception of two features:
> the Asclepieia had buildings attached to them which

---

[53]See R. A. Tomlinson, *Greek Sanctuaries*, 101. P. Cavvadias (το ἱερον τοῦ 'Ασκληπιοῦ, 121) estimates the length at 70 meters and the width at 9.5 meters.

[54]So Burford, *The Greek Temple Builders*, 63. Tomlinson (*Epidauros*, 66) prefers to interpret the Tholos as a structure with a ritual function associated with dead heroes. A funerary cultic interpretation of the Tholos is also favored by G. Roux, "Trésors, Temples, Tholos," in G. Roux, ed., *Temples et sanctuaries* (Paris: Maison de l'Orient, 1984) 153-171.

[55]Pausanias, *Descriptio Graeciae*, II, 27, 1-7 = T. 739.

[56]Tacitus, *Annales*, IV, 14, 1-2 = T. 798.

were intended to house patients and to provide the
necessary means for their treatment; besides, there
was the hall in which the patients slept.[57]

Pausanias says that within the precincts of the Asclepieion
near Tithorea were dwellings for both the suppliants and his
servants.[58] Indeed, as Burkert notes, it was unusual for
sanctuaries to provide housing for the priests.[59]

    Guest quarters in Asclepieia were necessary for a
variety of reasons. One was that demand was high because
incubation was a usual mode of treatment.[60] According to
Jayne,[61] it was the frequent visitation of suppliants that may
have led to the building of accommodations for the pilgrims,
and eventually to temples with quarters for priests and
guests. Indeed, priests were needed much more
continuously than at other types of temples. In view of our
functional analysis, one may say that it was the therapeutic
function of the temple that was mainly responsible for the

---

[57]*Asclepius*, II, 191.

[58]*Descriptio Graeciae* X, 32,12 = T. 499.

[59]W. Burkert, *Greek Religion* (Cambridge, Mass.: Harvard, 1985) 96.

[60]Aside from the comments by the Edelsteins, some of the early
studies on incubation that are still useful include: R. Caton, *The
Temples and Ritual of Asklepios at Epidauros and Athens* (2nd ed.;
London: C. J. Clay and Sons, 1900); M. Hamilton, *Incubation or the
Cure of Diseease in Pagan Temples and Christian Churches* (London:
W. C. Henderson & Son, 1906); For a modern psychiatric evaluation,
see R. Rouselle, "Healing Cults in Antiquity: The Dream Cures of
Asclepius of Epidauros," *The Journal of Psychohistory* 12 (3, 1985)
339-352; H. J. Stam and N. P. Spanos, "The Asclepian Dream
Healings and Hypnosis: A Critique," *The International Journal of
Clinical and Experimental Hypnosis* 30 (1, 1982) 9-22.

[61]A. Jayne, *The Healing Gods of Ancient Civilizations* (New Haven:
Yale University Press, 1925) 254-255.

investment in guest accommodations. Indeed, the petitionary and thanksgiving functions could be executed during the day, and they probably would not have necessitated much time on the part of the patient. In contrast, the overnight stay was an essential component of the therapy at Asclepieia. Moreover, shrines located at some distance from population centers made guest accommodations necessary.

b) Administration

At the best known, and most popular temples, the administrative apparatus usually consisted of a chief priest (ἱερεύς) and his assistants. At Pergamum the chief priest directed the schedule, supervised the sacrifices and festivals, and acted as treasurer for the valuables that were given to the temple. He also acted as groundskeeper.[62] Similar duties may be attributed to the chief priest at Epidauros and other major Asclepieia.

Insofar as the selection and oversight of the priesthood is concerned, there does not seem to be a uniform standard among all of the sites. At Athens, for example, the state, and, more precisely, the Council of the Boule, seems to have had oversight of the Asclepius temple, and it appointed the chief priest.[63] At Cos the priest was selected by lot or by an oracle. There are reports of buying the office (e.g., T. 491).

The chief priest usually had assistants at the best known temples. The assistant priest was called the

---

[62]See *Inscriptio Pergamena* = T. 491 [2nd c. B.C.?]; and T. 786.
[63]See *Inscriptiones Graecae*, II, no. 1163 = T. 494 [288-7 B.C.E.]

neokoros, or, at Athens, a *zakoros.* At Pergamum there were two of these *neokoroi* according to Aristides.[64] Sometimes a secular officer, called the *hieromnemon,* acted as clerk for the receipts (cf., T. 562). Another officer, a *propolos,* seems to have been charged with tending the lamps according to Aristophanes.[65] Sometimes boys termed *pyrophoroi* were responsible for lighting and maintaining the altar fires, and bearing incense. Other assistants, usually boys, would be responsible for bearing relics and other objects used in ceremonies and processions. The remuneration for the temple personnel usually consisted of gifts and food left by the suppliants (T. 490).

Insofar as health care is concerned, one should note that the temple personnel were partly responsible for accommodation of the patients, and for other aspects of their therapy. According to Aristophanes (*Plutus,* 400-14), the priest, for example, would bid the suppliants good night. At Cos, the *neokoros* offered prayers for the suppliant, and interpreted dreams and omens.[66] The Asclepieion, therefore, provided patients with access to human beings who were acting on behalf of the patients in some manner. This must have been an attraction not found at other temples where the priests might not have been as interested in providing personal care to the suppliants. No doubt, the expertise of the priests was also an important attraction.

---

[64]*Oratio,* XLVIII, 29 = T. 495.

[65]*Plutus,* 660 = T. 421.

[66]Aristides, *Oratio,* XLVIII, 35 = T. 497.

B. THE ROLE OF THE TEMPLE IN HEALING

In order to elucidate how a particular constellation of socio-religious concepts resulted in the known forms of the Asclepius cult and its temples, one must be cognizant of the interplay of the specific functions of the temple with the larger social and religious dimensions of the society in which the temples flourished.

1. Petitionary function

The petitionary function of the Asclepius temples can be established on the basis of numerous sources. Such sources indicate that a patient could go to the temple, or s/he could send a proxy if mobility was a problem. For example, Marinus reports that a girl named Iphigenia was too ill to go to the Asclepieion, and so two persons (Proclus and Pericles) went in her stead.[67] The case is interesting in that Marinus notes that the temple was the option chosen after non-temple physicians were unable to help her. It was permissible for someone too ill to walk to the temple to be carried by some means (T. 423, 25). The prayers could be long and complicated,[68] or short and simple (e.g., T. 582).

As in the case of the biblical Hannah, women went to the temple to pray for healing from infertility. For example, a woman named Andromache of Epirus went to the temple to ask for a child (T. 423, 31). During her incubation, Andromache was said to have been impregnated by Asclepius himself. Another woman from Troezen went

---

[67]*Vita Procli*, Cp. 29 = T. 582.

[68]Arnobius, *Adversus Nationes*, I. 49 = T. 584.

to the temple to ask for a child. The god asked her whether she wanted a male or a female, and she said that she wanted a male. Her wish was subsequently fulfilled (T. 423, 35).

A vow (εὐχή) was often made by the suppliant in return for healing.[69] Vows, in fact, combine the petitionary and thanksgiving aspects of healing. The vow was intended to persuade the god to heal (petitionary), and yet it promised some act of gratitude on the part of the patient (thanksgiving). The specific vows that were offered could include offering sacrifices, making figurines, or a variety of other acts.

2. Therapeutic function

The therapeutic function of the Asclepius temples is very clear, and it is one of the distinctive features of Asclepieia. In addition to being a place where petitions for health were made, procedures and prescriptions were administered at the temple that were intended to heal the patient. Illnesses that the temple serviced included lice infestation (T 423, 26), "leprosy" (T. 436), blindness (T. 423, 4), aphasia (T. 423, 5), lodged implements and weapons (T. 423, 12), alopecia (T. 423,19), tapeworm (423, 23), headaches and insomnia (T. 423, 29), and war wounds (T. 423, 30). There are indications that some Asclepieia specialized in certain diseases. Thus, Rouse notes the preponderance of eye votives at Athens, while

---

[69]The word εὐχή means both vow and prayer, but the history of the word is more complicated than it seems, see L. Muellner, *The Meaning of Homeric EΥXOMAI through its Formulas (Innsbrucker Beiträge zur Sprachwissenschaft* 13, 1976).

genitals and breasts predominate at Corinth.[70]   However, it is difficult to ascertain how representative such samples are. People usually slept there overnight, and healing usually was thought to be accomplished during a dream.

One description of a healing incubation required that the supplant or his proxy be dressed in white.[71] The patient was assigned a pallet in the Abaton. Some reports say that a *neokoros* would come in at twilight, and he would light the lamps. The supplant placed an offering on the table, then he retired to his couch. Some depictions of the couch show that it was covered with animal skins.[72] After a prayer by the supplant and priest, the lamps were extinguished, and the priests departed to their quarters. During the night some sources (e.g., T. 421) report that the priests dressed in the god's attire would visit the supplant and perform rites.

Yet, there has been a resistance to viewing the priests as physicians, as if the two roles could not be combined. This seems to be part of a more basic resistance to using the word *physician* or *medicine* for practices which involved supernatural or religious assumptions. For many scholars, the only legitimate medicine in ancient Greece apparently is that which most resembles the "naturalistic" or "scientific" type. Note the remarks of the Edelsteins:

---

[70]W. H. D. Rouse, *Greek Votive Offerings*, 212.

[71]Aristides, *Oratio*, XLVIII, 31 = T. 486.

[72]See U. Hausmann, *Kunst und Heiltum. Untersuchungen zu den griechischen Aslepiosreliefs* (Potsdam: Eduard Tichnote, 1948) 46-48, pl. 1. For a comparative discussion of incubation on animal skins, see Susan Ackerman, "The Deception of Isaac, Jacob's Dream at Bethel, and Incubation on an Animal Skin," in G.A. Anderson and S. M. Olyan, eds., *Priesthood and Cult in Ancient Israel* (Sheffield, 1991) 92-120.

There is no evidence whatever that the physicians
participated in the temple healings...One would have
to postulate a *medicina altera* different from that
known from Hippocrates and Galen, an invention of
the priests and physicians who presumably worked
together at the Asclepieia.[73]

But, as our discussion on Mesopotamia will illustrate
more clearly, the role of the physician and the priest cannot
be separated so easily at healing temples. Excavations at the
Asclepieia at Pergamum and at other places reveal probable
evidence of surgical procedures. For example, at least five of
the metal implements found in the Asclepieion at Pergamum
could be surgical instruments.[74] Depictions of surgical
instruments and physical therapy in some votive reliefs
suggests that surgery and physical therapy were practiced in
at least some Asclepius shrines.[75] Excavations at Corinth
have uncovered an inscription (Cor. Ins. 1035 and 1134) in
which the priest was also called a physician (ιατρον).[76]
There should now be little doubt that, at least at some
sites, the Asclepieion was served by priests who sometimes
may have used religious rites in conjunction with surgical
procedures. Far from being an invention of priests at
Asclepieia, surgical therapy administered by priests was
probably much more ancient than its use in the type of

---

[73]*Asclepius*, II, 158.

[74]See O. Ziegenaus and G. de Luca, *Altertümer von Pergamon*, XI, 2:
pages 136 -137 and Tafel 75, 1.

[75]See, for example, a votive relief from Paros in U. Hausmann,
Griechische Weihreliefs (Berlin: De Gruyter, 1960) 58 and *Abbildung*
28. A depiction of surgical instruments from the Asclepieion at
Athens may be found in Sigerist, *A History of Medicine*, II: 314 # 2.

[76]Carl Roebuck, *Corinth* XIV, 156.

medicine attributed to Hippocrates and Galen. The use of surgery and other practices associated with "naturalistic" medicine may never have posed the type of logical problem that the Edelsteins seem to assume.

The testimonies indicate that treatment at Asclepieia was very flexible and varied. Asclepius prescribed drugs (T. 432) that could be invented extemporaneously or that were already known. He prescribed, for example, the eating of partridge with frankincense (T. 434). Wine mixed with ashes from the altar was prescribed for a man named Lucius (T. 438). Less conventional prescriptions included running, and the composition of odes was not an unusual prescription.[77]

Bathing in springs, rivers or the sea was also prescribed by the god.[78] Water from the well in Pergamum was reputed to heal the blind and lame (T. 409). One could drink it or bathe in it. Encomia intended for the well are also extant (e.g., T. 804). A report in Aristides suggests that eating at certain spots within the temple may have had some significance.[79] Treatment could include herbal preparations applied to the affected area (T. 423, 18), and the divine kiss at Epidauros (T. 423, 41).

Of particular interest is the association of dogs and snakes in the healings. A number of sources report the therapeutic effect of a licking by a dog (e.g., T. 423, 26). Pausanias and tablets found at Epidauros speak about the role of dogs in effecting cures.[80] Dogs are often depicted

---

[77]For example, Galenus, *De Sanitate Tuenda*, I, 8, 19-21 = T. 413.

[78]Aristides, *Oratio*, XLVIII, 80 = T 408a; and *Inscriptiones Graecae*, IV, 1 no. 126 = T. 432.

[79]*Oratio*, XLIX,28 = T. 411.

[80]*Descriptio Graeciae*, II, xxvi 4 = T. 19; xxvii, 2 = T. 630.

accompanying Asclepius in coins and on reliefs.[81] Sextus
Empiricus reports that, based on the presuppositions of the
Asclepiads, Diocles recommended that some patients eat the
flesh of puppies.[82] The dog also functioned as a guard for
the temple (cf., T. 731). In fact, according Aelianus, the
dog was honored as "a truly faithful guard and inferior to
none of the sacristans in watchfulness."[83]

The Edelsteins believe that the dog, as an attribute of
Asclepius, was inherited from Apollo Maleatas.[84] Such a
connection is not discussed by the ancient sources. If, as
suggested by Szemerényi, Asclepius came from Anatolia or
further east, then the dog may have been an attribute of
Asclepius from the beginning of the cult in Greece. We shall
speak of the parallel association of dogs with Gula, the
Mesopotamian healing deity, in the relevant section. The
Edelsteins speak of the dog as a possible nurse to Asclepius
during his infancy (cf., the Romulus myth).[85]

Equally important was the therapeutic effect of
licking by a serpent (e.g., T. 423, 17). The serpent of
Asclepius may have been the species *Elaphes longissima*

---

[81]For a good example of a relief depicting the dog of Asclepius, see F.
R. Walton, "A Problem in the *Ichneutae* of Sophocles," *Harvard
Studies in Classical Philology*, XLVI (1935) Plate I. A coin from
Epidauros depicting the dog of Asclepius from ca. 350 B.C.E. may be
found in Sigerist, *A History of Medicine*, II:80 # 2.

[82]*Hypotyposeis*, III, 225 = T. 225: Διοκλῆς ἀπὸ τῶν κατὰ τοὺς
Ασκληπιάδας ὁρμώμενος τισὶ τῶν πασχόντων σκυλάκεια
δίδοσθαι κελεύει κρέα.

[83]*De Natura Animalium*, VII, 13 = T. 731: φύλαξ πιστὸς καὶ τῶν
νεωκόρων οὐδενὸς τήν ἐπιμέλειαν.

[84]*Asclepius*, II, 227.

[85]*ibid*, II, 227.

longissima, which is harmless to humans.[86] Live serpents may have been kept in the Tholos. Some of the medicines at Pergamum were made from vipers (τῶν ἐχιδνῶν φαρμάκου) according to Galenus.[87] Bronze serpents have been found, at the Asclepieion of Pergamum.[88] The posture and other features of the bronze serpents at Pergamum evoke obvious parallels with bronze serpents found at Timna and other places in the ancient Near East, and these serpents will be discussed more fully in our chapter on Israel. Depictions of serpents accompanying Asclepius are common in reliefs and coins.

    Sacrifices often preceded the incubation ritual at Asclepieia, and the most common offering was the cock.[89] However, in place of the usual sacrifice, people gave a wide variety of items such as "money, frankincense, laurel, olive shoots, oak leaves, garlands, songs, branches, chaplets, pictures on which Asclepius was painted as a well-doer (T. 539), or brass rings (T. 542), candles (T. 544), offerings of gold and silver."[90] The main food offerings to Asclepius consisted of honey-cakes, cheese-cakes, roasted meats and figs that were laid upon the table of the god (T. 514; 490). Although such food offerings usually fed the priests, sometimes cakes were also given to the dogs.[91]

---

[86]See G. Majno, *The Healing Hand* (Cambridge, Mass.: Harvard University Press, 1975) 203.

[87]*Subfiguratio Empirica*, Cp. X, p. 78 = T. 436.

[88]For example, see O. Ziegenaus and G. de Luca, *Altertümer von Pergamon*, XI, 1 (1968) p. 169 and Tafel 61 no. 465.

[89]Artemidorus, *Onirocritica*, V, 9 = T. 523.

[90]Edelstein and Edelstein, *Asclepius*, II, 190.

[91]*Inscriptiones Graecae*, II, no. 4962 = T. 515; beginning of 4th c. B.C.E.

When patients did go to the temple, they usually
performed preliminary purification rites. The fact that these
purification rites were standard at Epidauros is highlighted in
the case of a voiceless boy who came to the temple to be
healed. According to the inscription, the boy first "made
sacrifices and [performed] the prescribed (rituals)."[92]
Pausanias says that people may not go up to the temple of
Asclepius at Pergamum unless they have bathed.[93]
Although the entire ritual at any one Asclepieion cannot be
reconstructed with certainty, an inscription, unfortunately
incomplete, from Pergamum appears to give the order of
rituals from the arrival of the patient to his/her incubation.[94]
The order of the main components of the rituals in this
inscription seems to be as follows:

> 1. Bathing, accompanied by rituals involving
> brimstone and laurel and dressed in a white
> garment.
> 2. Presentation before the god (presumably
> before his image in the temple);
> 3. Entrance into the incubation room (the
> Abaton).

Presumably, the offerings of cakes or other types of
sacrifices also preceded the incubation ritual as indicated by
other inscriptions (e.g.,T. 515). The priority of ritual
bathing may also be reflected archaeologically in that bathing

---

[92]*Inscriptiones Graecae*, IV, 1, no. 121,5 = T. 423,5: ὡς δε
προεθύσατο καὶ [ἐπόησε τὰ] νομιζόμενα.
[93]*Descriptio Graeciae*, V, 13,3 = T. 512: ἔστι γὰρ δὴ οὐδὲ τούτοις
ἀναβῆναι πρὸ λουτροῦ παρὰ τὸν Ἀσκληπιόν.
[94]*Inscription Pergamena* [*Inschriften von Pergamon*, II no. 264] = T.
513.

structures preceded the temple entrance. In his description of the Asclepieion at Corinth, Roebuck notes:

> The buildings of the Hellenistic sanctuary and of Lerna seem to provide for all these [rituals]. Upon entering the sanctuary from the east, a ceremonial ablution, preliminary to sacrifice, would have been performed at the east water basin.[95]

It is important to note that purification rites do not seem to be required for healings away from the temple. As we shall show below, the distinction between the necessity of purification rituals at the temple and the lack of necessary purification rituals away from the temple is related to the fact that illness *per se* usually was not regarded as a ritual impurity. In other words, the purification rituals at the temple seem to be required because the worshipper (ill or healthy) must not defile the sacred locus, rather than because the healing of the disease requires the purification. For example, Marinus reports that an arthritic man placed a bandage on his foot at the request of certain advisors.[96] This was a sufficient ritual, and soon thereafter, Asclepius healed him at home. An inscription indicates that prayer away from the temple by a man named Diophantus of Sphettus was sufficient to effect a healing. Indeed, the patient wanted to be healed in order to visit the temple again (πάλιν εἰσάγειν).[97]

---

[95]Roebuck, *Corinth* XIV, 157.
[96]*Vita Procli*, Cp. 31 = T. 446.
[97]*Inscriptiones Graecae*, II, no. 4514 = T. 428; 2nd c. C.E.

3. Thanksgiving function

After a healing, the patient was expected to bring a thank offering. In fact, such thank offerings sometimes were commanded by the god. For example, Aelianus notes that when a man named Aristarchus was ill, Asclepius commanded him to provide a thank offering (προστάσσει χαριστήρια τῆς ὑγείας).[98] Epidauros Asclepius enjoined a woman to send a thank offering after she was cured of worms (T. 423, 25). In effect, such commandments served to emphasize and maintain the thanksgiving function of the temple. Since thanksgiving offerings often provided food and money, the commandments to provide thanksgiving offerings also, in effect, commanded economic support for the temple.

These thank offerings/vows could be variable. Models of the parts healed, in terracotta, ivory, bronze, gold or silver, sometimes inscribed with the name of the donor, were part of these thank or votive offerings.[99] Thank offerings included money, paintings and figurines. Some of the figurines depicted the suppliant (including statuettes of children at Athens[100]), while others depicted the god. We shall speak about figurines of body parts below. Thank offerings could range from an inexpensive cock to expensive oxen.[101]

Hymns were often sufficient as a thank offering. Many of these hymns were inscribed on stones. The

---

[98]*Fragmenta*, 101 = T. 455.

[99]Jayne, *The Healing Gods of Ancient Civilizations*, 293.

[100]See W. H. D. Rouse, *Greek Votive Offerings* (Cambridge: Cambridge University Press, 1902) 210.

[101]See Polybius, *Historiae*, XXXII, 15, 1-5 = T. 546.

honoring of gods with song is an ancient tradition, and it is not peculiar to healing deities. However, the use of songs as payment for healing helped to insure the accessibility of the cult to the poor.

4. Figurines of body parts

Of special interest are the distinctive figurines that seem to predominate at Asclepieia. It is well established that many of the figurines of body parts at Asclepieia do represent an afflicted part of the body. In fact, for almost every text that mentions the healing of a specific body part by Asclepius, one can find an Asclepieion that contains a figurine of such a body part. The following are a few examples:

Body part healed by Asclepius	Attestation of body part figurine
Eyes (T. 423,2)	*Pergamum* XI, 1 (Tafel 62, B)
Foot (T. 423,6)	*Corinth* XIV, pl. 41
Ear (T. 424)	*Pergamum* XI, 1 (Tafel 62,A)
Hand (T. 423,3)	*Corinth* XIV, pl. 66
Genitals (T. 474)	*Corinth* XIV, pl. 44

The chart does not imply that there is a direct correlation between the body part in a text and the body part in an Asclepieion, but the general correlation is best explained by the practice of representing afflicted body parts with figurines.

The following inscriptions found on figurines of body parts also attest to the fact that many of these figurines represented afflicted body parts:[102]

Body part	Inscription (Source)	English
Pair of eyes	ὑπὲρ τῆς γυναικὸς Πραξίας ᾿Ασκληπιῶι (*CIA* ii. 1453)	For Asclepius, on behalf of the woman, Praxias.
Leg	Μενεστρατος εὐχὴν ανεθηκεν (*CIA* ii. 1503)	Menestratos (as) a vow has offered (it).

One cannot always claim that a particular figurine represents an afflicted body part because many of the figurines are found in other types of temples. Many of the figurines may represent other aspects of the cult. For example, one figurine at Pergamum depicts an ear, and bears an inscription dedicated to Asclepius by a woman named Fabia Secunda, who apparently was healed during a dream.[103] Ziegenaus and de Luca note correctly that such ear votives are found at many non-healing temples, and that they may symbolize the gracious hearing of the suppliant by the gods (θεοὶ ἐπήκοοι), rather than an afflicted body part.[104] Although one cannot

---

[102]*CIA* as cited in Rouse (*Greek Votive Offerings*, 213), who dates the first inscription to the fourth century B.C.E. and describes the second as "late."

[103]Greek: ᾿Ασκληπιω. σωτῆρι. φαβια. σεκουνδα. κατ᾿ ὄνειρον. See Christian Habicht, *Die Inschriften des Asklepieions* (Berlin: W. de Gruyter, 1969) 119 and Tafel 30.

[104]See O. Ziegenaus and G. de Luca, *Altertümer von Pergamon*, XI, 1 (1968) page 171.

simply equate such figurines exclusively with healing deities
or with afflicted parts, neither can one automatically deny
that such body parts may also be an expression of thanks
for a healing at the Asclepius temple.

Similarly, some nude female figurines show hand
placement on the right breast.[105] Since other temples have
figurines with hand placement on the right breast (including
males), it is difficult to argue that these figurines always
depict an afflicted body part rather than some typical
pose.[106] On the other hand, one also finds figurines of
breasts alone at various sites that are almost certainly
depictions of afflicted body parts. At Athens, for example,
one finds a breast dedicated to Asclepius by a patient named
File (φίλη 'Ασκληπιοιῶι).[107] At Corinth one can find at least
11 such votive breasts.[108]

Also common are figurines of feet. These may also
represent healed portions, or symbolize the presence of the
suppliant.[109] A pair of eyes with an inscription is certainly
to be interpreted as a thanksgiving for a healing according to

---

[105]For examples, see O. Ziegenaus and G. de Luca, *Altertümer von
Pergamon*, XI, 1(1968) Tafel 51:299 and 53: 368.

[106] It should be noted that in his study of the Hippocratic corpus W.
H. S. Jones (*Hippocrates* I, Introduction, xlviii; Loeb Classical Library)
notes that the two most common complaints in ancient Greece are
"chest troubles and malaria."

[107]*CIA* ii. 1482, as cited in Rouse, *Greek Votive Offerings*, 213.

[108]See Roebuck, *Corinth* XIV, 121-22, and accompanying plates.

[109]O. Ziegenaus and G. de Luca, *Altertümer von Pergamon*, XI, 2
(1975) page 134 and Tafel 73: 4 and 5.

de Luca.[110] At Pergamum heads are also common.[111] And most persuasive are models of the disease itself. For example, a lady named Timothea dedicated an ulcer (καρκίνος).[112]

In summary, it is difficult to say that every depiction of a body part is a depiction of an afflicted body part, especially if there is no accompanying inscription. Yet, there is much compelling evidence that a great many of these depictions of body parts at Asclepieia represented afflicted body parts. As we shall demonstrate, some figurines depicting or highlighting body parts in Mesopotamia may also represent afflicted body parts.

The exact function of the depictions of body parts is not always easy to decipher. Some may have been simple testimonies of the healing of a specific part of the body. The written testimonies usually do mention the specific body part that Asclepius healed. The figurines of body parts and many of the testimonies from Epidauros reflect the idea that illness was localized in a specific area of the body (in contrast to a systemic disorder). Since many figurines were marked by the word εὐχὴν, the votive figurine also may have acted as a sort of receipt for the fulfillment of a vow. As we have mentioned, the word εὐχή means both vow and prayer. According to a comparative study of votive figurines from Cyprus and the Near East by J. B. Connelly, many votive figurines may have represented the prayer of the worshipper

---

[110]The inscription reads: Ταπαρι 'Ασκλήπιω εὐχὴ[ν]. De Luca *Altertümer von Pergamon*, XI, 2 (1968) 172, states: "es sich zweifellos um das dankbar gestiftete Ex-Voto für erfolgete Heilung."

[111]*Altertümer von Pergamon*, XI, 2 (1975) 117-121 and Tafeln 62 and 63.

[112] See Rouse, *Greek Votive Offerings*, 214.

rather than the worshipper himself.[113] But the presence of
the votives may also guarantee the presence (ἀνάθημα) or
proximity of the patient, or his afflicted parts, to the healing
god.[114]

Insofar as votive inscriptions are concerned, Plinius
says that it was a custom for those who had been freed from
an illness to inscribe in the temple of their god whatever it
was that had helped them so that other persons might profit
from that experience.[115] Another effect of votive figurines
and inscriptions was that it provided a sort of advertisement
for the success of the temple. Indeed, the fame and success
of the temple was sometimes associated with the number of
its votives. Thus, in his description of the Asclepieion at
Cos, Strabo notes the great number of votives (σφόδρα
ἔνδοξον καὶ πολλῶν ἀναθημάτων μεστὸν [ἱερόν]).[116]

The artisans also probably benefited from the sale of
the votives. The burial of votives meant that older votives
were periodically replaced in the temple by newly
manufactured votives. Libanius, for example, mentions that
a patient would willingly pay the painter the fee needed to
commemorate the god's beneficence in return for health.[117]
However, some votive figurines could be made by the
patient himself.

---

[113]J. B. Connelly, "Standing Before One's God: Votive Sculpture and
the Cypriot Religious Tradition," *BA* 52 (4, 1989) 211.

[114]See W. Burkert, *Greek Religion* (Cambridge, Mass.: Harvard
University, 1985) 92-95.

[115]*Naturalis Historia* XXIX, 1 (2) 4 = T. 795: *liberatos morbis
scribere in templo eius dei quid auxiliatum esse, ut postea similitudo
proficeret.*

[116]*Geographica*, XIV, 2, 19 = T. 794.

[117]*Declamationes*, XXXIV, 35-36 = T. 539.

5. Social accessibility

Part of the attraction of many Asclepieia was that they served patients from a wide range of social classes. Of course, one cannot claim that such egalitarianism obtained in all periods and in all places. Some of the Asclepieia in the Roman period (e.g., Pergamum during second century C.E.) seem to be social centers for the upper classes.[118]

But the services offered, even if only an ideal, to the poor and rich, may have been an important factor in the initial stages of the cult of Asclepius at Epidauros and elsewhere. Even Aelius Aristides, who constantly praised the Asclepieion of Pergamum in the second century C.E., speaks of the ideal of distributing holy portions to fellow pilgrims.[119] Aelianus and other writers from the periods of most prosperity for Asclepieia emphasized that Asclepius healed the poor (τινὰ τῶν ἀπόρων ἰάσαιτο), [120] and that the god did not receive gifts in exchange for healing.[121] Spiritual purity, not wealth, was demanded of those who came in search of healing. The range of gifts found at many of the excavated Asclepieia indicates that the Asclepius temples did, in fact, contain gifts of varying economic value. The thanksgiving song, which is often emphasized as a payment for healing, perhaps functioned as an inexpensive and democratic means of payment for a healing. In fact, Lucianus (2nd c. C.E.) states that those who did not have the talent to compose good thanksgiving songs could simply

---

[118]See Radt, *Pergamon*, 270-71.

[119]Aristides, *Oratio*, XLVIII, 27 = T. 504.

[120]*Fragmenta*, 100 = T. 405.

[121]*Fragments*, 101 = T. 455.

sing ones that had already been composed by Sophocles and others.[122]

Of course, one cannot claim that fees were consistent throughout all places and periods. Some of the sources we have discussed indicate that expensive gifts were also accepted. Undoubtedly there were periods and places that may have moved towards increasing fees and the value of thanksgiving offerings. Some authors do evince sustained polemics against high fees or even the necessity of fees altogether. For example, a discussion by Libanius shows that there were apologetic strategies to defend the necessity of paying fees at the temple even if Asclepius did not have need for wealth.[123] Libanius also says that the gods are prone to beneficence of their own free will, but that they are even better when petitioned and when a fee is paid at the temple. In other words, the payment of fees at the temple was defended as a means to show Asclepius the patient's good will rather than because of some need for wealth on the part of Asclepius.

If one assumes that unquestionable customs need not be commanded, then the enjoining of thanksgiving offerings also seems to be an attempt to persuade patients to provide the offerings that, as we have seen, formed the economic well being of the temple. The explicit reference to the fact that Asclepius did not demand expensive gifts may reflect an attempt to assuage the differences between the rich and poor that seemed to have plagued many communities in Greece.

---

[122]*Demosthenis Encomium*, 27 = T. 588.
[123]*Declamationes*, XXXIV, 23-26 = T. 539.

C. MEDICAL THEOLOGY

1. Cause and morality in illness

The testimonies of healing are remarkable in that very little explicit discussion of sin or immoral transgressions are associated with an illness. The majority of the 43 best preserved testimonies on the stela (2nd half of the fourth century B.C.E.) from Epidauros have the following pattern:[124]

1. Name of the patient;
2. Place of residence of the patient;[125]
3. Description (and history) of medical condition and afflicted part;
4. Description of the healing action of Asclepius (e.g., prescription, ritual);
5. Affirmation of healing (and departure from the temple)

The following report is an example:

Alcetas of Halieis. This blind man saw a dream. It seemed to him that the god came up to him and with his fingers opened his eyes, and that he first saw the

---

[124]*Inscriptiones Graecae* IV, 1, II = T. 423. The stela actually contains over one hundred testimonies, but most were too fragmentary to be translated (cf., Edelstein and Edelstein, *Asclepius*, I, 229 n. 1).

[125]About a dozen of the testimonia on the Epidauros stele do not mention a place of origin. The social significance, if any, of such an omission is uncertain, though one must not overlook the existence of a significant population of homeless or errant individuals who may have received care at Asclepieia.

trees in the sanctuary. At daybreak he walked out
sound.

Some of the testimonia do place some responsibility on the
patient when they speak of the aggravation of a pre-existing
condition. For example, according to Philostratus a person
complaining that Asclepius did not heal him was
reprimanded because he irritated and aggravated his
condition.[126]   On the other hand, Marinus believed that
Proclus, an arthritic, suffered from a disease that was
transmitted in many cases from father to son.[127] Eustratius
said that health is an attribute of chance.[128]   Julianus
reported that Asclepiads believed that disturbances in
breathing (ἐκ τῆς τοῦ πνεύματος εἶναι τροπῆς) were the
cause of all or most diseases (μάλιστα μὲν πάσας τὰς
νόσους).[129] This study of the testimonia confirms the
following assessment of morality in the Asclepius cult by
Parker: "To questions of morality he [Asclepius] had in
general the professional indifference of the true doctor."[130]

---

[126]*Vita Apollonii*, I, 9 = T. 397: σὺ δὲ ἐναντία τῇ νόσῳ
πράττεις.

[127]*Vita Procli*, Cp. 31= T. 446: δὲ τὰ πολλὰ εἰς παῖδας ἐκ
πατέρων χωρεῖν.

[128]*Commentarium in Aristotelis Analytica Posteriora*, B11, 95a 3 = T.
222: πολλὰ μέντοι τῶν κατὰ προαίρεσιν γένοιντ᾽ ἄν καὶ ἀπὸ
τύχης, οἷον ὑγεία.

[129]*In Matrem Deorum*, 178 C = T. 224.

[130]R. Parker, *Miasma: Pollution and Purification in Early Greek
Religion* (Oxford: Clarendon, 1983) 249.

2. Purity and illness

The question of whether in ancient Greece illness was believed to produce an impure state in patients has been discussed by various scholars. According to the Edelsteins:

> But in antiquity, disease was never understood as a defilement of the body. Nor would it have discouraged people from coming to the sanctuaries had Asclepius imposed an elaborate ritual.[131]

The Edelsteins may be overstating the extent to which disease was viewed as pollution or "defilement of the body" everywhere in antiquity, but it is not far from accurate in depicting the attitude toward illness found in Asclepieia.

Some sources note that, despite their accessibility to the people with illnesses, Asclepieia did observe standards of purity. However, the definition of purity is not as obvious as one might think.[132] Not surprisingly, birth and death were regarded as impurity. Pausanias reports that a special building was provided for women to give birth or for the sick to die because birth and death were not to take place in his precinct.[133]

But illness *per se* was not regarded as an impurity if by this term we refer to any state which renders a person unfit to be present in a sacred area or which displeases the gods in some manner. In fact, Porphyrius notes that purity

---

[131]*Asclepius*, II, 149 n. 16.

[132]For a general examination of purity in Greek religion, see R. Parker, *Miasma*.

[133]*Descriptio Graeciae*, II, 27, 1-7 = T. 739: οὐδὲ ἀποθνήσκουσιν ἄνθρωποι οὐδὲ τίκτουσιν αἱ γυναῖκές σφισιν ἐντὸς τοῦ περιβόλου.

was defined as purity of thought at Epidauros.[134] That is to say, thinking "holy" thoughts was sufficient to render a person pure. Being physically clean or pure meant little if one's thoughts were not pure. Such a definition of purity seems to emphasize the fact that illness itself was not an impurity that excluded one from the temple. Indeed, the sick were admitted to the temple.

Purification rituals were not limited to the ill, but were incumbent on all those who entered the temple. Purification rituals were also performed at "non-healing" temples even if the person was not ill. Illness *per se,* therefore, did not render a patient impure of body in the Asclepius cult. The idea of purity of thought as holiness would certainly not discourage service to those who had illnesses.

Although the location of springs may have been related to the water as cleanser of moral pollution in the early history of the Asclepius cult, purification during the Classical and Hellenistic periods had more to do with the general cleanliness of the sacred locus and with the restoration of the proper balance of bodily substances, than with the extirpation of a stigmatizing pollution. As in the Hippocratic corpus, Asclepius testimonies usually did not view disease as producing, or deriving from, substances that could lead to the destruction of the sacredness of a temple. Instead, impurity related to disease was often viewed as an imbalance between an otherwise normal substances. Water could wash away any excess in these normal substances and thus restore the proper balance.

---

[134]*De Abstinentia,* II, 19 = T. 318: ἐν γοῦν Ἐπιδαύρῳ προεγέγραπτο. ἁγνὸν χρὴ ναοῖο θυώδεος ἐντὸς ἰόντα ἔμμεναι. ἁγνεία δ' ἐστὶ φρονεῖν ὅσια.

The water of certain locations was regarded as miraculous and healthy for both the sick and the healthy. In his discourse on the well of Asclepius, Aristides says: "This water alone is equally pleasant to the sick and to the healthy, and it is most useful for one as for the other." [135] Aristides adds: [136]

τὸ δὲ τῷ σώζειν τοὺς χρωμένους, οὐ τῷ
μηδένα αὐτου ψαύειν, ἱερόν ἐστιν. καὶ τὸ
αὐτὸ καθαρσίοις τε ἐξαρκεῖ τοῖς περὶ τὸ
ἱερὸν καὶ ἀνθρώποις καὶ πίνειν καὶ λούεσθαι
καὶ προσορῶσιν εὐφραίνεσθαι

[The water] is sacred because it saves those who use it and not because no one touches it. And the same water suffices both for purifications of what belongs to the shrine and for men to drink and be bathed in it and to rejoice over when they behold it.

Note that "purity" is defined as an ability to heal. Again, such a notion of the purity of the water had the effect of inviting the sick to use the temple facilities, and it emphasized that the temple was meant for the sick.

As we have noted, purification does have its place, but it does not always seem to be a necessary component of a healing ritual *per se*. One finds purification ceremonies when the patient goes to the temple, but not always when the healing is executed away from the temple. The implication of this distinction shall become more important

---

[135]*Oratio,* XXXIX, 1-18 = T. 804: μόνον δὲ τοῦτο τὸ αὐτὸ
νοσοῦσι καὶ ὑγιαίνουσιν ὁμοίως, ἥδιστον καὶ
λυσιτελέστατον ἑκατέροις τε καὶ συναμφοτέροις ἐστίν.
[136]*Oratio,* XXXIX, 1-18 = T. 804.

when we look at the biblical material. In any case, R. Parker is probably correct in noting that "purification played little part in the temple medicine of the classical period."[137]

The idea that moral transgressions could produce illness was also not very prominent at Asclepieia. One should note that by the time of the proliferation of Asclepius temples, there was already a widespread tradition that did not always explicitly connect illness with only supernatural causes. The Hippocratic corpus, probably produced in part by Asclepiads, attempted to explain many illnesses on the basis of natural phenomena.[138] Diseases resulted from imbalances in bodily substsances or from environmental changes according to much of the Hippocratic corpus. While some diseases (e.g., madness) may have been viewed as the result of some sort of moral transgression, the same was not the case for most of the illnesses treated at Asclepieia.

The cases mentioned in the inscriptions rarely presuppose some moral transgression on the part of the patient, and the prescriptions given rarely enjoin a change in moral life. In effect, there were a variety of concepts available that did not place a moral burden on the patient for his or her condition. The causes of disease delineated in texts pertaining to Asclepius do not always differ from causes discussed in the Hippocratic corpus and in other author deemed as "rational" by many modern scholars.

---

[137]Parker, *Miasma*, 213.

[138]For recent discussions on the nature and diversity of the Hippocratic Corpus, see Wesley D. Smith, *The Hippocratic Tradition* (Ithaca, NY: Cornell, 1979); and G. E. R. LLoyd, "The Transformations of Ancient Medicine," *Bulletin of the History of Medicine* 66 (1992) 114-132.

3. The efficacy of the temple locus

A natural theological tension existed between the efficacy of the temple locus in healing and the potential of divine healing to be effected at any locus. One stream of thought emphasized the efficacy of the locus. This is exemplified by the rationale found in the story of Alexander Severus related by Cassius Dio.[139] Alexander complained that he had not received help from Asclepius or Sarapis while living abroad. He first tried prayer. Then he tried sending sacrifices and votive offerings through couriers. Finally, he went to the temple himself, "hoping to prevail by appearing in person" (ἦλθε δὲ καὶ αὐτὸς ὡς καὶ τῇ παρουσίᾳ τι ἰσχύσων). This text exemplifies the concept that the healing efficacy of the locus centered on the proximity to the god. The temple was the house of the god, and it was where the god was most likely to be present and entreated. Moreover, the text indicates that there was a gradation of efficacy that was proportional to the proximity to the god at his temple. The text also exemplifies the hierarchy of options that develops when the first option does not yield satisfactory results. In the case of Alexander Severus these options yield a hierarchical strategy that may be schematized as follows:

> Prayer away from the Asclepieion > INR > dispatch of gifts through a third party > INR > personal visit to the Asclepieion.[140]

---

[139]*Historia Romana* LXXVIII, 15, 6-7 = T. 395.
[140]INR = If no result.

Hierarchies in therapeutic options are a very normal part of the therapy-seeking behavior of patients in most health care systems, ancient or modern.[141]

The proliferation of Asclepius temples, along with other factors, also raised the question of whether Asclepius was able to heal at more than one temple at the same time. Some answered in the negative. For example, the stela at the Asclepieion at Epidauros from the fourth century B.C.E. (T. 423, 23) reports that Aristagora of Troezen had her head cut off by the sons of the god (= physicians) in order to expel a tapeworm. But because Asclepius was away in Epidauros, a messenger was sent to Epidauros to fetch the god so he could effect the cure. In other words, this text supposes that Asclepius could not act in two places at the same time. This interpretation is confirmed by Aelianus who quotes an earlier writer (Hippys of the 5th or 3rd centuries B.C.E.) who says that the god was not present (οὐ παρῆν ὁ θεός) in this instance at Epidauros.[142]

The multiplicity of Asclepius temples also led to the question of whether the new shrines (e.g., Cos) were as efficacious as the old ones (e.g., Epidauros). Even though it is of late date (fourth c. C.E.), the following discourse in Themistius reflects the problem:[143]

εἰ τὰ σώματα ἐνοσοῦμεν καὶ ἐδεόμεθα τῆς παρὰ
τοῦ Θεοῦ βοηθείας, ὁ δὲ ἐνταῦθα παρῆν ἐν τῷ νεῷ
καὶ τῇ ἀκροπόλει καὶ παρεῖχεν ἑαυτὸν τοῖς
κάμνουσιν, ὥσπερ δήποτε καὶ λέγεται, πότερον ἦν

---

[141]For different types of hierarchies which may be found in the therapy seeking process, see A. Kleinman, *Patients and Healers*, 187ff.

[142]*De Natura Animalium*, IX, 33 = T. 422.

[143]*Oratio*, XXVII = T. 385.

ἀναγκαῖον εἰs Τρίκκην Βαδίζειν καὶ διαπλεῖν εἰs
'Επίδαυρον κατὰ τὸ παλαιὸν κλέοs, ἤ δύο Βήματα
κινηθέντas ἀπηλλάχθαι τοῦ νοσήματοs

If we were bodily sick and we needed the help of the
god, and he was present here in the temple, and in the
acropolis, and he were offering himself to the ill, as
he was said to have done [in the past], then what need
is there to go to Tricca and to sail to Epidauros just
because of their ancient fame, or to move two steps
to expel the illness?

The polemic presupposes that there was a tendency to view
the oldest temples as most efficacious by virtue of their
antiquity. The underlying presupposition is that the god
favored the most ancient site or that Asclepius was present
more frequently in the older sites.

But the reasoning of Themistius also exemplified yet
another tendency that questioned the advantage or necessity
of the temple locus itself, and it questioned the petitionary
function of the temple locus in particular. Themistius argued
that if Asclepius could act in more than one place at the same
time, then his good will alone should suffice to negate any
advantage of visiting any one temple locus. By increasing
the democratization of the god's action at various temple
sites, the petitionary function for a particular healing temple
could decline or disappear. In other words, the extension of
the range of Asclepius' healing powers to many or to all
loci, along with the belief in Asclepius' willingness to help
the ill, could lead logically to a position that negated any
advantage in the petitionary function of any particular temple
locus. If the efficacy of the god's action was no longer
confined to a locus or proportional to the proximity to his

temple, then the temple would lose any superiority over the effectiveness of praying from any other locus to an omnipresent (or nearly omnipresent) god.

Although Themistius' thinking could affect the petitionary function of a temple, the other main functions could still provide sufficient reason to maintain the viability of the Asclepieion in general. As we have mentioned, although Diophantus of Sphettus (T. 428) believed that one could be healed away from the temple, he still wanted to go to the temple afterwards, presumably to give thanks. The calibre of the water source and other therapy could still justify the existence of the Asclepieia.

Another reason for the perceived advantage of a temple locus was the existence of the idea that the patient should do as much as was physically or economically possible for him/herself. This aspect of patient behavior can be described as an effort to maximize the utilization of healing resources. That is to say, a particular patient may attempt to utilize as many potential sources of healing as are available within his or her perception of theological and economic possibilities.[144] Thus, even if patients believed in the omnipresence of the god, they might increase the chances of healing by also going to the temple.

One can also detect another concept wherein the image of Asclepius was the ultimate locus in which healing power centered. For example, in cases of plagues, the image of Asclepius was brought to the scene (T. 845). It was obvious that bringing the image to the scene would be

---

[144]For a modern example of the phenomenon of eclecticism and the maximization of healing resources, see R. Frankenberg and J. Leeson, "Disease, Illness and Sickness: Social Aspects of the Choice of Healer in a Lusaka Suburb," in J. B. Loudon, ed., *Social Anthropology and Medicine* (New York: Academic Press, 1976) 223-256.

advantageous in a plague when most people would not be able to travel to a temple.

It was also to the priestly establishment's advantage to promote the efficacy of the temple. For example, in the case of Demandrus the patient is commanded by the god to go to Lebena to receive healing.[145] This may have been part of an effort to legitimize Lebena's Asclepieion. Economically, it may been advantageous for the priests to maintain the idea of the god's preference for the locus.

We may summarize the attitudes towards the efficacy of the temple locus as follows:

LOCUS CENTERED CONCEPTS
1. Proximity to the god increases the chance of the success of a personal appeal;
2. Asclepius has a preference for ancient sites;
3. The god appreciates the effort of the patient to visit the site;
4. The experience of the physician/priests at Asclepieia (i.e., the therapeutic function) is superior.
5. The superiority of the temple equipment (e.g., water source).

NON LOCUS-CENTERED CONCEPTS
1. The god's power and goodwill extend to any locus.

---

[145]*Inscriptiones creticae*, I, xvii, no. 9 [2nd c. B.C.E.] = T. 426.

2. Other gods are better (e.g., Sarapis in Egypt).

3. Non-temple health care is superior.

As one can see, there were many specific aspects that helped maintain the high status of the Asclepieion for centuries. In fact, the theological inconsistency discussed by Themistius did not become sufficiently problematic to cause the decline of the Asclepius temples in pre-Christian centuries or even in the early centuries of Christianity. These conceptual polarities (omnipresent action vs. localization of the god's actions) were not always either-or-propositions, and one should view them as a dynamic tension within the Asclepius cult. One can still see this conceptual tension in modern Catholicism between an omnipresent God and the existence of healing shrines at Lourdes, for example. Asclepius temples survived well into the sixth century C.E., and Christian ascendance and opposition constituted the main factor in the decline. The dynamics of the tension between the efficacy of the locus and the ubiquity of the god's healing powers shall be explored further in the case of the Israelite temples.

4. Temple and non-temple health consultants

As we have mentioned, the distinction between the type of medicine practiced at the temple and outside of the temple in ancient Greece is not always clear. We have already mentioned that the Edelsteins see naturalistic therapy as the only practice deserving of the name *medicine.*

Likewise, the noted medical historian Henry Sigerist stated: "Medicine was a secular craft."[146]

We have argued that the boundaries between secular and religious therapy cannot always be drawn so neatly. For example, was the extraction of lodged weapons (e.g., arrow points in wounds) performed at Asclepieia much different from extractions performed by therapists at places away from the temple? Should we classify the extraction of lodged weapons in a temple as non-medical because prayers might have been recited by the surgeon-priest? The surgical implements found at Asclepieia do not seem to differ much from those found outside of those shrines. Herbal remedies were prescribed by therapists at the temples of Asclepius as well as by therapists not associated with temples. Sigerist himself notes that at Cos, non-temple physicians worshipped Asclepius, even though they were not priests.[147]

At the same time, there were traditions (e.g., Hippocratic traditions) that attributed the causes of disease to non-supernatural factors (e.g., climate), and which used therapy that did not mention the gods or any religious rituals. But, as we shall show more clearly in our chapter on Mesopotamia, the mention of non-supernatural factors did not mean that supernatural ones were not assumed. Whether or not religious assumptions were lacking in non-temple medicine, it is clear that most patients saw no contradictions in using temple and non-temple physicians. G. E. R. LLoyd states:

> Temple medicine was as popular as any... Thereby giving the lie to any who might suppose that the

---

[146]*A History of Medicine*, II:57.
[147]*A History of Medicine*, II:58.

rationalist, scientific, medicine of some Hippocratic authors would mean the end of such basically religious medical practice.[148]

Lloyd also cautions us against seeing Hippocratic and other naturalistic (or "rationalist") traditions as unified, because they differed on "not just on points of detail, but on fundamentals."[149]

Even if the specific procedures and tasks of the temple and non-temple healers were not always the same, the non-temple physicians and the temple priests were probably seen as complementary modes of healing. More precisely, there was a hierarchy of consultants. When an illness could not be cured by a local non-temple physician, for example, one could go to the Asclepieion. In one instance Aelianus speaks of the case of Euphronius who was afflicted with what was termed pneumonia (περι πνευμονίαν καλοῦσιν).[150] But it was only after the disease proved stronger than the knowledge of the non-temple physicians that his friends brought him to the temple. Similarly, many other testimonia also report that the temple was consulted after local non-temple physicians were unable to help.[151]

As Sigerist notes, the temple may have sometimes benefited from the non-temple Asclepiads.[152] At Cos, for

---

[148]LLoyd, "The Transformations," 117.

[149]LLoyd, *Ibid.*

[150]Fragmenta, 89 = T. 399.

[151]Plato (*Republic*, III, 406D) speaks of the tendency of some craftsmen to avoid treatments which would interfere with livelihood. Indeed, unless the condition was disabling, many working people would probably tolerate suffering as long as possible to avoid the economic burden of illness.

[152]H. E. Sigerist, *A History of Medicine*, II:68.

example, Asclepius guilds preceded efforts to build an Asclepieion. Any conflict that existed was not so much between the temple and non-temple physicians but between non-temple physicians and patients. Such conflicts centered around the fees charged by physicians. It seems that the temple may have been less expensive in terms of fees (provided one overcame the cost of travel and the loss of income from one's employment). Libanius reports a discussion on the fees charged by Asclepius and the non-temple physicians.[153]

However, blame rarely falls on the regular physicians in the testimonies when a healing does not occur. As we have noted, there existed the concept that the healing efficacy of Asclepius was proportional to the distance from the Asclepieion. Such a concept could have helped to deflect blame from the physicians. Moreover, the mode of therapy was flexible. If one remedy did not work, another one could always be prescribed. Thus, physicians usually were not castigated for following the method of trial and error.

Another reason for the lack of competition is that the sick probably outnumbered the consultants available. In a study of the physicians of ancient Greece, L. Cohn-Haft concludes:

> For better or worse, the secular physicans produced by apprenticeship and the schools were all the Hellenistic world had, and the weight of the evidence indicates an insufficient number of such trained doctors to meet the need for their services. [154]

---

[153]*Declamationes*, XXXIV, 35-36 = T. 540.
[154]"The Public Physicians of Ancient Greece," *Smith College Studies in History* 42 (1956) 31. In contrast, Libanius (*Declamationes*,

The Asclepieia at Athens probably could not serve all of the patients in a city which, as we have noted, had a population of about 200,000 in the fourth century B.C.E. According to Walton and subsequent investigators, some 300 Asclepieia existed in Greece and its dependent territories in pre-Christian times.[155] However, most of these Asclepius temples were relatively small, and they probably did not have the reputation of the larger sites. Strabo notes how crowded the temple at Epidauros was. One may say tentatively, therefore, that the sick usually exceeded the capacity of Asclepieia throughout most of the pre-Christian era. Moreover, some sites seem to have been considered more effective, something that would have caused some sites to be more crowded than others. The building of Asclepieia in many cities does not seem to have adversely affected sites such as Epidauros.

If competition among Asclepius temples did exist, the sources do not see it as much more than a friendly rivalry, and such rivalry never reached violent confrontation in the extant sources. Epidauros and Cos, for example, were seen as rivals in prestige. As we have seen, Themistius seems not only to have doubted the advantage of the ancient Epidauros temple, but he also questioned the very necessity for an Asclepieion, no matter what the location. Asclepius did come into conflict with Christianity and the Sarapis cult.

XXXIV: 38-42 = T. 540) complains of being cramped by innumerable physicians (πόδεν οὖν τῷ πλήθει τῶν ἰατρῶν στενοχωρούμεθα;) in the fourth century C.E.

[155]A. Walton, *The Cult of Asklepios* (Ithaca: Cornell University Press, 1894) 95-98.

D. SYNTHESIS

The discussion above illustrates how petitionary, thanksgiving, and therapeutic functions interacted to produce the particular constellation of material and ideological features of famous Asclepieia. The figurines of body parts, for example, are related to the particular ideas about thanksgiving and petitionary modes. The use of incubation for therapy is mainly responsible for the building of overnight accommodations. Contrary to the opinion of the Edelsteins, some of the personnel at Asclepieia probably did perform surgical procedures sometimes. We may now summarize the components of the conceptual framework that led to the success of the Asclepius cult in the delivery of health care of ancient Greece.

1. A god who specialized in the personal care of the ill. Healing, and not political and other social differences, was the focus of his cult. He was called the most man-loving of the gods (θεῶν φιλανθρωπότατε) according to Aelianus.[156] The cult of Asclepius may be categorized as utopian in its view of the etiology and prognosis. Indeed, Asclepius was so devoted to healing that the etiology of an illness usually mattered only insofar as it enhanced Asclepius' miracles. All illnesses could be cured, and there was a prescription for every type of illness. Asclepius usually did not use illness as an instrument to accomplish his purposes. It is natural to suppose that these factors would be inherently attractive for those who were ill.

---

[156]*De Natura Animalium*, IX, 33 = T. 422.

2. A theology that did not automatically regard the patient as morally impure, or sufficiently impure to be excluded from the temple. Indeed, it is difficult to establish a healing temple if the ill are considered so impure as to be excluded from the temple.

3. A flexibility that allowed various forms of payment and treatment. Economic flexibility may have allowed the poor and the rich to receive equal service in the initial phases of the cult. The therapeutic flexibility may also have created the sense that treatment was tailored for the individual.

4. A social context in which the Asclepieion was an acceptable part of the overall health care available in the society. No stigma or penalty seems to be attached for going to the Asclepius temples, and the temple and the "secular" physicians were seen as "legitimate" components in a hierarchy of health care consultants. The eclecticism and the maximization of utilization of health care consultants, secular and sacred, were acceptable practices for the sick.

5. The Asclepius cult reflected a tendency toward the maximalist pole in its view of the state's responsibility in the health care system. City states cooperated in the building of temples. In effect, city states sponsored therapeutic loci and often paid the personnel who operated them. The Asclepieia had a staff of persons who were devoted to the ill. The attendants often are seen counseling, and interpreting the dreams of the ill. They help them secure accommodations, and guide the ill in the healing rituals. In other words, Asclepieia provided an apparatus to which a patient could turn to receive answers on a human level.

6. A community of ill people. The fact that the Asclepieia provided contact with other persons who were undergoing the same experience is something rarely noted in Asclepius scholarship. The Abata conducted multiple incubations, and the physical proximity of patients would seem to provide more than sufficient opportunity for interaction. However the overcrowding of a local temple may also provide a reason for making trips to distant Asclepieia. Services such as a theater probably increased the sense of community with the cult, and may have helped to diminish the anxieties of illness.

In addition to mutual moral support, the Asclepieion was a place where people could trade prescriptions and discuss medical cases and precedents that could be useful for many patients. This in turn may have led to a great expectation of expertise and knowledge available at an Asclepieion.

7. A reputatation that was crafted by the ancient equivalent of a modern advertising campaign. As we have noted, the testimonia at Epidauros were famous and quoted. Vitruvius notes that Asclepieia were not above augmenting their reputation.[157] The numerous votives also must have helped to promote the successes of particular temples.

8. Asclepius scholars rarely mention another probable social function of the Asclepieion. This is to provide a respite from the stress and travails of daily life in ancient Greece. The existence of conditions that may be characterized as depression was recognized in ancient

---

[157]*De Architectura*, I, 2, 7 = T. 707:*uti ex natura loci maiores auctasque cum dignitate divinitas excipiat opiniones*.

Greece. For example, the Hippocratic tractate on *Epidemics* (III, Case XI) mentions the case of a woman who was treated for conditions relating to grief (λυπής). The Asclepieion may have been a place to rejuvenate one's psychological life, and to escape the various forms of strife and stress in ancient Greece.

In summary, the most important aspect of the Asclepieion is that it welcomed the sick individual. The sick were not regarded as so impure as to be excluded from the cult or the temple.   The existence of non-temple physicians did not impair the popularity of Asclepius temples because the sick probably outnumbered the supply of consultants in the Classical and Hellenistic periods.   Violent competition seems not to have developed between the temple establishment and the physicians on a theological level. The notion that the probability of healing was directly proportional to the distance from the temple may also have deflected blame from the "secular" physicians if the desired results were not realized.

Despite the fact that questions about the efficacy of a particular locus did exist, such questions affected mostly the petitionary function.   Even if the purely petitionary function of the temple were assailed (e.g., Themistius), the temple could still maintain its importance by emphasizing the thanksgiving and therapeutic functions (e.g., community of the ill, social accessibility, the quality of its water etc.). In general, the tension between the omnipresence and localization of the god's power and goodwill favored the latter, something that also helped to maintain the importance of local temples.

EXCURSUS

Specialization and the avoidance of socio-political strife by the Asclepius cult

In the section on the social context of the first temples (A. 3) we sought to explain why the Asclepius temple (and cult) at Epidauros attracted devotees from different socio-economic strata and from cities that were sometimes hostile to the town of Epidauros. We suggested that specialization in healing was a crucial factor in the palatability of the cult to many socio-political groups. By "specialization in healing" we refer to the focus by Asclepius on healing in general, and not to the specialization in a particular disease. The cult was interested in the patient as a sick individual, and not as a member of a particular city or socio-economic stratum. That specialization in healing was the key factor in avoiding socio-political conflict can be argued on four grounds:

1) On purely conceptual grounds, the degree of specialization of a cult in any principal feature X is directly proportional to the exclusion of concerns perceived to be outside of feature X.

2) The only main feature of Asclepius that is mentioned and explicit in the texts is his interest in healing the ill, and the furthering of specific political interests of Epidauros or specific political parties involved in conflicts is not expressed. This situation justifies the characterization of Asclepius as sufficiently specialized to exclude the

promotion of the political interests of one city against another or the interests of one socio-political group against another.

3) Hostility towards the town of Epidauros seems not to have affected the status of the Asclepius cult that was under the care of the town of Epidauros, and such would not likely have been the case if non-Epidaurians saw him as interested in anything other than healing.   It would be especially difficult to retain such wide appeal if Asclepius was viewed as a god interested in furthering the political or military interests of one city (e.g., Epidauros) or political group against another city or political group.

4) Asclepius was patronized by all types of socio-economic groups and cities, and such would not likely be the case if his known specialization in healing was not viewed as neutrality or indifference in socio-political matters.

The first element above is justified, as indicated, on conceptual grounds. The justification of the second element is based on the direct observation of the attested texts, many of which we have quoted and discussed within the chapter. The data to support the third and fourth elements of the hypothesis can be schematized in the following chart that summarizes hostilities and related events that involved the town of Epidauros:[158]

Year (B.C.E.)	Events
425	Athens invades and lays waste to the town of Epidauros (Thucydides IV, 45, 1)

---

[158]The chart represents a shorter adaptation of the chart in Burford, *The Greek Temple Builders*, 26-29.

420	Epidaurian cult of Asclepios introduced into Athens (cf. *Inscriptiones Graecae*, II^2 4969 = T. 729; middle of 4th c.)
419/418	War between Argos and Epidauros; Athens blockades Epidauros (Thucydides V, 56-7)
393	Epidauros attacked by the Athenian general Iphikrates (Polyaenus III, 9, 48)
374-70	Wide cooperation from a number of Greek cities helps Epidauros to build the temple of Asclepius (Burford, Inscription VI; middle of 4th c.).[159]
368	Thebans lay waste to the town of Epidauros, and Argos invades Epidauros (Diodorus Siculus xv, 69,1; Xenophon, *Hellenica* vii, 1, 25)
365	According to an inscription cited by Tomlinson (*Inscriptiones Graecae* IV^2 94 [365 B.C.E.]), the following cities had "*Theorodokoi*, i.e., individuals in other Greek cities who received and otherwise supported ambassadors (*theoroi*) sent out by Epidauros to promote the cult and

---

[159]Burford, *The Greek Temple Builders*, 65-66.

to collect funds for the improvement of the
sanctuary." [160]

Megara
Athens
Boeotian cities
Thessaly
Macedonia
Thrace
Sicily
Italy

Consider also the following list of cities which sent
craftsmen to help build the temple of Asclepius at Epidauros
(Burford, Inscription VI; middle of fourth century): [161]

Argos
Athens
Paros
Troizen

In addition, there is a (partial) list of persons who,
according to the Epidauros stela (= T. 423; 4th c. B.C.E.)
sought treatment at the Epidauros temple even though they
were from cities that had been at war with the town of
Epidauros probably within their lifetimes:

Cleimenes of Argos (Κλειμένης ᾿Αργεῖος; T. 423,37)
Ambrosia of Athens (᾿Αμβρόσια ἐξ ᾿Αθανᾶν; T. 423, 4)
Cleinatas of Thebes (Κλεινάτας Θηβαῖος; T. 423, 28)

---

[160]See Tomlinson, *Epidauros*, 25.
[161]Burford, *The Greek Temple Builders*, 65-66.

As one can see, hostilities with the town of Epidauros rarely had any attested negative impact on the status of the Asclepius cult at Epidauros. Note that Athens was involved in hostilities with Epidauros in 425. Yet Athens imported the cult of Asclepius from Epidauros in 420. A year later, Athens was again involved in hostilities with Epidauros. Similarly, Argos was at war with Epidauros in 419 and 368, yet users of the temple included people from Argos, and that city also cooperated in building the temple, most probably between 374 and 370 B.C.E. Similarly, craftsmen and patients came from other cities that had been otherwise engaged in hostilities with the town of Epidauros, probably within their lifetimes.[162]

      This situation indicates that the cities outside of Epidauros were able to distinguish between Epidauros as a political entity and Epidauros as the home of a god of healing. It would be difficult to find a reason for the attraction to Asclepius on the part of so many different, and often warring, cities and socio-economic groups if Asclepius had been associated with bestowing military or other types of political power to Epidauros or to certain socio-economic groups. It seems reasonable to suppose, therefore, that the widely attested specialization in healing by the Asclepius cult, especially at the time of its initial ascendance in the fifth-third centuries B.C.E., was sufficiently exclusive to

---

[162]The testimonies of the stela of Epidauros may represent actual persons, although the ascription of their cure must be viewed from the viewpoint of the Asclepius cult's beliefs in miraculous cures. Even if the cases are entirely fictitious, the fact that the stela recorded healings of persons coming from these towns indicates that that the town of origin was not held against the patients even though such a town had had hostilities with Epidauros.

avoid the socio-political strife in which the town of Epidauros was involved. This would explain, therefore, why cities that were sometimes hostile to the town of Epidauros had no qualms about patronizing, supporting or adopting the Asclepius cult of Epidauros.

Our explanation is slightly different from and yet complementary to that of Burford, who makes the following observation about the wide support for the construction of the temple of Asclepius at Epidauros:

> Epidauros did not bear the whole expense alone for Asklepios was Panhellenic, and investments in the healing cult came from all over the Greek world.[163]

It is true that a Panhellenic god would have attracted funds from most cities. Yet it seems that part of the reason he was "Panhellenic" was that he was a specialist first. Historically, Asclepius was a healing specialist before he was a Panhellenic healing specialist. Moreover, this specialization, rather than just his Panhellenic status, also explains why his cult extended beyond the borders of Greece. Asclepius exemplifies how specialization (in this case in healing) can be an asset in the growth and adoption of a cult by a variety of different socio-political entities and groups.

---

[163]Burford, *The Greek Temple Builders*, 81.

CHAPTER II

MESOPOTAMIA
The Temples of Gula/Ninisina

A. INTRODUCTION

1. General purpose

The temples of Gula, an important healing deity in Mesopotamia, are natural candidates for the topic of this study. Since our work focuses on the role of the temple in healing, it is not the intention of this chapter to provide a comprehensive review of medicine in Mesopotamia.[1] The vast amount of material demands that one be selective without creating a distorted portrayal. This chapter will focus on those features of Mesopotamian medicine that will illuminate the role of the temples of Gula in the health care system of Mesopotamia in the relevant periods. As such, it

---

[1]Among the general works that may be consulted on Mesopotamian medicine are: R. D. Biggs, "Medizin, A. In Mesopotamien," *RLA* 7 (7.8.) 623-630; *idem*, "Babylonien," in H. Schipperges et al, *Krankheit, Heilkunst, Heilung* (Freiburg: Munchen, 1978) 101-109; J. M. Durand, "Maladies et médecins," in *Archives épistolaires de Mari* I/1 (Paris: Éditions Recherche sur les Civilisations, 1988) 543-584; D. Goltz, "Studien zur altorientalischen und griechischen Heilkunde:Therapie-Arzneibereitung-Rezeptstruktur," *Sudhoffs Archiv/ Zeitschrift für Wissenschaftsgeschichte* 16 (Wiesbaden:Franz Steiner, 1974); P. Herrero, *La thérapeutique mésopotamienne* (Paris: Editions Recherche sur les civilisations, 1984).

intends to be a contribution to the larger study of how socio-religious factors produced the type of health care one sees in Mesopotamia.

2. Sources

Although written sources concerning Gula and her temples are not as abundant as sources concerning Asclepieia, there is sufficient textual and non-textual evidence to warrant our attention. Textual evidence comes in the form of votive inscriptions, prayers, rituals, and economic texts (e.g., ration texts) from various periods. The reign of the Neo-Assyrian king Esarhaddon, in particular, produced a number of important texts that help to clarify the place of Gula and the role of the healing professions. Esarhaddon, who gave financial support for the temple of Gula in Assur, also suffered a number of illnesses (or perhaps symptoms of one major illness) treated by consultants who frequently invoked Gula.

Archaeological evidence becomes very important in light of the relative paucity of written sources concerning the temples of Gula.[2] One of the primary archaeological sources for the study of the association of the temple of Gula with healing comes from the recent German excavations, led by

---

[2]On general methodological issues concerning the reconstruction of Mesopotamian social history from archaeological and written materials, see Maria DeJong Ellis, "Correlation of Archaeological and Written Evidence for the Study of Mesopotamian Institutions and Chronology," *AJA* 87 (1983) 504-507; N. Yoffee, "Social History and Historical Method in the Late Old Babylonian Period," *JAOS* 102 (1982) 347-353.

B. Hrouda, of the temple of Gula at Isin.[3] Fortunately, this temple was excavated using modern methods that are cognizant of interdisciplinary studies. Another temple of Gula was recently discovered at Nippur by McGuire Gibson of the University of Chicago, but the excavations are at such an early stage that they will not be of much significance in our study.[4] However, we hope to provide points of departure for further research at Nippur.

3. Gula/Ninisina

Gula, Ninisina, Ninkarrak, Bau, and Nintinugga may be viewed as different names of a single female healing deity who was envisioned as a dog.[5] Although the melding of the identity of these deities was not always uniformly maintained, these goddesses were almost indistinguishable

---

[3]The main excavation reports are as follows: B. Hrouda et al., eds., *Isin-Išān Baḥrīyāt I: Die Ergebnisse der Ausgrabungen 1973-1974* (hereafter = *IB* I; München:Bayerische Akademie der Wissenschaften, 1977); B. Hrouda, et al., eds., *Isin-Išān Baḥrīyāt II: Die Ergebnisse der Ausgrabungen 1975-1978* (hereafter = *IB* II; München: Bayerische Akademie der Wissenschaften, 1981); B. Hrouda, et al., *Isin-Išān Baḥrīyāt III: Die Ergebnisse der Ausgrabungen 1983-1984* (hereafter = *IB* III; München: Bayerische Akademie der Wissenschaften, 1987); and B. Hrouda, et al., *Isin-Išān Baḥrīyāt IV: Die Ergebnisse der Ausgrabungen 1986-1989* (München: Bayerische Akademie der Wissenschaften, 1992). The last volume was not available to us at the time most of our study was completed, but a brief review of that volume indicates that none of our main conclusions need revision, especially since most of the data on the temple of Gula is contained in *IB* I and *IB* II.

[4]See M. Gibson, "Nippur 1990:The Temple of Gula and a Glimpse of Things to Come," *OIAR* (1990) 18.

[5]Frankena, *RLA* 4, 695.

by the OB period. For the sake of simplicity, we shall
henceforth use the name Gula/Ninisina (= G/N) in generic
references to this healing goddess.[6] This section will
concentrate on the character of the deity only insofar as that
character affects the role of her temple in the health care
system, and many references to G/N were eliminated to
limit our scope. Nonetheless, we shall include some
important references that were published or re-studied after
the publication of the article on Gula by Frankena in *RLA*.

According to the standard description provided by
R. Frankena, Gula (written as: *gu-la* = "great,"[7] and
ideographically as *dME.ME*) was an ancient healing deity
who is probably the same deity attested by the name of *gú-lá*
in texts as early as the Early Dynastic period from Fara.[8]
Copies of hymns to Gula exist as late as the Seleucid and
Parthian periods.[9] Cult centers for Gula include Isin,
Umma, Lagash, Larsa, Uruk, Borsippa, Assur, and
Babylon.

Nintinugga is a name attested as early as the ED
period in tablets from Fara,[10] and she is mentioned
alongside Gula (*dNin-tin-ug5-ga dGu-l[a]*) in a late

---

[6]We shall use specific names of the healing goddess when citing textual
references which preserve those specific names.

[7]On the suggested etymology of "the great one" for *gu-la*, see R.
Frankena, *RLA* 4, 695.

[8]See R. Frankena, *RLA* 4, 695; For attestations in the ED period, see
F. R. Kraus, "Zur politischen Geschichte der Städte Nippur und Isin
unter den Königen von Isin und Larsa," *JCS* 3 (1951) 64. See also J.
J. M. Roberts, *The Earliest Semitic Pantheon* (Baltimore: The Johns
Hopkins Press, 1976) 17.

[9]See W. G. Lambert, "The Gula Hymn of Bullutsa-rabi," *Or* 36 (1967)
105. The name should best be transcribed as *Bullutsu-rabi*.

[10] For references, see Kraus, "Zur politischen Geschichte," 70.

Babylonian text from Uruk.[11] As Bergmann notes, Nintinugga and Gula are equated in a Sumerian lexical text.[12] Another text mentions that Enlil-bani built the *Enidubu* ("House of relaxation)" for Nintinugga, and describes her as "the lady who revives the dead" (l. 2: *nin ti-la ug5-ga*).[13]

   The most widely attested name of the female healing deity is Ninisina. The name *Ninisina* is first attested in the Fara period,[14] and reflects her patronage of the city of Isin (= Sumerian *Nin-Isin-a(k)* = Lady of Isin). As W. H. Ph. Römer notes, the name ^{d}nin-in-si-na-$umma^{ki}$ also attests

---

[11]Published as Text 29 (W 22758/5) in E. von Weiher, *Spät-babylonischer Texte aus Uruk* (Berlin: Gebr. Mann, 1983) vol. II, p. 138, Col. III, line 2.

[12]This lexical text (*Emesalserie* I 100 [*MSL* IV 9]) from the Neo-Assyrian period is discussed by E. Bergmann, "Untersuchungen zu syllabisch geschriebenen sumerischen Texten," *ZA* 56 (1964) 31. On the meaning of Nintinugga as "The lady (of) the lofty wine", see M. E. Cohen, "The Name Nintinugga with a Note on the Possible Identification of Tell Abū Salābikh," *JCS* 28 (1976) 82-92.

[13]*RIME* E4.1.10.6 (p. 83).

[14]We follow P. Steinkeller's reading [personal communication] of ^{d}Nin-in as ^{d}Nin-$Isin_x$ in the following references from the Fara period: R. D. Biggs, *Inscriptions from Tell Abū Salābīkh* (*OIP* 99; Chicago: U. of Chicago, 1974), p. 51, l. 187; A. Alberti, "A Reconstruction of the Abū Salābīkh God-List," *SEL* 2 (1985) p. 10, l. 155B. We also read Nin-$Isin_x$ in an Old Akkadian seal published in D. Collon, *First Impressions:Cylinder Seals in the Ancient Near East* (Chicago:U. of Chicago, 1987) p. 33 # 95. For attestations during the Ur III and Old Babylonian periods, see W. H. Ph. Römer, "Einige Beobachtungen zur Göttin Nini(n)sina auf Grund von Quellen der Ur-III Zeit und der Altbabylonischen Periode, " In M. Dietrich and W. Röllig, eds., *lišān-mithurti-Festschrift W. von Soden* (AOAT 1; Kevelaer/Neukirchen Vluyn, 1969) 279ff.

her place in the pantheon of Umma.[15]   Other important cult centers of G/N are located at Ur, Uruk and   Larsa. According to D. Frayne, *Eunamtila* ("House of the plant of life") is probably the name of her temple at Larsa.[16]   In Babylon she had three temples (*É.sa.bad, É.ḫur.sag.sikil.la and É.ḫur.sag.kù.ga*). There were also at least three temples in Assur (*É.gal.maḫ, É.sa.bad* and *É.nam.ti.la*).[17] The temple of G/N at Isin was called *É.gal.maḫ* ("the lofty palace").[18]   The popular reports concerning the temple at Nippur indicate that there was a major installation dedicated to Gula in that city.

G/N was part of a divine family at Isin. She is regarded as the daughter of An and Uraš in some texts (e.g., *SRT* 6 III 11-12//7,22-23). One of the earliest consorts is Pabilsag. Ninisina and Pabilsag were already paired in the Neo-Sumerian period.[19] Numerous inscriptions from the Kassite and Neo-Assyrian periods pair Gula with Ninurta, her consort, and the shrine of Gula at Isin was paired with that of Ninurta.

Damu and Gunura, respectively, are the son and daughter of G/N. Damu, however, is described as a daughter (*mārtu*) of G/N in various texts (e.g., Ebeling,

---

[15]Römer, "Einige Beobachtungen zur Göttin Nini(n)sina..." 280.

[16]The provenience of the text which bears the name of the temple (*RIME* E.4.2.13.22, l. 12) is not certain, but Frayne argues for Larsa in *RIME* 4, p. 244. On the importance of Ninisina at Larsa see also W. Hallo, "The Royal Correspondence of Larsa:A Sumerian Prototype for the Prayer of Hezekiah?" *AOAT* 25 (1976) 209-224

[17]See Frankena, *RLA* 3, 696.

[18]See J. Krecher, "The Sumerian Names of the Temples in Babylon and Ashur," *Sumer* 41 (1985) 42.

[19]For example, in *SLT* 123 II 17-21 = 124 II 8-12; See Kraus, *JCS* 3, 79.

KAR 15/16, 14f). As we shall see below, Damu is paired with G/N in numerous therapeutic incantations. For example, one finds Damu and Ninkarrak in an OB incantation against a variety of ailments.[20] As in the following incantation against various diseases (*CT* 17, 33 Rs. 32ff), sometimes Damu is paired with Gunura, his sister:

^d*Da-mu ina pa-ás-tu₄ li-im-ḫa-as-s[u]*
^d*Gu-nu-ra dimgul-gal-bi ḫu-mu-un-dar-r[a]*

May Damu strike him (i.e., the disease-demon)
with the axe,
May Gunura smite him with the mace.

Damu is called ŠIM.SAR *gal-la* (= *a-ši-pu ra-bu-ú* = "the great exorcist") in *Šurpu* 7:71. Damu's cult is mentioned at Isin, Girsu, Larsa and Ur.[21]

The epithets of G/N provide ample evidence of her role as a healer. These epithets include: *azugallatu* ("the great healer" in *IB* I, E8), *azu kalam-ma* ("healer of the country"),[22] and *azu gal kalam-ma* ("the great healer of the land") in *TCS* 3, p. 40, 1. 392. Similarly, Nintinugga is called *azu kalam-ma* (e.g., *UMBS* 1² 134, 1). Ninisina is

---

[20]A. Goetze, "An Incantation against Diseases," *JCS* 9 (1955) p. 10, 1. 30.

[21]On Damu, see also E. Lipínski, "Le dieu Damu dans l'onomastique d'Ebla," in L. Cagni, ed., *Ebla 1975-85* (Naples:Atti del Convegno internazionale [Napoli, 9-11 ottobre 1985] 1987) 91-99.

[22]The latter epithet is attested in *CT* 23, II, 15. For a collection of other epithets of Gula, see W. Mayer, *Untersuchungen zur Formensprache der babylonischen Gebetbeschwörungen* (Rome: Biblical Institute Press, 1976) 387-88.

called *a-zu-gal   sag-gi₆-ga* ("the great healer of the black-headed ones") in *TCS* 3, p. 105b, l. 268. The same epithet is applied to Bau in *UMBS* 10⁴ 14 Obv. 6.

The epithet *šim-mú* ("herb grower") indicates the involvement of G/N with medicinal plants. Note the following occurrence in an incantation published by M. J. Geller:

> *šim-m[ú lú-ti-la kalam-ma-ke₄ me-en]*
> *maš-maš [gal-gal-la uru-a DU-DU]*

> [I am] the incantation priest [who is the life restorer of the Land],
> [The chief] exorcist [walking about in the city]²³

Geller says:

> Although *šim-mú* might be thought to correspond more closely to *asû* than *āšipu*, the original function of *šim-mú* may have been more pharmaceutical than exorcistic.²⁴

A large number of royal inscriptions also mention her function as a healer. In *RIME* E4.1.7.2001 Enlil-ennam dedicates a dog to Ninisina for the life of Bur-sin, and describes the goddess as "the lady who makes the 'broken-

---

²³Transliteration and translation is that of M. J. Geller, *Forerunners to Udug-hul: Sumerian Exorcistic Incantations* (Freiburger Altorientalische Studien 12; Stuttgart:Franz Steiner, 1985) 24-25, lines 93-94.

²⁴M. J. Geller, *Forerunners*, 92-93. The possible connections of the *šim-mú* with the *bārû* and the *sā'ilu* are mentioned by A. Falkenstein, *La divination en Mesopotamie ancienne (XIV Recontre Assyriologique Internationale,* Strasbourg, 2-6 juillet 1965 (Presses Universitaires de France, 1966) 52.

up' whole (again)." (line 3: *nin lú-kus-da(?) dím-dí[m]*).[25] Another royal inscription mentions that Ninisina "creates life in the land" (*RIME* E4.2.13.22, 1.3: *zi-gál kalam dím-dím-me*).[26]

According to one prayer, G/N was entreated to heal, among other illnesses, headaches (*muruṣ qaqqadi*), toothache (*muruṣ šinni*, "heart" sickness (*muruṣ libbi*), and "bowel sickness?" (*kīs libbi*).[27] According to K 232 she is also charged with the promotion of fertility (1. 23: *mu-šak-li-lat ta-lit-ti*).[28] There is a long association of G/N with the care of pregnant women and infants. In an OB incantation, Gula and Damu work together to expel a worm responsible for the blindness of a baby.[29] Gula appears in a number of incantations against the Lamaštu-demons, which were notorious for their attacks on babies.[30] *LABS* 293, a text which we shall discuss in greater detail below, apparently describes a ritual involving Gula that is performed in order to grant a safe birth.

---

[25]The transliteration and translation follow corrections to the Sumerian text in *RIME* (p. 72) made by P. Steinkeller (personal communication).

[26]Transliteration and translation follow corrections to the Sumerian text in *RIME* (p. 245) made by P. Steinkeller (personal communication).

[27]Text (c) of C. J. Mullo-Weir, "Four Hymns to Gula," *JRAS* (1929) 8.

[28]Text (d) of Mullo-Weir, "Four Hymns to Gula," 12, 1. 23.

[29]*YOS* 11, 5, p. 19.

[30]For some interesting examples, see W. Farber, *Schlaf, Kindchen, Schlaf: Mesopotamische Baby-Beschwörungen und -Rituale* (Mesopotamian Civilizations 2; Winona Lake, Indiana: Eisenbrauns, 1989) 69 and 103-105.

According to a Neo-Assyrian text, Gula performs the following duties for humanity.[31]

> be-lit re-e-ši ut-nin-ni a-na ši-si-it ḫa-an-ṭa-at
> i-šim-me taṣ-lit niše(UN.MEŠ) i-nam-din bul-ṭu
> i-nam-din te-e šá šup-šu-ḫi ši-pat balāṭi(TI.LA)
> i-paṭ-ṭar ri-kis nam-ra-ṣi mu-ru-uṣ ta-az-bil(!)-ti
> ab-kal-lat ba-ra-at muš-ši-pat mu-us-sa-at ka-la-
> ma

She is the mistress of joy and supplication, she hastens at the call (of the suppliant).
She listens to the supplication of the people, she provides health;
She provides the soothing incantation, the incantation of health;
She will untie the bond of trouble, the lingering sickness;
She is wise, the diviner, the exorcist, the one who finds out everything.

These duties assigned to G/N are very ancient. In an OB text published by Römer (= SRT 6//7), Ninisina exhorts her son Damu to heed all of the duties of the "healer's craft" (l. 16: ᵈda-mu níg nam-a-zu-ka gizzal ḫé-em-ma-ak). The duties are described as follows:[32]

---

[31] The cuneiform text (K 232) is provided by C. J. Mullo-Weir ("Four Hymns to Gula," *JRAS* [1929] 15, lines 25-29).

[32] Following the readings of Römer, "Einige Beobachtungen..." 284, ll. 17-21; and P. Steinkeller's revisions (personal communication).

*túg*bar-si-ge šu im-ma-an-ti šu <im->gur-gur-re
*túg*bar-si-ni í-e im-ma-ak-e
im al-du₁ ₁-ga im-ku₇-ku₇-e
úš-lugud-e šu im-šú-ur-šú-ur-re
GIG-GIG-ma šu bil mu-na-ak-e

He(?) takes the bandage and winds it around;
He anoints his bandage with oil;
He soothes (the wound) with the...ointment(?);
He dries(?) the blood (and) the gore;
He ... his hand upon the carbuncle.

In addition, the text states that Ninisina sharpens her scalpel
(l. 11: ^{d}nin-in-si-na-ke₄ gír-DU-e ù-sar im-ma-ak-e).³³
Another OB text (*YOS* 11, 14:l. 5) attests to the use of the
scalpel by Gula (na-ag-la-bu [ša ^{d}Gu-la) to heal the
maškadu-disease.

In *The Hymn of Bullutsu-rabi* Gula states:³⁴

79. a-sa-ku-ma bul-lut a-le- ʾ-i
80. na-šá-ku šammi(Ú ḪI.A) kul-lat-su-nu
    ú!-né-es-si mur-ṣu
81. ez-ḫe-ku tu-kan-nu šá ši-pat ba-la-ṭu
82. na-šá-ku maš-ṭa-ru šá šá-la-mu
83. a-nam-din bul-ṭu a-na ba- ʾ- ú-la-a-tú
84. el-lu rik-su sim-ma ú-na-aḫ
85. rap-pu ṣi-in-di murṣa(GIG) ú-pa-áš-šá-aḫ

79. I am an *asû*, I can heal
80. I bear healing substances, I expel all illness

---

³³On the meaning of *gír-DU* as "scalpel," see CAD s.v. *karzillu*.
³⁴W. G. Lambert, "The Gula Hymn...," *Or* 36 (1967) 120.

81. I strap on a sack which contains healing
    incantations;
82. I carry texts which provide health;
83. I provide medicine for humanity;
84. The pure tourniquet soothes the injury;
85. The soft bandage alleviates illness.

In line 183 of the same hymn one finds:*[a]-sa-ku ba-ra-ku
a-ši-pak* ("I am a 'physician,' a diviner, an exorcist").

As Lambert notes, "Bulluṭsa-rabi was merely
reproducing existing ideas in his hymn."[35]   In fact, the
tradition of a hymn of "self-praise" by Ninisina was in
existence in the OB period.[36]   Lambert has dated the original
composition of *The Hymn of Bulluṭsu-rabi* to between 1400
and 700 B.C.E.[37] *The Hymn of Bulluṭsu-rabi* is noteworthy
because, although Gula describes herself as an *āšipu* and a
bārû, it is her profession as an *asû* which receives the most
elaboration of the three professions. Thus, perhaps the hymn
was composed by an *asû* whose very name, *Bulluṭsu-rabi*,
also suggests such a profession. As Ritter notes, Gula is
most common in the incantations of the *asû*.[38]

Although G/N was known as a healer, she could also
be a destroyer. A Sumerian execration text (lines 3-4) from

----

[35]W. G. Lambert, "The Gula Hymn...," 110.

[36]See the example published by Römer, "Einige Beobachtungen zur
Göttin Nini(n)sina, 302-303.

[37]W. G. Lambert, "The Gula Hymn...," 109.

[38]E. Ritter, "Magical Expert = (*Āšipu*) and Physician (= Asû): Notes
on Complementary Professions in Babylonian Medicine," in H. G.
Güterbock and T. Jacobsen, eds., *Studies in Honor of Benno
Landsberger on his 75th Birthday, April 21, 1965* (*A S* 16; Chicago:
U. of Chicago, 1965) 315.

the time of Iddin-Dagan (1974-1954 B.C.E.) describes her as follows:[39]

> *nin* $^{IM}ul_x$ *(GIŠGAL)-lu-ni u₄-mir-a-gim an- x -a*
> *ki(?)-dúb-bu- x*
> ^{d}*gibil-gim igi [ḫus(?)-íl(?)]-la-ni erím-ma su dar-dar-re*

> Queen whose 'tempest,' like a raging storm, makes heaven
> [tremble(?)], makes the earth quake,
> Whose [lifted (?) awesome(?)] face, like Gibil, cuts the
> flesh of the enemy;

She is also depicted as having lethal claws in line 6: "Lion -paw, sharp knife, claws constantly dripping blood" (*šu pirig-gá gír ù-sar-ak(!) unₐbin-úš bi-bi-bi*). The scalpel that Ninisina uses to heal could also be a weapon, and it is described in the same text (lines 8-9) as:

> *gír-zal bulug kin-gur₄ gír pirig-gá-gim GALAM*
> *è-a-zu-uš un-sag-gíg su ma-ra-sìg-sìg-ge*

> When you bring forth skilfully(?) the scalpel,[40] the
> rotating(?) pointed(?) needle, like a lion's 'knife,'
> The people, the 'blackheaded ones'-(their) flesh
> winces(?) because of you.

The connection of G/N with the dog is very ancient. The deity is often indistinguishable from the dog, and she

---

[39]The edition of the Sumerian text and the English translation follows that in O. R. Gurney and S. N. Kramer, *Sumerian Literary Texts in the Ashmolean Museum* (*OECT* 5, text 8; Oxford:Clarendon, 1976) 20-26.
[40]For the meaning of *gír-zal* as "scalpel," see *CAD* s.v. *karzillu*.

probably was envisaged as a dog from the earliest stages of her biography. As early as the reign of Enlil-bani (19th c. B.C.E.), for example, one finds the mention of the construction of the "Dog house" (*é-ur-gi7-ra*), undoubtedly a reference to the temple of Ninisina at Isin.[41] In a contract (*YOS* 8, 76) for the sale of an orchard from Larsa one also finds the divine dog of Gula (line 2: *dKa-al-bu-um ša dGu-la*)[42] as one of the divinities by which the participants swear. T. Jacobsen suggests that the name *Bau*, another name for G/N at Uruku in the Lagash region, derives from the sound of the bark of a dog.[43] In *YOS* 11, 69:1. 1, Ninisina is said to have "a big snatching mouth" (*ka gal zú kar-kar dnin-i-si-na-kam*). It is probable that it is G/N who is depicted in a Middle-Assyrian seal that shows a worshipper before an altar on which a dog is sitting; the sign *dingir* appears above the dog.[44] Numerous dog figurines are dedicated to G/N as part of petitionary or thanksgiving rituals.

G/N also has a large progeny of dogs that help her in her healing duties. According to *YOS* 11, 5, 1. 9, the dog follows Gula (*kal-bu il-li-ku wa-ar-ki-i-ša*) when she acts against enemies. The dogs of Gula are apparently distinguished from "ordinary" dogs in an incantation published by Farber against the Lamaštu demon: [45]

---

[41]See D. R. Frayne, *RIME* 4, pp. 80-81; and A. Livingstone, "The Isin 'Dog House' Revisited," *JCS* 40 (1, 1988) 54-60.

[42]D. E. Faust, *Contracts from Larsa Dated in the Reign of Rim Sin* (*YOS* 8; New Haven: Yale University Press, 1941) plate xxxiv.

[43]T. Jacobsen, *Toward the Image of Tammuz*, 33.

[44]The seal appears as 150b in H. Frankfort, *The Art and Architecture of the Ancient Orient* (Harmondsworth, Middlesex, England: Penguin, 1970) 132. Discussion also by I. Fuhr, *IB* II, 137.

[45]Following the interpretation of Farber (*Schlaf, Kindchen, Schlaf*, Text 34, p. 105) who notes that the reference may be to magical dog-

11k *ù ni-i-nu* NU UR.G[I7]
12k UR.GI7.MEŠ *šá* ^{d}g[*u-la*]

We are not a (an ordinary type of?) dog;
(We are) hounds of Gula.

As Farber notes, dogs are mentioned frequently in rituals
and incantations against the Lamaštu demons.[46] A seal from
Tell Halaf shows a dog standing on top of a hut in which a
man lies on a bed. Two men, perhaps healing consultants,
appear to perform rituals within the hut.[47] An example of
her iconography from a *kudurru* (10th c. B.C.E.) depicts a
lady seated in profile on a throne with a dog lying beside
her.[48] As we shall see below, dog figurines were also used
in thanksgiving offerings. We shall discuss below other
aspects of the connection between G/N and dogs.

The foregoing discussion indicates that G/N was an
ancient female healing deity who, for still unclear reasons,
was identified and/or associated with the dog from the
earliest known stages of her biography. We shall provide
further discussion below on the impact of the goddess'
character (including the role of dogs) on the health care

---

figurines used in rituals against the Lamastu demons.   Farber also
assumes that the *nīnu* in line 11 is the subject in line 12.

[46]W. Farber, "Tamarisken-Fibeln-Skolopender," in Rochberg-Halton,
ed., *Language, Literature and History* (AOS 67; New Haven,
CT:American Oriental Society, 1987) 89 n. 10. The article by Farber
provides illustrations of amulets depicting rituals against Lamastu
demons and a discussion of their interpretation.

[47]The seal is published as #803 in D. Collon, *First Impressions*, 173.
See further, I. Fuhr, *IB* II, 138.

[48]For a discussion of such depictions, see I. Fuhr, "Der Hund als
Begleiter der Göttin Gula und anderer Heilgottheiten," in *IB* I, 135-145;
See further, U. Seidl, *BaM* 4 (1968) 143.

system. As we shall demonstrate, at times Gula was simply an intercessor for the suppliant or acts in concert with deities such as Ea and Marduk (Asalluhi).

4. Preliminary description of the temple at Isin

a) Site and plan (see Figure 2)

The best known temple of G/N is at Isin (now Isan Bahriyat), a city some 200 kilometers south of modern Baghdad. Since the best archaeological remains yet excavated come from the Kassite and Isin II periods, most of our discussion will center on those periods, but we will also discuss references from other periods. The temple at Isin was found during the 1975-76 excavations led by B. Hrouda.[49] The temple of Gula at Isin experienced its main building phases during the Kassite period (more specifically, ca. 1400-1150 B.C.E.) and the Second Dynasty of Isin (ca. 1150-1025 B.C.E).[50] The earliest structure probably dates to the Early Dynastic period,[51] and the latest known construction was undertaken by Nebuchadnezzar II. Isin itself dates back to Ubaid-Uruk periods. Unlike the Asclepieia at Epidauros, Cos and Pergamum, the temple of Gula was situated in the midst of the city. The shrine of Gula itself was actually a small room (about 7.5 x 3 m) within a building that also housed the temple of Ninurta. B.

---

[49]See M. Haussperger, B. Hrouda, and E. Strommenger, "Gula Tempel 1975-1978 (4.-6. Kampagne)" in *IB* II, 9-25.

[50]B. Hrouda (*IB* II, 199) comments: "Die Hauptbauphase datiert ins 14. Jahrhundert v. Chr. und ist einem der Kurigalzu zuzuweisen." On other dates for the temple of Gula, see Hrouda, *IB* II, 199-201.

[51]B. Hrouda, "The First Preliminary Report..." *Sumer* 45 1/2 (1987-88) 38.

Hrouda says: "The temple was erected on a large and high terrace, as we specially (*sic*) know from buildings in 'Aqr Quf, Nippur and from Ur."[52]

b) Socio-historical context of the Isin temple

As we have argued in the previous chapter, demographic shifts and civil unrest in Greece during the 5th-4th centuries B.C.E. helped to illuminate the rise of the Asclepius cult. Since the best known phases of the temple of G/N at Isin are situated in the Kassite and Isin II periods, one should explore the socio-historical context of the temple of G/N during these periods to search for any data that might illuminate the function of the temple of G/N. One should note that the temple seems not to have been functional for some time prior to the time of Kurigalzu (I or II). One of Kurigalzu's inscriptions, for example, states that prior to his restoration, the temple of Gula had been in ruins for a long time.[53] At the same time, it should be noted that the temple probably had been in use (even if not continuous) since the ED periods. This is consistent with the long record of worship of G/N at Isin and other cities.

Although the rise of the Asclepius cult can be related to certain crises in health that can be, in part, attributed to increases in population density, the relationship between demographic shifts and the rise (or enhancement) of the cult of G/N cannot be established on the basis of present

---

[52]B. Hrouda, "The First Preliminary Report about the Results of the Excavations at the Site of Ancient Isin (Sept. 15-October 15 1986)," *Sumer* 45 (1-2, 1987-1988) 38. This report was published in English.
[53]Text is published as Kurigalzu D in C. B. F. Walker and C. Wilcke, "Preliminary Reports on the Inscriptions 1975-1977, 1978," in *IB* II, 98.

demographic data. According to J. A. Brinkman, "Mesopotamian demography is still at a primitive level."[54] Nonetheless Brinkman, R. McC. Adams, and others, have made some tentative assessments of demographic issues in, among others, the Kassite and Isin II periods.[55] It is useful to state one of Brinkman's conclusions:

> Although in the early Iron Age the gross settled area in each region of lower Mesopotamia declined as compared with the preceding period, the rate of decline exhibits pronounced regional variation and is progressively more severe as one moves from south to north. The extreme proportions vary from Ur, where the settled area was 78 percent as large as it had been in Kassite times, to the lower Diyala, where the area was only 23 percent of its fomer size.[56]

He adds:

> It is also clear that these shifts should be viewed not as a unique catastrophic decline, but as the final phase of a long-term trend whereby the gross settled area of lower Mesopotamia--and presumably the population level--steadily decreased over a period of 1500 years,

---

[54]J. A. Brinkman, "Settlement Surveys and Documentary Evidence: Regional Variation and Secular Trend in Mesopotamian Demography," *JNES* 43 (3, 1984) 179. For methodological comments on life expectancy in between the 7th and 4th centuries in Mesopotamia, see M. A. Dandamayev, "About Life Expectancy in Babylonia in the First Millennium B.C.," in *Mesopotamia* 8 (1980) 183-186.

[55]Brinkman (see note above); Robert McC. Adams, *The Heartland of Cities* (Chicago: U. of Chicago, 1981).

[56]Brinkman, "*Settlement Surveys...*," 172-73.

from the high point in the period beginning ca. 2100
B.C. to a low point in the period ending ca. 625
B.C.[57]

In particular the gross settled area in the Nippur-Uruk
corridor was 1308 hectares in the Kassite period, but fell to
616 hectares in the Post-Kassite period (1150-625 B.C.E).
The percentage of settled surface area occupied by
settlements of 10 hectares or less was 56.8% in the Uruk-
Nippur corridor during the Kassite period, but it was 64.3%
in the Post-Kassite periods.[58] In other words, the large
urban centers lost population, while small villages gained
population. Speaking of the urban centers, Brinkman
suggests that "famine and plague in the eleventh and tenth
centuries may also have hastened their wane."[59]

The population decline cited by Brinkman has been
correlated with climactic changes by J. Neumann and S.
Parpola. They conclude that:

> The political, military and economic decline of
> Assyria and Babylonia in the twelfth through tenth
> centuries appears to coincide with the period of

---

[57]Brinkman, *ibid.*, 173.

[58]Statistics as presented by Brinkman, *ibid.*, 173.

[59]J. A. Brinkman, *A History of Post-Kassite Babylonia* (Rome:
Pontificium Institutum Biblicum, 1968) 318. The abandonment of
cities as a response to epidemics is apparently attested in Mari. Note
for example, Text A. 675 rev. 1. 1: *a-lam i-[zi-bu-ma]* in A. Finet, "Les
médecins au royaume de Mari," *AIPHOS* 14 (1954-57) 28.

notable warming and aridity which set in about 1200
and lasted till about 900.[60]

The synergism between malnutrition and disease in history
has been explored by a number of nutritionists.[61] Neumann
and Parpola, basing themselves on previous work by L.
Cagni and J. J. M. Roberts, conclude that the Poem of Erra
reflects the following sequence: "heat > scorched earth >
famine > epidemics > death as the ultimate source of
Babylonia's woes." [62] If this interpretation of the Poem of
Erra is correct, it shows that, regardless of the date one
assigns to Erra, the link between nutritional crises and
epidemics was known in ancient Mesopotamia.[63]

     This scanty paleodemographic survey suggests that it
is difficult to correlate any increased building activity on the
temple of Gula with some specific crisis in health during the

---

[60]J. Neumann and S. Parpola, "Climactic Change and the Eleventh-
Tenth-Century Eclipse of Assyria and Babylonia," *JNES* 46 (3, 1987)
177.

[61]For a collection of essays exploring the complex relationship
between malnutrition and disease see Rotberg, R. I. and T. K. Rabb
Hunger and History (Cambridge: Cambridge University Press, 1983).
Useful comments on the relationship between the evolution of the state
and nutrition may be found in M. N. Cohen, *Health and the Rise of
Civilization* (New Haven:Yale, 1989) 55-74.

[62]J. Neumann and S. Parpola, "Climactic Change...," *JNES* 46 (3,
1987) 180.

[63]For a proponent of the view that the Poem of Erra may reflect some
events in the Isin II period, see W. G. Lambert," Review of F.
Gössmann, *Das Era Epos* [Würzburg, 1956]" *AfO* 18 [1957-58] 396-
400). W. von Soden argues for a date during the disturbances in Uruk in
765-763 B.C.E. (*UF* 3[1971] 253-263). For a recent interpretation of
the Poem of Erra, see Peter Machinist, "Rest and Violence in the Poem
of Erra," *JAOS* 103 (1, 1983) 221-226.

Kassite period. The Kassite period, in general, seems to have been prosperous.[64] But the Kassite period was a time when a movement towards organizational improvements of various aspects of Mesopotamian society (e.g., the provincial system, and the calendar) was implemented. In particular, the efflorescence of educational pursuits and the accumulation of new information and literary texts during the Kassite period are reflected, as Brinkman notes, in that "many of the great scribal families of first-millennium Babylonia traced their descent to famous forebears who were active during the fifteenth and fourteenth century."[65] Such heightened scholarly activities may have encompassed the temple of G/N, and we shall provide more discussion below on the relationship between scholarly activities and medicine.

Insofar as the kings of the Isin II period are concerned, it is reported that early in his reign Nebuchadnezzar I (1126-1105 B.C.E.) suffered a significant setback against the Elamites when a plague broke out among his troops in Elamite territory.[66] Adad-apla-iddina (1069-1048 B.C.E.), who undertook improvements on the temple of Gula at Isin,[67] experienced raids from the Suteans that ravaged a number of shrines, notably the temple of Šamaš at

---

[64]See J. A. Brinkman, "Kassiten," *RLA* 5, 468. For a larger collection of materials concerning the Kassite period, see J. A. Brinkman, *Materials and Studies for Kassite History* (Volume I; Chicago:U. of Chicago, 1976).

[65]J. A. Brinkman, "Kassiten," *RLA* 5, 468 For texts bearing scribal genealogies, see W. G. Lambert, "A Catalogue of Texts and Authors," *JCS* 16 (1962) 59-67.

[66]For details, see J. A. Brinkman, *A History of Post-Kassite Babylonia*, 106.

[67]This is attested in an inscription (*IB* 148) published by D. O. Edzard and C. Wilcke in Hrouda, *IB* I, 90.

Sippar.[68]   The Second Dynasty of Isin was marked by numerous petty battles among Assyrians, Elamites and Arameans. Military strife is almost always accompanied by health crises precipitated by disruptions in food supply, and by the contamination of water, among other factors. Nevertheless, it is not possible, on the basis of present evidence, to correlate any health crises resulting from strife during the Isin II period with any increased or renewed building activity on the temple of G/N.[69]

c) Comments on paleopathology

Data concerning nutritional and other health related aspects are only beginning to be studied intensely. One such study, by R. Ellison, notes that some of the workers who depended heavily on barley rations for their sustenance, something especially documented between 3000 and 1400 B.C.E., may have developed deficiencies of Vitamin A (which can lead to eye problems) and Vitamin C (which can result in scurvy) in certain seasons. [70] Yet, one must await more refined and larger samples in order to make more

---

[68]See J. A. Brinkman, *A History of Post-Kassite Babylonia*, 138.

[69]For general brief surveys of epidemics in ancient Mesopotamia (and the difficulties posed by the study of ancient epidemics for historians and paleopathologists), see   R. M. Martinez, "Epidemic Disease, Ecology, and Culture in the Ancient Near East," in *ANETS* 8 (1990) 413-457; and   D. Snell, "Plagues and Peoples in Mesopotamia," *JANES* 14 (1982) 89-96.

[70]R. Ellison, "Some Thoughts on the Diet of Mesopotamia from c. 3000-600   B.C.E.,"   *Iraq*   45   (1983)146-150;   *idem*,   "Diet   in Mesopotamia: The Evidence of the Barley Ration Texts (c. 3000 to 1400 B.CE)," *Iraq* 43 (1981) 35-45.

accurate assessments of the nutritional status of the various population and social groups in Mesopotamia.

Osteological remains of more than 50 individuals have been identified thus far at Isin, some 46 of which dated from the Akkadian through late Babylonian periods.[71] At least one skull (*G* 100),[72] dated as later than the Isin II Dynasty, bears evidence of post-mortem trephination.[73] The individual was found in the vicinity of the dog burials. It is still unclear whether the personnel of the temple of Gula were responsible for the trephination, though Ziegelmayer suggests a ritual significance associated with the area of the dog burials.[74]

Two skeletons in the Old Babylonian period (*G* 113 and *G* 116) had lesions in the eye sockets known as *cribra orbitalia*. These are classified as the mildest of the three degrees assigned by H. Nathan and N. Haas.[75] The cause of these lesions, which produce an area of "strainer-like" bone changes in the roof of the eye orbits, is now usually assigned to various forms of anemias, especially those induced by parasitic infections.[76] What is remarkable is that six individuals in the Islamic period at Isin had *cribra*

---

[71]The main reports are in: G. Ziegelmayer, "Anthropologische Auswertung des Skelettmaterials aus Isin," *IB* II, 103-129; and G. Ziegelmayer, "Die menschlichen Skelette 1983-1984," *IB* III, 121-136.

[72]*G = Grab* (Graves as numbered by the excavators).

[73]G. Ziegelmayer, "Anthropologische Auswertung..." *IB* II, 107, 108-109 and Tafel 41:4 and 6.

[74]G. Ziegelmayer, "Anthropologische Auswertung...,"*IB* II, 109.

[75]H. Nathan and N. Haas, "Cribra orbitalia, a Bone Condition of the Orbit of Unknown Nature," *Israel I. Med. Sci.* 2 (1966) 171.

[76]See D. P. Hengen, "Cribra orbitalia, Pathogenesis and Probable Etiology," *Homo* 22 (1971) 57.

orbitalia, something that may indicate the increasing incidence of sickle cell anemia and malaria according to Ziegelmayer.[77] Assuming that few or none of the cases are pseudopathological,[78] the most we can conclude is that presence of *cribra orbitalia* in the Isin skeletal material may reflect the incidence of malaria or malnutritional anemias (especially iron deficiency) in the Old Babylonian period. A skeleton dated in the Kassite period (*G* 114) belongs to a child of about 7 years of age buried on a mat inside of a room.[79] No unusual pathological conditions were reported.

Three skeletons attributed to the Isin II period by K. Karstens (*G* 90, *G* 91 and *G* 92) are generally in a poor state of preservation.[80] They do not provide sufficient data on which to base precise statements about the paleodemography or paleopathology of Isin's inhabitants. These three skeletons were buried in large clay vessels and two were accompanied by objects such as beads (*G* 90 and *G* 91). The remains of textiles could be seen in *G* 91, and the skeleton in *G* 92 had the hands in front of his face. Pathological conditions are not reported.

One adult male was found buried in an earthen grave (*G* 96), dated as slightly later than the Isin II period by G. Ziegelmayer, inside the Gula temple building (Room

---

[77]G. Ziegelmayer, "Die menschlichen Skelette..." *IB* III, 133.

[78]Ziegelmayer does not note that the condition may be simulated by post-mortem erosion processes of the soil, on which see C. Wells, "Pseudopathology," in D. R. Brothwell and A. T. Sandison, eds., *Diseases in Antiquity* (Springfield, Illinois:Charles Thomas, 1967) 7.

[79]G. Ziegelmayer, "Die menschlichen Skelette 1983-1984," *IB* III, 129.

[80]Raw data provided by K. Karstens, "Gräber, Nordabschnitt II, nördl. Teil," in Hrouda, *IB* II, 40-48.

XXIX).[81] This individual bore evidence of illness, particularly skoliosis and kyphosis.[82] In addition to noting that the individual probably had a visible deformity of the chest, Ziegelmayer reports the wedgelike (*"Keilform"*) shape of some of the thoracic vertebrae.[83] Although Ziegelmayer wisely refrains from providing a firm diagnosis, this wedgelike appearance of the thoracic vertebrae may be indicative of a number of diseases known in antiquity, including rheumatoid arthritis and tuberculosis. The number of diseases that may result in such deformities of the vertebrae however, makes it difficult to ascertain a specific disease based on these data alone.[84] In addition, the individual in *G* 96 suffered from dental caries.[85]

Unlike the solid evidence for the founding of some Asclepius temples soon after plagues or other health-related crises, the foregoing discussion indicates that one cannot, on the basis of present paleopathological evidence, trace the efflorescence of the temple of G/N during the Kassite period (or any other period) to specific instances of plague with much confidence. Plagues may have been more common

---

[81]G. Ziegelmayer ("Anthropologische Auswertung...," *IB* II, 108 and Tafel 39:1.

[82]Ziegelmayer, *ibid*, 113.

[83]Ziegelmayer (*ibid*, 113) says: "*Zum einen sind die Wirbelkörper des mittleren Brustwirbelbereichs in ihrer Randhöhe recht unterschiedlich, ventral und seitlich relativ niedrig, so dass die einzelnen Wirbel Keilform haben.*"

[84]See D. Morse, "Tuberculosis," in D. R. Brothwell and A. T. Sandison, *Diseases in Antiquity* (Springfield, Illinois: Charles C. Thomas, 1967) 249-271. For an analysis of the conditions which can mimic tuberculosis in skeletal material, see J. E. Buikstra, "Differential Diagnosis: An Epidemiological Model," *Yearbook of Physical Anthropology* 20 (1976) 316-328.

[85]G. Ziegelmayer, "Anthropologische Auswertung...," *IB* II, 114.

than our extant records indicate. As we have noted, the temple of G/N seems to have been quite ancient, even if it was not in continuous use. It is also difficult to surmise how much of the attention garnered by the temple of G/N was due to her association with Ninurta.

One can surmise on analogy with other ancient cultures that there will always be a sufficient population of sick individuals in a given area to produce a demand for a deity that heals.[86] However, the temple was probably not used as a large-scale infirmary. As we will argue below, the movement to centralize medical knowledge, something that may have been the product of an intrinsic bureaucratic evolution, rather than simply specific crises in health, may have been a prime factor in the role of the temples of G/N within the Mesopotamian health care system.

d) Administration

Not   much   is   known   at   present   about   the administration of the temple of G/N at Isin during the Kassite and Isin II periods. Our best information is based on some cogent analogies with other periods at Isin and elsewhere in Mesopotamia. According to Renger, G/N at Isin was served by an *en*-priest during the reign of Damiq-ilišu (19 c. B.C.E.), and by a *lú-maḫ*-priest as well.[87] The

---

[86]For the widespread existence of healing deities in the ancient world, see W. A. Jayne, *The Healing Gods of Ancient Civilizations* (New Haven: Yale, 1925).

[87]On the nature and duties of these types of priests, see J. Renger, "Untersuchungen zum Priestertum im der altbabylonischen Zeit, 1. Teil" *ZA* 58 (1967) 121-122; *idem*, "Untersuchungen zum Priestertum im der altbabylonischen Zeit, 2. Teil" *ZA* 59 (1968) 126-129; *idem*,

en-priest(ess) was chosen by oracle in a number of texts, and s/he was often the offspring of the king.

As was generally the case in Mesopotamia, a temple was regarded as the residence of the god(s), but large numbers of priests/ administrators and other servants of the temple could live within the temple complex which surrounded or was near the shrine of the god(s). In the Kassite period, for example, Kurigalzu's *giparu*, the section of the temple complex normally reserved for *en*-priests or *entu*-priestesses, at Ur probably served the Ningal temple, and was able to house a large number of individuals.[88] Large cooking ovens near the temple of G/N at Isin indicate that large quantities of food may have been prepared for the residents of the temple complex.[89] Animal remains of sheep and goats near the temple of G/N may attest the remains of offerings or meals.[90]

During the period of Hammurabi and his dynasty, the temple of G/N at Sippar had a *šangû* (among them, Awil-damu, Iddin-Šamaš and Šubiša).[91] A ration text from the period of Esarhaddon reveals that G/N had a *šangû* at

---

"Die Priesterschaft babylonischer Tempel," in *Le Temple et le Culte* (XXth Recontre assyriologique internationale; Nederlands Historisch-Archeologisch Institut (Leiden, 1975) 111.

[88]See E. Heinrich, *Die Tempel und Heiligtumer im Alten Mesopotamien* (2 volumes; Berlin: De Gruyter, 1982) Vol 1:228 and Vol 2: Abbildung 309.

[89]See *IB* II, Tafel 9:1.

[90]See J. Boessneck and R. Ziegler, "Tiersknochenfunde III. Serie III," *IB* III, 147-48.

[91]J. Renger, "Untersuchungen zum Priestertum im der altbabylonischen Zeit:2. Teil," *ZA* 59 (1968) 114.

Assur during his reign.[92] A text found at Uruk, and perhaps composed about 1200 B.C.E., indicates that the temple of Gula at Isin had a *šangû* (LÚ SANGA [d]ME.ME).[93] This text, which we will designate as *The Story of the Bitten Man from Nippur,* as well as other evidence, indicates that the temple of G/N at Isin probably had a *šangû,* and perhaps a *lú-maḫ*-priest as well, throughout most of the Kassite and Isin II periods.

The role of the *šangû* is that of a chief administrator of the temple, and he probably was well educated as a scribe. At Sippar Iddin-šamaš, the *šangû* of G/N, was involved in land transactions.[94] As we will see below, the *šangû* of the Middle and Neo-Assyrian periods could also administer certain forms of therapy. The fact that Esarhaddon provided rations to the *šangû* of temple of G/N also indicates that the latter's office as chief administrator continued in the Neo-Assyrian period, at least in Assur. The *šangû* of G/N at Sippar during the OB period probably served between 20 to 30 years according to Renger.[95]

---

[92]B. Menzel, *Assyrische Tempel* II: Kultische Texte, T 18, vs. 15 reads: 1 BAN [d]*Gu-la* SANGA-*ša.* The text reveals that this ration was equal to that received by the *šangû* of ZA.BA4.BA4 and by the *šangû* of Adad([d]IM). A broken inscription published by Borger (*Die Inschriften Asarhaddons Königs von Assyrien* [*AfO* 9 [1956]; p. 105, lines 8-11]), suggests that Esarhaddon also provided the temple of Gula at Assur with the spoils of war.

[93]The text (W 23558) was published by A. Cavigneaux, "Texte und Fragmente aus Warka," *BaM* 10 (1979) 111-117.

[94]See R. Harris, *Ancient Sippar: A Demographic Study of an Old-Babylonian City (1894-1595 B.C.)* (Istanbul: Nederlands Historisch-Archaeologisch Instituut, 1975) 184.

[95]J. Renger, "Untersuchungen zum Priestertum...2. Teil," *ZA* 59 (1968) 121.

Information for the *lú-maḫ*-priest is more scarce than for the *šangû*. However, it appears that he dressed in special attire and participated in various ceremonial and ritual aspects of the temple. Renger reminds us that, at least in early periods, the *lú-maḫ*-priest had a high status (e.g., Lugalzaggesi and his father had been *lú-maḫ*-priests of Nisaba).[96]

The various economic and administrative texts found in the temple of G/N at Isin support the idea that the temple of G/N functioned much like other temples insofar as it was an economic and administrative center in the city.[97] As we have mentioned, Iddin-Šamaš, the *šangû* of G/N at Sippar, in the OB period, was involved in land transactions. Dandamayev has argued that certain temples, particularly at Uruk, of the first millennium were more involved in the economics of the country than those in the second millennium.[98] The temple of G/N at Isin may have shared in such a trend, though sufficient data are not available at present to confirm this.

It was the king who was generally responsible for the general maintenance and repair of the temples during most periods in Mesopotamia. In the case of G/N, this is indicated by the various inscriptions in which the king takes

---

[96] J. Renger, "Untersuchungen zum Priestertum...,2. Teil" *ZA* 59 (1968) 128-129.

[97] For examples, see B. F. Walker and C. Wilcke, "Preliminary Report on the Inscriptions..." 101.

[98] M. A. Dandamayev, "State and Temple in the First Millennium B.C.," in E. Lipinski, ed., *State and Temple Economy in the Ancient Near East* (2 volumes; Leuven: Departement Oriëntalistiek, 1979) Volume II: 588.

responsibility for building the temple.[99]   Unlike the temples of Asclepius, therefore, the initial building (or rebuilding) of the temple of G/N did not depend on a large international or pan-Mesopotamian effort to raise funds. A text (Nbn 804:1) from the reign of Nabonidus mentions that ten hired workers ([lú]a-gar-ru-ú-tu) participated in the construction of the temple of G/N at Sippar.[100]

The Asclepius temple priests also were responsible for clerical administration, but it appears that the Mesopotamian temple was a much more complex organization. On the basis of the economic and administrative texts found in many Mesopotamian temples, one may hypothesize that, in general, administrative, socio-legal and other bureaucratic matters involving multiple parties (e.g., contract witnessing) probably predominated over personal services for individuals in Mesopotamian temples. The connection of the *asû* and *āšipu* with the temple will be discussed in a section below.

B. MESOPOTAMIAN MEDICAL THEOLOGY

1. General comments

The medical theology of the temple of G/N must be seen in the context of the wider scope of the medical theology of Mesopotamian cultures. In the broader context

---

[99]C. B. F. Walker and C. Wilcke, "Preliminary Reports on the Inscriptions 1975-1977, 1978," in *IB* II, 98.

[100]Text as cited in M. A. Dandamaev, "Free Hired Labor in Babylonia during the Sixth through Fourth Centuries B.C.," in Powell, *Labor in the Ancient Near East* (New Haven, Conn.: AOS, 1987) 274-75.

we may begin with van der Toorn's statement that illness "comprises all deviations from an ideal of individual fulfilment, the physiognomy of which is to a large extent culturally determined."[101] Such a definition fits well with that suggested by various anthropologists discussed in our Introduction.[102] In Mesopotamia, illness had a variety of explanations which often mixed ostensibly empirical causes with hidden and supernatural ones.

In Mesopotamia illness was often, if not normally, viewed as ultimately rooted in the will of the gods. There were illnesses, notably *saḫaršubbû*,[103] that almost always were regarded as definite indications of divine punishment.[104] Although long illnesses carried the stigma of divine reproval, K. van der Toorn argues that most illnesses were not viewed as divine punishment. In order to understand the connection between the divine will and illness one may begin with the popular diagnostic series called *SA.GIG* (= "The symptoms"), much of which was published by R. Labat.[105]

---

[101]K. van der Toorn, *Sin and Sanction in Israel and Mesopotamia* (Aasen/Maasricht:Van Gorcum, 1985) 67.

[102]For example, A. Kleinman, *Patient and Healers* (Berkeley: U. of California, 1980) 72.

[103]This word is sometimes translated as "leprosy," by scholars. For a study of the identification of the disease, see J. V. Kinnier Wilson, "Medicine in the Land and Times of the Old Testament," in T. Ishida, ed., *Studies in the Period of David and Solomon* (Winona Lake, Indiana:Eisenbrauns, 1982) 354-357.

[104]K. van der Toorn, *Sin and Sanction*, 72-80.

[105]R. Labat, *Traité akkadien de diagnostics et pronostics médicaux* (= *TDP*; Leiden:Brill, 1951). We will follow most scholars in quoting the transcription from *TDP* by **page number and line**; For a recent discussion of the identification and history of the series *SA.GIG*, see I. L. Finkel, "Adad-apla-iddina, Esagil-kin-apli and the Series *SA.GIG*,"

Here we find a recurrent expression in the diagnosis of an illness--namely *qāt DN*. The following example is typical: "If the face is filled with 'marks,' it is the hand of Marduk."[106] Other symptoms are spoken of as the hand of Šamaš (e.g., *TDP*, 78:68), Adad (*TDP* 62:26), Ištar (*TDP* 80:8) and numerous other supernatural beings. The diagnosis *qāt DN* often is followed by a prognosis which usually notes whether the patient is expected to live (e.g., *iballut* in *TDP* 74:47) or die (e.g., *imât* in *TDP* 26:74). Sometimes one only finds a prognosis in the apodosis. The form of the diagnoses and prognoses which are based on symptoms (rather than on other types of omens) follows the sequence of protasis-apodosis known from Akkadian omens and laws, and the sequence may be schematized as follows:

If symptom X is present, then diagnosis Y   (usually *qāt DN*) and/or prognosis Z (usually notes that the patient will live (*iballut*) or die (*imât*).

Before one can determine the pervasiveness and precise nature of the concept of illness expressed by the ubiquitous expression, *qāt DN*, in *SA. GIG* and elsewhere, it is important to note that the meaning of *qāt DN* has been the subject of some disagreement. J. V. Kinnier Wilson views the expression as a general indication of divine displeasure, and he says: "In fact, Akk *qātu*, lit. "hand" may be thought to express the idea of both 'disease' and

---

in E. Leichty, M. de J. Ellis and P. Gerardi, *A Scientific Humanist: Studies in Memory of Abraham Sachs* (Philadelphia, 1988) 143-59.
[106]*TDP* 76: 51: *šumma*(DIŠ) *pânû*(IGI.MEŠ)-*šú* [*ziq*]-*ti malû*(SI.A) *qāt*(ŠU) ^d*Marduk*(AMAR.UTU).

'punishment' in such contexts."[107] He would translate the phrase *qāt DN* as "disease or punishment of DN."[108] However, K. van der Toorn argues that *qāt DN* cannot always be seen as indicating punishment by the particular god in the expression, and that it should not be an automatic indicator of sin on the part of the afflicted. In his view, "The *qāt DN* constructions, then, intend to localize the source of the signs rather than to give a definite answer concerning the nature and cause of the disease."[109] In particular, he cites a text from Tell Rimah in which a boy diagnosed with a *qāt DN* seeks further counsel which concludes with *mimma ḫiṭum ul ibašši* ("There is no sin").[110] In summary, he argues that *qāt DN* is an expression analogous to "NIG.ŠU = *ša qāti*, 'committed to the charge of, under the responsibility of.'"[111]

The views of Kinnier Wilson and K. van der Toorn need some refinement. First, one must note that a *qāt DN* does not represent one specific disease (e.g., malaria, leprosy, or one specific disease associated with the god in the formula) in all texts. Illnesses which are apparently not otherwise related can be attributed to the same god with the same expression. For example, the same expression *qāt Ninurta* was applied in instances (e.g., *TDP* 66:68') when one patient had an ailment which manifested itself in speech disturbances (*šumma dabab-šu itta*[*kki*]*r*), and in the case of

---

[107]J. V. Kinnier Wilson, "Medicine in the Land and Times of the Old Testament," 349 n. 37.

[108]Kinnier Wilson, "Medicine...", 349.

[109]van der Toorn, *Sin and Sanction*, 78.

[110]S. Dalley, C.B.F. Walker and J. D. Hawkins, *The Old Babylonian Tablets from Tell Al-Rimah* (British School of Archaeology in Iraq, 1976) no. 65.

[111]van der Toorn, *Sin and Sanction*, 199 n. 304.

another patient who had an illness which manifested itself in inflamed face and eyes and perhaps had trouble urinating.[112] Of course, Kinnier Wilson's translation of "disease of DN" does not require an attribution of sin to the suppliant.

Although K. van der Toorn is sound in arguing that *qāt DN* should not always be viewed as punishment, he may mislead the reader into thinking that Mesopotamians did not view *qāt DN* as more than simply a reference to "the source of the signs." In particular, one must note the following features in the context of *qāt DN* expressions.

1.   The situations in which the expression *qāt DN* is used are usually a negative, namely, an illness. K. van der Toorn's arguments would be better served by examples where wholly positive omens are characterized with the phrase *qāt DN*. Moreover, if the expression is so analogous to NIG.SU = *ša qāti*, then why is that latter formula (which was presumably available and not unusual in Akkadian) not used more often in contexts identical to *qāt DN* in these medical texts?

2.   K. van der Toorn also cites *KTS* 24 to show that illness need not be sent because of wrongdoing on the patient's part. At issue is the delay in the repayment of a loan, and the crucial portion reads:[113]

> *a-šu-mi kaspim ša ik-ri-be*
> *a-na-kam Bé-la-tum*

---

[112]*TDP* 78:69-70: *šumma panū*(IGI.MEŠ)-*šu u enâ*(IGI-II-MEŠ)-*šu ittanpaḫu*(MU.MEŠ... *šinati?* (KAŠ?.MEŠ)-*šu ta-ba-ka la ilê*(ZU-e).
[113]*KTS* 24 = H. Hirsch, *Untersuchungen zur altassyrischen Religion* (*AfO* 13/14 [1961]) 71 n. 385, lines 4-8.

ta-am-ra-aṣ i-na ú-tù-ke
ù i-na e-ṭá-me
ša-am-du-a?-ni

In regard to the money of the
ikribu (offering), here Belatum
is ill. By the utukku-demon
and the ghost (of the ancestors)
we have been struck.

Yet the example also shows that, even if the failure to repay the loan was not a sin, illness could be sent to motivate the patient to serve the interest of the supernatural beings (in this case repayment of the loan). Although such an illness may not be punitive in the strict sense, the case simply reinforces the notion that supernatural beings could send illnesses for a wide variety of reasons, even if the patient did not do anything wrong. Far from lessening the anxiety of the patient, such a concept would increase it. Indeed, the patient would be more prone to find out how he had displeased the deity responsible for the illness.

3. K. van der Toorn's example from Tell Rimah, in which no guilt was found in a boy who was given the diagnosis *qāt eṭemmi*, does show that a sin need not always be held responsible for an illness designated by *qāt DN*. But the case also shows that the person suffering from *qāt DN* did not simply wish to localize the signs. Indeed, the patient was interested in finding out which sin, or if a sin, was responsible for the illness--hence the response *mimma ḥiṭum ul ibašši*. Thus, the case again confirms that the belief that sin was the reason for the illness designated by *qāt DN* was

a common presupposition that required further investigation (e.g., determining which sin).

In light of this review of van der Toorn and Kinnier Wilson, one may say that *qāt DN* describes an adverse condition, and illness in particular, that was somehow of special interest to the god (which we will designate "sender/controller")[114] in the formula. The specific illness or other adverse condition could change from case to case (e.g., *qāt Ninurta* could refer to a headache in one instance and to a bowel disease in another). We may also say that the pervasive use of *qāt DN* in Mesopotamia for so many different types of symptoms reflects a belief that most illnesses were divine instruments or messages of which punishment was one, though not the only, sub-category or motive. Such a view avoids unwarranted specificity (e.g., specific diseases or punishment for specific sins), and it explains why the formula is usually not found in situations wholly favorable to the person.[115] Illnesses, as instruments or messages, sometimes were intended to motivate the patient to an action that promoted the sometimes arbitrary (at least from a human standpoint) interests or pleasures of the god(s) that were not punitive (e.g, repayment of a loan). Of

---

[114]The term "controller" accommodates K. van der Toorn's notion that *qāt DN* may designate the deity under whose charge the signs are placed.

[115]In regard to illness, Goltz (*Studien zur altorientalischen und griechischen Heilkunde*, 264) would see it as one of the most important instruments of the gods in their dealings with humans ("*Sie ist eines ihrer wichtigsten Instrumente in ihrem Handeln am Menschen*").

course, there were large classes of purely malevolent sources of illness such as witchcraft and sorcery.[116]

Equally important, however, is the fact that the "sender/controller" of an illness was the key to its treatment. Even if one accepts K. van der Toorn's idea that *qāt DN* simply identified the sign of the deity associated with the illness, it was imperative that such a deity be contacted, appeased, or entreated properly in order to regain one's health. In any event, significant practical consequences attended a patient's belief that his illness might have been caused by some hidden sin or that it was a message to fulfill some supernatural being's wish.

One consequence was that the large array of sometimes conflicting symptoms meant that determining which god was responsible, or which god was an appropriate contact, in the case of an illness could be a cumbersome task in terms of diagnosis and therapy. The identification of the correct *qāt DN* functioned as a crucial step in the medical process that was followed by the performance of rituals to the appropriate gods that would hopefully bring permanent relief. The *SA.GIG* series can

---

[116]In order to control the scope of our thesis, we will not enter into a full discussion of witchcraft and sorcery, except as it is relevant in our discussion of the Mesopotamian health care system. For full treatments on witchcraft and sorcery, see J. Bottero, "Magie A," *RLA* 7:200-234; Marie-Louise Thomsen, *Zauberdiagnose und Schwarze Magie in Mesopotamien* (Carsten Niebuhr Institute of Ancient Near Eastern Studies, 2 Museum Tusculanum, 1987); and T. Abusch, *Babylonian Witchcraft Literature:Case Studies* (Brown Judaic Studies 32; Atlanta:Scholars Press, 1987). For an anthropological discussion of the difference between witchcraft (the use of magic as a power intrinsic to a special group of individuals) and sorcery (the use of magic through techniques available to anyone), see G. P. Murdock, *Theories of Illness* (Pittsburgh:U. of Pittsburgh, 1980) 64-71.

be seen as an attempt to develop some type of systematic determination of the numerous omens and symptoms. Such an attempt was not perfect because, as Labat notes, the manual may recommend contradictory prognoses for the very same symptoms.[117] Nonetheless, the *SA.GIG* series, even if sometimes contradictory and ambiguous, was part of an ancient "flow chart" in which the step of identifying the god responsible (whether this means that the god sent the disease or had knowledge of the prognosis) for the illness led to the particular ritual in the next step of the medical process.

Indeed, after the identification of the DN and what the *qātu* of this DN signified in this particular case, the next step in the process were the execution of rituals such as described in the namburbi texts. Caplice notes:

> since physical illness could be conceived as
> foreshadowed by a portent, there is sometimes
> overlapping between strictly medical texts and the
> namburbis.[118]

As van der Toorn notes, penitential prayers such as the ones known under the rubric *dingir.šà.dib.ba* probably "represent the therapeutic counterpart of the diagnostic texts."[119] In any event, the most important aspect of *SA.GIG* was the

---

[117]Labat (*TDP*, xxxi): "*Il n'est pas rare que, d'une même symptomatologie, le traitè infère des pronostics contradictoires, donnés comme egalemente probables.*"

[118]R. Caplice, *The Akkadian Namburbi Texts:An Introduction* (Los Angeles:Undena, 1974) 9.

[119]K. van der Toorn, *Sin and Sanction*, 123. For a significant collection of such prayers, see W. G. Lambert, "*Dingir.šà.dib.ba* Incantations," *JNES* 33 (1974) 267-322.

supposition that identifying "the sender/ controller" of an illness was the key to therapy.

From a patient's point of view, the numerous possible, and sometimes contradictory, causes were also psychologically burdensome, especially if the illness persisted. This burden is expressed in incantations that are specifically intended for the uncertainty concerning the supernatural causes or divine motives for the misfortune. For example, one *dingir.šà.dib.ba* prayer by a person suffering illness, among other misfortunes, is entitled: "Incantation. What are my iniquities that I am thus treated?"[120] Another *dingir.šà.dib.ba* prayer is recited by a man who counts illness[121] among his misfortunes, and it is titled "Incantation: Oh Ea, Šamaš, and Marduk, what are my iniquities?"[122] Later in the text (l. 29) he exclaims: "My infractions are many, I do not know what I did" (*ma-a-du ár-nu-u-a e-ma e-pu-šú ul i-di*). In line 114 the suppliant exclaims: "Drive from my body illness due to known and unknown iniquities" (*murṣi*(GIG) *an-ni i-du-u la i-du-u u*[*k-kiš*] *ina zumri*(SU)-*ya5*).

The following passage in a prayer (*LKA* 139) is recited by a person who had been unsuccessful in learning the cause of his misfortunes from an *āšipu*, misfortunes that were apparently economic and physical:[123]

---

[120]ÉN *mi-nu-ú an-nu-ú-a-ma* [*ki-a-am*] *ep-še-ku*; Akkadian text (cuneiform copy and transcription) in W. G. Lambert, "*Dingir.šà.dib.ba* Incantations," *JNES* 33 (1974) 284:10.

[121]W. G. Lambert, "*Dingir.šà.dib.ba* Incantations," *JNES* 33 (1974) 274:10: "paralysis has gripped my side"/*mun-ga is-sa-bat i-di-ya5* .

[122]l. 1: ÉN ^d^*E-a* ^d^*Šamaš u* ^d^*Marduk mi-nu-u an-ni-ya;* W. G. Lambert ("*Dingir.šà.dib.ba Incantations*," 275).

[123]The transcription is from the recent and improved edition of the prayer by van der Toorn, *Sin and Sanction*, 147-154, lines 25-30.

[am-mi-n]im ni-ziq-tu la tú-ub-ba-tu ta-aš-ku-na
iá-ši ina MAŠ.GE$_6$ li-šab-ru-nin-ni-ma liq-bu-ni
[a]r-ni ZU-ú u NU ZU-ú li-šá-pu-nim-ma lu-ši-ib
ana še-er-ti ^{d}UTU a-na GIDIM.[MEŠ] kim-ti-ya
qí-bi-ma a-lak-tí A.ḪUL[MEŠ]-ti ša
NAM.LÚ.U$_{18}$.LU ša šú-pu-šá-ku ana-ku li-šab-ru-
nin-ni-ma li-ip-šu-ru-ni-ma

[Wh]y have you imposed upon me such unpleasant
anxiety? Let them reveal it to me in a dream, and let
them speak to me. Let them reveal my [s]in, whether
it was conscious or inadvertent, and I will live with
my punishment. Šamaš, speak to my ancestral
ghosts, that they may show me, and interpret for me
the oracle[124] of human misfortunes which I have
been made to endure.

Prolonged undiagnosed illness is naturally very
psychologically burdensome. The texts above show,
however, that the patient was burdened not only with the
anxiety of a prolonged illness, but also with questions about
what acts that s/he might have committed were responsible
for this prolonged illness. In addition, the prayers reflect the
concern that the appropriate god(s) had not been contacted or
moved to action.

Letters between Esarhaddon and his exorcists also
show that such anxiety did not exempt kings. In one letter,
for example, an exorcist attempts to comfort Esarhaddon by
telling him that his disease is a seasonal one (mur-ṣi šat$^!$-ti

---

124Rendition of alaktu; cf. T. Abusch, "alaktu and hālākhā:Oracular
Decision, Divine Revelation," HTR 80 (1987) 15-42.

šu-ú]), and not one caused by cultic negligence on the part of the king.[125] The various phrases seem to belabor the point that the disease should not be seen as punishment. Although the response suggests that non-punitive causes could be elicited as explanations, such responses suggest that offensive actions on the part of the patient were a natural supposition in times of illness even for the king.

Commenting on the theme of ignorance of one's sins in penitential prayers that often deal with illness, K. van der Toorn aptly remarks: "The sheer omnipresence of the theme can hardly fail to impress the student."[126] In summary, a wide variety of evidence (letters, diagnostic texts, prayers, and rituals) from Mesopotamia indicates that the notion that illness was an instrument of supernatural beings was pervasive, affecting king and commoner alike.

2. Principal general healing strategies

Two main and sometimes overlapping strategies were used to deal with this medical theology that centered on the often unknown "sender/controller" of an illness. One strategy was to maximize and lengthen prayers and rituals for the cure. By praying to all the possible gods or beings who could be responsible for the malady, the patient (or his consultant) hoped to contact and entreat the "correct" god(s). Such a strategy is seen in the *Šurpu* texts, which have long litanies (e.g., *Šurpu* 2: 129-192) intended to appease a large

---

[125]*LABS* 236: 11-12; See also *LAS* II, 174.
[126]*Sin and Sanction*, 94.

number of gods.[127]   Another aspect of such a maximalist strategy was that every possible sin that might have offended the sender was sometimes enumerated (e.g., *Šurpu* 2:5-103).   In the *dingir.šà.dib.ba* prayers one finds a patient concerned that even iniquities committed by family members might have been responsible for the suppliant's illness:[128]

> *ár-ni abi-ya₅ abi-abi*(AD.AD)*-ya₅*
> *ummi*(AMA)*-ya₅ ummi-umm[i*(AMA.AMA)*-ya₅]*
> *ár-ni aḫi*(ŠEŠ)*-y[a₅] rabî*(GAL-*i*)
> *aḫāti*(NIN)*-ya₅ rabītu*(GAL-*tu*)
> *ár-ni kimti*(NÍ.RI.A)*-ya₅ nišūti*(NÍ.RI.A)*-ya₅*
> *u salāti*(NÍ.RI.A)*-ya₅*
> *ša ki-ma sa-ba-si ki-mil-ti ili-ya₅* ᵈ*ištari*(15)*-ya₅*
> *iš-ni-qu-ni ya-a-ši*

The sin of my father, my grandfather, my mother, my grandmother,
The sin of my elder brother, my elder sister
The sin of family, clan and kin
which has been placed upon me because of the fury of
the anger of my god and goddess.

It also appears that the most labor intensive rituals for health, among other things, were those performed on behalf of the largest institutions or the most elite persons in Mesopotamia. The maximalist strategy, therefore, is used

---

[127]All references to *Šurpu* are from the standard edition by E. Reiner, *Šurpu: A Collection of Sumerian and Akkadian Incantations* (AfO 11; Graz, 1958).
[128]W. G. Lambert, "*Dingir.šà.dib.ba* Incantations," *JNES* 33 (1974) 280, lines 115-118.

by persons or institutions that had a large number of resources available to conduct the lengthy rituals. Because of their perceived importance to society, these institutions and persons were often believed to require a larger dose of protection from a large number of possible malevolent sources. In particular, such institutions included kingship, the city, and the empire. It is in such a light that lengthy and complicated rituals in *Maqlû*,[129] and *Bīt rimki*[130] may be understood.

The second strategy hoped to achieve the same range with a relatively simplified method of a divine intermediary. A divine intermediary could be entreated to locate the correct supernatural beings responsible for the malady. Such an intermediary was thought to possess special influence and/or special knowledge. Instead of numerous rituals to all the possible gods, a ritual to the intermediary may have been considered an efficient step to reach the "correct" god(s) either in the initial stages or when other strategies had failed.

Once such a god was located by the intermediary, then the proper ritual could be performed. One example of this strategy can be seen in a divinatory ritual where the suppliant, having exhausted other means of ascertaining the cause of his maladies, begs Šamaš to "speak to the ghosts of

---

[129]T. Abusch ("Mesopotamian Anti-Witchcraft Literature:Texts and Studies, Part I:The Nature of *Maqlû*: Its Character, Divisions and Calendrical Setting," *JNES* 33 [1974] 251-262) has shown that *Maqlû* was a unified ceremony performed over a night and the following morning in the month of Abu. See further, T. Abusch, *Babylonian Witchcraft Literature.*

[130]J. Laessøe, (*Studies on the Assyrian Ritual and Series bit rimki* [Ejnar Munksgaard, 1955:page 102] concludes that "occasions for performing the *bīt rimki* ritual seem to have been major events affecting the king, country, and people alike."

my kin" (dUTU *a-na* GIDIM[.MEŠ] *kim-ti-ya qí-bi-ma*).[131] The simplest strategy, entreating the one deity responsible (directly or through a consultant) for an illness in the initial stage of an illness, is the one used when the deity is thought to be obvious. This may be the case in *The Story of the Bitten Man from Nippur* that we will discuss below. While the elite could use the maximalist or minimalist strategies, one can surmise that the poor would not have had the option of using the maximalist strategy without the difficulty of obtaining resources and the time of the consultant(s).

3. Medical theology and the medical professions

An accompanying feature of the complex medical theology of Mesopotamia is that rituals became very complicated. As we shall demonstrate, these and other features of the medical theology led to the formation of a significant bureaucracy and the necessity of more than one type of health care consultant. The complex medical theology required that an enormous amount of confidence and trust be placed in the medical bureaucracy. Such a bureaucracy could control the agenda of a patient to an enormous degree, even in the case of a king.

a) E. Ritter's classification of the medical professions

One of the best established theories in the study of Mesopotamian medicine was expounded by Edith Ritter in 1965 in an article titled "Magical Expert (= *Āšipu*) and

---

[131]Text (g) in K. van der Toorn, *Sin and Sanction*, 148:28.

Physician (= *Asû*): Notes on Two Complementary Professions in Babylonian Medicine."[132] As the title and tenor of the article indicates, Ritter proposed that the relative presence or absence of magical and supernatural assumptions and operations by each profession was the key to their distinction. On the most general level, Ritter articulates the basic viewpoint of the *āšipu* as follows:

> The *āšipu* qua healer views disease as a particular expression of the wider beliefs that he holds, namely that a chain of events, initiated under the influence of 'supernatural' powers or forces, proceeds on a predetermined course to an outcome that can be predicted by the skillful reading of 'signs.'[133]

In contrast, the viewpoint of the *asû* can be described as follows according to Ritter:

> The *asû*, without reference to a more general system of notions,views disease as a complex of presenting symptoms and findings; by his 'practical grasp' (intuition plus accumulated experience) of the immediate situation he proceeds with treatment.[134]

For Ritter, therefore, the *āšipu* was primarily working under supernatural and magical assumptions, while the *asû* was more akin to healers who operate relatively free of supernatural assumptions--namely physicians.

---

[132]*A S* 16: 299-321.
[133]E. Ritter, "Magical Expert...," *A S* 16:301.
[134] Ritter, *ibid*, 302.

Ritter's theory has garnered an impressive consensus,[135] and most dissenters do not provide sustained critiques. For example, H. W. F. Saggs briefly cautions those who would see the two main healing professions as rooted in the distinction between a supernatural approach (*āšipu*) vs. a secular one (*asû*),[136] but he does not provide a sustained critique. Olof Pedersén restricts to a footnote the incisive objection that many of the texts on which Ritter bases her distinction originate from a single library which belongs to a family of *āšipu*s in Assur.[137] He notes, moreover, that the library of that family had an extensive collection of texts on botanical remedies, a collection that, on Ritter's theory, would not be expected of an *āšipu*.

As we shall demonstrate, recent advances in medical anthropology and the comparative study of healing consultants in many cultures suggest that Ritter's model is in need of a thorough re-examination, particularly insofar as she overlooks the dynamic manner in which societies with

---

[135]Among the scholars who espouse Ritter's definitions are R. D. Biggs, "Babylonien," in H. Schipperges, E. Seidler and P. U. Unschuld, eds., *Krankheit, Heilkunst, Heilung* (Freiburg: Munchen, 1978) 101-109; P. E. Dion ("Medical Personnel in the Ancient Near East," *ARAM* [1.2, 1989] 206-16); D. Goltz, "Studien zur altorientalischen und griechischen Heilkunde: Therapie-Arzneibereitung-Rezeptstruktur," *Sudhoffs Archiv/ Zeitschrift für Wissenschafts-geschichte* 16 (Wiesbaden:Franz Steiner, 1974); P. Herrero, *La Thérapeutique mésopotamienne*, (Paris: Editions Recherche sur les civilisations, 1984); and M. Moore, *The Balaam Traditions: Their Character and Development* (Atlanta: Scholars Press, 1990).

[136]H. W. F. Saggs, *The Might that Was Assyria* (London: Sidgwick and Jackson, 1984) 227-229.

[137]See O. Pedersén, *Archives and Libraries in the City of Assur* (2 volumes; Uppsala: Almqvist & Wiksell, 1985 and 1986) volume 2:58 n. 36.

multiple health care consultants can operate within one
conceptual system. It is especially misleading to suggest that
the *āšipu* worked within a conceptual framework which
supposed and assigned supernatural causes, while the *asû*
did not. In order to provide some refinements of Ritter's
model, let us re-examine some of the attested strategies that
were employed in the medical consultation process in the
following texts, most of which are cited by Ritter herself.[138]

The Poor Man of Nippur [139]
(Kassite?/patient:mayor)

Main diagnosis	>	Cons./Rec.	>	Result
physical		*asû*		Not
beating				applicable

PBS I/2, No. 72:6-9
(Kassite/ patient: official?)

Main diagnosis	>	Cons./Rec.	>	Result
chest ailment		*asû*/ bandage,		?
(*i-ra-as-su*		potions		
mar-ṣa-tu₄)				

---

[138]For the sake of succinctness, we have employed the following
symbols and abbreviations to express the sequence as described in the
text itself: Cons. = Consultant(s) working in the text; Rec. = the
recommendation of the consultant(s), including any treatment performed
in the text; > = sequence of action reported in the text; * = the task of
each profession when these are engaged in a cooperative action; ? =
result is not recorded or ambiguous in the text.

[139]Principal editions of the story include O. R. Gurney, "The Tale of
the Poor Man of Nippur," *Anatolian Studies* 6 (1956) 154-64; and J. S.
Cooper, "Structure, Humor, and Satire in the Poor Man of Nippur,"
JCS 27 (1975) 163-174.

PBS I/2, No. 72:18-26

(Kassite/ patient: official's daughter?)

Main diagnosis >	Cons./Rec. >	Result >	Con./Rec. >	Result
coughing (*i-ga-an-ni-ḫu-ma*)	*asû*/potions	cough is worsening (*su-a-lam it-ta-da-a*); new report of abdominal pain[140]	*asû*/request for *šarmadu* herb from king; concern that the disease might turn into the "hand of the power of the curse. " (ŠU.NAM.ERÍM.MA)	?

PBS I/2, No. 72:27-30[141]

(Kassite/ patient: princess)

Main diagnosis >	Cons./Rec. >	Result
repeated fever (*um-mu iṣ-ṣa-na-ba-tu-ši*)	*asû*/dressing and potion (*na-aṣ-ma-at-ti ù ma-aš-qí-ti*)	Positive

BAM 9:55ff

(Neo-Assyrian/patient:common citizen)[142]

Main diagnosis >	Cons./Rec. >	Result >	Con./Rec. >	Result
qāt eṭemmi	*āšipu*/rituals	Negative	*asû*/list of remedies	?

---

[140]P.B. Adamson ("Anatomical and Pathological Terms in Akkadian:Part II," *JRAS* [1979] 4) argues that *su'alu* refers to a cough accompanied by phlegm.

[141]*PBS* 1/2, 72 is a letter from Nippur which speaks of more than one case.

[142]The designation "common citizen" in *BAM* 9:55ff, *CT* 23, 44 a 8 and *AMT* 24, 1:3ff is based on the phrase: *šumma*(DIŠ) *amēlu*(NA) in the headings; these texts report typical, not actual cases.

CT 23, 44 a 8

(Neo-Assyrian/patient:common citizen)

<u>Main diagnosis</u> >	<u>Cons./Rec.</u> >	<u>Result</u> >	<u>Con./Rec.</u> >	<u>Result</u>
qāt eṭemmi,	*āšipu*/	Negative	**āšipu*/	?
headaches	rituals	more rituals		
		*asû/rubbing		
		with "tallow"		
		(Ú DIL.BAD)		

AMT 24, 1:3ff

(Neo-Assyrian/patient: common citizen)

<u>Main diagnosis</u> >	<u>Cons./Rec.</u> >	<u>Result</u>
Mouth and	**āšipu* for	Positive
jaws do not	rituals for	
function well,	6 days	
and cannot speak	**asû* uses	
(*da-ba-ba la il[e 'i*)	bandages	
	beginning	
	on the 7th day,	
	while *āšipu*	
	continues rituals.	

ABL 341

(Neo-Assyrian/ patient:official's daughter?)

<u>Main diagnosis</u> >	<u>Cons./Rec.</u> >	<u>Result</u>
serious illness	*asû*	?
(*mar-ṣa-at*		
a-dan-niš),		
no appetite		

LABS 241 (= *LAS* 181)[143]

(Neo-Assyrian/patient: king)

Main diagnosis	>	Cons./Rec.	>	Result
"strong fever?"		*āšipu*/		?
(*ṣa-ri-iḫ*		*ṣillibānu*		
a-dan-niš)		medication		

LABS 243 (= *LAS* 183)

(Neo-Assyrian/patient:king)

Initial diagnosis	>	Cons./Rec.	>	Result
"eye inflammation"		*āšipu*/ritual		?
ḫu-un-ṭi ša		against eye		
[*e-na-a-te*][144]		inflammation"		
		(*né-pe-še* ⌈ *ša*⌉		
		ITI⌉.GU[D] *ša*		
		ḫu-un-ṭi ša		
		[*e-na-a-te*]		
		né-ep-pa-áš)		

LABS 315 (= *LAS* 246)

(Neo-Assyrian/patient: king)

Initial diagnosis	>	Cons./Rec.	>	Result	>	Con./Rec.	>	Result
serious?		*asû*/presumably		Negative		*asû*/another		?
		usual treatment				treatment		
						(*ṣilbu*		
						medication)/		
						follow-up		
						visit/referral		
						to the haruspices		
						for "signs"		

---

[143]The addressee of *LABS* 241, 243 and 315 is Esarhaddon.

[144]Parpola's original reading in *LAS* 183, lines 5-6 is: *ḫu-un-ṭi* [*ša eṣ*]-*ma!-te* = "fever [of the bones]."

Before we propose our own view of the distinction between the *asû* and *āšipu*, we must note that Ritter's model pre-dated many of the recent advances in medical anthropology, and consequently many of her general assumptions about healing consultants are overly simpified.

The *āšipu*, according to Ritter's basic definition, sees illness as a chain of events, initiated under the influence of "'supernatural' powers or forces, which proceeds on a predetermined course to an outcome that can be predicted by the skillful reading of 'signs.'" Yet the same view can be seen in the *asû*, particularly in *LABS* 315. In that letter it is the *asû* who recommends that the king consult the haruspices (LÚ.ḪAL.MEŠ) to help determine the diagnosis. This presupposes that, even if the *asû* does not specialize in reading signs, this consultant can, and perhaps routinely does, view disease as a chain of events whose outcome can be predicted by a skillful readings of signs.

According to Ritter's basic definitions, the *āšipu* is distinct from the *asû* because the latter "views disease as a complex of presenting symptoms and findings." However, one could also describe in a similar manner the basic viewpoint of the *āšipu*. The series *SA.GIG* is a lengthy treatise which lists diagnoses that show that the *āšipu* is quite interested in the presenting of physical symptoms and findings of patients. In effect, Ritter has restricted to the *āšipu*, and so treated as distinctive, a viewpoint that may characterize both the *āšipu* and the *asû*.

Note that Ritter's definition of the *asû* states that he "proceeds with treatment" on the basis of his empirical findings. But *BAM* 9:55ff, *CT* 23, 44 a 8, and *AMT* 24, 1:3ff indicate that the *āšipu* also proceeds with treatment once he, presumably by the skilfull reading of signs, has ascertained the agent. As Caplice notes, a primary purpose of reading signs was to help select the appropriate therapy.[145] The rituals of the *āšipu* in *BAM* 9:55ff, *CT* 23, 44 a 8, and *AMT* 24, 1:3ff should be considered no less of a treatment than the actions of the *asû*. Yet, Ritter does not mention in her basic definition that the *āšipu* also proceeds with treatment on the basis of his empirical findings--namely, the physical symptoms of the patient. Again, Ritter has restricted to one profession, and so treated as distinctive, a *modus operandi* that characterizes both the *āšipu* and the *asû*.

Ritter's basic definition of the *asû* also suggests that only that profession worked by "intuition plus accumulated experience," but *CT* 23, 44 a 8 indicates that the *āšipu* tries other rituals when prior ones did not work, a sort of trial-and-error approach. This *modus operandi* is something that also may be characterized as a combination of "intuition plus accumulated experience," and consequently it would not distinguish him from the *asû*.

The data cited by Ritter herself also do not lend much support to her four specific distinctions or "corollaries," the first of which may be summarized as follows:

āšipu	*asû*
Frequently assigns "a cause or agent responsible for the symptoms..."[147]	"Does not affix supernatural 'causes...'"[146]

---

[145]R. Caplice (*The Akkadian Namburbi Texts:An Introduction* [Los Angeles:Undena, 1974] 9) says: "since physical illness could be conceived as foreshadowed by a portent, there is sometimes overlapping between strictly medical texts and the namburbis."
[146]Ritter: "Magical Expert...," *A S* 16: 302.
[147]Ritter: "Magical Expert...," *A S* 16: 301.

Although the definition of the terms "supernatural"
and "magical" has come under intense scrutiny in recent
years,[148] it is clear that for Ritter "supernatural causes"
referred to the operation of primarily invisible personal
beings or forces.[149] In contrast, Ritter views the *asû* as one
who was not concerned with supernatural causation, but
instead used that *materia medica* that his empirical experience
had shown to be beneficial. The *modus operandi* of the *asû*,
according to Ritter, was sufficiently free of supernatural
assumptions to merit the designation of "physician."

In particular, Ritter argues that one does not find in
the *asû*'s work an analogue for the frequent "directive to the
āšipu: āšipūssu teppuš, 'you perform for him (the patient)
the magical act of healing.'"[150] However, her statement rests
on the seemingly *a priori* assumption that *āšipūtu* is
essentially a magical act of healing, while *asûtu* is not. In
order to support her contention that the *asû* is less interested
in magical therapy, Ritter minimizes the part that the
incantation (*šiptu*), which is a clearly magical endeavour for
her, plays in the work of the *asû*, and further claims that "the

---

[148]For general discussions of the definition of "magic", see G. P.
Murdock, *Theories of Illness: A World Survey* (Pittsburgh: U. of
Pittsburgh, 1980) 20-22; L. Petzoldt, ed., *Magie und Religion*
(Darmstadt, 1978); A. Ünal, "The Role of Magic in the Ancient
Anatolian Religions According to the Cuneiform Texts from Bogazköy-
Hattusa," in H. I. H. Prince Takahito Mikasa, ed., *Essays on
Anatolian Studies in the Second Millennium B. C.* (Wiesbaden:
Harrasowitz, 1988) 52-85.

[149]Ritter does not appear to distinguish "supernatural" and "magical,"
and, unless otherwise noted, we shall treat them as synonyms in our
discussion.

[150]Ritter: "Magical Expert...," *A S* 16: 309.

šiptu in *asûtu* tends to be a random thing."[151]   However, as we have seen in *The Hymn of Bullutsu-rabi,* Gula states that, as an *asû,* she routinely carries, and presumably uses, incantation texts (*ši-pa-at ba-la-ṭu*).[152]   The routine use of such incantations by the *asû* indicates that he is no less of a user of magical procedures than the *āšipu.*

Ritter cites *BAM* 110, *BAM* 124 , *BAM* 125, *BAM* 171 and *BAM* 174[153] as examples of those treatments of the *asû* whose purpose mentions only the relief of physical symptoms. Yet those texts are precisely some of the ones that Pedersén lists as part of the *āšipu's* library at Assur.[154]   Thus, Ritter appears to have assigned texts to each profession on the basis of a preconceived notion of a magical/non-magical dichotomy, not on the basis of direct evidence. And, at least in these texts, the distinction of magical vs. non-magical is not very useful because the non-supernatural view of causation, if it exists at all, may apply as much to *āšipu* as it does to the *asû.*

Indeed, some of the cases characterized as "natural" show how difficult it is to separate "supernatural" from purely "natural" causes. For example, Ritter cites[155] *TDP* 28:91 as an example of the assignment of "natural" causes (presumably an infection contracted from sexual contact with a woman) by the *āšipu,* and yet the same diagnosis is

---

[151]Ritter: "Magical Expert...," *A S* 16: 309.

[152]For the text, see W. G. Lambert, "The Gula Hymn of Bullutsa-rabi," *Or* 36 (1967) 120.

[153]Ritter: "Magical Expert...," *AS* 16: 308,

[154]The locations are discussed by Pedersén, *Archives and Libraries* II: 65 (*BAM* 110), 61 (*BAM* 124), 59 (*BAM* 125), 26 (*BAM* 171), 73 (*BAM* 174).

[155]Ritter: "Magical Expert...," *A S* 16: 306.

concurrently attributed to the hand of the moon god.[156]   In fact, it is quite probable that the mention of only physical symptoms does not exclude the assumption of a supernatural agent by the *āšipu* or the *asû*. For example, in *LABS* 243 a diagnosis that mentions only physical symptoms requires rituals of the *āšipu*. Likewise, the type of cooperation depicted in *AMT* 24, 1:3ff suggests that both the *asû* and the *āšipu* have accepted the same ostensibly "natural" etiology, and yet the supernatural component is still evident in the *āšipu*'s performance of rituals for six days.

The fact is that many texts that Ritter uses indicate that the *asû* worked within a framework that assigned and presupposed supernatural causes. For example, *CT* 23, 44 a 8, which attributes the illness to *qāt eṭemmi*, was probably written for an *asû*, because it refers to the *āšipu* in the 3rd person sg. ("Let the *āšipu* do as he knows"/*āšipu ki ša idû liteppuš*), while the reference to the *asû* is in the second singular ("you rub him [the patient]"/*tapaššassu*).[157] The second singular is usually addressed to the user, and identifies the professional authorship of the tablet (in this case the *asû*).   Consequently, the text implies that a premier supernatural diagnosis, *qāt eṭemmi*, is one that could be assigned or supposed by the *asû*, and one within which the *asû* could work.

In *PBS* I/2, No. 72:18-26, a letter from the Kassite period, the *asû* is concerned that the illness will turn into the

---

[156]*TDP* 28:91 reads: *šumma* [*iš*]t*u qaqqadišu adi šēpīšu bubu'ta sāmta imtanalli*(DIR.DIR) *u zumuršu peṣi itti šinništi ina mayāli kašid qāt* ᵈ*Sin* /If red blisters chronically cover him [the patient] from his head to his foot and his body is pale, he was reached (by) being in bed with a woman: hand of Sin [it is].

[157]On the use of term *pašāšu* in medical texts, see D. Goltz, "Studien zur altorientalischen und griechischen Heilkunde," 64-65.

"hand of the power of the curse" (ŠU.NAM.ERÍM.MA), a diagnosis that supposes a magical or supernatural etiology. The text also shows that he was not unwilling to "affix a supernatural cause," and it is reasonable to suppose that such a concern rested on the reading of signs in a manner akin to the *āšipu*.

Another set of distinctions made by Ritter is more difficult to evaluate:

āšipu	*asû*
Based on his understanding of signs, "he then makes a prognosis."[159]	"Does not make prognosis before treatment;"[158]

She may be correct, though sufficient information is lacking to render a decisive conclusion. The notion that the *āšipu* does specialize in prognoses is well supported, principally by *SA.GIG*. However, it is difficult to believe that in those cases where the *asû* worked alone, he rendered no prognosis. One would think that such a prognosis would at least be requested by the patient. But if the *asû* did render a prognosis, it is difficult to claim that it was always done after treatment. In fact, in *BAM* 9:55ff, *CT* 23, 44 a 8, and *AMT* 24, 1:3ff, the prognosis seems to precede the *asû*'s treatments, though he may not have made the prognosis himself. But as *PBS* I/2, No. 72:18-26 demonstrates, even if an *asû* renders a prognosis only after treatment, this does not mean that his endeavours or prognosis are devoid of a supernatural component.

---

[158]Ritter: "Magical Expert...," *A S* 16: 302.
[159]Ritter: "Magical Expert...," *A S* 16: 301.

A third set of distinctions expressed by Ritter may be summarized as follows:

āšipu	*asû*
"When [prognosis] is hopeful...he institutes appropriate treatment directed toward freeing the patient from the malevolent forces that grip him."[161]	"His therapy is directed toward the relief of acute and pressing symptoms, for which he has a long list of alternative healing prescriptions;"[160]

Ritter implies that the relief of acute and pressing symptoms by the *asû* does not involve the expulsion of malevolent agents. Similarly, Ritter implies that the *āšipu* is not interested in treating "acute and pressing symptoms." In part, Ritter apparently assumes that the use of botanical substances and bandages reflects a view that is sufficiently non-magical or non-exorcistic to merit the comparison to a modern physician.

But the focus on botanical substances and bandages by the *asû* does not imply that his treatments were non-magical or non-exorcistic. As Pedersén noted, the libraries of *āšipus* could also house extensive collections of texts dealing with botanical substances. Moreover, an incantation of Gula recited upon the application of medicines by an *asû* (*AMT* 9,1: 27-28) says:[162]

---

[160]Ritter: "Magical Expert...," *A S* 16: 302.

[161]Ritter, "Magical Expert...," *A S* 16: 301.

[162]The reading and translation follows that of B. Landsberger, "Corrections to the Article: 'An Old Babylonian Charm against Merḫu,'" *JNES* 17 (1958) 56.

liddi(ŠUB-di) ^{d}*Gu-la tê(TU₆) balaṭi* (TI.LA)
en-qu-ti ṣim-de-ti li-qer-ri-bu
at-ti taš-ku-ni ba-laṭ bu-ul-ṭi

May Gula lay down the charm of life,
may the sages apply the bandages!
You (Gula) have brought about health and healing.

Thus, the *asû's* treatments, just like those of the *āšipu*, are executed with the full recognition that their actual healing power is provided by Gula or other deities. Even if the *materia medica* used by the *asû* had real medicinal value from a modern scientific standpoint, the *asû* might attribute such a value to magical powers provided by the gods. As Ritter herself notes, the *asû* could recommend herbs for dispelling witchcraft (e.g., *ABL* 1370 rev. 16: *šammī*(Ú)...*ana* UŠ₁₁.BÚR.[RU].DA). Such prescriptions presuppose that the *asû's* treatments could be meant to expel malevolent causes. In simpler terms, the *asû's* treatments also can be viewed as exorcistic and magical rituals. At the very least, we cannot suppose that the distinction between the *asû* and the *āšipu* resided in the fact that the treatment of the former was never meant to expel malevolent causes, while those of the latter were.

A final set of distinctions proposed by Ritter may be summarized as follows:

āšipu	*asû*
He seems concerned with "exacerbations and remissions, and recurrences"[164]	"He does not treat conditions which are prolonged;"[163]

---

[163]Ritter: "Magical Expert...," *A S* 16: 302.
[164]Ritter: "Magical Expert...," *AS* 16: 302.

Her definition of *prolonged* is not very precise. If one defines *prolonged* as those conditions that persist despite treatment, then *LA BS* 315 shows that the *asû* was sought in conditions which were prolonged, and he was willing to treat conditions that did not get better. In *BAM* 9:55ff one finds the *asû* treating a patient for a condition that persisted after the treatment of the *āšipu* has proven ineffective. In *CT* 23, 44 a 8 one finds an *asû* working on a case that persists after at least one treatment by an *āšipu*. Indeed, there is no inherent reason why an *asû* cannot work to alleviate the discomfort of a patient who has been ill for months.

In sum, both the *āšipu* and the *asû* work within a conceptual framework that clearly supposes and assigns supernatural causes. Indeed, one never finds explicit denial of supernatural causes of illness on the part of the *asû*, but, as we have seen, one does find repeated explicit references to, or assumptions of, magical causation on the part of the *asû*. As we shall argue in more detail below, the difference between the *āšipu* and the *asû* resides in the distinct, yet overlapping, distribution of their labors within the same conceptual system, and not in the use of a different conceptual system in the labors of each profession.

b) Refining the distinction between the asû and the āšipu

Ritter's distinctions place the highest value on texts in which each profession worked alone, viewing those texts in which the professions cooperated as somewhat less useful.[165] But one of the salient insights of the comparative

---

[165]Most of the texts which Ritter uses for the identification are those in which each profession works alone, whereas cooperation requires

anthropological study of societies with multiple healing professions is that one must be sensitive to the stages of an illness, and the socio-economic status of patients. Cross-cultural studies of illnesses show that the same patient may often consult different healers at different stages of an illness, and that availability and access to consultants can play significant roles in the selection.[166]

Accordingly, it is precarious to draw distinctions between the *āšipu* and the *asû* when each is working alone. In particular, a text about an illness that mentions only an *asû* (e.g., *ABL* 341) or only an *āšipu* (e.g., *LABS* 243) may simply represent a selection at a particular stage of an illness, and omit reference to a different selection at another stage. Similarly, *CT* 23, 44 a 8 indicates that *qāt etemmi* may be treated by both the *asû* and the *āšipu*, though one may find only one of these consultants at different stages of the illness.

In the case of Esarhaddon (*LABS* 241, 243, 315 and other letters), in particular, Parpola has attempted to show that the illnesses reported in different letters are in fact different aspects and symptoms of one continuing or recurrent illness--namely, lupus erythematosus.[167] Even if

---

"special circumstances" (cf. Ritter: "Magical Expert...," *A S* 16: 315) which are presumably not useful for clarifying the distinctions.

[166]For examples, see A. Kleinman, *Patients and Healers* (Berkely: U. of California, 1980) especially 179ff; R. Frankenberg and J. Leeson, "Disease, Illness and Sickness: Social Aspects of the Choice of Healer in a Lusaka Suburb," in J. B. Loudon, ed., *Social Anthropology and Medicine* (New York: Academic Press, 1976) 223-256; and A. R. Beals, "Strategic Resort to Curers in South India," in C. Leslie, ed., *Asian Medical Systems* (Berkeley: U. of California, 1976) 184-200.

[167]Parpola, *LA S*, Part II, 229-238. It is, of course, difficult to know whether each of those symptoms was regarded as part of one larger syndrome by Esarhaddon or his consultants. *LABS* 315 (= *LA S* 246)

Parpola's diagnosis is incorrect, his analysis serves as a caution against identifying a particular case in isolation, and against the assumption that only the professional mentioned in that particular text was consulted in the course of the entire illness. Ritter's treatment of letters from Urad-nana (an *asû*) and Marduk-šākin-šumi (*āšipu*) to Esarhaddon should be read in light of the possibilities outlined by Parpola.[168]

Similarly, in *LABS* 243, where it is apparently an *āšipu* who is managing the illness, one can find evidence that labor requirements might have limited the availability of the consultant. His lack of immediate availability to the patient is reflected in the use of messengers and in the fact that the *āšipu* promises to come on the next day. Such texts also show that availability of any particular consultant could be a recurrent, if not a pervasive, problem, and one which may have affected the choice of consultant at a particular time by a sick king, let alone patients of lesser status and wealth.

Conversely, patients with resources may seek to maximize the medical consultants available. Such a phenomenon may be exemplified in a Neo-Assyrian text in which an official requests that the king appoint one *āšipu* and one *asû*.[169] Patients of lower status may not have been economically or politically able to command the presence of two consultants. Thus, one ought not to assume that a selection of a single type of consultant was always based on the presumed magical or non-magical cause of an illness.

---

does appear to register the king's annoyance at the persistence of his condition, however, it is difficult to determine how many or which illnesses reported in the other letters were viewed as part of the same "condition."

[168]See E. Ritter, "Magical Expert...," *A S* 16:319-320.

[169]*ABL* 1133 rev. 11:*ištēn*(DIŠ-*en*) *āšipu*(LÚ.MAŠ.MAŠ) *ištēn*(DIŠ-*en*) *a-sú ina panī*(IGI)-*ya lip-qid-ma.*

Availability and socio-economic status alone could affect choices at particular times.

Once one is aware of the many factors that could affect the selection of a consultant and the dynamic nature of health care systems with multiple health care consultants, one realizes that the presence of two types of healers need not imply the use of different conceptual frameworks (e.g., magical vs. non-magical).

The labor demands of health care in Mesopotamia were such that a single profession usually couldn't do it all. The Mesopotamian medical theology was heavily burdened with a myriad of possible causes, of which the divine "sender(s)" was the key to the treatment. Therapy consisted in finding which of many possible supernatural beings had "sent" the disease, and in contacting, appeasing or repelling those beings.

One example of the labor requirements of the Mesopotamian medical system may be seen in a ritual against disease (and) "malaria" (GIG *di 'u*) performed in the month of Addaru.[170] In order to perform this ritual, one needs:

> a figurine of the daughter of Anu
> a figurine of Namtar
> a figurine of Latarak
> a figurine of Death
> a substitute figurine made of clay
> a substitute figurine made of wax

---

[170]Following Parpola's translation in *LABS* 296 rev. 1-20; Parpola (cf. *LAS*, II, 212) does not document his diagnosis of *di 'u* as malaria. It is apparently a malady which affects the head (*muruṣ qaqqadi*) as noted by *AHw*, 174 s.v. On the presumed endemicity of malaria in ancient Mesopotamia, see P. B. Adamson, "Anatomical and Pathological Terms...Part II" *JRAS* (1979) 3-4.

...15 drinking tubes of silver
[....for?] Gula (and) Belet-seri .
... 7 twigs]of tamarisk
7 twigs of date palm
[7 bot]tles of wine
7 bottles of beer
[7 bottles] of milk
7 bottles of honey

The text above suggests that labor intensive rituals were related, in large part, to the number of supernatural beings that were to be contacted, appeased or repelled in a single case.

The rituals for most other illnesses and occasions could be just as intensive, and sometimes even more so. *KAR* 44 contains a catalogue of rituals categorized by, among other things, illnesses.[171] Dozens of entries show the large number of rituals that an *āšipu* theoretically could or was expected to perform as part of his duties. Indeed, sometimes the consultant had to spend much of the time in the performance of complicated rituals and in the procurement of paraphernalia for different gods, even if a single illness was the object of the ritual.

We have already noted how *LABS* 243 indicates that labor requirements affected availability of consultants. The fact that such labor intensive rituals affected the immediate availability of some health care consultants also is evident in *LABS* 255 where the king orders that Marduk-šākin-šumi, an *āšipu*, perform an anti-witchcraft ritual (*ušburrudû*)

---

[171]For an edition, see H. Zimmern, "Zu den 'Keilschriften aus Assur Religiösen Inhalts,'" *ZA* 30 (1915/16) 184-229.

before the 24th day of the month (*ma-a a-na* UD.24.KAM
ep-ša). The *āšipu* replies, in part, as follows:[172]

> 8. *la-áš-šu la nu-šá-an-ṣa*
> 9. *tup-pa-a-ni ma-a ʾ-du-ti šu-nu*
> 10. *im-ma-ti* ⸢*i!-šaṭ!-ṭu!-ru!*⸣
> 11. *ù šá-aṣ-*⸢*bu*⸣*!-*⸢*tú šá*⸣ NU.MEŠ-*ni*
> 12. *ša* LUGAL *e-mur-*[*u-n*]*i ina* ŠÀ UD.MEŠ
> 13. *5 6 re-e-šú ni-*[*i*]*t-ti-ši*

We cannot execute it (the ritual);
the tablets are (too) many.
How will they copy them (in time)?
Even the preparation of the figurines which
the king saw (yesterday) took us 5-6
days.

The text again reflects how the complexity of the
Mesopotamian theology resulted in a labor intensive system
of rituals which affected the availability of the *āšipu* to the
king as well as the schedule of rituals. In fact, even with
helpers, one profession could not always accomplish the
numerous tasks needed in exorcism in the time requested by
the king.

However, most therapeutic rituals *per se* were not
the only ones that could be labor intensive and time
consuming. Rituals that petition for oracles and prognoses
could also be quite complex. This is exemplified in a
petition found at Sultantepe (*STT* 73) for oracles concerning

---

[172]*LABS*, pp. 201-202.

illness published by Erica Reiner.[173] The lengthy petition seeks counsel from a number of deities including apparently Gula.[174] In general, the rituals of the diviner could, indeed, be labor intensive.[175] The practical logistics of such a theology seem to have made the specialization in different aspects of the health care system inevitable.

Ritter is correct in noting that the *asû* does seem to function more often in the realm of drugs and bandages which are applied to the patient. Such a focus of labor is also supported by texts in which the interaction of both professions may be seen. Thus in *CT* 23, 44 a 8 and *AMT* 24, 1:3ff. the *āšipu* performs rituals to contact and/or appease the sender of the illness, while the *asû* applies *materia medica* and bandages directly to the patient.[176] In

---

[173]E. Reiner, "Fortune Telling in Mesopotamia," *JNES* 19 (1960) 23-35.

[174]*STT* 73, 1. 1: [*ÉN il-tum] rím-ni-tum mu-bal-li-ṭa-at* LU.UG7. Although the name of the goddess is not explicit, the identification of the goddess as Gula/Ninisina is probable because (a) "*muballiṭat* X" (X = usually humanity) is a known description of Gula/Ninisina, and (b) the colophon indicates that the text was copied from Esabad, a name for the temple of Gula. For a collection of epithets of Gula/Ninisina, see W. Mayer, *Untersuchungen zur Formensprache der babylonischen Gebetbeschwörungen* (Rome: Biblical Institute Press, 1976) 387-88.

[175]For a general discussion, see I. Starr, *The Rituals of the Diviner* (Malibu, Calif.:Undena, 1983).

[176]The purpose of the dressing and bandage (*ṣimdu*) used by Gula, the divine *asû*, is described in *The Gula Hymn of Bulluṭsu-rabi* (Lambert, *Or* 36 [1976] 120) as follows: Line 84. *el-lu rik-su sim-ma ú-na-aḫ/ 85. rap-pu ṣi-in-di murṣa ú-pa-áš-šá-ah* (= "the pure ointment alleviates the injury, the delicate bandage soothes the malady"). A letter (113) from Tell Rimah reports that a lady requested an oil-soaked bandage (l. 9: *ri-ki-is* ì) from a certain Amisum, and the latter does not appear to have been a healing consultant. This may indicate that traffic in bandages may have involved non-healing consultants. The text was

LA BS 315, the *asû* appears so busy collecting and preparing *materia medica* that he advices the patient to seek a diagnosis with the haruspices. It is reasonable to suppose that in this case the king probably did resort to another consultant because the *asû* that he requested was not available.

Another important factor in the maintenance of different consultants in modern and ancient health care systems is the simple fact that one type of consultant may not provide satisfactory results. In the absence of scientific methods and modern pharmacology, "magical" rituals and substances, while they may have relieved some symptoms, did not always, if ever, eradicate the underlying causes of a disease, especially if serious.[177] Patients usually attempt to maximize their therapeutic options if they have the resources to do so. In the face of persistent illness, Mesopotamian polytheism provided a ready system of alternative options for a patient, even if such options were not effective from a modern scientific standpoint.

In order to illustrate how the search for options was related to a division of labor, note the description by the emblematic sufferer in *Ludlul bēl nēmeqi* (*BWL* 38:4-9) of the distribution of labors among the different professions:

> *ila al-si-ma ul id-di-na pa-ni-šú*
> *ú-šal-li* ^d*iš-tar-ri ul [ú]-šá-qa-a ri-ši-sá*
> ^{lú}*bārû*(ḪAL) *ina bi-ir ár-kàt ul ip-ru-us*
> *ina ma-áš-šak-ka* ^{lú}*šā 'ilu* (EN.ME.LI) *ul ú-šá-pi di-i-ni*

---

published in S. Dalley, *The Old Babylonian Tablets from Tell Rimah* (British School of Archaeology in Iraq; Hertford: Austin and Sons, 1976) 90.

[177]In fact, even today, alternative cures and consultants are often sought when modern medicine cannot effect a cure in a patient.

za-qí-qu a-bal-ma ul ú-pat-ti uz-ni
^{lú}*mašmaššu ina ki-kiṭ-ṭe-e ki-mil-ti ul ip-ṭur*

I implored my god, but he did not acknowledge me,
I prayed to my goddess, but she did not raise her head,
The *bārû* has not determined the cause by divination,
The *šā'ilu*, with libations, has not illuminated my case,
I sought the *zaqīqu*-ghost, but he did not inform me,
And the *mašmaššu*,[178] through rituals, has not soothed the
anger against me.

The task of immediate relief, the task of seeking the correct
"signs," and the task of restoring a favorable relationship
with the supernatural world, then, were seen often as
related, but different labors within the same conceptual
framework which viewed illnesses as ultimately rooted in
supernatural causes.

    LABS 315[179] shows how the use of alternative
professions resulted from the inadequacy of the therapy of a
particular profession.   In this letter an *asû* answers the
king's repeated queries concerning diagnosis:

    7. *ka-a-a-ma-nu* LUGAL *be-lí*
    8. *i-qab-bi-ya ma-a a-ta-a*
    9. *ši-ki-in* GIG-*ya an-ni-u*
    10. *la ta-mar bul-ṭe-e-šú la te-pa-áš*

Thus the king, my Lord,
keeps speaking to me, "Why have you

---

[178] On the equivalence of the *mašmaššu* and the *āšipu*, see our brief
discussion in section B.3.d. of this chapter.
[179]See also *LAS* I, p. 188.

not diagnosed this illness of mine,
and accomplished its cure?"

The *asû* recommends that the king consult the haruspices, and he further asks the king to apply some *silbānu*-medication that he will send with the messenger who carries the letter. The recommendation of the *asû* also may have served to deflect responsibility or blame (deserved or undeserved) from himself, without excluding himself from the treatment of the king. In fact, the *asû* recommends another of his own treatments even though his previous ones have not been helpful.

So in contrast to Ritter we view the differences between the *asû* and *āšipu* as rooted, not in the relative use of magical and non-magical assumptions, but rather in different foci of labor required by a complex medical and theological system that did not normally distinguish natural and supernatural operations. Both the *āšipu* and *asû* are providers of magical treatment.

The *āšipu* is the healing consultant who primarily labors to identify the sender of an illness, provide a prognosis, and effect a reconciliation with, or expulsion of, the sender, though he may also prepare *materia medica* as a secondary focus of labor. Note that the *mašmaššu* (= *āšipu*)[180] is specifically charged with performing rituals to restore the patient's relationship with supernatural beings, and with providing the cause of illness (*BWL* 44:110: *ši-kin mur-ṣi-ya*).

The *asû* is the healing consultant who primarily labors to collect, prepare and apply directly the *materia*

---

[180]On the equivalence of the *mašmaššu* and the *āšipu*, see our brief discussion in section B.3.d. of this chapter.

medica intended to magically expel discomfort, though he may, when necessary, be expected to diagnose the supernatural causes of an illness (e.g., *LABS* 315).

The selection of the professions by a patient is a dynamic process that involves socio-economic factors (availability, status of the patient) rather than a judgment about the magical or non-magical viewpoint of the professions. An *asû*, for example, may assume the primary responsibilities of the *āšipu* when the latter is not available, and vice versa.

By understanding the *asû* and *āšipu* as designations for different roles within the same conceptual system, one can also understand how it is that they can work separately at times, and cooperatively at times. Such cooperation need not exclude rivaly or competition between the professions. However, the presence or absence of any competition may be a dynamic process as well, depending, for example, on the variation in the number of consultants in particular areas and times.

Thus, it is best to discontinue the use of the term *physician* to describe the *asû*, preserving the native Mesopotamian term instead. The *asû* is not really a physician in the western sense, and the use of the term is misleading. In actuality, the *āšipu* is more analogous to a modern physician in that he attempts to provide a general portrayal of an illness, while the *asû* is more akin to a combination of a modern pharmacist and nurse. The modern physician attempts to read "signs" on the body to diagnose illness and to direct the general course of therapy, and so the *āšipu* is no less a physician in this sense.[181]

---

[181]On the modern physician as a reader of signs, see M. Foucault, *The Birth of The Clinic* (New York:Vintage, 1973).

c) The bārû

Thus far we have concentrated on the two main therapists in the Mesopotamian health care system. But there were a number of other consultants (e.g., sā'ilu) who also played a role, albeit a smaller one, in the Mesopotamian health care system. Perhaps the most important of these other consultants was the bārû ("seer" or "soothsayer"). Like the āšipu, the bārû was a type of priest at various temples.[182] In The Hymn of Bullutsu-rabi, Gula states that she was a bārû as well as an asû and an āšipu.[183] We have already seen that the patient in Ludlul (BWL 38:6) explicitly mentions the purpose the bārû as follows: "The bārû has not determined the cause through divination." Thus, the bārû seems to be involved in the diagnostic phase of the patient's strategy. As such, the bārû differs from our two main healing consultants insofar as they actually administer therapy. One can also view the āšipu's task of discovering identifying "signs" as a subset of the bārû's. That is to say, the bārû was probably interested in a variety of omens, but the āšipu probably specialized in omens concerning illness. Alternatively, we may say that the āšipu usually combines both diagnosis and therapy in his endeavours, while the bārû does not.

---

[182]For a more complete treatment of the bārû, see J. Renger, "Untersuchungen zum Priestertum im der altbabylonischen Zeit, 2. Teil" ZA 59 (1968) 203ff.

[183]W. G. Lambert, "The Gula Hymn...," 128, l. 183: [a]-sa-ku ba-ra-ku a-ši-pak.

d) The history of the professions

Although we cannot provide a detailed historical reconstruction of the origin of the two main professions, there are a few historical notes that are of relevance to our study. The *asû* is mentioned as early as 2500 B.C.E.[184] In a text that may be assigned to the reign of Shulgi, there is a reference to the existence of 33 *asûs* in Umma.[185] The Code of Hammurabi has laws regarding his fees, and he appears there as someone in charge of conditions that require immediate relief. Newly published letters from Mari indicate that the *asû*, the *wāšipu* (*mašmaššum*), and the *bārû* were part of the health care system of that society in the 18th century B.C.E.[186]

Following R. Caplice and other scholars, we assume that *āšipu*, *mašmaššu*, and the Sumerogram LÚ.MAŠ.MAŠ were variant designations for the same profession.[187] The

---

[184]R. D. Biggs, "Babylonien," 105.

[185]*TCL* 5: Plate XLVI, 6166 r. col. 4, l. 3l; The date follows P. Steinkeller (personal communication).

[186]For a general survey of the medicine of Mari, see most recently J. M. Durand, "Maladies et médecins."*AEM* I/1 1988) 543-584; and the earlier treatment of A. Finet, "Les médecins au royaume de Mari," *AIPHOS* 14 [1954-57] 123-144. On the supposed trend towards the lessening importance of the *asû* during the course of the 2nd millennium, see A. L. Oppenheim, *Ancient Mesopotamia:Portrait of a Dead Civilization* (Chicago:U. of Chicago, 1977) 295-96.

[187]For a brief review of the evidence, see R. Caplice, "Participants in the Namburbi Rituals," *CBQ* 29 (3, 1967) 42 n. 15'; and *CAD* A 1/2, 431. For the occurrence of the term *āšipu* in the OB period, see AHw, 1487 s.v. As we have noted, the equivalence between the *āšipu* and the *mašmaššu* also may be seen in *Ludlul* (*BWL* 44:108-111) where parallel lines form the following structure: 108-109: *mašmaššu/bārû*, 110-111: *āšipu/bārû*.

use of the term *āšipu* is quite rare in the Old Babylonian period, but attestations begin to increase in the Middle Assyrian and Middle Babylonian periods.[188] During the early Kassite period, the *āšipu* may have been primarily a temple scribe who eventually developed expertise in therapeutic rituals.[189] One can only speculate that such expertise was derived from his task of copying numerous tablets treating magical rituals. Nonetheless, the existence of persons who performed the work of the *āšipu* was probably as old as the existence of the *asû*.

Although the exact circumstances under which the *āšipu* began to be seen as a primary health care consultant are still obscure,[190] it seems clear, at least in the texts from the Kassite and NA periods that we have discussed, that the therapeutic logistics of the Mesopotamian system were directly related to the necessity and maintenance of the two roles (along with others). As we have mentioned, the *bārû* was interested in a variety of omens, but the *āšipu* probably specialized in omens concerning illness. The *āšipu* may have been able to assume the labors involved in medical divination and restoration of the relationship of the patient with the supernatural world, even if not always promptly, but the *āšipu* may not always have been able to assume the labors involved in preparing *materia medica*. It is quite likely that both basic tasks (divination and preparation of *materia medica*) were served by different specialists by the dawn of Mesopotamian civilization. While the *āšipu* and the *asû*

---

[188]For the occurrence of the term *āšipu* in the OB period, see AHw, 1487 s.v.

[189]Cf. Ritter, "Magical Expert...," *A S* 16:303 n. (3)

[190]P. Michalowski ("Adapa and the Ritual Process," *Rocznik Orientalistyczny* XLI [1980] 77-82) argues that the story of Adapa depicts the institutionalization of *āšipūtu*.

apparently remained important at least as late as the Hellenistic period in Babylonia, G. J. P. McEwan notes that the position of the *bārû* is virtually unattested in texts from the Hellenistic period.[191]

There are a number of indications that the *asû* and *āšipu* received fees for their work. In laws 215-217 of the Code of Hammurabi, for example, one finds that fees were fixed for the *asû*, depending on the procedure and the socio-economic class of the patient. For example, if an *asû* has cured a free citizen (*a-wi-lam ub-ta-al-liṭ*) through the use of surgical instruments (*i-na* GÍR.ZAL.ZABAR), then the *asû* may take 10 shekels of silver; 5 shekels if the patient is a commoner (DUMU MAŠ.EN.KAK); 2 shekels from the master if the patient is a slave. At least in the ideals expressed in the Code, medical care was graduated to the patient's socio-economic status.

The continuity in the use of fees in subsequent periods may be seen in a namburbi text (*KAR* 3 Nr. 144) dated between the 8th and 6th centuries B.C.E. where one finds a ritual to promote good business for, among others the *barû*, the *asû*, and the *mašmaššu* = *āšipu* (*ana iš-di-iḫ...lu* ᴸᵁ*barû lu* ᴸᵁ*asû lu* ᴸᵁ*mašmaššu*).[192]

According to *LABS* 289, the *āšipu*s who worked in the palace apparently also received payment in goods, the distribution of which was apparently controlled by the *rab*

---

[191]G. J. P. McEwan, *Priest and Temple in Hellenistic Babylonia* (Wiesbaden: Franz Steiner, 1981) 15.

[192]Akkadian text is that of E. Ebeling, "Beiträge zur Kenntnis der Beschwörungsserie Namburbi," *RA* 49 (1955) 178. Additional notes in R. Caplice, *The Akkadian Namburbi Texts: An Introduction* (Los Angeles:Undena, 1974)p. 1; See pp. 23-24 for a discussion of the date of the texts.

āšipī.[193] According to *LABS* 324, *asûs* were also apparently required to perform *ilku*-service, possibly medical in nature, on certain fixed days. The same may be said of the *āšipu*.[194] One can see that, at least in Neo-Assyrian times, healing consultants, especially those in the employ of the king, had organizations with a hierarchy, but they also had to perform some public services at certain intervals.

4. The main loci of therapy

a) The home

The primary locus of health care in Mesopotamia was the home, and it appears that it was also the consistent locus of care, especially for the elderly. More specifically, in Mesopotamia the home usually remained the locus of therapy regardless of the progressive deterioration of the patient. A secondary and temporary locus of therapy was the river. The river was a place where rituals were performed, but the patient usually returned home soon afterwards. The dominance of these two loci *vis-à-vis* the temple of the healing deity is one of the *differentia* of the Mesopotamian health care system as opposed to the one in Greece.

The dominance of the home is very apparent in a variety of sources. For example, the centrality of home-centered medical care in Mesopotamia is the principal presupposition of the series *SA.GIG*, which is also known as *enūma ana bīt marṣi āšipu illaku* ("When an *āšipu*

---

[193]See Parpola, *LAS* II, p. 217.
[194]See Parpola, *LAS* II, p. 244, and an earlier reference in Falkenstein, *LKU* 51:12, which refers to "the *ilku* -service of the exorcist" (*ilki ša* LÚ.MAŠ).

goes to the home of the sick") and which was in use as early as the 8th century B.C.E.[195] None of the texts in this manual recommends that one go to the temple for treatment even when the case seems hopeless. Note, for example, the numerous passages in which the *āšipu* enumerates the significance of being sick a certain number of days. For example, *TDP* 150:42' says:

> *šumma* UD.5.KAM *mariṣ-ma*
> *ina* UD.6.KAM *uš-tar-di-ma*
> *ia-ú ia-ú lā ú-kal-la*
> *imât.*

> If he [the patient] has been sick 5 days,
> 6 days, and he continues to vomit,
> (and) he does not stop (crying) 'Ay, Ay,'
> then he will die.

The tablet continues to enumerate cases when the patient has been ill 5 and 10 days (*TDP* 150:44'), and 1-2 months (*TDP* 154:14), and it includes diagnoses where the patient is expected to recover (e.g., *TDP* 152:7). What these diagnoses reflect is that patients were not expected to go to the temple even after many days, weeks, and months of being ill. It does not seem to matter whether the patient is expected to recover or become worse. At the very least, the tablets indicate the *āšipu* expected to find patients at home even after long illnesses, whether or not these patients were expected to recover. The consistent centrality of home care

---

[195]The *editio princeps* is that of R. Labat, *TDP*; remarks on dates on p. xiv.

was indeed the dominant presupposition of the *āšipu*'s manual.

The centrality of home care was also evident in the behavior of the king. In a Neo-Assyrian incantation from Sippar, a city with a temple of G/N, to the god Ṣalbatānu (Muštabarru), Šamas-šum-ukin, who is suffering from a "serious illness" (*muršu lemnu*), exclaims the following:[196]

> 8. *ina erši*(NÁ) *anḫ[ute...na]-da-ku-ma a-ša-si-ka*
> 9. *ana ili idû*(ZU-*u*) *u la i-du*
>
> From my bed, exhausted I lie, (and) I cry to you
> (and) to a known and unknown god.

Again, the option of going to the temple in this stage of severity is not mentioned.

Texts that mention the initial stages of serious illnesses also indicate the importance of home care. For example, it is clear that the ritual against "epilepsy" (AN.TA.ŠUB.BA) was executed at home in the early stages of the illness. The text says: "as soon as something has afflicted him (i.e., the patient), the exorcist arises and places a mouse (and) a piece of a thornbush on the vault of the (patient's) door."[197] Similarly, except for the search for

---

[196]Text 2, in V. Scheil, *Une saison de fouilles à Sippar*, (Cairo: L'Institut Francais d'archéologie orientale, 1902) 94, and Plate II (photograph); instead of Scheil's *ta-šu-ma* in l. 8, we read [*na*]-*da-ku-ma* with K. van der Toorn, *Sin and Sanction*, 202 n. 383.

[197]*LABS* 238: 10-13: *ki-ma mi-i-nu il-ta-pat-šu* LÚ.MAŠ.MAŠ *i-tab-bi* PEŠ.QA.GAZ!! NUNUZ ^giš^NIM *ina šib-še-ti ša* KÁ *e-'i-la*.

signs, most other extant prayers and rituals do not mention going to a temple as part of the healing process.[198]

The centrality of home care is also reflected in legal provisions for persons with chronic illnesses in the Old Babylonian period. For example, the Code of Hammurabi (Law 148) states that if a married woman contracts "*li ʾbu* disease,"[199] then her husband may not divorce her even if he does decide to marry another. Instead the Code demands that the husband "support her in the home which he has made for the rest of her life."[200] She may also opt not to live with her husband, and go back to her father's household with her dowry.

A Neo-Babylonian text from the reign of Nabonidus reflects the importance of the home in medical treatment of the elderly:[201]

---

[198]R. D. Biggs, personal communication (July 25, 1989) also affirms that he does not know of any texts in which going to the temple was discussed as part of the petition for healing by a patient.

[199]Akkadian: *la-aḫ-bu-um iṣ-ṣa-ba-as-sí* (If the *li ʾbu* illness seizes her"). On the possibility that *li ʾbu*-disease also affects the skin, see P. B. Adamson, "Anatomical and Pathological Terms in Akkadian:Part IV," *JRAS* (1984) 12.

[200]*i-na É i-pu-šu uš-ša-am-ma a-di ba-al-ṭa-at it-ta-na-aš-ši-ši.* Akkadian text provided by the edition of the Code of Hammurabi of R. Borger, *Babylonisch-Assyrische Lesestücke* (Second edition; Roma: Pontificium Institutum Biblicum, 1979).

[201]The Akkadian text (VS 5, 21) is provided in J. Greenfield, "*Adi balṭu*-Care of the Elderly and its Rewards," *AfO* 19 (1982) 309-316.

marṣūka,[202] *Zēru-ukin aḫuya undašširani*
u Rēmût-Uraš māruya iḫtaliqanni
ana pānika abka 'inma[203] *suddidinni.*

> I am ill. Zēru-ukin, my brother has abandoned me
> and Rēmût-Uraš, my son has left me,
> take me in and support me.

The text illustrates that at least some of the elderly who were physically ill had to rely on their family for long-term medical care during the Neo-Babylonian period. Thus, Mesopotamia exhibits a long tradition in which individual households, not a state institution or the temple, bore direct responsibility for the long-term care of the ill. The state, however, utilized its bureaucracy to adjudicate and perhaps enforce legal provisions and contracts dealing with home care for the ill.

According to I. J. Gelb, there was a tradition known as the *arua* institution (attested in texts as early as the ED period) by which the temple apparently functioned as a collecting center for "widows, orphans, old people, especially old women, sterile and childless women, cripples, especially blind and deaf persons..."[204] However, the function of the *arua* institution should not be confused with the function of a sanatorium. The former functioned to incorporate disadvantaged individuals into the temple

---

[202]The reading, *mar-ṣu-ka*, instead of the expected *marṣāku*, is provided in M. San Nicolò and A. Ungnad, *Neubabylonische Rechts- und Verwaltugnsurkunde* (Leipzig: J. C. Hinrichs'sche Buchhandlung, 1935) 21 n. 3.

[203]From *abāku*; J. Greenfield, ("*Adi balṭu...*" 315 n. 29) attributes the form to Aramaic influence.

[204]I. J. Gelb, "The Arua Institution," *RA* 66 (1972) 1-32.

complex (e.g., as servants), while the primary function of a sanatorium is to rehabilitate the sick so that they may return to their previous "healthy" role in life.

Also relevant to this discussion of the centrality of the home is the tale of the *Poor Man of Nippur*.[205] In this well known story, a man goes to the home of the mayor of Nippur disguised as a physician from Isin (*a-su-u i-lit-ti I-si-in*[ki]).[206] If one argues that the situation must have had plausibility in order to make its point, then the implications are interesting. First, the story is consistent with the fact that home care is central even to the extent that it was not regarded as unusual for physicians (in this case unsolicited) to come from Isin to see patients in Nippur. This visit may attest Isin's reputation outside of Isin. But it is curious that Nippur, with its temple of G/N and apparently large collection of medical tablets, would be in need of doctors from Isin.

Why was the home so central in Mesopotamian health care? In the first place, this position is not surprising as it is attested in many cultures, especially in the initial stages of treatment. However, one can also see that the Mesopotamian medical theology could provide strong motivations for the home to remain the center at stages of an illness where other cultures (e.g., Greece) might have recommended longer-term treatment outside the home.

In particular, the view of illness as a social indicator of misconduct or lack of piety, or as a mark of an unsuccessful person, probably functioned to keep the patient bound to the home, especially in cases where the illness

---

[205]See O. R. Gurney, "The Sultantepe Tablets V: The Tale of the Poor Man of Nippur," *Anatolian Studies* 6 (1956) 145-164.
[206]Gurney, *The Tale of the Poor Man of Nippur*, 156:122

persisted. If the patient is regarded in negative terms, then this attitude may discourage the patient from venturing to a place where his/her fellow citizens may ridicule, or abhor him or her. A prolonged stay at a temple might thus be a sure public indicator of the patient's ill standing, and would have the added disadvantage of exposing him/her to public ridicule. Thus, consistent home care would be a plausible response for the patient who wishes to receive treatment without exposing himself to the unwanted publicity.

The reality of such behavior towards the ill is apparently attested in *Ludlul bēl nēmeqi*, which dates from the Kassite period.[207] As we have noted, the Kassite period was one where the temple of G/N was functional and active in Isin (and perhaps other cities in southern Mesopotamia). The following passage concerning a sick individual (*BWL* 34:79-81) is instructive:

> *a-na rap-ši ki-ma-ti e-te-me e-da-niš*
> *su-qa a-ba-ʾa-ma tur-ru-ṣa ú-zu-na-a-ti*
> *er-ru-ub ekal-liš i-ṣa-pu-ra i-na-a-ti*
>
> As far as my friends at large are concerned,
> I have become ostracized;
> If I walk on the street, ears stiffen;
> If I enter the palace, eyes stare.

In addition, the reluctance or inability to leave the house is expressed in *BWL* 44:95-96:

---

[207] Arguments for a date of the Kassite period are presented in *BWL*, p. 15.

a-ḫu-uz ^{giš}*erši*(NÁ) *me-si-ru*
mu-ṣe-e ta-ni-ḫu
a-na ki-suk-ki-ya i-tu-ra bi-i-tu

I have taken an imprisoning bed.
Venturing out is wearisome.
The home has turned into my own prison.

It is, of course, possible to interpret the hostility of the citizens and friends of the patient as one which is not caused by his illness, or as a hostility which represents simply another misfortune of the suppliant. However, it seems that the illness was an instigating factor in the gloating and scorn heaped on the suppliant in the poem.

In view of the recently discovered fragments of the initial portions of the poem, it is clear that health forms a dominant topic from the beginning (e.g., the praise of Marduk as a healer in lines 21-28).[208] The initial loss of health, therefore, apparently leads directly to the negative social consequences that subsequently afflict him. The fact that his own family has rejected him is best explained if it is the illness itself which has prompted them to view him as cursed, and, therefore, as someone to be rejected. In any event, the motivation to remain at home is natural whether the illness was viewed by his friends as the cause of his scorn, or whether it simply provided an opportunity for the local citizenry to take advantage of his weakness.

If a ruler feared such an adverse reaction to illness, he may also have wished to mask his condition by remaining

---

[208]See D. J. Wiseman, "A New Text of the Babylonian Poem of the Righteous Sufferer," *Anatolian Studies* 30 (1980) 101-107.

at home. Parpola has speculated that illness may have been the cause of the bitter criticism of which Esarhaddon complains in one of his inscriptions.[209] On the other hand, there were opposing incentives to leave the home (e.g., for rituals at the river). As in most societies, the choice between avoiding exposure to public scorn and the social obligations which may force patients (especially rulers) to face public scorn created a tension. In any event, one can see that the negative social reaction that illnesses, especially prolonged ones, could engender was probably a strong motive to remain at home whenever possible.

Closely related to the negative connotations of illness for the patient are ideas about purity. The fact that a variety of illnesses were thought to produce ritual impurity is attested in a number of texts. For example, note the description about a person with a skin disease in an Old Babylonian omen text (*VAT* 7525):[210]

> *šumma*(DIŠ) *awilum*(LÚ) *pa-ga-ar*
> *ši-ru-šu pu-ṣa-am ku-ul-lu-u[m]-ma*
> *ù nu-uq-di i-ta-ad-du*
> *awilum*(LÚ) *šu-ú it-ti i-lí-šu sà-ki-ip*
> *it-ti a-wi-l[u-t]i sà-ki-ip*

> If white spots appear on the flesh of a man, and
> it (his flesh) is afflicted with *nuqdu*-marks,
> this man is rejected by his god
> (and) he is rejected by humanity.

---

[209]Parpola, *LAS*, Part II, 235.

[210]See F. Köcher and A. L. Oppenheim, "The Old Babylonian Text VAT 7525," *AfO* 18 (1957/58) 66:42-45.

At least in the case of this skin disease, participation in the
cult or entering a temple might not be an attractive option. A
dingir.šà.dib.ba prayer counts entering a temple in a state of
impurity (*i-na la elluti*(KÙ)-*ya₅ e-te-ru-ub a-na* É-KUR)[211]
as one of the sins for which a suppliant may be suffering
illness, among other maladies. According to *BBR* 24:30ff,
there were a number of medical conditions   or physical
defects, including those affecting the eyes (l. 31: *zaq-tu īnā*)
and defective dentition (l. 31: *ḫe-pu šinnā*),   which were
sufficient to exclude a person from being a *bārû* (l. 37: *ana
purussē ba-ru-ti la te-ḫe-e*).[212] Another text provides a long
list of conditions (not all of them extant in the text) which
were sufficient to exclude persons from the office of *nešakku*
or *pāšišu*-priest in Enlil's temple (I:44: *ana* É ᵈMIN *u*
ᵈMIN *ul ir-ru-ub*).[213] Defects included facial blemishes (I:
42: *šim-ta bu-un-na-nu-ú/né-e*). All of these texts suggest
that Mesopotamian temples and cultic activities in the temple
had definitions of purity or physical standards which did not
permit the presence of the ill.

Another factor in the centrality of home care is that in
Mesopotamian medical theology it is not sufficient to expel
the malady from the body. Illness is seen as an invasion of
the home as well as the body.   Thus, the ritual against

---

[211]W. G. Lambert, "*Dingir.šà.dib.ba*   Incantations," *JNES* 33 (1974)
282:144. It is uncertain how many illnesses failed to meet the
requirement of the concept expressed by the word *ellu*, though sexual
discharges were certainly regarded as such failures (e.g., *CT* 39, 45:28:
šumma(DIS) *amēlu*(NA) *gi-na ig-da-na-lut* NA.BI NU *el* = "If a man
constantly has emissions, this man is not pure").

[212]H. Zimmern, *Beiträge zur Kenntnis der babylonischen Religion* (*A B*
12; Leipzig:J.C. Hinrichs'sche, 1901) 118.

[213]The text is published by R. Borger, "Die Weihe eines Enlil-
Priesters," *BO* 30 (1973) 165.

malaria in *LABS* 296 is described as the ritual "for disease and malaria not to approach a man's home" (*šiptu* ...GIG *di 'u ana* É NA NU TE-*e*). This ritual is probably related to an incantation which guarantees that "disease, 'malaria,' 'insomnia' and pestilence will not approach a man and his house for one year."[214] Similarly, many namburbi rituals were specifically recited to prevent evil from approaching a man and his house.[215]

b) The river

Outside of the house, a frequent locus of therapeutic rituals was the river. Numerous types of texts attest to this fact. R. Caplice notes that when the portended evil did not involve a specific place, namburbi rituals, which were sometimes meant to undo or avoid portended illnesses, "may be directed to a more specific site which accords with the actions to be performed, usually a rooftop or a canal bank."[216] In one medical namburbi, a man must immerse himself in the river seven times (*a-na* ÍD *ur-rad-ma* 7-*sú i-tè-bu*).[217] In *LABS* 275 an exorcist instructs the king to

---

[214]*KAR* 298 r 1ff: GIG *di-ḫu di-lip-tú u* NAM.UŠ.MEŠ *ana* NA *u* É-*šú* MU.1.KAM. NU.TE-*šú*. See Parpola, *LAS* II, p. 212.

[215]See Caplice, *The Akkadian Namburbi Texts* (Texts 4, 5, 6, 7, and 11).

[216]R. L. Caplice, *The Akkadian Namburbi Texts: An Introduction* (Los Angeles: Undena, 1974) 9-10. Caplice also notes (*ibid*, p. 9) that: "since physically illness could be conceived as foreshadowed by a portent, there is sometimes overlapping between strictly medical texts and namburbis."

[217]Caplice,"Namburbi Texts in the British Museum," *Or* 34 (1965) 121, l. 17'.

participate in exorcistic rituals[218] at the river (*ina* UGU ÍD *ú-rad*).[219] A divinatory ritual concerning illness published by van der Toorn also describes acts that are to be performed at the river.[220]

The importance of rivers and canals in removing evil substances and forces becomes transparent in some of the incantations. For example, note the following incantation addressed to the river in Text 10 of the namburbi texts published by Caplice.[221]

> *i-na qí-bit* ᵈ*E-a* ᵈ*Asar-lú-ḫi* ḪUL *šá-a-šú*
> *šu-ši-ri* KI.A!*-ki* NU BAR*-šú šu-ri-di-šú* ZU.AB*-ki*

> By the word of Ea and Asarluhi, remove that evil!
> May your banks not let go of it, plunge it into your abyss.

This incantation helps us gain insights into the socio-geographical motives for the river's importance in exorcism. The waterways formed a dominant aspect of Mesopotamian culture, especially in the south, and one action of the river seems to have provided a powerful analogy to exorcism-- namely, the removal of materials of all types, and their transportation into the watery abyss downstream. This observation of rivers was direct, and it was experienced by the society in general because of the geographical dominance

---

[218]*LABS* 275, l. 9: *dul-lu a-ši-pu-ti* .

[219]*LABS* 275, r. l. 7.

[220]K. van der Toorn, *Sin and Sanction*, 150:lines 45 and 90.

[221]Caplice,"Namburbi Texts in the British Museum," *Or* 34 (1965) p. 127, reverse lines 10-11; see also p. 126, l. 6.

of the rivers and canals.[222] Although water, in general, is
seen as a great purifier in many cultures, it was only natural
that the ever-present and powerful rivers and canals of
Mesopotamia were the places where the most efficient
removal of bad substances was thought to take place,
whether directly or by sympathetic magic. As indicated in
the incantation above, the direct observation of the river
removing substances out of one's immediate sight in the
exorcism rituals may explain why going to the river was
often deemed better than simply bringing water to the
patient.[223]

c) The šutukku

The šutukku = dag-agrun(É.NUN)-na may also be a
significant locus of therapy in Mesopotamia. É.NUN[224]
may be the equivalent of the tarbaṣu ("enclosure") of Gula
mentioned in AMT 41, 1 v. 38, and in an incantation
dealing with healing.[225] This enclosure may be the hut seen
in the seal from Tell Halaf published by D. Collon.[226] The

---

[222]On the processes by which simple observed analogies can become
powerful stimuli for ideological structures, see Paul Ricoeur, The
Symbolism of Evil (Boston:Beacon Press, 1967).

[223]Text 11 (Caplice,"Namburbi Texts..." Or 34 [1965] 130, r. 1. 5),
shows that the river could be a place of exorcism rituals even when the
purpose was to prevent evil from approaching a man's home.   For
instances where the water drawn from the Tigris and Euphrates was
sprinkled upon the patient, see A. Goetze, "An Incantation against
Disease," JCS 9-10 (1955-56) 15-16.

[224]On É.NUN, see H. Waetzoldt and F. Yildiz, "Eine neusumerische
Beschwörung," Oriens Antiquus 26 (1987) 295.

[225]See A. R. George, ZA 80 (1990) 156.

[226]First Impressions, #803.

seal, which shows a man resting on a couch while a group of men seemingly attend to him, may depict an actual healing ritual. A dog (Gula?) stands on top of the hut. The hut may have been placed by the river or near the home of the patient.

C. THE MEDICAL THEOLOGY OF G/N

1. General

The previous discussion on the general medical theology of Mesopotamia allows one to explore the role of G/N in the Mesopotamian health care system with more precision and confidence.

G/N was an active participant in a conceptual system which supposed that gods could use illness as a divine instrument. For example, G/N could inflict punishment on transgressors of the law in Mesopotamian society. Thus, the epilogue of the Code of Hammurabi mentions that, if anyone violated his statutes, Ninkarrak (= G/N) could bring "a sore wound which none can alleviate (and) no *asû* shall know what is within it."[227] Similarly, G/N was charged with punishing those who did not fulfill covenant obligations in the Neo-Assyrian period. For example, a vassal treaty of Esarhaddon includes Gula in curses against those who do not fulfill their obligations.[228] *Šurpu* 3:160 also mentions the existence of "the curse of Gula" (*mamit* ^{d}*Gula*), which could cause illness and other misfortunes. Moreover,

---

[227]Col xxviiib: 57-60: *sí-im-ma-am mar-ṣa-am ša la i-pa-aš-še-ḫu A.ZU qí-ri-ib-šu la i-lam-ma-du.* See G. R. Driver and J. C. Miles, *The Babylonian Laws* (Oxford: Clarendon, 1955) 107.

[228]D. J. Wiseman, *Iraq* 20 (1958) 63.

SA.GIG records a number of diseases which are described as "the hand of Gula." Thus, "If his urinary tract? is consumed, (it is the) hand of Gula".[229]   Another prayer (*RTA* 71:6) bids G/N:

> 5. ^{d}[nin]-*kar-ra-ak ṣu-bi-ti mi-ra-ni-ki*
> 6. *ina pī kalbē-ki dannūte i-di-i ḫar-gul-lu* [230]

> O, Ninkarrak, halt your young whelps,
> place a muzzle on the mouth of your mighty dogs.

The impact of the concept that a deity could send/permit illnesses had a number of consequences for the patient which we have already discussed in a general manner. As we have mentioned, one strategy in such a system was to confess all, or a large number, of possible sins, and prayers to G/N are no exception. For example, one prayer to Gula is recited on behalf of a patient who has committed "numerous sins, and numerous infractions."[231] The sins enumerated included failure to help her special animal, the dog.[232] More specfically, *LKA* 20:10 mentions that the patient saw dogs, among other things, fighting (UR.GI$_7$ *im-taḫ-ṣa*), but he pretended not to notice (*īmur*(IGI)-*ma pa-ni-šu ana la*(NU)

---

[229]*TDP* 108:16: [*šumma* UR. KU]N-*šú ikkal*(KU)-*šú* ŠU ^{d}*Gu-la.*

[230]*VAT* 8258 was published as Text Nr. 71 by E. Ebeling, "Religiose Texte aus Assur, " *ZDMG* 74-75 (1920-21) 175-177. B. Landsberger ("Zu Ubersetzungen Ebeling's *ZDMG.* 74, 175ff" *ZDMG* 74 [1929-21] 440) provided improved readings in line 6 and elsewhere in the text.

[231]*LKA* 20: Obv. 20: [*ma'du*] *ḫi-ṭa-tu-su ma'du gil-l*[*atušu* (...)].
See van der Toorn, *Sin and Sanction*, 82 and 201 n. 373.

[232]See van der Toorn, *Sin and Sanction*, 26.

idê(ZU-*e*) *ša-kan*).[233] Gula, the mistress of dogs, was not pleased.

G/N is not the only deity to be implored when an illness occurred. As we have noted, the ritual against "malaria" (*LA BS* 296) involved rituals not only for G/N but for a number of other deities. Other gods were supposed to heal the sick. In particular, Ea and Marduk, were the *āšipu*s of the pantheon. For example, according to *Šurpu* 4:16 one of Marduk's prerogatives was to heal the sick (LÚ.GIG *bul-lu-ṭu*). Equally important is that a large number of prayers and rituals for illness do not mention G/N at all. For instance, a complete prayer (*BAM* 516 ii 30) for the healing of *sinlurmâ* disease, which affected the eyes, addresses or mentions only Šamaš and Ea.[234]

Ritter also notes that some incantations assigned to G/N have "disclaimers" which indicate that the incantation really belongs to Ea, not Gula (*šiptu ul yattun, šipat Ea*).[235] The implications of such colophons are significant for the study of Gula's evolution. Since most of these incantations involve *materia medica,* such notations may reflect a movement towards centralization of the magical powers of most drugs in G/N. Such a specialty may be seen in incantations addressed to G/N which are recited when applying substances ranging from herbs (*AMT* 9, 1:25ff) to suppositories (e.g., *BAM* 105:7).

---

[233]On the idiom and other aspects of the prayer, see van der Toorn, *Sin and Sanction*, 26 and 168 n. 223.

[234]The effect on the eyes is clear: *šumma*(DIS) *amēlu*(NA) *ūma*(U4) *kalama*(DU.A.BI) *là*(NU) *immar*(IGI.DU8)= "If a man cannot see throughout the day." See further M. J. Geller, "Review of P. Herrero, *Thérapeutique mésopotamienne,*" in *BO* 43 (1986) 738-742.

[235]Ritter, "Magical Expert...," *A S* 16:312.

In another text Gula leads the patient to the temple of Asalluhi, and it appears to be Marduk's glance which effects the healing:

> ^{d}*Gula nādinat balāṭi amēlūti ina bīt*
> ^{d}*Asalluḫi ūbil eṭlu* ^{d}*Mar[duk] rēmēnû*
> *ippalissuma igsâmma*(!) *ibluṭ eṭlu.*[236]

> Gula, the giver of life, led the man
> to the house of Assaluhi; Marduk,
> the merciful, looked upon him. The
> young man belched and recovered.

The cooperation between G/N and Ea and Marduk may parallel the cooperation one expects between the *āšipu* and the *asû*. Even if pure hyperbole, some texts imply that G/N (and other gods) were excluded from healing in certain instances. For example *AMT* 97, 1:10-11 says:

> *šá la* ^{d}*E-a man-nu u-na-aḫ-ka šá la*
> ^{d}*Asar-lú-ḫi man-nu u-šap-šaḫ-ka*

> If Ea does not, then who will soothe you? If
> Asalluhi does not, then who will cure you?

The foregoing evidence demonstrates that even if G/N was a main patron of healing, she was certainly not the only deity who could heal.

---

[236]Ritter, "Magical Expert...," *A S* 16:311-312. The complete text, not available to me at the time of writing, was published earlier in F. Küchler, *Beiträge zur Kenntnis der assyrisch-babylonischen Medizin* (Leipzig, 1904) Pl. 2, l. 25.

Another important aspect of G/N is that she is often an intermediary figure in the search for healing. Because of Gula's role as an intermediary, patients sometimes ask her to entreat other gods to relieve their anger against the suppliant as in the following example: [237]

lu-uš-pur-ki ana ili-ya zi-ni-i
ištari-ya zi-ni-ti
ana ili ali-ya šá šab-su-ma kam-lu itti-ya

Let me dispatch you to my angry god,
(and to) my angry goddess;
To the god of my city who is angry and
furious with me.

The intermediary role of G/N in healing is directly related to the Mesopotamian medical theology. The most central aspect of this medical theology is the perceived actual and potential multi-causation of illness. An illness could be caused by a host of gods, ancestors, hidden sins, as well as obvious physical causes. This use of G/N as an intermediary may be an attempt to simplify the search for a cure. If G/N can petition many gods for the patient, the patient may be able to forego or eliminate some of the complicated rituals to all the gods who might be responsible for the illness.[238]

We already have noted that the "multi-causal" presuppositions of Mesopotamian medical theology also produced two general strategies. One was a maximalist

---

[237]Text (a) in C. J. Mullo-Weir, "Four Hymns to Gula," *JRAS* (1929) 2. Another example of the same intermediary status is present in *LKA* 19.

[238]On the nature of such personal gods as intercessors, see T. Jacobsen, *The Treasures of Darkness* (New Haven: Yale, 1976) 159-64.

strategy which sought to appease through labor intensive rituals as many of the potential "senders/controllers" as possible, and to enumerate as many of the potential transgressions as possible. The maximalist strategy could be pursued by kings or the wealthy who had sufficient resources to pay for exorcists and the materials needed for the complicated rituals. As we shall discuss in more detail below, there are instances where the healing consultant asks the king or other officials to supply or help to supply medicinal substances.

Although maximalist and minimalist strategies could be employed by persons of wealth, maximalist strategies probably would not be very attractive to those who did not have many resources. Indeed, common citizens may not have received priority when medicinal substances were in short supply or when the healing consultants were occupied with other rituals. The minimalist strategy (direct appeal to one known deity in the initial stage of an illness) may be used when the "sender/controller" is thought to be obvious, as may be the case in *The Story of the Bitten Man from Nippur*. In view of the number of features of the Mesopotamian health care system (e.g., the frequent inefficacy of "non-scientific" therapies, the common search for alternatives, the wide selection of deities one could use as alternatives), the minimalist strategy was probably very rare.

In any event, the use of G/N to entreat the many deities who could be responsible for an illness could help to reduce the number of petitions and rituals necessary for appeasing a number of gods at once. Such a simplifying strategy, which can be viewed as a sort of compromise between the maximalist and minimalist strategies, would be especially useful when the specific gods are not easily identifiable, or when the patient does not have the economic means and resources to pursue maximalist strategies.

The theology which centered on the "sender/ controller" as the key to healing also explains why G/N never became the sole or even the dominant deity of healing in the degree that Asclepius did in Greece. Since the "sender/controller" could be almost any god, known or unknown, it was difficult for a healing deity *per se* to gain dominance in the health care system because healing depended on locating and appeasing the "sender/ controller," and not only the healing deity. So long as the "sender/ controller" was the key to the healing, a healing deity (as a direct healer or as an intermediary) could only be part of the solution.

Moreover, it is clear that G/N did not specialize in healing to the degree that Asclepius did. G/N was charged with a number of non-healing tasks such as helping to enforce socio-legal instruments like covenants. Thus, she could use illness as punishment, something that made her a danger as well as a potential helper in illness. As *LKA* 20 shows, the patient was not always even sure whether an illness was, in fact, sent by G/N for various sins.

It is also important to realize that the prime visible manifestations of G/N by the patient were not necessarily at the temple. G/N was visible as a constellation. Many rituals were performed at night on rooftops of homes "before Gula." For example, one prescription recommends that the mixture be placed "before the constellation of the goat, the enclosure of Gula."[239] Gula's power, therefore, was not

---

[239]*AMT* 41 1 v. 38: *ana*(DIŠ) *pani*(IGI) *kakkab*(MUL) *enzi*(UZ) *tarbaṣ*(TUR) d*Gu-la* (*tuš-bat*). Gula was represented in the sky by

limited to the temple, but was probably viewed as in effect anywhere G/N, the constellation, could be seen.

2. The function of the temple of G/N

Even if G/N was not the sole or dominant deity in the relief of illness, one must realize that she had a temple in a number of cities. We must now turn our attention to the role of such a temple in the health care system of Mesopotamia, especially insofar as our three main functions are concerned, namely, petitionary, therapeutic, and thanksgiving.

a) Petitionary function

As we have mentioned, a variety of sources indicate that the home was the primary place of petitions and prayers at various stages of an illness. However, there is some evidence that "signs" were sought at temples in cases of illness. This is indicated in *Šurpu* 2:127 where a suppliant, who has apparently not been successful in identifying the precise "sender/controller," has apparently sought signs at a variety of places including a temple (*ina* É. DINGIR *ša-[a ']-il*). The use of the temple of G/N for the purposes of seeking such signs, presumably in regard to health, is supported by a text (*STT* 73) that mentions an oracle of G/N, and is apparently a copy of an original in the temple of G/N.[240]

Another possible indication of a petitionary function comes from *LABS* 293, which was published with new

---

the constellation now known as Lyra according to E. F. Weidner, "Eine Beschreibung des Sternenhimmels aus Assur," *AfO* 3-5 (1926-29) 84.

[240]See E. Reiner, "Fortune-Telling in Mesopotamia," *JNES* 19 (1960) 23-35.

joins and collations by Parpola.[241] Despite some of the
improved readings, it is still enigmatic and fragmentary in
places, which makes a complete interpretation very
precarious. The text apparently is a reply from Urad-nanna
to the king's inquiry about a pregnant woman, possibly the
queen.[242] Line 16' (É ^{d}gu-la i-na-šú-n[i -ši] = "[X] will
bring [her? to?] the temple of Gula") may suggest that the
woman was brought to the temple, although where the birth
was to take place is unclear. In the reverse lines an issue is
apparently made of a basket which is not present:

> 3. ...MA.SAB-ma[243] la ta-az-zi-[iz x x]
> 4. ina ŠÀ É.GAL i-tar-bu MA.SAB TA* É ^{d}[gu-la]
> 5. na-ṣu-u-ni us-se-ši-bu ˹É?˺ x ˺ [x x x x x]

> ...A basket was not availa[ble...]
> They entered the palace, (and) they brought a basket
>   from the temple of [Gula?) ...they placed it [in the palace?]

Perhaps the newborn is placed in the basket, which may also
have a role in other rituals associated with the birth. The
tablet ends with the mention of "many rituals" (l. rev. 14:
dul-la-a-ni ma-a[ʾ-du-t]e). It should be noted, moreover,
that a terracotta relief found at Isin (IB 314) depicts a woman
with a child being breast-fed, and an object that appears to be
a basket beside her (see Figure 3).[244] Courtyard B of the

---

[241]See also LAS II, pp. 354-56 and 377-78.

[242]l. 24' ma-a ša a-ri-at-u-ni te-pá-aš X [............])

[243]The gender of masabbu (MA.SAB) is unclear, rendering the role of
the basket even more uncertain in the ritual.

[244]B. Hrouda (IB I, 49) describes the object as: "Korb?". No specific
date is assigned to this relief, although Hrouda (IB I, 48)) suggests that

temple of G/N at Isin also had a terracotta relief of a naked female suppliant.[245] Although it is uncertain whether such a depiction represents part of petitionary or thanksgiving ritual, the relief and the other evidence discussed suggest that the temple of G/N did have a role in rituals concerning fertility and child-bearing.

One can only tentatively suggest that this text describes a ritual petitioning G/N for safe birth. It is relevant that in *BAM* 244 r 70, G/N appears at the end of an incantation for a safe delivery.[246] Dust from the door of the temple of Gula (SAHAR KÁ ^{d}ME.ME)[247] was used in rituals against miscarriage. Thus, one may tentatively suggest that the temple of G/N had a petitionary function, something attested especially in concerns of pregnant women. Even if the patient was not required to be present at the temple in such rituals, it appears that materials (e.g., baskets, dust) may have been brought from the temple to the site of the petitionary ritual.

b) Therapeutic function

(1) General

As we have mentioned, if, in addition to providing a place for simple petitions, a temple provides services designed to restore the ill, then the temple may be said to

---

such terracotta reliefs may date to the Old Babylonian period or earlier periods.

[245]The figurine is catalogued as IB 1163; See also *IB* II, 13

[246]For additional comments, see Parpola, *LAS* II, p. 356.

[247]See Farber, *Schlaf, Kindchen, Schlaf*, p. 69, l. 234; also Parpola, *LAS* II, p. 356.

have a therapeutic function. Such a temple, for example, may be a place for the application of *materia medica*, exorcism, incubation, and other rituals. Likewise, the temple may provide surgical or other procedures that presuppose or presage some of the modern ideas about medicine that we call "rational" (e.g., the physical extraction of lodged weapons).

If there were any temples that, in addition to simple petitions, provided services to heal patients, then the temple of G/N, as the shrine of a renowned healing deity, naturally would be the most appropriate temple to be used in such a manner. But was the temple of G/N used to house patients or for extensive therapeutic purposes? In order to answer the question, one must differentiate between short-term care and long-term care. By the former, we mean care that did not require an overnight stay or a stay of multiple days. Long-term care required an overnight stay or multiple days. The long-term type of care, as the Asclepieion exempifies, could be manifested in an architecture designed to house large numbers of patients.

There are at present no texts that provide any direct evidence that long-term therapy was exercised at the temple of G/N. Without unequivocal textual data, the question requires an analysis of the archaeological remains of the temple of Gula at Isin, and particularly an analysis of the function of the individual rooms of the temple. The function of most rooms was not specified by the excavators, and the contents do not provide much indication in most rooms. This problem is complicated by the fact that the temple seems to have suffered significant robbery in antiquity and in modern times.[248] Even if the site had suffered no modern

---

[248]See comments in Hrouda, *IB* II, 20.

disturbances, the function of ancient architecture is often notoriously difficult to ascertain on the basis of its contents.[249]

However, for the sake of our topic on the function of the temple, we will make a brief survey of the meagre indications available to see if we can uncover any credible evidence for the long-term therapeutic function of the temple of G/N, especially evidence that might indicate the internment of patients for a day or more. Our basic strategy will be a process of elimination wherein we can determine how many rooms, if any at all, might have served as guest quarters for patients for long term stays (overnight or more days).

(2) Long-term therapy /Architectural analysis

At its largest extent the temple building at Isin consisted of 29 rooms (numbered I-XXIX) and two large courtyards (A and B). The building measured some 68 x 52 meters.[250] We can summarize the published contents of the rooms as follows:

---

[249]For a general theoretical discussion of determining the function of architectural remains, see M.B. Schiffer, *Behavioral Archaeology* (New York: Academic Press, 1976).
[250]Hrouda, *IB* II, 199.

Room	Significant features/contents[251]	Possible function
I		
II	Dog figurine (IB 749)	
III	Offering stand	cultic?
IV	Inscription of Adad-apla-iddina	annex to Ninurta
V		"Durchgangs-raum"[252]
VI		"Vorzella"[253]
VII	Seals of Kurigalzu	"Allerheiligste des Gula Tempels"[254]
VIII		
IX		
X	Kurigalzu bricks	?
XI	Asphalt debris, charcoal (palm wood)	?
XII/XXI/XXII	"Diese Räume in der Nordecke des Tempels sind im aufgehenden Mauerwerk nicht mehr erhalten."[255]	?
XIII	Adad-apla-iddina inscription; Entrance trough Ninurta temple only	?
XIV	Remains of door installation	Restricted access to Ninurta portion?
XV	Remains of door hinges	"Vorzella"[256] to Ninurta temple.

[251] A lack of entry under a category indicates that no significant features or contents were noted by the excavators insofar as function is concerned. Quotation marks under the *Possible Function* column are those assigned by the excavators themselves in M. Haussperger, B. Hrouda and E. Strommenger, "Die Grabung im Gula Tempel 1975-1978," in *IB* II, 7-25.

[252] *IB* II, 10.

[253] *IB* II, 12.

[254] *IB* II, 12.

[255] M. Haussperger, B. Hrouda and E. Strommenger, "Die Grabung im Gula Tempel 1975-1978," in *IB* II, 15.

[256] *IB* II, 19.

XVI		
XVII	seal of Ur-nammu	"Verbindungs-raum"[257]
XVIII		"Vorzella"[258]
XIX	Ninurta inscription	"Die Zella des Ninurta"[259]
XX		
XXI	(See XII)	
XXII	(See XII)	
XXIII		?
XXIV	Dog figurine (IB 1176) at entrance; A treasure hoard with many dog figurines and fragments from a mask; A large vessel with human bone remains; Another large vessel filled with sand and ashes; A figurine of a kneeling man (IB 1260); A figurine of a female dog nursing young (IB 1267).	Cultic? Storage? Priest's quarters?
XXV		
XXVI		
XXVII		
XXVIII		"Haupt-eingang"[260]
XXIX	Grave (G 96); A large vessel filled with small offerings.	

As one can infer, most rooms do not reveal much indication of function. Let us begin with those rooms whose function was assigned by the excavators, namely, V (a connecting room), VI (an ante-cella), VII (the Gula Temple),

---

[257] *IB* II, 17.
[258] *IB* II, 19.
[259] *IB* II, 20.
[260] *IB* II, 16.

XV and XVIII (ante-cellas), XVII (a connecting room) and Room XIX (the Ninurta temple). Rooms IV, VIII, and XIII, which are "dead-end" rooms next to the Gula and Ninurta shrines respectively, are typical of other temples in Mesopotamia, including Kassite temples, and do not appear to be accessible to the public.[261] Room XI appears to be an entrance foyer, and room XIV is a connecting room. Room XXVIII may have been the main entrance. It is clear that these types of rooms are typical of many other Mesopotamian temples which do not house a specialized healing deity, and these rooms do not have any contents which indicate any type of patient care whatsoever (e.g., surgical instruments).

Rooms I, IX, XX, XXIII, XXV, XXVI and XXVII have not been described in much detail, but there is also no indication of any accommodations for patients. The function of rooms XII, XXI, and XXII is unclear. If one draws on analogies to other temples, one may surmise that at least one room housed the priest,[262] and at least another room housed

---

[261]For parallels, see Abbildung 301 (Ningal temple of Kurigalzu at Ur), and Abbildung 308 (Kassite shrine at Ur) in E. Heinrich, *Die Tempel und Heiligtümer im Alten Mesopotamien* (2 volumes; Berlin: De Gruyter, 1982) volume 2.

[262]A model analysis of the room function of the Inanna temple (Ur III period) in Nippur has been undertaken by R. Zettler, "Administration of the Temple of Inanna at Nippur under the Third Dynasty of Ur: Archaeological and Documentary Evidence," in McG. Gibson and R. D. Biggs, *The Organization of Power: Aspects of Bureaucracy in the Ancient Near East* (Chicago: U. of Chicago, 1987) 117-133. The temple, which has a number of analogies with Neo-Assyrian temples, has a square plan like the Gula temple, and multiple courtyards. Zettler's analysis reveals that family quarters of the administrators probably required a number of rooms. The study also indicates that a

an archive,[263] and at least one was used for storage. Thus, about 20 of the numbered rooms were typical of other Mesopotamian temples, or had no function which could be called distinctive of large-scale patient housing and care.

If there were any care beyond simple rituals that might have required more than a day's stay in the temple, then there are 9 numbered rooms which might have served such a purpose (Rooms II, III, X, XII, XVI, XXI, XXII, XXIV, and XXIX). Yet, we do not have any evidence for medical function for 7 of these rooms. Two of these rooms (XXIV and XXIX), however, do have relatively significant numbers of seemingly cultic objects. Room XXIV bears many dog figurines, masks, a figurine of a kneeling man, and other seemingly cultic paraphernalia. As we have mentioned, Room XXIX has a grave with a person bearing spinal deformities, and other cultic objects as well. Yet one must realize that these contents *per se* do not necessitate the explanation as rooms for guest patients, and room XXIV might well have been used for the storage of sacred objects or as the residence of one of the priests. Thus, at most, one can suggest Rooms XXIV and XXIX have the only extant evidence that might reflect patient care, though other functions are possible too.

Courtyards are, of course, typical of many temples in Mesopotamia, and so cannot be deemed to be distinctive

---

large number of rooms is not unusual even for temples that do not specialize in housing sick guests.

[263]The location of the archive of the temple of Gula is still uncertain, and tablets could be stored in a number of rooms in a temple. See discussion by K. R. Veenhof, "Cuneiform Archives: An Introduction," in K. R. Veenhof, ed., *Cuneiform Archives and Libraries* (30[e] Recontre Assyriologique Internationale, Leiden, 4-8 July, 1983; Leiden: Nederlands Historisch-Archaeologisch Instituut, 1986) 1-36.

of a patient care facility. But as mentioned, Courtyard B had the terracotta relief (IB 1163) of a naked female suppliant. Courtyard A also had a distinctive feature, namely, a sort of long trough (*Wanne*) and box-like structure (*Kasten*) dug into the floor.[264] Libations do not appear to have been performed here according to the excavators, and the function of these features is still unclear.[265]

In any event, the meagre archaeological evidence is consistent with the view that the temple of G/N was probably not a place where crowds of sick individuals would come for therapeutic services which required an overnight stay or more. Indeed, once one considers the space devoted to the normal functions of temples in Mesopotamia, the non-typical space would not permit the use of the temple of G/N as a sprawling center which took care of crowds of sick people for long periods of time.

Unlike the Asclepius temples which did have some differences from non-healing temples, the temple of G/N at Isin does not seem to have any differences which can be attributed to a healing temple *per se*. It is not the largest temple in southern Mesopotamia, nor does it have more space than other temples, which might indicate the housing of a large number of individuals. One does not find large quantities of furniture, depictions of patients in the temple, or surgical implements. This may simply be due to the fact that the temple has been robbed, or has not been entirely excavated.[266] One should not exclude the possibility of

---

[264]*IB* II, 9.

[265]*IB* II, 9.

[266]In response to my inquiry about findings which post-date the major reports on Isin, Barthel Hrouda (Written communication, August 8, 1990) comments: "*Keine Räume im Tempel weisen auf Krankenbehandlung hin.*"

nearby buildings being used in such a manner, but such evidence is not available at present.[267] The recently discovered temple of G/N at Nippur may shed more light on these issues, or reverse some of our tentative conclusions, once the investigations are more fully published.

(3) Short-term therapy

Although the balance of present evidence indicates that the temple of G/N at Isin was probably not a place where a large number of patients would spend the night, this does not exclude the possibility that the sick or their intermediaries used the temple for short-term therapeutic rituals that did not require an overnight or a longer stay.

Of particular significance are dog figurines that are known to have been used in healing and exorcism rituals in Mesopotamia. The connection of G/N with dogs is well known.[268] Dog figurines devoted to G/N have been found

---

[267]Many temples, including some Kassite temples, did have a *giparu* nearby (e.g., Kurigalzu's *giparu* at Ur which probably served the Ningal temple), which was able to house a large number of individuals. See E. Heinrich, *Die Tempel und Heiligtümer im Alten Mesopotamien* (2 volumes; Berlin: De Gruyter, 1982) Vol 1:228 and Vol 2: Abbildung 309.

[268]For a study of this association, see I. Fuhr, "Der Hund als Begleiter der Göttin Gula und anderer Heilgottheiten," in *IB* I, 135-145.

at Isin, Sippar,[269] and Nippur,[270] among other places.[271] It would be useful to review briefly the role of dog figurines in such rituals. The function of dog figurines in probable apotropaic rituals (e.g., against sickness) is certainly attested during the Neo-Assyrian period. Such dog figurines were buried near or in the buildings that they were protecting.[272] One section of the so-called barrack rooms at Fort Shalmaneser, which may have functioned as a sick bay, had a large number of apotropaic figurines buried within it.[273] In addition, *LKU* 33 speaks of the apotropaic use of "two dogs for the outer door, two dogs for the inner door, two dogs for the door of the bedroom."[274]

One should also note that dogs were seen by many texts as a portent of evil or of punitive actions by

---

[269]For some examples of inscriptions and photographs of dog figurines from Sippar, see V. Scheil, *Une saison de fouilles à Sippar* (Cairo: Imprimiere de l'Institut Français d'archéologie orientale, 1902) 91-94.

[270]A recent popular discussion about baked-clay and bronze dog figurines from Nippur may be found in M. R. Yoe, "Ancient Medical Dogma?" *The University of Chicago Magazine* (summer, 1990) 9.

[271] Though Gula is not the main theme, a recent discussion of dog figurines of Gula may be found in B. Mallowan, "Three Middle Assyrian Bronze/Copper Dogs." in M. Kelly-Bucellati ed., *Insight through Images* (*Bibliotheca Mesopotamica* 21; Malibu:Undena, 1986) 221-228.

[272]See A. Green, "Neo-Assyrian Apotropaic Figures," *Iraq* 45 (1983) 94. On apotropaic figurines, see also F. A. M. Wiggermann, *Babylonian Prophylactic Figurines: The Ritual Texts* (Amsterdam:Free University Press, 1986).

[273]A. Green, "Neo-Assyrian Apotropaic Figures," *Iraq* 45 (1983) 89.

[274]2 UR.GI₇ ME ša bābi kamê....2 UR.GI₇ ša bābi bītani....2 UR.GI₇ ša bāb bīt erši; Portion of text and translation of *LKU* 33 r. 21, 22, 23 as cited in *CAD* K, 71; The entire text in *LKU* was not available to me.

supernatural beings. For example, one namburbi text published by Caplice is specifically against the "evil of the dog."[275] In this case the dog has approached the man and/or his house and urinated on the man. The namburbi ritual consists, among other aspects, in making clay figurines of the dog. After the making and dressing of the dog figurine, the ritual may be summarized as follows:

> 1) The exorcist sets up a reed altar for Šamaš near the river and prepares a number of substances for the ritual (e.g., loaves of bread, dates, fine flour, beer, honey and ghee).
> 2) Incantation for Šamaš recited by suppliant.
> 3) Incantation recited over the figurine by the liturgist.
> 4) Procession to the river, and request that the river carry away the evil of the dog, and repeated three times.
> 5) Casting of the dog into the river by the liturgist.
> 6) The suppliant leaves river, being careful not to look behind him, and proceeds to a tavern.

It is clear that the dog figurine was part of a ritual of imitative magic, where the removal of the dog figurine by the river was supposed to remove the evil of the dog. The aforementioned prayer to G/N (*RTA* 71:6), which requests that G/N lock the jaws of her dog, also suggests that the dog was seen as an instrument which brought punishment.

---

[275]R. Caplice, "Namburbi Texts in the British Museum II," Or 36 (1967) 1-8; also R. Caplice, *The Akkadian Namburbi Texts*, 16-17.

Insofar as the dog figurines in the temple of G/N at Isin are concerned, one may mention the following types of depictions.

A. Solitary dogs

1) Dog sitting or or lying down without attachments (e.g., IB 1047;*IB* II:Tafel 27 found in the Gula Temple Room XIX).[276]

2) Dog figurine with "attachment" rings on its back (e.g., IB 800;*IB* II, Tafel 27).

B. Dog with company

1) Dog with suckling puppies (e.g, IB 1267/ *IB* II, p. 67 and Tafel 27)

2) Dog with a human (e.g., IB 29/*IB* I, Tafel 12 and Tafel 25)

These dog figurines may have been used as part of petitionary or thanksgiving rituals. If any of these figurines was used for exorcism rituals of the type described in namburbi rituals, then it would probably be the solitary dog without attachments. A Kassite votive inscription (in Sumerian) for Gula (line 1:^{d}gu-*la*) published by E. Sollberger also mentions the fashioning of a dog figurine. We present a crucial portion of Sollberger's inscription and translation for the convenience of the reader:

14. *n*[*am*]-*ti-la*
15. [^{d}na-*z*]*i-ma*-[*r*]*u-ut-ta-aš*
16. [*lugal*] *šár*

---

[276]See B. Hrouda, "Rundplastische Figuren aus verschiedenen Material," *IB* II, 66.

17. [*lugal-l*]*a-ni-ir*
18. [*alam*(?)] *ur x-x-ni*
19. *gú* ^{íd}*]UD.KIB.NUN^{ki}-gé*
20. ^{íd}*dağal-la-na*
21. [*é-mu*]-*pà-da*
22. [*é ki-á*]*ğ-ğá-ni*
23. [*nam-ti-l*]*a-a-ni-šè*
24. [*ù nam-ti-la k*]*alam-ma-šè*
25. [*ḫu-mu-u*]*n-dí*[*m*]

For the life of Nazi-maruttaš, king of the world, his
king, (Ninurta-rēṣušu) did fashion an image(?) of
her...dog on the bank of the Euphrates, her wide river,
in the É-mupada her beloved temple, for his life and
the life of the land.[277]

If the dog figurine was made at the river, then this figurine
may be part of an exorcism ritual similar to that described in
the namburbi text mentioned, though petitionary or
thanksgiving purposes cannot be excluded.[278]

Perhaps the solitary type of dog figurine (IB 1176)
found at the entrance of Room XXIV in the Gula temple[279]

---

[277]Transliteration and translation follow E. Sollberger, "Two Kassite
Votive Inscriptions," *JAOS* 88 (1968) 192-193.

[278]F. A. Ali ("Dedication of a Dog to Nintinugga," *ArOr* 34 [1966]
289-293) published an inscription from Nippur dedicated to Nintinugga,
identified with Gula, which mentions the making of a dog figurine
named *Tu$_6$-ni-lú-ša$_6$* (= "her incantation heals the people"). Ali
suggests a scribal exercise as the purpose, but it is unclear whether it
was a model of a petitonary or thanksgiving inscription. On
Nintinugga, see also M. E. Cohen, "The Name Nintinugga...," *JCS*
28 (1976) 82-92.

[279]See B. Hrouda, "Rundplastische Figuren..." *IB* II, 66.

may have been part of petitionary of thanksgiving rituals. On the other hand, one cannot exclude the possibility that these figurines were simply apotropaic figurines that functioned in the same manner as those mentioned in *LKU* 33. The dog figurines with rings on their backs suggest that they were intended to be attached, perhaps to the human body. Evidence for such a practice may be found in a text (*KAR* 213 1 i 10) which mentions "a stone dog (to wear) on the throat, (set in?) gold" ((NA4)UR.GI7 ZI KÙ.GI).[280]

A group of metallic figurines (IB 29; see Figure 4) found in a non-temple locus, tentatively dated to the early first millennium by Hrouda,[281] may be interpreted only on a very hypothetical basis as a depiction of suppliants and dogs. One man in IB 29 is seen with his left hand on his head while his left torso leans over the back of the dog. IB 29 depicts another man with his right arm around the dog (see Figure 5). If IB 29 represents any kind of healing rituals, then the live dog may have been part of a ritual that involved kneeling and touching the dog.[282]

Although Hrouda does not cite textual parallels, a text which may reflect such a practice is *CT* 39, 38 r 8, part

---

[280]See "*kalbu*" in *CAD* 8:71h. A duplicate copy (Text A 231) published by K. Yalvac, ("Eine Liste von Amulettsteinen im Museum zu Istambul," in *A S* 16) 333 ii 37 reads: NA4 UR.GI7 ZI KÙ.GI.

[281]B. Hrouda, *IB* I, 52-3, and Tafel 12 and Tafel 25. Hrouda labels it "Beter-Hundegruppe." The group of figurines may be associated with a grave.

[282]Hrouda (*IB* I, 52) suggests that IB 29 has a parallel at the temple of Hera of Samos (See U. Jantzen, *Samos* VIII [Bonn: Rudolf Habelt, 1972] Tafel 72). However, in the example from Samos, the person is standing, and the connection of the latter figurine with healing is uncertain at best.

of the series *šumma amēlu ana bīt ilišu itbima*, which has the following omen: [283]

> *šumma*(DIŠ) *amēlu*(NA)
> *ana bīt*(É) *ili*(DINGIR)-*šu itbi*(ZI)
> UD KA MA *ilappat*(TAG)-*ma el*
> KIMIN UR.GI₇ *ša* ᵈ*Gu-la ilappat*(TAG)-*ma el*

> If a man goes to the temple of his god,
> and if he touches....?, he is clean (again?);
> Likewise, if he touches the dog of Gula,
> he is clean (again?)

It is difficult to determine whether the dog was touched at the temple, or on the way to the temple. Many of the signs in *enūma ana bīt marṣi āšipu illaku* are encountered, not at the patient's house, but on the way to the patient's house. However, the identification of a "dog of Gula" might indeed indicate that it was a dog that could be identified or distinguished from other dogs. Such an identification would best be made at the temple of Gula. If there was a ritual at the temple in which an unclean person became clean, then the temple of G/N would form an exception to texts which indicate that impurity was not welcome in various temples. If IB 29 and *CT* 38, 8 r 12 reflect the same type of ritual (and if they reflect a ritual at all), then they furnish some tentative evidence for the use of the temple of Gula as a place for therapeutic rituals, albeit not necessarily long-term therapy.

     The dog and dog figurines also had other functions in Mesopotamian religious practices. One interesting practice

---

[283]See "*kalbu*" in CAD 8:71f.

is the mention of the dog and the swine in fertility
incantations. For example, in a text published by Ebeling,
one finds: "Incantation: I impregnate myself, I impregnate
my body as when a dog and bitch, and a boar and sow
copulate." (*šiptu a-ra-aḫ-ḫi ra-ma-ni a-ra-ḫi pag-ri kīma
kalbu u kalbatu šaḫu saḫī[tu i]r-tak-bu-u*).[284] One should
note that figurines of both pigs and nursing bitches have
been found at Isin, though it is difficult to determine whether
they were linked chronologically or in fertility rituals.[285]

Figurines depicting persons with hands on different
parts of their bodies are attested at various sites with Gula
shrines. It should be noted that Mohammed Ali Mustafa
theorizes that sometimes Kassite figurines for Gula from the
time of Nazimaruttaš (1323-1298) were manufactured as
part of the petition for healing, and not simply as a
thanksgiving offering after healing.[286] The figurines from
the vicinity of ʿAqar Quf published by Mustafa show
suppliants with their hands on different portions of their
body, and he concludes that such hand positions indicate the
area of affliction. The same conclusion is reached by
McGuire Gibson concerning a figurine found at the temple
of G/N at Nippur which depicts a man holding his throat

---

[284]Following transcription of E. Ebeling, "Keilschrifttafeln
medizinischen Inhalts," *Archiv für Geschichte der Medizin* 13
(1921/Heft 1 and 2)142, line 26.

[285]A pig figurine (labeled IB 1469) dated to the Jamdet Nasr period
was recently reported by J. Boessneck, "Ergebnisse der Ausgrabung in
Isin 1984," *Sumer* 45 (1-2, 1987-88) 15, and photograph on p. 16.

[286]M. Ali Mustafa, "Kassite Figurines: A New Group Discovered near
ʿAqar Quf," *Sumer* 3 (1947) 19ff.

with the left hand.[287]   The variety of figurines depicting
hand placement in different areas of the body is consistent
with pointing to afflicted portions of the body (rather than a
stereotyped hand placement in prayer). Figurines of body
parts (e.g., feet and legs) from the Isin II period have been
recovered from the area of a ramp (see below) to the temple
of Gula at Isin. Agnes Spycket interprets them as ex-voto
figurines associated with the healing activities of Gula.[288]

A terracotta figurine (IB 1260) of a man in
genuflection (Height: 16.5 cm.) was found in Room XXIV
of the Gula building and was tentatively assigned to the
Kassite period, though earlier dates are possible.[289] The
possibility that it represents a sick individual or a healed
individual is presented by Braun-Holzinger.[290] In all of
these cases one can only provide very precarious hypotheses
on their actual function.

Among the other important finds at Isin are 33 dog
burials from around 1000 B.C.E., which are associated with
a paved ramp which may have led directly to the temple of
G/N.[291] The thoroughfare was probably built by Adad-

---

[287]The best depiction of this figurine thus far is published in M.
Gibson, "Nippur 1990:The Temple of Gula and a Glimpse of Things to
Come," *OIAR* (1990) 18.

[288]Agnes Spycket, "Ex-voto mésopotamiens du iie millénaire av. J.-
C.," in O. Tunca, ed., *De la Babylonie à la Syrie en passant par Mari:
Melanges offerts à Monsieur J.-R. Kupper à l'occasion de son 70e
anniversaire* (Liège, 1990) 79-86.

[289]E. A. Braun-Holzinger, "Terrakotte eines knieenden Mannes aus
Isin," *IB* II, 62-65.

[290]E. A. Braun-Holzinger, "Terrakotte," 65.

[291]The basic report is that of J. Boessneck, "Die Hundeskelette von
Išān Baḥrīyāt Isin) aus der Zeit um 1000 v. Chr.," in *IB* I, 97-109.

apla-iddina.[292] Slightly less than half of the dogs (15) were puppies, and 9 were full adults. The precise function of these dogs while they were alive is very difficult to interpret, especially in light of the significant number of fractures found in the dogs. Since most of the fractures had healed well, Boessneck concludes that such fractures did not lead to the immediate death of the dogs.[293] The injuries were usually sustained in the limbs of the dogs, and the ages of the injured dogs range from 6-8 months (Nr. 33) to a full adult (Nr. 18). One young adult dog also had signs of "rickets" on the radii.

Boessneck's hypothesis is that the dead dogs may be associated with healing rituals. Although Boessneck does not adduce evidence for this belief, the existence of incantations which mention the death of dogs that bite men (see below) may be consistent with his hypothesis. However, there is also another possibility that also has some textual support. In *LKA* 20 a suppliant is punished by Gula because, among other infractions, he did not help dogs in need. In particular, the patient apparently saw a dead dog but "did not bury (it)" (l. 12: *la iq-bir-ma*).[294] It may, therefore, be suggested that the dead dogs buried in the area of the ramp leading to the temple of G/N were sick, and/or abused dogs which were interred near a structure leading to the known patroness of dogs--G/N.

---

[292]*IB* I, 17ff.

[293]*IB* I, 102: *"nicht unmittelbar zum Tode führten."*

[294]Following K. van der Toorn (*Sin and Sanction*, 26). As it appears in Ebeling's copy of *LKA* 20:12, the sign translated as "did not" (*la*) may have two horizontal strokes in the far left, and if so, it may be read as *at*. Since the preceding extant portions of the text recount a series of acts which neglect dogs in trouble, van der Toorn's reconstruction is plausible, though by no means certain on the basis of the copy.

In view of Gula's love of dogs, and her concern with preventing harm to the animals reflected in *LKA* 20, one can safely eliminate any thought of ritual abuse. The skeletal material does not show any evidence of systematic sacrifice. If all of the dogs were sacred animals which were taken care of by the G/N temple establishment, then one would not expect the significant number of injured or sick dogs in the burials. In view of the mixture of healthy and injured animals, and of injured animals of varying ages, one may also suggest that the temple of G/N may have taken care of a variety of dogs in the city, rather than just the injured ones or sacred ones. This may also explain why her temple is called the "Dog house" (*é-ur-gi₇-ra*) in inscriptions as early as the reign of Enlil-bani (19th c. B.C.E.).[295]

Unlike the Asclepieion, unequivocal textual evidence for the use of the temple of G/N for short-term rituals is very limited. Perhaps the strongest evidence thus far is *The Story of the Bitten Man from Nippur*. The text, perhaps composed about 1200 B.C.E.,[296] speaks of a certain Ninurta-sagentarbi-zaemen,[297] a resident of Nippur who was bitten by a dog. He went to Isin where Amel-bau, "the šangû of Gula, examined him, recited an incantation over him, and

---

[295]See A. Livingstone, "The Isin 'Dog House' Revisited," *JCS* 40 (1, 1988) 54-60.

[296]E. Reiner, "Why Do You Cuss Me?" *Proceedings of the American Philosophical Society* 130 (1, 1986) 1; Akkadian text (W 23558) represents that in A. Cavigneaux, "Texte und Fragmente aus Warka," *BaM* 10 (1979) 115.

[297]The precise transliteration of the name is ᵈ*Nin-urta-sag-èn-tar-bi-za-e-me-en.* For a discussion of the name, see W. G. Lambert, *JCS* 11:12f.

healed him."[298] Unless the story has abbreviated the length of the healer's procedures, the healing ritual seems to have been short, and remuneration was promised by the suppliant. The attempt by the priest to collect the promised remuneration complicates the plot of the story.

To what extent may we use the text to determine the therapeutic activities of the temple of G/N at Isin? One should begin by noting that the injury is not a usual illness. As we have seen, dogs could be viewed as negative omens, especially if the dog performed some negative activity on a man (e.g., urination). In such a case, a namburbi ritual could be performed.[299] The idea of the biting dog as a punitive action by Gula is attested in *RTA* 71. With these facts in mind, seeking the help of the temple of G/N would not be unexpected in the case of a bite from a dog.

There are a number of rituals known to have been performed in case of a dog bite. One OB example reads, in part, as follows:[300]

> *e-ma iš-šu-k[u m]e-ra-nam i-zi-ib*
> *ú-su-úḫ ša-ar-k[a]-am*
> *ša pa-ni-š[u]*
> *ù bu-ul-ḫi-ta-am*
> *ša ša-ap-ti-šu*
> *ka-al-bu-um li-mu-[ú-ut]*
> *a-we-lum li-ib-luṭ*

---

[298] A. Cavigneaux, "Texte und Fragmente aus Warka," *BaM* 10 (1979) 115, line 5: LÚ SANGA ᵈME.ME *imur*(IGI)-*šú-ma* ÉN ŠUB-*sú-ma ú-bal-liṭ-su.*

[299] See R. Caplice, "Namburbi Texts in the British Museum II," *Or* 36 (1967) 1-8

[300] Text no. 4 in O. R. Gurney, *Literary and Miscellaneous Texts in the Ashmolean Museum* (Oxford:Clarendon, 1989) 22, lines 7-13.

Where it bit, it left a pup. Remove the wound
of his face and the blister of his lips.
May the dog die, (but) the man should live.

The reference to the puppies left by the dog's bite probably
reflects the belief that the rabid dog carried semen in his
mouth that could produce progeny when it was left in the
wound of the bitten man. This belief is more explicit in an
OB text published by M. Sigrist which reads:

i-na ši-in-ni-šu
e- ʾi-il ni-il-šu
a-šar iš-šu-ku
ma-ra-šu e-zi-ib

In his teeth
he hangs his semen;
Wherever he bites,
he leaves his offspring. [301]

The belief that the saliva of the dog was semen may have
been due to the similar appearance of semen and the white
thick sputum of a rabid dog.

Thus, *The Story of the Bitten Man from Nippur*
raises the question: Did Ninurta-sagentarbi-zaemen go to the
temple of G/N because he needed healing, regardless of the
cause? That is to say, was the dog bite simply one of many
illnesses that might prompt this patient to go to the temple of
Gula? Or did Ninurta-sagentarbi-zaemen go to the temple of

---

[301]M. Sigrist, "On the Bite of a Dog," in J. H. Marks and R. M.
Good, *Love and Death in the Ancient Near East: Essays in Honor of
Marvin H. Pope* (Guilford, Conn.:Four Quarters, 1987) 86.

Gula because it specialized only in healing from a dog bite? In favor of the seeking of non-specialized healing is the fact that the text speaks simply of healing (*a-na bu-tal-lu-ṭi-šú*). The text also uses language about the procedures of the *šangû* which is commonly used by the normal healing consultants in a variety of illnesses (e.g., IGI-*šú*),[302] and he uses an incantation (ÉN), which is a normal treatment for a variety of illnesses. So although the temple of Gula may have been consulted in a variety of illnesses, the connection between G/N and dogs perhaps was so well known that a bitten man who consulted a temple would most likely consult the temple of G/N.

So unless the *The Story of the Bitten Man from Nippur* is telescoping a lengthy procedure, the latter does provide some tentative evidence that short-term rituals, at least in the case of dog bites, were performed at the temple of G/N.[303] However, if one looks at the evidence cumulatively (the figurines, *CT* 39, 38 r 8, etc.), then one

---

[302]R. Labat, (*La médicin babylonienne* [Paris:Université de Paris, 1953] 8) views *amārum* as analogous to a clinical examination.

[303]The story also raises a number of literary issues which can only be mentioned briefly. One is the reason for the trip to the Gula temple at Isin when Nippur, the home of the bitten man, also appears to have had a Gula temple. Was the latter not active during the period of the story, or was the Isin temple more renowned? Not to be excluded is the possibility of inter-city satire as the motive for the tale. In the *Poor Man of Nippur* it is a healer from Isin (more precisely, a Nippurian disguised as a healer from Isin) who mistreats a citizen of Nippur, and in *The Story of the Bitten man of Nippur* it is a healer-priest from Isin who is mistreated at Nippur. In both stories the medicine of Isin seems to be praised. But if there was an active Gula temple at Nippur at the time of the composition of the story, could a pro-Isin writer be implying that Nippurian medicine was not as worthy as that of Isin, or do the stories reflect the actual reputation of Isin?

may say that short-term healing rituals may also have been conducted for other illnesses at the temple of G/N at Isin.

c) Thanksgiving function

Some votive inscriptions strongly suggest that the temple of G/N had a thanksgiving function during the Kassite, Isin II and post Isin II periods. One Middle Babylonian example (*IB* I, E8), found inscribed on a dog figurine in the temple of G/N, manifests this clearly:[304]

1. [a-n]a ^{d}gu-la GASAN? é-g[a]l-m[a]ḫ
2. be-le-et ba-[la-ṭ]ì
3. a-z[u-g]al-la-at x(x) x ti
4. qa-i-ša-at na-ap-ša-at ba-la-ṭì
5. be-el-ti-i-šu
6. ì-lí-x-x-da-a-ya
7. [i]k-ru-um-ma ik-ri-bi-i-šu iš-m[e]
8. [x]x a-ta-na-aḫ-AN ÌR TUR X [(x)]
9. kalba(UR.GI₇) ú-še-li

For Gula, mistress of the Egalmah,
Mistress of life, the great physician...,
Bestower of the breath of life, his mistress,
Ili...daya prayed, and she heard his petition.
[..].. Atanah-ili ...(this) dog I offered.

304E. O. Edzard and C. Wilcke, "Vorläufiger Bericht über die Inschriftenfunde 1973-1974," *IB* I, 90.

The inscription, and particularly the G preterit of *šemû* in line 7, indicates that the temple had a thanksgiving function, and that the dog figurines were used as offerings of thanksgiving for answered prayers (presumably for healing). The prayer here is called an *ikribu*, which can denote a special type of prayer according to Starr.[305]

Other more general offerings and feasts, though not necessarily for thanksgiving after a healing, were also provided for G/N. For example, a text (*VAT* 10138), which is unfortunately incomplete, of the Neo-Assyrian period mentions the *qarītu*-offering.[306] This type of offering is attested in various locales, and in this particular case appears to be brought by an ordinary devotee.[307] According to Menzel, this form of the offering varied according to the deity or city.[308] The text, however, is significant in that it shows the interaction between the devotee and the *šangû* in the temple of G/N.

Insofar as our purpose is concerned, one may say that, based on the presence of figurines of kneeling people, body parts, and other indirect evidence, the temple of G/N had a thanksgiving and/or petitionary function at least in

---

[305]Starr, (*The Rituals of the Diviner*, 44ff), suggests that an *ikribu* is a prayer-cum-ritual. If this is so, then the patient may have participated in a healing ritual.

[306]The cuneiform text is provided by E. Ebeling, *PKTA* 21; B. Menzel (*Assyrische Tempel, Text 48; 1:T 104-T105*) has provided the first transliteration and notes based on a new collation by S. Parpola. No modern language translation of the text has been published to my knowledge.

[307]For further details on the type of offering, see B. Menzel, *Assyrische Tempel*, I:21-23.

[308]B. Menzel, *Assyrische Tempel*, I, 21: "*Doch mag dies von Gottheit zu Gottheit und/oder Stadt zu Stadt variiert haben.*"

Kassite times, and the temple of G/N in Assur held *qarītu* feasts at least in Neo-Assyrian times.

d) The temple of G/N as a resource for healing consultants

The best textual evidence available suggests that the temple of G/N functioned as a resource center for healing consultants. More specifically, the temple of G/N was a library and an educational center for the healing professions. To understand the value of such a centralized source of information one need only look again at the logistics of rituals. For example, speaking of one apotropaic ritual (*LABS* 240 = *ABL* 23) against all types of evil (l. 14: NAM.BUR.BI H̬[UL.DÙ.A.BI]), an *āšipu* says: "I will search for, collect, and copy numerous-(that is,) 20 or 30-canonical and non-canonical tablets" (lines 23-27: *ú-ma-a re-eš tup-pa-a-ni ma-a'-du-ti lu 20 lu 30* SIG5.MEŠ *a-ḫi-ú-ti ú-ba-'a a-na-áš-ši-a a-ša-ṭar*). If one multiplies this ritual by the large numbers of other rituals for healing, witchcraft, etc. that may have been undertaken in a short period of time, one begins to understand the need for a centralized system of information storage, retrieval and reproduction.

The use of the temple of G/N to store medical information is reflected in a medical text which speaks of copying medical texts which are in the temple of Gula.[309] Another medical text speaks of an item that is "recorded and collated from a wooden tablet with prescriptions from the

---

[309]*BAM* 131: rev. 10: TA GIŠ.ZU *sa bul-ṭi ša* É ^dME.ME *šà-ṭir.* *BAM* 131 (= VAT 13775) belongs to the library of Kisir-Assur, an *āšipu* who was active about 658 B.C.E. The text is mentioned under the reference N4:601 in O. Pedersén, *Archives and Libraries in the City of Assur,* II: 46. The date of the original may be considerably older.

temple of Gula, (which was) retrieved urgently."[310] The latter portion of the passage may suggest a medical emergency. As we have mentioned the colophon of an omen text concerning a sick individual (*STT* 73) says that it was copied from an original in the temple of G/N named *Esabad* (GABA.RI É-*sa-bad šà-ṭar*).[311] Though most are still unpublished, incantation tablets have been found in the Gula temple building at Isin.[312] Thus, it appears that the temple of G/N did function as a library which was used to keep prescriptions and ritual texts used by the healers. Unlike the stele at the Asclepius temple in Epidauros, however, the tablets apparently were not meant for public consumption, but only for the use of technicians.

As we have mentioned, *LABS* 293 apparently suggests that a basket was taken from the temple of G/N in at least one case involving an impending birth. In this case it was also apparently the healing consultant(s) who actually were responsible for bringing the basket from the temple.

As a resource center the temple of G/N may have focused not on providing an infirmary to the community's patients, but on supporting endeavours connected with the healing professions. In its primary role as a storage and

---

[310]*BAM* 201 rev. 44'-45': TA ŠÀ GIŠ.ZU *šá bul-ṭi ša* É ᵈME.ME SAR È *ha-an-ṭiš na-às-ḫa. BAM* 201 (= *VAT* 13787) also belongs to the library of Kisir-Assur, and may have been copied when he was a student, on which subject see Pedersén, *Archives and Libraries in the City of Assur*, II: 45 (reference under N4:492). The date of the original may be considerably older.

[311]Reiner, "Fortune Telling..." *JNES* 19 (1960) 35. On É.SA.BAD, see E. Ritter, "Magical Expert...," *AS* 16:312 n. 18.

[312]A preliminary report is provided in C. Wilcke, "Bericht über die in der 8. Ausgrabungskampagne Isin-Ishān Baḥrīyāt gefundenen Inschriften," *Sumer* 45 (1-2, 1987-88) 17.

distribution center for medical information, the temple of G/N distributed medical knowledge directly to the healing consultant rather than directly to the ultimate consumer (i.e., the patient). The temple of G/N interposed a bureaucracy between the primary commodity of the deity (health) and the ultimate consumer of that commodity (i.e., the patient). The Asclepieion, in contrast, was usually seen as a direct dispenser of the primary commodity of the god (health) to the ultimate consumer (i.e., the patient). The temple of G/N, therefore, continues a Mesopotamian tradition of using temples as bureaucratic centers.

e) The relationship of the temple to the consultants

The healing consultants who invoked G/N were not always bound to the temple of G/N, and this marks a major difference from the Asclepius temple consultants. Most Mesopotamian consultants were apparently freelancers and expected to go to the patient's home as a matter of routine. The healing rituals were complicated, and, for this reason, few of these rituals could be carried out by the patient himself.

Various texts attest that the king had his own exorcists. For example, in a colophon to a tablet of the Middle Assyrian period one finds mentions of "Rišeya, the exorcist of the king" (^{I}Ri-*še-y[a]* $^{[I]ú}$MAŠ.MAŠ *šarri*).[313] As Parpola has noted, Esarhaddon and other Neo-Assyrian kings, had their own *āšipu*s and *asû*s.[314] Judging by the occurrence of the *āšipu* before the *asû* in joint letters (e.g.,

---

[313]VAT 10035 as cited in O. Pedersén, *Archives and Libraries in the City of Assur*, I: 30.
[314]Parpola, *LAS* II, pp. XVI-XIX.

LA BS 297) to the king in the Neo-Assyrian period, Parpola also surmises that the *āšipu* had a higher status than the *asû* in that period.[315]

As noted by Ritter, it is the invocations of the *asû* (in contrast to the *āšipu*) which mention G/N most often.[316] This may suggest that G/N may have been the predominant patron of the *asû*. The patronization is also suggested by the letters of the king's *asû* which almost always mention G/N in the salutation, while those of the *āšipu* rarely do so. For example, among the letters collected in *LA BS* which are ascribed to *asû*s (some 20), numbers 315, 316, 318, 319, 320, 321 322, 324, 329, 333, and 334 mention Gula (and Ninurta). Usually Gula and Ninurta are the only deities mentioned in the salutation. In contrast, of the letters from the *āšipu*s (at least 128), only 227, 228, 240, 254, 286, 293, 296, and 297 mention the goddess, and usually in the latter portion of a long list of gods in which Ea, Marduk (Asalluhi) and Nabu feature prominently.[317] Although such a survey is not scientific, it is consistent with the view that Gula was primarily a patron of the *asû*,[318] while Ea, Marduk, and Nabu were primary patrons of the *āšipu*.

There is evidence that healing consultants were dependent on the king for the supply of medicinal materials. For example in a letter from Nippur of the Kassite period, the consultant (an *asû* ?) says: "As to the herbs about which

---

[315]Parpola, *LAS* II, p. XVI.

[316]Ritter, "Magical Expert...," *A S* 16:315.

[317]Instances where deities occur in reconstructed passages have not been counted, but they would not affect the relative proportions outlined even if they were.

[318]A. L. Oppenheim (*Ancient Mesopotamia*, 304-5) states: "Gula...has no function as a patron deity," but he does not offer any reasons for his conclusion.

I spoke to the king, my lord will not forget (them)."[319] This
request is followed by over a dozen ingredients. The same
letter complains that another medication was lacking for a
bandage, and the consultant made the request from the
gardener through the mayor.[320] One can see that the
consultant was not always self-sufficient in his supply of
medicines or medical tablets, and he depended on other
bureaucracies for support.[321] This again is a reflection of
the labor requirements of the healing professions (e.g.,
growing herbs and preparing them for medicinal purposes
required different labors and professions).

D. SYNTHESIS

We are now ready to provide a brief history and
summary of the theology of G/N and the function of her
temple. We begin by noting that G/N was a healing goddess
from the earliest known attestations. Her original home is
uncertain, but the earliest attestations are mostly in southern
Babylonia. In view of the antiquity of the temple of G/N at
Isin, the latter may have well been one of her earliest homes.

It is clear that G/N is not the only deity who could
heal, but the total number of gods who specialized in healing
within the Mesopotamian pantheon was quite limited. Gods

---

[319]*PBS* I/2, No. 72:30-31: *aš-šum šammi*(Ú.ḪI.A) *ša be-lí-ya aq-bu-
u be-lí la i-ma-aš-ši.* The text is from a new publication of the letter in
Parpola, *LAS* II, p. 496.

[320]*PBS* I/2, No. 72:16-17: *ḫa-za-an-na ki e-ri-šu-x* [...] *ana*
LÚ.N[U.GI]Š.SAR *ki iš-ta-pa-ru.*

[321]The same seems to be the case in Mari, on which see Finet, "Les
médecins au royaume de Mari," 135-37; See also W. Farber, "Drogerien
in Babylonien und Assyrien," *Iraq* 39 (1977) 223-228.

such as Ea and Marduk were depicted primarily as *āšipu*s, while G/N and Damu were depicted primarily as *asû*s. Just as in the human sphere, the gods apparently were divided into *āšipu*s (e.g., Ea and Marduk) and *asû*s (e.g., Gula and Damu). G/N was never able to replace totally other healing gods such as Marduk, and many healing rituals mention other gods alongside of her in incantations dealing with illnesses.

It is not clear why Marduk was associated primarily with the *āšipu*. Such links are undoubtedly complex, and beyond our scope. In the case of Gula, we can only speculate that Gula was originally associated with birth and midwifery, activities which can involve herbs and other types of remedies, and then the link progressed to more general types of healing.

It is still not clear how G/N extended her domain from one city to a wide number of cities. Perhaps the key is the *asû*. As in the case of Asclepius, the cult of G/N may have been spread by the profession that was patronized. The patronization of G/N by the *asû* is probably very old. The profession was active as early as 2500 B.C.[322] As exemplified in Ninisina's encouragement of Damu to practice the craft of the *asû* (SRT 6//7), the special relationship of G/N with the *asû* was already well established by the OB period. This relationship is also corroborated by the numerous invocations of G/N by *asû*s upon the application of *materia medica*, and by G/N's ancient epithet, *azugallatu*. We have cited additional tentative evidence in the larger frequency of references to G/N in Neo-Assyrian letters

---

[322]See R. D. Biggs, "Babylonien," in H. Schipperges et al, *Krankheit, Heilkunst, Heilung* (Freiburg: Munchen, 1978) 105; *idem*, "Medizin, A. In Mesopotamien," *RLA* 7 (7.8.) 623-630.

written by *asûs* compared to those written by the *āšipu*s. Her best known hymn (*Bulluṭsu-rabi*) also elaborates her characteristics as an *asû*, while identification with other professions seems to be secondary.

Even if it is not abundant, the evidence discussed indicates that the temple exercised the three main functions that we have outlined for healing temples (petitionary, therapeutic, and thanksgiving). We have evidence that signs concerning health were sought in the temple of G/N. There is evidence for the use of the temple of G/N in short-term rituals, at least in the case of dog bites. The use of the temple for short-term healing rituals in other types of illnesses may be reflected in figurines and omen texts, among other sources. One finds direct evidence of the thanksgiving function in inscriptions and votive figurines.

But the best attested function was as a place to store and retrieve information about medical matters. We have attempted to show how the complexity of the Mesopotamian theology required experts, and the copying of the appropriate tablets is well attested. The centralization of a large quantity of information may have been especially useful to those consultants who could not afford to have archives of their own. In essence, the temple of G/N may have been not only a library, but a sort of medical school. The educational function is attested in various scribal exercise texts found in the temple of G/N. In addition, the temple of G/N may have provided a place to store and retrieve paraphernalia in the medical trade.

The function of the temple of G/N as a resource center for the healing arts may reach back to the third millennium.[323] During the Kassite period the temple of G/N at Isin may have been the beneficiary of a renewed building program by Kassite rulers. Although royal sponsorship of physicians is known from the Mari period and earlier, Kassite rulers may have sought to increase efficiency of the health care system as part of a movement to centralize or simplify a variety of other aspects of Mesopotamian society (e.g, the calendar, the provincial system).[324] It was during the Kassite period that, according to Brinkman, "Babylonian medicine achieved a high reputation, and the skills of Babylonian physicians were in demand at home and abroad."[325] The excavations of the temple of Gula at Nippur may illuminate the extent of the use of the temple of Gula as a resource center for medical consultants in other periods as well.

In 1977 W. Farber's survey of the distribution of medicines in Mesopotamia concluded that the responsibility for medical ingredients was a sort of monopoly subject to the state or temple bureaucracy.[326] The evidence that we have discussed permits us to suggest that it was the temple of G/N which was assigned a key role in the centralization and distribution not just of "medical ingredients" but also of a wide range of goods (e.g., texts, education, paraphernalia) pertaining to the healing arts.

---

[323] As M. Civil ("Prescriptions médicales sumériennes," *RA* 54 [1960] 57-72) notes, the practice of collecting medical prescriptions is recorded already by the Ur III period.

[324] See J. A. Brinkman, "Kassiten," *RLA* 5, 467-68.

[325] J. A. Brinkman, "Kassiten," *RLA* 5, 468.

[326] W. Farber, "Drogieren in Babylonien und Assyrien," *Iraq* 39 (1977) 227: "*Man könnte fast den Eindruck bekommen, dass die Versorgung mit medizinischen Ingredienzien einer Art Monopol der staatlichen oder Tempelverwaltung unterlag.*"

Althought the temple of G/N had a long history at Isin, the improvements made to that temple in the Kassite period may have been a part of a more general program to increase the efficiency of a number of aspects of Mesopotamian life. One cannot claim that the Kassites paid any more attention to the temple of G/N than they did to most other temples. Despite the increase in strife during the Isin II period, various kings of the period, and by the time of Adad-apla-iddina in particular, continued to support the temple of G/N at Isin. By the first millennium the use of the G/N temple as a resource center may have been well established in Assyrian capitals, and one can cite the medical establishment at Assur as a good example.

A wide-ranging investigation of the archaeological remains and written sources suggests strongly that the temple of G/N at Isin did not function as a large-scale infirmary. As has been mentioned, even when one finds a rare reference to a visit to a temple in the case of an illness, it is sometimes G/N who is said to lead the patient to the temple of another god. At first sight, it is surprising that the temple of G/N, as the home of a healing deity, did not become a large-scale healing center which housed patients for overnight or longer periods. Indeed, the data available at present suggest that the center of therapeutic rituals was primarily the home. The river and other non-temple loci were also utilized in such rituals.

The non-use of the temple of G/N as a large-scale infirmary, *à la* the Asclepieion, can also be understood very well in view of the following components of the Mesopotamian socio-religious conceptual framework:

1. A medical theology which tends toward the realist pole in its view of illness etiology, prognosis and the use of illness

as a divine instrument. Mesopotamia had a medical theology in which the large variety of possible "senders/ controllers" of an illness were the key to therapy. Thus, regardless of the existence of a healing deity, ultimate relief was centered in contacting and entreating the correct "sender/controller" of an illness, and not only the healing deity. This is the reason why assigning the correct *qāt DN* was a crucial step in the healing process. This being the case, no healing deity and her/his temple could become the only center of magical healing. The more persistent or serious the disease the larger the number of alternative gods, rituals, magical loci that were used (maximalist strategy), especially if the patient had the resources to do so.

Moreover, G/N was often an intermediary deity herself. Even if her temple was deemed as a place to make petitions, it was obviously also important for the patient to go to the temples of the gods which G/N was to entreat. As a divine *asû*, G/N often worked in concert with the divine *āšipu*s (e.g., Ea and Marduk), and so the temples of the latter would also be important if the patient wished to maximize his/her options. These factors, therefore, help to explain why any movement towards the centralization of healing in the G/N cult never reached the success of the Asclepius cult.

2. A conceptual framework that allowed G/N a virtually universal range of efficacy. However important her temples were, G/N's efficacy was not viewed as confined to a single locus. In fact, medical consultants, as a matter of course, prayed to G/N at many non-temple locations. G/N could be seen directly in the sky as a constellation over the entire northern hemisphere, and so rituals could be performed "before her" at many locations outside of the temple. The

relationship between efficacy and proximity to the temple of G/N was never the issue that it was in the Asclepius cult.

3. A theology in which illness was regarded not only as an attack on a person, but as an attack on the entire household. As such, the home was a most natural place to expel the agents causing illness, and rituals at the temple locus could only be part of the solution at best.

4. A geographical situation in which the main waterways were experienced as dominant transporters of evil or impurity into the abyss, something that also logically deprived the temple of being the only center of magical healing.

5. A theology that regarded many illnesses as generators of impurity, and/or as stemming from sin. Persons with physical flaws were not always welcome in the cultic activities of the temple. Patients, especially those with persistent or other repugnant diseases (e.g., *saḫaršubbû*), probably preferred to remain at home rather than be exposed to ridicule or other criticisms.

6. A long tradition that regarded the temples as bureaucratic centers which were involved in land transactions and the management of a variety of commodities which were not always ostensibly related to the primary characteristics of the resident deity. If there was an effort to distribute to the public the commodity most closely related to the resident deity, the temple seems to have been predisposed to do so in a manner consistent with its bureaucratic and administrative

traditions.[327] Many temples probably sponsored scholarly activity,[328] and, since G/N was a healing deity, the use of her temple as a library or resource center for the medical bureaucracy (rather than as a locus of healing for the public at large) was quite consistent with the bureaucratic traditions of temples and with the primary commodity of its resident deity.

Despite the population loss of the large urban centers during the course of the late 2nd millennium, many administrative institutions remained rooted within the city. As a bureaucratic center, the temple's was understood to have its prime function within the large urban centers, not in distant places (cf. Asclepieia). In light of this fact, there was no need to house a large number of patients if most of these lived nearby. Except, for short-term rituals, therefore, most long-term care was efficiently managed in the home.

7. A long tradition in which the kinship or household group were responsible for health care, especially in the long-term. Such home-care was not simply a family preference; but it could also be legally mandated. The household, not the state, was apparently the institution favored by the patient and suggested by the state itself in some of its laws. However, healing consultants may have been obligated by the state to perform public service at least within the Neo-Assyrian period. In this manner, the state probably affected the availability and distribution of consultants in certain periods.

---

[327]On the long tradition of temples as administrative centers, see essays in E. Lipinski, ed., *State and Temple Economy in the Ancient Near East* (2 volumes; Leuven: Departement Oriëntalistiek, 1979).

[328]E. Sollberger, "The Temple in Babylonia," in *Le Temple et le Culte* (XXth Recontre assyriologique internationale; Nederlands Historisch-Archeologisch Institut, 3-7 July, 1972; Leiden, 1975) 34.

This study shows that there is much to learn about G/N. This analysis may be distorted by the relative lack of texts which would attest to the use of the temple of G/N as a predominant locus for long-term healing rituals. The excavations at Nippur, when they are fully published, may confirm or overturn many of the conclusions, tentative as they are.

Although the temple in Mesopotamia had an important role in the health care system, Mesopotamian cities bore less responsibility than Greek city-states in funding and maintaining therapeutic loci. The Mesopotamian state(s) sponsored short term petitionary and therapeutic loci (at least in the case of dog bites); the Mesopotamian state(s) sponsored thanksgiving loci for former patients, and resource centers for health care consultants. The Mesopotamian state(s) also propounded laws concerning prices for health care and provided protection against malpractice. But unlike Greece, Mesopotamia had laws by which the state reinforced the social custom that households were responsible for the care of their sick members, especially in the long-term. More importantly, the Mesopotamian state(s) did not sponsor an institution which could house the ill for long-term care. We shall provide further comparative observations concerning state reponsibility and illness etiology and prognosis in our final synthesis.

SYNOPSIS OF THE MESOPOTAMIAN HEALTH CARE SYSTEM
(hypothetical model of selected features set in the late Kassite period)

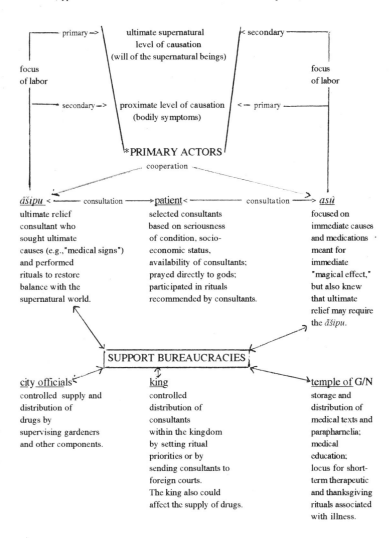

primary → | ultimate supernatural level of causation (will of the supernatural beings) | ← secondary

focus of labor

focus of labor

secondary → | proximate level of causation (bodily symptoms) | ← primary

*PRIMARY ACTORS

cooperation

āšipu ← ——— consultation ——→ patient ← ——— consultation ——→ *asû*

| ultimate relief consultant who sought ultimate causes (e.g.,"medical signs") and performed rituals to restore balance with the supernatural world. | selected consultants based on seriousness of condition, socio-economic status, availability of consultants; prayed directly to gods; participated in rituals recommended by consultants. | focused on immediate causes and medications meant for immediate "magical effect," but also knew that ultimate relief may require the *āšipu*. |

SUPPORT BUREAUCRACIES

city officials

| controlled supply and distribution of drugs by supervising gardeners and other components. |

king

| controlled distribution of consultants within the kingdom by setting ritual priorities or by sending consultants to foreign courts. The king also could affect the supply of drugs. |

temple of G/N

| storage and distribution of medical texts and parapharnelia; medical education; locus for short-term therapeutic and thanksgiving rituals associated with illness. |

*The *bārû*, *šā 'ilu*, and other diviners may also be consulted, particularly for diagnosis and prognosis.

CHAPTER III

ISRAEL
The Temple(s) of Yahweh

A. INTRODUCTION

1. General purpose

The foregoing chapters have demonstrated how different socio-religious conceptual frameworks produced and interacted with the role of the temple in different systems of health care. The role of the temple in Greece and in Mesopotamia was related to a complex of factors that have to be examined as a system. As should be apparent by now, we are using the temple and its roles as instruments to study wider questions regarding illness and health care systems.[1] Since new insights come not only from the accumulation of new data, but also from new ways of viewing data that

---

[1] On the methodology of the study of the social history of ancient Israel, see R. E. Clement, ed., *The World of Ancient Israel: Sociological, Anthropological and Political Perspectives* (New York: Cambridge, 1991); G. A. Herion, "The Impact of Modern and Social Science Assumptions on the Reconstruction of Israelite History," *JSOT* 34 (1986) 3-33; A. H. Mayes, *The Old Testament in Sociological Perspective* (London: Marshall Pickering, 1989).

already exist, we shall re-view and pose new questions to biblical passages that refer to illness.

As mentioned in our Introduction, we have devised a number of questions concerning health care that hopefully will help to place the role of the temple in better perspective.[2] We have provided a typology to compare illness etiology and prognosis and views concerning the use of illness as a divine instrument. Although these typologies were intended to compare the different cultures in our study, Israel also provides an opportunity to apply them to different traditions within the same culture. We shall explain the particulars of these polarities, and their relevance to the role of the temple, as our chapter progresses.

In order to assess the role of the temple in the health care system of ancient Israel, we shall describe as much as possible that health care system and its complex historical development. While we will focus on the biblical period, our treatment of the role of the temple and the health care system of ancient Israel will also extend briefly into the late Second Temple period. Such a range will not only help us to see the diversity of views concerning the role of the temple in health care, but it will also help us to trace some of the long-term effects of various ideas about health care that were put forth during the biblical period.

---

[2]For studies which discuss various theoretical and mythological aspects of the temple which we shall not treat in detail, see M. V. Fox, *Temple in Society* (Winona Lake: Eisenbrauns, 1988); J. Levenson, "The Temple and the World," *Journal of Religion* 64 (1984) 275-298; *idem, Sinai and Zion* (New York: Harper and Row, 1985); T. G. Madsen, ed., *The Temple in Antiquity* (Provo, Utah: Brigham Young University, 1984).

2.   Sources

a) Hebrew Bible and extra-biblical sources

The Hebrew Bible is a necessary point of departure for discussions concerning the health care system of ancient Israel. This does not suggest, however, that one ought to assume that the Hebrew Bible is an accurate depiction of the health care system of Israel in all the instances where biblical texts discuss or provide clues regarding the subject. Political motivations, literary motifs, and hyperbole, among other features of the Bible, may mislead one about actual socio-historical conditions if not critically examined.

We shall view each text relevant to the health care system in light of its larger literary context. If it is relevant or controversial, we shall provide reasons for assigning a text to a specific period, source, or tradition. Given the number of texts involved, an exhaustive discussion of the reasons for some of the assignments can not always be provided. Nonetheless, we will discuss briefly the chronological and literary implications of F. M. Cross' double-redaction theory for the Deuteronomistic History (DtrH), which is a primary source of data for our study.[3]

Aside from various inscriptions from the Second Temple period, the main corpus of extra-biblical texts that is useful for our study is that from Qumran. Some of the texts

---

[3]*CMHE*, 287ff; see also J. D. Levenson, "Who Inserted the Book of the Torah," *HTR* 68 (1977) 203-233; R. D. Nelson, *The Double Redaction Theory of the Deuteronomistic History* (JSOT Suppl. 18; Sheffield: JSOT, 1981); and S. L. McKenzie, *The Chronicler's Use of the Deuteronomistic History* (HSM 33; Atlanta: Scholars Press, 1983). For a critique of important aspects of the double-redaction approach, see John van Seters, *In Search of History* (New Haven: Yale, 1983).

from Qumran, for example, provide a very specific view of the role of the temple in the health care system. The Temple Scroll, in particular, treats the exclusion of various types of patients from the ideal sanctuary.

b) Comments on paleopathology

Work on paleopathology is not yet at a stage where one can use it to draw precise conclusions regarding the range or incidence of illnesses in ancient Israel. Paleopathological information, however, can provide tangible evidence for the existence of various diseases that may not be mentioned in the biblical texts, or corroborate certain hypotheses regarding the existence or non-existence of illnesses mentioned in the Bible.

B. Arensburg and Y. Rak have discussed what they describe as "Jewish skeletal remains," from the 7th c. B.C.E.[4] They noted that 31.5% of the cases exhibited *cribra orbitalia*. As we mentioned in the previous chapter, the condition (assuming it is not pseudopathological) has been correlated with anemias, some of which may be induced by malaria. Dental and arthritic problems were also noted.

Paleopathology and archaeology have helped to provide some insights into the types of conditions that were likely to have existed, even if their direct attestations are difficult to discover in many instances. Some archaeological remains may also alert us to the types of problems that were likely to afflict ancient populations. For example, some types of water systems in Israel may have been vulnerable to

---

[4]B. Arensburg and Y. Rak, "Jewish Skeletal Remains from the Period of the Kings of Judea," *PEQ* 117 (Jan.-June, 1985) 30-34.

numerous types of bacterial contamination.[5] Sources of contamination may have included human and animal fecal matter. Studies of water supplies in East Africa, some of that are similar in structure and location to those found in ancient Israel, show a great vulnerability to a wide range of diseases such as cholera, amoebiasis, and worm infections.[6]

K. Y. Mumcuoglu and J. Zias have recently published evidence for the existence of ecto-parasites in ancient Israel.[7] The existence of such parasites is not surprising, and it should be noted that some of these produce rashes that might have been classified as "leprosy."

Another type of illness that may reflect a real phenomenon is poisoning by eating quail. Numbers 11:31-34 mentions that a plague struck great numbers after eating quail. The phenomenon, known as coturnism, has been

---

[5]For a recent thorough study of Israelite and ancient Near Eastern water systems, see Y. Shiloh, "Underground Water Systems in Eretz-Israel in the Iron Age," in L. G. Perdue, L. E. Toombs, and G. L. Johnson, eds., *Archaeology and Biblical Interpretation* (Atlanta:John Knox, 1987) 204-244; R. Miller, "The Prehistory of Public Health--Water and Waste in the Ancient Near East," in S. Ball and J. Pickford, eds., *The 7th WEDC Conference: Water People and Waste in Developing Countries* (University of Technology, Dept. of Civil Engineering: Loughborough, 1982) 11ff. E. Neufeld, "Hygiene Conditions in Ancient Israel (Iron Age)," *BA* 34 (2, 1971) 42-66.

[6]G. F. White, D. J. Bradley, and A. U. White, *Drawers of Water:Domestic Water Use in East Africa* (Chicago:U. of Chicago, 1972) especially 151-199. In particular, White et al., provide detailed studies of the incidence of contamination and diseases related to the use of open pools (and wells) that is analogous to the use of open cisterns and pools in ancient Israel. Evidence of parasitic worms in Israel is discussed by J. Cahill, K. Reinhard et al., "It Had to Happen--Scientists Examine Remains of Ancient Bathroom," *BARev* 17 (3, 1991) 64-69.

[7]K. Y. Mumcuoglu and J. Zias, "How the Ancients Deloused Themselves," *BARev* 15 (6, 1989) 66ff.

documented in various locations around the Mediterranean in the 20th century, though the precise causes are not known.[8]

Recent explorations of health have also found relationships between low caloric intake and infertility. Accordingly, the recurrent mention of infertility in biblical texts may be more than a literary motif; infertility may have been a useful motif because it reflected a recurrent and real problem.[9] The recent interest in paleopathology of the ancient Near East shows great promise, and we hope to provide questions that might be asked of such data in the future. The most useful aspect of paleopathology in its present stage is that it alerts us to the difficulty of making facile diagnoses of ancient conditions.

B. THE ISRAELITE HEALTH CARE SYSTEM

1. General comments

As have discussed earlier, a health care system consists of, among other things, the etiology of illness, the consultative options available to the patient, and the attitudes toward the patient in the society. The role of the temple in health care cannot be undersood very well unless we outline the health care system of Israel as far as the data will permit. In particular, we shall outline how the concept of Yahweh,

---

[8]For comments on coturnism in the Bible and in modern times, see L. E. Grivetti, "Coturnism:Poisoning by European Migratory Quail," in E. F. P. Jellife and D. B. Jelliffe, eds., *Adverse Effects of Foods* (New York:Plenum Press, 1982) 51-58.

[9]See M. Cohen, *Health and the Rise of Civilization* (New Haven:Yale, 1989) 71.

views of disease, and various therapeutic options available in ancient Israel interacted with the role of the temple.

a) Yahweh: Preliminary remarks

Our study concentrates on the interrelationship of the theology of Yahweh and the health care system. The main source for the theology of Yahweh is the Hebrew Bible, though we shall mention briefly a few important non-biblical sources concerning the "pre-history" of Yahweh that might be of relevance for the study of illness and health care.

If F. M. Cross is correct, the name *Yahweh* originated as a cultic name of El.[10]   The Hebrew god Yahweh may be viewed as a deity which evolved from the combination of various aspects of the personality and nature of the El and Baal figures known from Canaanite sources.[11] Insofar as our study is concerned, one of the most important features that Yahweh might have inherited from his Canaanite "ancestors" was the concern with healing. El, for example, was a god concerned with healing, especially infertility. In the Ugaritic Kirta Epic one finds a king (Kirta) who is ill.[12] His illness is depicted as a type of demon that must be beaten and expelled. In one episode (*KTU* 1.16 V 25-27), El seeks a divine volunteer to heal Kirta, but he finds none. He finally says:

---

[10]F. M. Cross, *CMHE*, 71.

[11]F. M. Cross, *CMHE*, 147ff.

[12]*KTU* 1.16 II, 22-23 (*ṯlṯ yrḫm km[rṣ]/ arbᶜ kdw k[rt]*) = "For three months he has been ill/ for four (months) Kirta he has been stricken." Ugaritic text is from the edition of G. del Olmo Lete (*Mitos y Leyendas de Canaan* [Madrid:Ediciones Cristiandad, 1981] 313). For further comments on Kirta's illness, see M. Dietrich and O. Loretz, "Kerets Krankheit und Amtsunfähigkeit," *UF* 17 (1986) 123-128.

ank iḫtrš waškn aškn ydt [m]rṣ [13]

I shall recite an incantation, and I shall appoint. I
shall appoint the one who shall expel the illness.

The being appointed is Šatiqatu who enters Kirta's house
and expels Kirta's illness (*KTU* 1.16 VI, 1-14). El also
demonstrates his interests in healing infertility in the same
Epic.

The story prefigures a number of motifs that we shall
encounter in Hebrew literature. One theme is that El certainly
is concerned with healing his devotees, and it is his
prerogative to give the command for healing.[14] Biblically,
this concern may also be reflected in personal names such as
Raphael[15] in 1 Chr 26:7, and in place names such as Irpeel
in Josh 18:27.[16] The Kirta Epic also shows El sending
another being to heal the devotee. Something comparable
occurs in Deut 32:23-24, Job 5:7, and other biblical
passages, which may derive from a tradition that included

---

[13]In G. del Olmo Lete, *Mitos y Leyendas de Canaan* (Madrid:
Ediciones Cristiandad, 1981) 318.

[14]H. Rouillard ("El Rofé en Nb 12, 13," *Semitica* 37 [1987] 16-46)
has recently argued that healing is more properly a feature of El than of
Yahweh. For a discussion of the possible relationship between the
Rephaim and healing, see N. Lohfink, "'Ich bin Jahwe, dein Arzt (Ex
15:26),'" *Stuttgarter Bibelstudien* 100 (1981) 13-73.

[15]Hebrew: רפאל (= El heals). Note that this was the name of the
angel sent by God to heal Tobit in the apocryphal book of the same
name. In I Enoch 40:9 Raphael has domain over all diseases.

[16]Hebrew: ירפאל (= El heals). The reason for the place name, which
appears to be located in Benjamin, is uncertain, and one can only
speculate that it might have been a petitionary locus for illness.

Rešep, a god of plague and healing, among Yahweh's lackeys.[17] It should also be noted that the story does not require that Kirta go to a temple to be healed, for he is healed at home.

Healing is also a part of the mythology of the Divine Warrior traditions that figure prominently in Yahweh's theology. The Divine Warrior's return from victory is marked by the revival of nature, which had been convulsed and "sickened" when he went out to war.[18] Yahweh is also a god of plagues, and as such, he has the power to reverse the plagues that he has sent. Job 5:18 says: "He [Yahweh] causes the wound, and he shall bandage it. He injures, and his hands heal" (כי הוא יכאיב ויחבש ומחץ ידו תרפינה).

The relationship between the Israelite health care system and its religious history was marked by a tension between strict monotheism (i.e., the belief that Yahweh was the only supernatural being that exists) and the belief that Yahweh lived alongside numerous divine beings who could act as his agents in healing (and in sending plagues), or who could act on their own volition, a volition that was sometimes contrary to that of Yahweh. For the most part, we shall concentrate on the effects of a theology that viewed Yahweh as the only "sender/ controller" of an illness, and the only healer as well. In historical terms, we shall concentrate on Yahweh from the stage where he was

---

[17]On Rešep, see W. J. Fulco, *The Canaanite God Rešep* (New Haven: AOS, 1976) especially 56-62.

[18]For a study of the relationship of the Divine Warrior traditions and healing, see L. Greenspoon, "The Origin of the Idea of Resurrection," in B. Halpern and J. D. Levenson, eds., *Traditions in Transformation:Turning Points in Biblical Faith* (Winona Lake, Indiana: Eisenbrauns, 1981) 247-321.

incorporated into a monolatrous theological system, and we shall view the biblical texts as the main representatives of this monolatry. But we shall also explore the effect of a tension between Yahwistic and non-Yahwistic (and polytheistic) consultative options that affected the Israelite health care system.

As did many deities in Mesopotamia and other cultures of the ancient Near East, Yahweh used illness as an instrument. In particular, Yahweh used illness to enforce covenants made with humans. Such covenants promised health and longevity to those who followed Yahweh's stipulations, but illness and death to those who did not. One classic statement of this theology is found in Deut 28:15:

והיה אם לא תשמע בקול יהוה אלהיך
לשמר לעשות את כל מצותיו חקתיו
אשר אנכי מצוך היום ובאו עליך
כל הקללות האלה והשיגוך

> If you do not obey the voice of Yahweh, your god, to observe all his commandments and statutes, which I am commanding you today, then there shall come upon you all the following curses, and they shall overtake you.

Deut 28:22 is explicit in including illness among these curses. These illnesses are described by Hebrew terms translated as "consumption" (שחפת), "fever" (קדחת), and "inflammation" (דלקת) by the RSV. Verse 35 threatens illnesses such as severe "boil(s)" (שחין רע) that cannot be cured (לא תוכל להרפא).

The reverse aspect of these curses for transgressions is that God will bless with health those who follow the stipulations of the covenant (Deut 28:1-13). In particular, this theme is reiterated in speeches and narratives throughout DtrH.

The view that health is related to righteousness (and sickness to unrighteousness) is present in the Mesopotamian model of illness etiology. However, scholars have overlooked the fact that the Deuteronomistic view of the relationship between righteousness and health bears a significant difference. Whereas in Mesopotamia the gods may use illness for a variety of reasons, which may be entirely arbitrary from a human standpoint, Deuteronomy 28 limits the use of illness to the enforcement of covenants. Deuteronomy 28 affirms that illness is not caused by any arbitrary reason that the deity may hide from the patient. Yahweh restricts his use of illness to the enforcement of stipulations that have been fully disclosed to the patient.

We may schematize this difference between Mesopotamia and Deuteronomy 28 (and DtrH, in general) as follows:

THE CAUSES OF ILLNESS

Mesopotamia	Deuteronomy 28
Transgression of	Only transgression
covenants +	of covenants
a myriad of arbitrary	whose stipulations
divine interests (from	are fully disclosed
a human standpoint)	to the patient.
that may not	
always be disclosed	
to the patient.	

The contrast above reveals the tendency of Dtr toward the utopian model of illness etiology and divine instrumentality that we described at the outset. The Mesopotamian model tends toward the realistic pole in the same aspects. However, as we shall show in more detail below, the view of health found in Dtr was not monolithic throughout Israel.

The extent to which illness was regarded as an arbitrary instrument of the gods forms one of the great issues in the medical theologies of the ancient Near East. As we shall see, not all biblical traditions expressed the same opinion on this issue. The tension between the reality and mystery of illness in pre-scientific societies and the explanatory system devised by an ancient society often resulted in a type of cognitive dissonance that made a single viewpoint untenable.

In any case, Deuteronomy and Mesopotamian traditions acknowledge that illness was an instrument of the deity. The view that illness was an instrument of Yahweh is pervasive in biblical texts of different traditions and chronological provenience. Yahweh employs illnesses to subjugate the Egyptians in Exodus 7-10, to punish evildoers in DtrH and in the Chronicler, and to test Job. As in Mesopotamia, therefore, the view that illness is a divine instrument permeated most aspects of the society.

As in the case of Mesopotamia, we shall show that this pervasive assumption had some concrete effects upon the health care system. One of the effects was that patients assumed that transgressions or a poor relationship with Yahweh was the cause of their illness. Under this conceptual system, searching for reconciliation with Yahweh became part of the therapeutic process itself. The petitions and thanksgiving rituals related to illness were permeated by the patient's search for reconciliation with the deity. The search also included a concern for "hidden" sins that might have caused the illness, and this theology interacted with socio-political agendas on various levels of Israelite society.

As mentioned, we shall focus on the impact of monolatry upon the health care system of ancient Israel. This concept had a profound effect on the mode of consultation as well as on the therapeutic system. In a monolatrous conceptual system, Yahweh was the only healing deity that could be consulted, and consulting any other deity was a grave offense. This is succinctly expressed in Exodus 15:26 ("I, Yahweh, am your healer"/אני יהוה רפאך).[19] Yahwism restricted options insofar as non-Yahwistic consultation was not acceptable.

Another significant feature related to monolatry which affected the health care system in some periods is that Yahweh did not specialize in healing to the extent that Asclepius did. Yahweh had to assume many of the functions that had been divided under polytheism. Yahweh's duties ranged from ensuring fertility, to representing the nation, to creating and maintaining the cosmos. As the main god of an *ethnos*, socio-political boundaries were important for Yahweh. The cumulative effect of these characteristics is that, among other things, it led to a dichotomous system of health care, consisting of "legitimate" and "illegitimate" consultative options for the Israelite patient. This dichotomous consultative system is one of the principal distinctions of the Israelite health care system relative to that of Gula and Asclepius.

---

[19]On the exegetical, literary, and theological issues posed by the passage, see J. Hempel, "Ich bin der Herr, dein Arzt (Ex. 15,26)" *ThLZ* 82 (1957) 809-26; and N. Lohfink, "'Ich bin Jahwe, dein Arzt (Ex 15:26),'" *Stuttgarter Bibelstudien* 100 (1981) 13-73.

Yet within the legitimate consultative sphere there was also room for some diversity. As we shall see below, options for healing included prayer, musicians, self-medication, Yahwistic prophets, and the temple in some cases. The temple's main functions (petitionary, therapeutic, and thanksgiving) also evolved as different socio-religious views alternated in dominance. The views of so-called Priestly texts (P), in particular, had far reaching effects which became pronounced in the late Second Temple period.

b) The general concept and terminology of illness

We have attempted to make a distinction between "disease" and "illness" in our study. We use "disease" to refer to modern biomedical classifications of physical and mental abnormalities (e.g., lupus erythematosus). We have reserved the word "illness" to refer to those conditions that an ancient society saw as abnormal. As we shall learn, not all of the illnesses that were identified in Israel have a direct equivalent in a modern classification, and many items that we would call a disease in modern classifications were not deemed to be an "illness" in ancient Israel.

The Bible had various general terms for illness as well as some relatively more specific ones. K. Seybold, among other scholars, has provided extensive study of this terminology,[20] and, except insofar as we relate the terminology to larger socio-religious issues, including the concept of illness itself, we cannot add to the substantial

---

[20]Some of the relevant studies include: "חלה," *TDOT* 4:399-409; *idem*, *Das Gebet des Kranken im Alten Testament* (Stuttgart:W. Kohlhammer) 17-62.

contribution already made in this area. However, it is useful to summarize the results of these inquiries on terminology.

One of the principal words to describe illness in the Hebrew Bible is חלה. However, the original Semitic root is unclear, and so is its original meaning. As Seybold notes, a variety of etymons have been proposed, ranging from *ḥlh/y* (cf. Arabic *ḥly* : "to make bright"), to *ḥlh* (cf. Arabic *ḥala 'a* : "rub, stroke").[21]

The various nouns and verb forms of the word are applied in a wide variety of situations that depict conditions ranging from one that does not appear to be serious (e.g., 1 Sam 19:14) to one that is potentially deadly (e.g., 2 Kgs 1:2f, 2 Kgs 8:7f, Isa 38:9). The word may be applied to conditions where the patient seems more depressed than physically ill (e.g., Neh 2:2). In Jeremiah 12:13 it is applied to someone who is exhausted from labor, though not necessarily suffering from a "disease" in the modern Western sense. The word can also be applied to physical defects in animals that render them unfit for sacrifice (e.g., Mal 1:8). Another word, דוה, is applied to women during their menses (e.g., Lev 12:12 and 15:23), as well as conditions involving psychological distress (Lam 1:22).

Other words emphasized the belief that illness was caused by a "sender/controller." Thus, נגע, which is usually translated as "plague," emphasizes that an illness was sent by God, usually for some transgression (e.g., Exod 11:1, 1 Sam 6:8). More specific illnesses, such as צרעת, could be described with נגע (e.g., Deut 24:8).

In addition to terms that are general descriptions of illness as it affects the whole person, there is a common term that often refers to the localization of pain. For example, one

---

[21]K. Seybold, "חלה," *TDOT* 4:400-401.

finds the term בְּאֵב applied to those suffering pain from circumcision in Gen 34:25 or from extraneous concrete causes such as a thorn (e.g. Ezek 28:24). But the term can also be applied to the general state of physical or mental pain (e.g., Ezek 13:22). Illnesses such as צָרַעַת could also be localized, and yet the whole person was regarded as ill.

The definition of illness in Israel is a complex one, and it involved social as well as physical factors. The terminology and references to illness in the Bible allow one to characterize illness as a condition with visible symptoms that rendered a human being physically and/or mentally unable to fulfill the normal *social and/or physical* role assigned by the society.[22] A normal state, in particular, was one that allowed the person to participate in the temple cult. A normal "healthy" state was one which valued the harmony (שָׁלוֹם) between Yahweh and his people.[23]

The social aspect of the definition of "illness" may be seen in the case of infertility. The illness may be linked to the malfunction of a specific body part (e.g., 1 Sam 1:5) that did not place the person in danger of imminent physical death, but it was the fact that this infertility prevented the woman from fulfilling her role as a mother which was the

---

[22]On illness as an impairment of social roles, see R. N. Wilson, *The Sociology of Health:An Introduction* (New York:Random House, 1970); and F. L. Dunn, "Traditional Asian Medicine and Cosmopolitan Medicine as Adaptive Systems," in C. Leslie, ed., *Asian Medical Systems:A Comparative Study* (Berkeley: U. of California, 1976). Despite the title, the latter study attempts to provide a cross-cultural definition of illness and health that may be applied to ancient and modern systems of health care.

[23]On various social and theological aspects of שָׁלוֹם, see P. D. Hanson, *The People Called:The Growth of Community in the Bible* (San Francisco:Harper and Row, 1986) 3ff.

most important aspect in her assignment to a sick role. Her inability to have children would lead to a sort of "death" for her lineage.

The Israelite idea of "health" is complicated by the fact that the idea interacted with notions of purity and impurity. There could be some skin conditions, for example, that might not pose much of a physical danger to the patient, or that would not render them physically unfit for most tasks. Yet Israelite ideology would view them as "sick" because there was a visible abnormality, which, even if not regarded as physically dangerous by a modern Western physician, was "dangerous" in other ways. For example, a hierocracy might propose that the presence of physically "defective" persons in the temple might bring the wrath of Yahweh upon the nation.[24]

The dividing line between someone who is simply impure and someone who is defined as "ill" in Israelite society is not always easy to discern. One may say that to be categorized as "ill," one had to show visible signs (or symptoms) that were regarded as indicative of a condition that rendered the person unable to execute the roles assigned to them. For example, lack of children, a sad countenance, and a headache (and its accompanying facial gestures) may all qualify as symptoms of an illness in ancient Israel. As we shall discuss in more detail below, impurity, while overlapping with conditions regarded as "illness," was viewed as that aspect of a person (place or thing) that rendered him/her (or it) fit or unfit to participate in the cult. Impurity need not be physically visible, and it can exist even after visible signs of an illness have disappeared. As we

---

[24]For a study of "deformity" as a literary motif in the Bible, see Lyn Holden, *Forms of Deformity* (Sheffield: JSOT, 1991).

shall argue, purity and socio-economic status were intimately linked and interactive.

In summary, illness is any condition that, regardless of physical danger as defined by modern Western medicine, renders a person physically or mentally unfit to execute a social role defined as "normal" by the society at issue, here ancient Israel. Such a definition allows for historical changes because the definition of a "normal role" underwent changes, as did the types of conditions that were regarded as sufficiently abnormal to exclude one from participation in the cult. It should be noted that any non-human entity that could not execute the role assigned to it was also deemed to be sick. This is the reason why the land (cf. 2 Chr 7:14) or a nation could be described as ill.

Accordingly, the general term for healing, רפא,[25] describes the act of restoring someone (or something) to a normal role and physical state in the society. The root is common in West Semitic languages, but not in Akkadian, which principally uses *bulluṭu* as an equivalent. The term is applied to those healed from infertility (e.g., Gen 20:17), to someone who recuperates from a physical assault (e.g., Exod 21:19), as well as to socio-political entities who are not able to fulfill their assigned functions (e.g., Hos 7:1, Ezek 34:14).

We shall provide more detailed discussion below concerning the conditions that were regarded as "illness" in Israelite society, focusing on those illnesses that afflict human individuals as opposed to the nation or the land.

---

[25]For a detailed treatment, see D. Brown, "רפא," *TWAT* 7:618-625.

2. The home as the main locus of therapy

a) Biblical evidence

As in most societies, the home is the first locus of health care for the patient. But in ancient Israel, as in Mesopotamia, it appears that the home was the only or main locus of health care for most of the duration of an illness. A variety of passages attest to the importance of the home as a locus of health care for a range of socio-economic classes.

One glimpse into the health care of the royal family is provided by the story of Amnon and Tamar (2 Sam 13). In this story Amnon has an incestuous ardor for his sister. He apparently made himself sick with his obsession (v. 2: ויצר לאמנון להתחלות בעבור תמר). Amnon had a friend named Jonadab to whom he confided his obsession, and the latter devised a plan to bring Tamar to Amnon. The plan was for Amnon to lie in bed at home and assume a "sick role" (v. 5: שכב על משכבך והתחל).[26]

In addition to any literary motives,[27] the story probably provides a portrayal of the accepted or normal manner in which a patient was treated in such instances. Amnon is placed under the care of a family member, his sister, and she is expected to prepare the food. The plausibility of the scenario is corroborated by the fact that the author does not betray any indication that the practice needs justification for the readers. If servants, for example, were

---

[26]RSV renders the Hithpael second masculine imperative of חלה as "pretend to be ill."

[27]Note, for example, that Michal's scheme involved a bogus illness for David in 1 Sam 19:13ff.

the only caretakers of the royal family in times of illness, one certainly would have expected some justification for depicting a departure from the tradition. The story indicates, therefore, that despite a large group of servants in a royal household, illness was a situation in which family members were expected, or perhaps even obligated, to bring personal care to the sick person.

Another case is found in 2 Sam 12:15-18 where David's child by Bathsheba becomes very ill after being struck by Yahweh. The child appears to be cared for at the palace, while David maintains a vigil that involves fasting and mourning. One also sees a large retinue of consultants attempting to provide moral support for the king. In the case of Hezekiah's illness (2 Kgs 20) it is clear that he remains at home for the duration of his illness. Hezekiah's petition is uttered at home, and the prophet visits the king at this home. In the case of Saul's emotional or mental distress (1 Sam 16:1ff), the musician is brought to the palace to relieve Saul.

But home care also appears to be normal for non-royal personnel. In the story of Saul's pursuit of David (1 Sam 19), for example, Michal attempts to provide an excuse for her husband by informing Saul's lackeys that he was sick in bed (v. 14: חלה הוא). The fact that this was a plausible excuse again indicates the viability of the practice in Israelite society.

The story of the Shunammite woman (2 Kgs 4:8-37) depicts a case involving a family of high status, though non-royal. The socio-economic class of her and her household is indicated in v. 8 where she is called "an important woman" (אשה גדולה). The father had servants at his disposal (v. 19). They apparently owned land and livestock, and earned enough income to improve their home (v. 10). According to v. 19 the child complains of some sort of severe head ailment (רֹאשִׁי רֹאשִׁי) while out in the fields with his father. The father commands that a servant take the boy to his mother (וַיֹּאמֶר אֶל הַנַּעַר שָׂאֵהוּ אֶל אִמּוֹ). It is the mother who selects the next option in deciding to go to the prophet. The option chosen is not a temple or a priest, but a prophet. The mother goes to seek Elisha, and the latter goes to the home of the sick child. The story ends with the short ritual by Elisha which successfully resuscitates the boy.

However, home care was not the accepted procedure for illnesses such as "leprosy."[28] As we shall discuss in more detail below, "lepers" were excluded from the "healthy" community altogether in the medical theology of P, though one cannot claim that this was the case in all periods. Such regulations meant that "lepers" had to formulate new communities and modes of livelihood.

Even a king struck with "leprosy" could be forced to live in a special dwelling. The story of king Uzziah's bout with "leprosy" (2 Chr 26:20-21) ends with the following notice in verse 21:

וַיְהִי עֻזִּיָּהוּ הַמֶּלֶךְ מְצֹרָע עַד יוֹם מוֹתוֹ
וַיֵּשֶׁב בֵּית [29]הַחָפְשִׁית מְצֹרָע כִּי נִגְזַר
מִבֵּית יהוה

So king Uzziah remained a "leper" until the day of his death, and consequently he lived in a "special

---

[28]For reasons which we shall explain in detail below, we shall use "leper" and "leprosy" with quotation marks througout the study to refer to the complex of conditions encompassed by the Hebrew צָרַעַת, and to distinguish the latter from the modern disease known as Hansen's Disease.

[29]Vocalization with the medial yod follows the qerê; the ketîb is הַחָפְשׁוּת.

abode."[30] (Because he was) a "leper, "he was certainly excluded from the temple of Yahweh.[31]

Although, the discussion concerning the meaning of the phrase בית החפשית has not yielded a consensus, the phrase suggests that the king was not able to live in a "normal dwelling or state." Nonetheless, it does not appear that the king was ostracized to the degree that common citizens might be.

b) "Self-medication" in Genesis 30:14-16

Some biblical texts assume that the use of botanical substances by the patient without the aid of a professional

---

[30]Unfortunately, the meaning of בית החפשית. has been the subject of a great debate which has not yielded a consensus. Among the meanings that have been proposed are (1) A house which was reserved for a king released from royal service (e.g., N. Lohfink, "Hopšî," *TWAT* 3 [1982] 125]); (2) A dwelling reserved for members of a stigmatized class (cf., O. Loretz, "Ugaritisch-hebräisch ḤB/PṮ, BT ḤPṮT--HPŠJ BJT ḤḤPŠJ/WT," *UF* 8 [1976] 129-31; (3) A place of impurity (cf., P. Grelot, "Hofšî [Ps LXXXVIII 6]," *VT* 14 [1964] 256-63). Further references and discussion may be found in David P. Wright, *The Disposal of Impurity:The Elimination Rites in the Bible and in Hittite and Mesopotamian Literature* (Atlanta:Scholars Press, 1987) 175 n. 25. Our rendition,"special abode," assumes that it was not a regular house, though more precision cannot be obtained.

[31]Most translators regard the second occurrence of מצרע as a further explication of why Uzziah lived in a בית החפשית, but his life in the special abode is a suitable consequence to the statement that he was a "leper" in the prior clause. We, therefore, regard מצרע as a new statement which is followed by another consequence. This provides two statements with a symmetrical pattern: "illness-consequence/ illness-consequence. A similar use of כי to emphasize result in an apodosis may be found in Isaiah 7:9.

consultant was a legitimate recourse, or at least one which was not denounced. One case is that of the use of "love plants" (דודי) to cure infertility in Genesis 30:14-16, a text usually assigned to J and/or E by traditional source critics.[32] The name of the plant suggests a type of aphrodisiac, though a modern botanical classification is unclear. The effectivity of the plant is not explicit in the text, though it is not denounced. According to the text, Leah gave Rachel these plants in return for the privilege of sleeping with Jacob. When Rachel does conceive, it is said that Yahweh opened her womb in v. 22 (ויפתח את רחמתה). Monolatry does not necessarily affect the legitimacy of natural remedies, and there is no reason why the latter could not have been used as long as the effectivity is ultimately attributed to Yahweh.

Cross-cultural studies by medical anthropologists indicate that the use of natural remedies is a very widespread mode of self-help, regardless of the socio-economic stratum of patients.[33] In modern societies, for example, every household usually has a range of "natural" remedies (e.g., insofar as these may be termed "natural": tea, chicken soup, and lemon juice) that are often selected and applied without the direct consultation of a professional. The "official religion" of ancient Israel may not have objected strongly to the use of *materia medica* when this did not involve "illegitimate consultants." The Wisdom of Solomon 16:12 (ca. 1 c. B.C.E.), however, may represent the existence of another, and perhaps equally ancient, tradition which denies

---

[32]For example, S. R. Driver, *ILOT*, 16; R. E. Friedman, *Who Wrote the Bible?* (New York:Summit, 1987) 248.

[33]For a brief general study, see N. L. Etkin, "Ethnopharmacology: Biology and Behavioral Perspectives in the Study of Indigenous Medicines," in T. M. Johnson and C. E. Sargent, *Medical Anthropology* (New York: Praeger, 1990) 149-158.

that *materia medica* (e.g., herbs) had any healing power at all.

c) Direct prayer

Direct prayer to Yahweh was probably the most frequent therapeutic strategy, especially in the initial stages of an illness. Such direct prayers by the patient may also be viewed as a form of self-help. As we have mentioned in previous chapters, this is the most economical form of consultation. The main deficiency is that direct prayer will usually not be regarded as sufficient to effect a healing.

The biblical texts have some examples of the prayers uttered by the patient. For example, in the narrative of Hezekiah's illness one finds a very short prayer uttered by Hezekiah who turned his head to the wall. The prayer focuses on the plea that Yahweh remember Hezekiah's good deeds (2 Kgs 20:3), though one cannot say that this plea constituted the whole of the prayer.

The Psalms contain various prayers that indicate the behavior of the patient, and also the type of health care that s/he sought.[34] Such psalms may also be classed with the genre of laments. One of these is Psalm 38. That illness is the occasion for the lament is explicit in a number of places within this psalm. The patient speaks of his tormented flesh and bones in v. 4 (אין מתם בבשרי...אין שלום בעצמי), wounds in v. 5 (חברותי), and calls his condition a plague in v. 12 (נגעי).

In Psalm 38 the suppliant describes his condition as one caused by Yahweh's anger against the patient. As in

---

[34]For a detailed literary study of these psalms, see Seybold, *Das Gebet des Kranken im Alten Testament.*

Mesopotamia, the illness is described as a type of *qāt DN* (v. 3: ותנחת עלי ידך). As in many cases of illness in Mesopotamia, the patient attributes the god's anger to the patient's own sin (v. 4: אין שלום בעצמי מפני חטאתי). Confession is regarded as part of the therapy (v. 19: כי עוני אגיד אדאג מחטאתי). As in other psalms which we have discussed, the patient complains about the social consequences of illness. For instance, friends have become distant (v. 11), and enemies view illness as an opportunity to gain advantage over the patient (v. 12).

Psalm 39 is probably also set during an illness. The setting during an illness is indicated by the fact that the suppliant uses vocabulary that is usually linked with illness. In v. 11, for example, the patient says: "Remove from me your plague, put aside your hand, for I am consumed" (הסר מעלי נגעך מתגרת ידך אני בליתי). The suppliant confesses his transgressions (v. 8).

Psalm 88 may also be intended as a prayer during illness. The language speaks of death and being shunned by friends. These concerns are similar to those expressed by the patient in the Mesopotamian poem, *Ludlul bēl nēmeqi*. The suppliant in Psalm 102 speaks of physical suffering in v. 5, and he uses imagery (e.g., the underworld) seen in Hezekiah's psalm. The sufferer argues that, by creating a grateful worshipper, healing is in God's interest (v. 21).

Stereotypes undoubtedly abound in these psalms, and one cannot claim that the psalmist is portraying his illness, or an actual particular patient, with clinical precision. But we may assume that such stereotypes are employed because they depict what the author views as the common experience of the stereotypical patient in ancient Israel.

These prayers indicate that Hebrew and Mesopotamian patients shared a number of features. Both groups of patients frequently assumed that sins, often hidden, are were responsible for the illness. This illness was an instrument of the god. But while in Mesopotamia the search for the "sender/controller" of an illness was a source of great psychological anxiety and involved a sometimes labor-intensive set of rituals, in Israel a monolatrous theological system eliminated the search for a variety of divine "senders/controllers" as a source of anxiety, and divinatory rituals were relatively simple. Although weighty by themselves, the main sources of anxiety that remained for the monolatrous patient (*vis-à-vis* the Mesopotamian situation) were the identification of the specific wrongdoings that led to the god's anger and whether the god would heal the patient. These psalms also constitute evidence that the home, not the temple, was the main center of health care in ancient Israel.

In summary, biblical literature provides a portrayal with no surprises insofar as the main locus of therapy is concerned. As in Mesopotamia, the sick were cared for in the home. As in Mesopotamia, the consultant usually went to the home of the patient, though in some cases (e.g., Naaman in 2 Kgs 5) the patient might go directly to the prophet's residence. Whenever an explicit selection of consultative-therapeutic options is made in the biblical texts, it does not involve the temple. One sees such strategies followed by both kings and commoners, though kings seem to have prophets and other consultants at their disposal much more readily than the common citizen.

3. The consultative options outside of the temple and the family

The existence of "sophisticated" health care consultants in Canaan probably precedes the rise of the

Israelite state. Evidence comes from the trephinated skulls found at Jericho from the Neolithic and Bronze periods.[35] Other indications come from liver models found at Hazor and Megiddo in the Middle and Late Bronze ages.[36] Liver models were well-known methods of divination in Mesopotamia, and the exemplars in Canaan surely derive, directly or indirectly, from the Mesopotamian models. Judging by the value of divination in the health care system of Mesopotamia, such methods undoubtedly would have been applied in health care consultations in Canaan. There is much evidence for the existence of vibrant scribal schools in LB Canaan that may have copied medical texts as part of their endeavours.[37] Finally, one may note that the Amarna letters report the traffic of health care consultants among royal courts (cf. EA 49:24).[38]

Biblical authors demonstrate an intimate knowledge of medical procedures used by non-Israelites. Ezekiel 30:21, for example, depicts the medical procedures (bandages for a broken arm) used by Egyptians. In all probability, such

---

[35]See D. R. Brothwell, "The Paleopathology of the E.B.-M.B. and Middle Bronze Age Remains from Jericho," in K. M. Kenyon, *Excavations at Jericho II. The Tombs Excavated in 1955-8* (London:British School of Archaeology in Jerusalem, 1965) 685-93. For trephinated skulls from Lachish which date from the seventh century B.C.E., see O. Tufnell, *Lachish* III (1963) 63, 405.

[36]The Hazor liver models from the Late Bronze Age I come from area H in Hazor (stratum 2), which is also the area where a bronze serpent was found, albeit in stratum 1B. See B. Landsberger and H. Tadmor, "Fragments of Clay Liver Models," *IEJ* 14 (1964) 201-218.

[37]See comments by B. Landsberger and H. Tadmor, "Fragments of Clay Liver Models," 201-218; and M. Kochavi, "Canaanite Aphek, Its Acropolis and Inscriptions," *Expedition* 20 (1978) 12-17.

[38]See also E. Edel, *Ägyptische Ärzte und ägyptische Medizin am hethitisches Königshof* (Berlin, 1976).

procedures were not uniquely Egyptian, but ones used throughout the Near East. Jeremiah 8:22 also reflects knowledge of medical procedures used within Israel.

In this section we shall attempt to provide an account of the consultative options that are attested to in ancient Israel, and we shall leave a synthetic discussion of their interrelationship and socio-historical developments for a subsequent section. The most important feature of the Israelite health care relative to that in Mesopotamia and Greece is that the textual evidence depicts a health care system that was divided into legitimate and illegitimate consultation options. We must note that by the word *legitimate* we are expressing the views of the authors of the canonical texts, but most of the Israelite population may have had, and probably did have, different views on what constituted a legitimate or illegitimate option.

a) Legitimate options

(1) Yahwistic prophet

Most ancient societies in which temples had a petitionary or therapeutic function usually also had consultants who operated outside of the temple. In Israel the most common legitimate health care consultant outside the temple was probably the person designated as a prophet (נביא) or man of God (איש האלהים).

The role of the prophet is still disputed. Issues have included the relationship of prophets to the ruling power structures, the priesthood, the origin and age of the institution. Fortunately, our discussion will not be affected by most of these controversies. The reason is that most scholars do agree that prophets were persons who claimed to be intermediaries and/or messengers on behalf of Yahweh.[39] Persons who were believed to have special access to a deity, therefore, would be seen as diviners and as natural candidates for consultation by the sick, especially when their prayers had not been answered.

In fact, Biblical texts are relatively uniform in assigning these figures a role as health care consultants. This includes figures primarily associated with the North and who operated outside of the ruling political structures (e.g., Elijah and Elisha), as well as those who operated within the royal court (e.g., Isaiah). In order to delineate the role and *modus operandi* of the prophet in the health care system, we shall use a simple inductive approach that focuses on the sources that provide information on the role of these consultants in illnesses.

(a) Illnesses

Although the variety of recorded illnesses for which a prophet was consulted in the Bible is not as great as those attested for consultants in Mesopotamia or Greece, one may still obtain some insights into the consultational process involving biblical prophets.

---

[39]For general discussions of the role of the prophets, see J. Blenkinsopp, *A History of Prophecy in Israel* (Philadelphia: Westiminster, 1983); K. Koch, *The Prophets I:The Assyrian Period* (Philadelphia:Fortress, 1983); David L. Petersen *The Roles of Israel's Prophets* (JSOT:Sheffield, 1981); and R. Wilson, *Prophecy and Society in Ancient Israel* (Philadelphia: Fortress, 1980). Wilson (*Prophecy and Society*, 301) argues that Judean prophets did not have an intercessory role, but that they did maintain a messenger role. Either role would be useful in health care consultation.

i) Infertility. Genesis 20 contains the story of the attempt by the king of Gerar to marry Sarah. Since Sarah was Abraham's wife, Yahweh punished Abimelech by making the latter's wife infertile. Abimelech called upon Abraham to help heal his wife. Although Abraham is not usually characterized as a prophet by the Pentateuchal sources, it is clear that the author of Gen 20 has cast him in the role of a prophet. Genesis 20:7 describes Abraham as a prophet (נביא הוא). It is reasonable, therefore, to assume that the author depicts a role which he would ascribe to others with the same title נביא. In fact, as a נביא, Abraham does act much like other persons designated by that Hebrew term who pray for those whom Yahweh has punished with illness (e.g., Moses in Num 12:13).

Abraham clearly functions as an intermediary, and the actions that he performs do not extend beyond a prayer to Yahweh. The story also shows that Abraham's role as an effective consultant resides in his personal relationship with Yahweh, and not in some elaborate ritual or technique. Note that the story assumes that Abimelech is able to communicate with Yahweh directly, something evinced by Abimelech's dialogue with Yahweh (Gen 20:3-7). However, the text indicates that the therapeutic process must involve an appeal by the prophet, and not simply by the patient. Yahweh's willingness to heal, therefore, is linked directly to his inclination to heed the prophet's plea. If the story has wider social implications for the health care system, it is that this system sometimes requires the consultation of the prophet-as-intermediary regardless of the existence of the patient's ability to contact Yahweh directly through prayer. Indeed, the narrator requires the presence of the prophet in the therapy seeking process.

ii) "Leprosy" (2 Kgs 5). The story of Naaman, the Aramean, attests to the consultation of the prophet for "leprosy." The story is probably tendentious in that it ascribes to Naaman a devotion to Yahweh. The story aims to prove Yahweh's power to neighboring religions and socio-political entities (v. 15). Indeed, the motive of the story is clearly to show that there was a God in the land of Israel. Nonetheless, the story clearly ascribes to the prophet a role as a principal, if not the principal, health care consultant in Israel. Note the statement (2 Kgs 5:3) of the servant girl who advertises the prophet's role to Naaman's wife:

אחלי אדני לפני הנביא אשר בשמרון אז
יאסף אתו מצרעת

Indeed, if my lord [Naaman] would consult the prophet who is in Samaria, then he [the prophet] would heal him [Naaman] of his "leprosy."

This statement divulges that the prophet was the person to consult for "leprosy." According to these biblical texts, the role of the temple is ignored or of no value in the therapeutic process in the North. The role of the prophet is again emphasized in verses 7-8 which again directs Naaman to the prophet, not the temple.

Verses 10-11 allow some insights into the consultative and therapeutic procedures of the prophet. Verse 11 describes what Naaman expected the prophet to do for a patient:

יצא יצוא ועמד וקרא בשם יהוה אלוהיו
והניף ידו אל המקום ואסף המצרע

> He shall come out [of his house] and he shall stand
> and call upon the name of Yahweh, his god; and he
> shall wave his hand over the [afflicted] area; and he
> shall remove the "leprosy."

Although this procedure is placed in the mouth of an Aramean, it is probable that it is the procedure that the Israelite listener/reader also expected or that was current in Israel at the time the author composed the story. The expected ritual also was quite simple, and not as labor-intensive as a Mesopotamian ritual might be.

The ritual that Elisha prescribes for Naaman consists of dipping oneself seven times in the Jordan. Note that such a procedure does not seem to be concerned with the laws of purity described in Leviticus. The simple ritual consists of the repetition of an action a specific number of times. This is not unlike some of the prescriptions of Asclepius. The latter's prescriptions may not always appear be the most obvious ones to use, but it was the fact that they were prescribed by Asclepius which was the reason for their supposed efficacy.

Similarly, Elisha's prescription may not have been the expected one, but it was one that worked because it was the prophet of Yahweh who provided it. In fact, Naaman's own servants advised him to follow the words of the prophet (v. 13), and it was obeying the word of the prophet that is credited in verse 14 (כדבר איש האלהים) with making the prescription successful.

The priest does not have a role in the story, though the opportunity to refer the patient to a priest was present if such a procedure was viewed as preferable or normal by the author. Another aspect of the consultative process that is interesting is that, even though Elisha rejected it, the offer of a gift to the consultant was a usual assumption or expectation on the part of the patient. It may be that the author did not wish to portray the prophets as healing for profit, but it is reasonable to surmise that such gifts were probably necessary, especially if the prophet did not have other means to earn a livelihood.

Other features of the story offer insights into the medical theology of the author. Naaman himself offers a crucial statement in v. 15: "Now I know that there is no God in all of the earth, except in Israel." Although Yahweh's healing power is not limited to a temple locus or to Israel, the healing power attributed to the Jordan River is part of a socio-religious framework that views Israel as the socio-geographic boundary that Yahweh has blessed with special therapeutic efficacy. The value of this socio-geographic boundary is also reflected in the fact that Naaman takes "two mules' load of soil" (v. 17: משא צמד פרדים אדמה)[40] from Israel back to Damascus. Although therapy in this story is best sought within Israel, it is not sufficient to step into that socio-geographic boundary to receive healing because access to this power is channeled through the prophet's word. So in DtrH obedience to Yahweh and his authentic prophet, not a routine prescription, is the determinant of therapeutic efficacy. This, of course, is quite different from the theology of Asclepius which placed a high value on the temple locus because the god could not be

---

[40]See M. Cogan and H. Tadmor, *II Kings* (*AB* 11; Garden City, NY: 1988) 62. LXX reads: καὶ σύ μοι δώσεις ἐκ τῆς γῆς τῆς πυρρᾶς/ "and you shall give me some red earth."

everywhere within a large geographic area. As we shall show below, obedience to a consultant in Mesopotamia was a very important part of the therapy, though the attested Mesopotamian prescriptions seem to be more formalized, and not as unexpected as some of the ones prescribed by the prophets or Asclepius.

    iii) "Terminal" illnesses. Terminal illnesses are very frequent in the biblical accounts of prophetic consultation. It is difficult to determine how much of this is due to the tendency to glorify the feats of the prophets in the literary strata. However, such consultations must have been plausible in view of the natural incentive to search for all means of restoration that a society offers in the case of potentially deadly illnesses. Anyone thought to have special influence with the deity would certainly not be excluded from such consultations.

    According to R. L. Cohn, the story of Abijah in 1 Kings 14 is part of a larger series of narratives with a discrete pattern unique to Kings which involve kings, terminal illnesses, and the consultation of prophets.[41] The pattern described by Cohn is also part of the prophecy - fulfilment theme seen in DtrH, and it may be schematized as follows:

I. Setting and preparation for inquiry
II. Audience with the prophet
    a. request for oracle
    b. delivery of oracle
III. Fulfilment of oracle

---

[41]R. L. Cohn, "Creation and Creativity in the Book of Kings:The Case of the Dying Monarch," *CBQ* 47 (4, 1985) 603-616.

This pattern is present in this story and in the stories of Ahaziah (2 Kgs 1), Ben-hadad (2 Kgs 8), and Hezekiah (2 Kgs 20). For our purposes, we assume that the pattern was selected by the author of DtrH because it reflects how actual consultations should, or would, proceed. The story of Abijah, the son of Jeroboam, illustrates the use of a prophet in the case of the terminal illness of an infant.

Although Schley would view the function of Ahijah as part of the tradition of oracular priests at Shiloh,[42] it is clear that Ahijah is referred to as a נביא (v. 2). The story also illustrates the custom of offering a נביא some sort of gift or remuneration when his consultation was sought, in this case, ten loaves of bread, cakes, and a bottle of honey. As in the story of the Shunammite woman (2 Kgs 4), it is the mother of the patient who is sent to seek out the prophet (1 Kgs 14:2ff).

Again, the temple does not appear to be an option for Jeroboam. Jeroboam, in fact, suggests that the reason for consulting Ahijah was that it was the latter who had prophesied that Jeroboam would be king over Israel (cf. 1 Kgs 11:29). But this need not be interpreted as a case where Jeroboam prefers a prophet, and not the temple, because he might have had fruitful dealings with prophets in the past. The text simply explains why, among all the prophets that Jeroboam could have consulted, it was Ahijah that was chosen. The choice to be made was not between prophet and temple, but between Ahijah and some other prophet.

One should note that the precise diagnosis is not important in the story. The prophet is not consulted to diagnose what illness the child had. The prophet is consulted

---

[42]D. G. Schley, *Shiloh:A City in Biblical Tradition and History* (Sheffield:JSOT, 1989) 166.

to learn whether the child would recover (or die). Although one does not find any sign that a highly developed typology of illnesses existed in Israel as depicted in the biblical materials, the question about the mortality of the illness is congruent with the traditions seen in Mesopotamia. As we have discussed, the series *SA.GIG* typically ends all prognoses with either of two alternatives: *iballuṭ* (he shall live/recover) and *imât* (he shall die). So rather than being simply a literary topos in "terminal illness" stories, one may see this literary feature as grounded in the diagnostic traditions that were also current in Mesopotamia. As we shall learn, this type of concern recurs in other biblical stories as well.

Another story of terminal illness is found in 1 Kings 17:17-24. As argued by R. L. Cohn, this story is part of a larger coherent narrative (1 Kgs 17-19) that focuses on the life of Elijah as an instrument through which Yahweh combats the forces of Baal.[43] Each episode, which corresponds roughly to present chapter divisions, involves journeys, two encounters with various entities, a central miracle, and an acknowledgment of Yahweh's power and Elijah's divine commission.

Regardless of the origin of the story in 1 Kgs 17, the narrative illuminates a number of issues pertaining to illness and health care in ancient Israel. First, no mention is made of taking the boy to a Yahweh shrine of any sort. Therapy is administered directly in the home. The prophet does not engage in elaborate rituals, and Elijah simply leans over the

---

[43]R. L. Cohn, "The Literary Logic of 1 Kings 17-19," *JBL* 101 (3, 1982) 333-50. A reading using the theories of V. Propp and A. J. Greimas may be found in D. Jobling, *The Sense of Biblical Narrative:Structural Analyses in the Hebrew Bible* (Sheffield:JSOT, 1986) 66-82.

youth three times (v. 21: ‏ויתמדד על הילד שלש פעמים‎).
A prayer is recited by Elijah, and Yahweh is said to hear
Elijah.

Even if one argues that the story exaggerates the role
of Elijah, one can draw some inferences about the editorial
intentions. Assuming it depicts an idealized role of the
prophet in this instance, one may say that the composer
would at least like to see the prophet as the intermediary of
choice in this case of illness. The prophet makes the prayer
that prompts Yahweh to act. Yahweh does not act on his
own.   One can see, therefore, that the text promotes the
prophet as the main intermediary in such cases, and the
patient (or family) does not have much recourse otherwise.
This, of course, may be due to the fact that it is Elijah who is
held responsible for the death of the boy, and so it is his
responsibility to reverse his own act.   Such an ideology is
similar to the one in Mesopotamia where the "sender/
controller" of an illness is the one that is entreated. But one
sees the same type of prerogative given to prophets in other
stories, where the prophet is not responsible for the malady.

The story of Ahaziah' terminal illness in 2 Kings 1:1-
18 illustrates the existence of the notion that not all
consultants were legitimate. The passage argues for the use
of Yahweh, and certainly his prophets, as the primary
consultants in health care. The fact that the prophet, not the
temple, was promoted by the author as the primary health
care consultant is illustrated by two features of the story.
One is that the story presents the prophet, not the priest, as
the legitimate Yahwistic alternative to Ahaziah's illegitimate
consultation. It is a prophet, moreover, who provides the
prognosis in which Ahaziah was interested in the first place--
namely, whether he will live or die. The prophet's answer is
that he will die. Finally, no recommendation is made to visit

the temple of Yahweh for any part of the prognosis. Insofar as the relative importance of the priest vs. the "man of god" is concerned, we are, of course, arguing *e silentio*. But, at the very least, the story supposes that "the man of God" alone was sufficient to provide the consultation needed by Ahaziah. We shall provide further comments on this story in a forthcoming section.

The story of Ben-hadad's illness (2 Kgs 8:7-25) allows another glimpse into the nature of the prophet's role as a consultant, at least in the view of DtrH. In the episode, Elisha goes to Damascus. The Aramean king is sick, and one finds the following procedure: First the king asks a messenger to procure the services of the prophet, and such a procurement includes a gift. The question that is emphasized is a simple one: "Shall I recover from this illness?" (האחיה מחלי זה). The question allows us to infer that the king saw the possibility that his illness was lethal, and later we learn that it was. But as in the other stories, one does not find any interest in ascertaining what type of illness it was.

The illness of Hezekiah (2 Kgs 20:1ff.) is particularly important in assessing the thoughts about illness and health care within the biblical materials. One reason is that it was Hezekiah who is credited with with a program of religious reformation that included the removal of the most famous therapeutic device in the biblical texts---Nehuštan. In light of these events, one must ask: How does DtrH depict Hezekiah's consultative/healing strategy in his illness?

First, one must note that the narrative concerning Hezekiah exists in two parallel versions that exhibit some literary disturbances. The principal discontinuity in the version in Kings is 2 Kgs 20:7, which reports that Isaiah applied a sort of ointment made of fig cakes, and Hezekiah recovered. However, the recovery reported as a past event

in verse 7 has not yet occurred in verse 8.[44] The parallel
story in Isaiah (38:21-22) places the episode with the fig
ointment at the end of the narrative. As Cogan and Tadmor
note,[45] the placement of the report of the fig ointment at the
end of the narrative in Isaiah reflects an effort by the narrator
in Isaiah to produce a more coherent account, and it also
indicates that the story in Kings is the earlier version. It
seems best, therefore, to regard 2 Kgs 20:7 as an
independent tradition. The motives for its placement in the
narrative are still obscure, though we shall offer a hypothesis
below.[46] The narrative may be schematized as follows:

verse(s)	feature
1	Notice of Hezekiah's illness
2-3	Prayer by Hezekiah;
4-6	Reply of Yahweh, who sends Isaiah to notify Hezekiah that he would be healed and that he would receive a sign;
8	Request of the specific sign by Hezekiah;
9	Description of the sign by Isaiah;
10	Doubt of Hezekiah concerning the sign;
11	Fulfilment of the sign (and presumed restoration)

---

[44]The LXX interprets the recovery as a future event (ὑγιάσει).

[45]M. Cogan and H. Tadmor, *II Kings* (*AB* 11; Garden City, NY: 1988) 256-57.

[46]IQIsa[a] omits the verse in its text, though a marginal note reflects an effort to supply the verse. S. Talmon (*Qumran and the History of the Biblical Text* [Cambridge, MA:Harvard U. Press, 1975] 330) attributes the omission to a homoioteleuton, while Y. Zakovitch (*Beth Mikra* 17 [1972]. 302-5) argues that the *Vorlage* of the text of IQIsa[a] lacked the verse.

The other important literary feature of the story of the illness of Hezekiah is the placement of a psalm of thanksgiving after the healing in the narrative in Isaiah (38:11-20).

In general, the story follows a familiar biblical scheme that describes a crisis which is followed by a request for help from Yahweh, and the reply from Yahweh. Insofar as our purpose is concerned, the most important feature of the story (excluding v. 7) is that the direct instrument of therapeutic efficacy is Hezekiah's prayer. Hezekiah prayed directly, and Yahweh acted directly upon his prayer. Isaiah does not have a direct role in convincing Yahweh to allow Hezekiah to live. Instead, Isaiah serves as a messenger and reader of omens. So the story indicates that, while the patient could relay messages to Yahweh without an intermediary, Yahweh's messages to the patient were through the prophet. The prophet's role in the consultative process is still necessary in order to interpret omens, and to provide a report on the patient's request to Yahweh.

Insofar as the temple is concerned, it is clear that Hezekiah does not intend to go to the temple to petition for health. 2 Kings 20:6 clearly states that Hezekiah was to go up to the temple on the third day, and verse 8 says:

ויאמר חזקיהו אל ישעיהו מה אות כי ירפא
יהוה לי ועליתי ביום השלישי בית יהוה

And Hezekiah said to Isaiah: "What is the omen [that shall confirm] that Yahweh shall heal me, and that I shall [be able] to go up to the temple of Yahweh on the third day?"

There are two sound reasons that suggest that the visit to the temple on the third day should be interpreted as a visit that was to take place the third day *after* Hezekiah had been healed. First, the verb "to go up" is placed in the "future tense" (imperfect) in v. 5 (תעלה) and follows the notice that Yahweh would heal Hezekiah. If the visit to the temple preceded the healing, then one would expect a corresponding order in the verbs. Second, the procedure that is attested to most often in the Bible places the visit to the temple after the healing. In the case of "leprosy," one cannot visit the temple at all until a specified amount of time has passed after the patient has been declared healed (= "clean"). Though the precise nature of the illness is not provided in the main narrative, the independent tradition in verse 7 admits the possibility that it was some type of skin ailment (שחין) that may have been categorized among the illnesses that required the patient to go to the temple after he had been healed.[47] Thus, it is best to interpret the three day period as one associated with the regulations regarding purification/ thanksgiving rituals after a healing. A message by Yahweh to visit the temple after the healing (v. 5) may have been regarded as a confirmation that the healing that must precede such a visit would be realized.

In effect, the story of Hezekiah's illness is consistent with the actions that have been attributed to Hezekiah in 2 Kgs 18:4ff, and that are emphasized in the psalm of thanksgiving in Isaiah. The temple is not viewed as a

---

[47]Verse 7 says that Hezekiah was suffering from שחין, which is usually translated as "boil" and in its other occurrences (e.g., Lev 13:18, Job 2:7) is regarded as painful, but not necessarily as deadly. שחין is mentioned in the laws of purity of Leviticus (e.g. 13:18). The suggestion by J. Leibovich (*Encyclopedia Miqra'it* 7:421-22) that it is pemphigus, a skin disease, lacks evidence. At most one may say that it is a type of painful disease which manifests itself in the skin in a sufficiently localized manner that ointments may be applied to it.

necessary or advisable petitionary or therapeutic locus. The story is consistent with the view, even if not stated explictly, that the temple's proper role in the health care system in DtrH is that of a thanksgiving and/or purificatory locus *after* an illness, especially if that illness is regarded as producing impurity.

(b) A comparative model of the operations of the נביא

We have noted that the stories in DtrH concerning the role of the נביא in the health care system exhibit some recurrent features. One is that the specific diagnosis of the illness is not of interest to the authors. There is rarely an effort to describe the specific symptoms by the authors. Most prognoses center on whether the patient would recover or not. One may simply explain this recurrent feature as due to a literary disinterest by the biblical author(s) in the particulars of an illness. However, it may be linked to the distinct Israelite aspects of the causes of illness in the biblical texts.

In Mesopotamia the search for the "sender/controller" of an illness was of paramount importance, and a large variety of such beings could be responsible for an illness. In the Mesopotamian series *SA.GIG*, the symptoms were important because they helped to identify the *qāt DN*. As we have mentioned, these omens had a very consistent form:

If symptom x occurs, then it is *qāt DN*
and/or the patient shall recover/die.

In the Israelite prophetic stories, in contrast, the "sender/controller" of an illness was well known--namely Yahweh. Since in the Yahwistic prophetic stories there could only be one *qāt DN* (i.e., Yahweh), the specific symptoms were not necessary for the determination of the *qāt DN*. The strict Yahwist assumed that if someone was ill, there was only one *qāt DN* possible. The only question left was whether Yahweh would permit a recovery, or why Yahweh had decided to strike the patient. The mono-causal aspect of Yahwistic illness etiology, therefore, was probably a main factor in the outward literary form of the prophetic pronouncements concerning illness, and also helped to shape the literary structure of the story.

The report of the fig-cakes (דבלת תאנים) is consonant with the idea that prophets could serve as more than intermediaries between the patient and Yahweh. They sometimes did recommend specific medicinal treatments. In this regard, Isaiah's actions seem to be like those of the *asû* in Mesopotamia. However, Isaiah also exhibits the functions of the Mesopotamian *āšipu*. Like the *āšipu*, Isaiah interprets omens for the patient. If medicinal expertise was not the normal purview of the prophet, still verse 7 may serve as a notice by Dtr that the prophet had such a wide variety of expertise that going to non-Yahwisitic healers and sorcerers was not necessary. If the story reflects an actuality, then one may see that the relatively simple procedures used by Hezekiah (and allowed by the relatively uncomplicated mono-Yahwistic medical theology) might have allowed a combination of the tasks of the *asû* and the *āšipu* in the נביא.

The stories that comment on the role of the נביא in the health care system also indicate that, although the patient could send a message to the healing deity through direct prayer, the prophet was still needed in the consultative system in order to relay answers, omens and other messages from the healing deity to the patient. Unlike the *asû* and the *āšipu*, the value of the Israelite נביא in the health care system did not reside in technical proficiency. Compare, for example, the following reply (*LABS* 276 = *ABL* 53)[48] from an *āšipu* to one of Esarhaddon's queries regarding his illness.

> *ina pa-an LUGAL né-ru-ba ⌐dul-lu⌐ [k]i!-i ša*
> *in-né-pa-šu-u-ni ⌐a⌐ -[na LUGAL b]e!-lí-i-ni*
> *nu-[šá]-ah-ki-im dul!-⌐lu! ma⌐-ah-du šu-ú ⌐de!-iq⌐*
> *a-ki-i LUGAL ša pi-i-ni i-šá-mu-u-ni*

> We will enter before the king; we shall instruct the king, our lord, how the ritual task is to be done. The ritual is cumbersome. It behooves the king to listen to our instructions.

Note that, while a personal relationship with a healing deity may be important, the Mesopotamian consultant emphasizes that his value is rooted in the technical proficiency to perform the healing ritual. In contrast, expertise in complex rituals is never mentioned as a reason to consult Hebrew prophets. In biblical texts the value of the נביא resided solely in the personal relationship of the consultant with the healing deity. The biblical stories constantly emphasize the consultant's ability to persuade the deity to heal and forgive.

On the other hand, both Israelite and Mesopotamian health care consultants extolled the virtue of heeding their instructions in order to achieve a good result. In effect, statements that indicate the importance of the consultant's instructions affirm and promote the value of the consultant in the respective health care system.

---

[48]*LABS* 276, Rev. lines 2-8.

Many commentators interpret these stories in DtrH as ones composed to glorify dead heroes, or to emphasize obedience to Yahweh. All of these are certainly legitimate interpretations. But it is also possible that the purpose of these stories may be to promote the role of the prophet as a consultant within the health care system, even when patients might believe that they are able to contact Yahweh directly. Indeed, the stories emphasize that the prophet is needed even when it is clear that Yahweh can, and has, heard the suppliants themselves. We have already mentioned that the stories of miracle healings inscribed at the temple of Epidauros served to promote the value of consulting that temple. Similarly, the stories of these prophets may advertise the value, or necessity, of the prophet within the health care system.

Such an interpretation gains credibility when one places the prophets in juxtaposition to the denunciations of many other consultative options that existed in ancient Israel. As we shall learn below, such alternative consultants probably competed for clients with Yahwistic prophets. Note also that some stories that decry the use of non-Yahwistic consultants (e.g., 2 Kgs 1) offer the prophet as the legitimate alternative.

(2) Musicians

The story of King Saul's "mental disturbance" in 1 Sam 16:14ff provides evidence that musicians were deemed appropriate consultants in DtrH for his condition. Psychiatric diagnosis is precarious even when patients are alive and able to be examined in a modern context.[49] We can only speculate that Saul's malady might fit within the general definition of a psychiatric disorder in modern Western medicine. The authoritative manual (often abbreviated as DSM-III-R), of The American Psychiatric Association, for example, generally defines a mental disorder as:

> A clinically significant behavioral or psychological syndrome that occurs in a person and that is associated with present distress (a painful symptom) or disability (impairment in one or more important areas of functioning) or with a significantly increased risk of suffering death, pain, disability, or an important loss of freedom. In addition, the syndrome or pattern must not be merely an expectable response to a particular event, e.g., death of a love one.[50]

The biblical text provides the following clues that indicate that Saul's affliction might fit within these general guidelines. First, Saul was deemed to be impaired "in one or more important areas of functioning," insofar as he apparently was not able to carry out his normal daily routines because of his malady. Also, no specific event that might be expected to be distressful (e.g., death of a loved one) is mentioned in the text. At the very least, the Hebrew author must have thought that his description was sufficient to convey the abnormality of Saul's behavior, and the latter

---

[49]On the theoretical and methodological difficulties involved in psychiatric evaluations, see Arthur Kleinman and B. Good, eds., *Culture and Depression* (Berkeley: U. of California Press, 1985).

[50]The American Psychiatric Association, *Diagnostic and Statistical Manual of Mental Disorders* (3rd edition; Washington: American Psychiatric Association, 1987) xxii.

surely involved signs of emotional distress. Whatever the
real cause, Saul's distress prevented him from functioning
effectively in the view of those who knew him, and he
appeared in jeopardy of being totally disabled as a king.

Saul's need for therapy and the therapeutic efficacy
of the music is explicit in the text itself (v. 16):

יאמר-נא אדננו עבדיך לפניך יבקשו איש
ידע מנגן בכנור והיה בהיות עליך רוח אלהים
רעה ונגן בידו וטוב לך

> Let our lord command the servants before you, that a
> man be sought who is skilled in the harp, so that
> when the troublesome spirit of God comes upon you,
> he can alleviate you with the playing of his hand.

Apparently, the therapeutic efficacy was believed to reside in
the musical melody itself because the work of the hands, not
the voice, seems emphasized. The supposed efficacy of
music seems most consistent with an illness that was mental
rather than physical. One cannot, however, exclude the
possibility that the music was thought to appease Yahweh
who sent the tormenting spirit. According to Pindar, a
writer who was active in the fifth century B.C.E., Greek
physicians also included singing in their therapeutic
repertory.[51] Thus, the Hebrew author indicates that this was
a customary or preferred mode of treatment for illnesses that
manifested themselves in the manner described in the story.

In sum, the depiction of Saul's malady seems to be
consistent with what might be *generally* classified today as a
psychiatric disorder, insofar as he suffered a type of distress

---

[51]Pindar, *Pythian Ode* III, 47-53.

that resulted in a radical alteration in his behavior and ability to function. However, we cannot be more specific (e.g., diagnosing him a person with schizophrenia, or depression) on the basis of the biblical data.[52] We, of course do not claim that Saul actually had any sort of malady at all, but only that the biblical author is depicting him as having it.

(3) Midwife

The "midwife" (מילדה) in Exodus 1:15ff was depicted as an acceptable consultant in the case of childbirth. We may infer that she was consulted on matters concerning birth, and concerning the pre/post-natal care of babies, but detailed information is not available. In two of the instances where midwives are mentioned (Gen 35:17 and 1 Sam 4:20) they are seen providing psychological support to women (Rachel and the wife of Phinehas) who eventually died. Although precise statistics are not available, the midwife may have been one of the most ubiquitous health care consultants in the ancient Near East.

b) "Illegitimate" consultants (human and divine)

For our purposes, we shall include human and divine consultative options in this section. Although most of these would be considered illegitimate by some sector of mono-Yahwism, a number of traditions show a tolerant attitude towards some non-Yahwistic consultants.

---

[52]We are generally skeptical of works (e.g., J. V. Kinnier-Wilson, "An Introduction to Babylonian Psychiatry," *AS* 16: 289-298), which seek to give highly specific diagnoses for ancient descriptions of symptoms.

(1) "Pagan" temples: Ekron (2 Kgs 1:2)

As mentioned, this episode in DtrH reflects a health care system that was divided into legitimate and illegitimate options. The story begins with the notice that king Ahaziah fell from a window and was injured. Thereupon, Ahaziah sends messengers to Baal-zebub, the god of Ekron. It is most probable that such a consultation was sought at the temple of Baal-zebub because gods are usually sought at their main places of residence (i.e., temples), and because the author does not deem more explicit directions to be necessary. Ahaziah requested an answer to a simple question: "Shall I survive this illness?" (אחיה מחלי זה). Again, the physical diagnosis seems to be obvious (injury from a fall), and so the diagnosis is not of paramount importance in the consultation of Baal-zebub.

It is unclear whether the temple of Baal-zebub was known as a petitionary or therapeutic center or whether Ahaziah sought information that any temple of Baal might have provided. An inspection of the geography suggests that Baal-zebub of Ekron may have had a special significance, for it was not the nearest temple of Baal to Samaria. The significance of the temple of Baal-zebub is supported by the etymology of the deity's name. The second element in the divine name may derive from the root designated in Ugaritic lexicons as *zbl* II ("disease") instead of from *zbl* I ("prince(ship)").[53] Thus, the name may mean

---

[53]An instance of *zbl* II may be found in the Kirta Epic (*KTU* 1.14, II, 45-46): *zbl 'ršm yšu* ("let the sick man bear (his own) bed"). This occurs in a list of tragedies, and is followed immediately by a reference to a blind man ((lines 46-47: *'wr mzl ymzl/* "let the blind man stumble around").

"Lord of illness," an epithet that would befit a god who heals.[54]

Archaeological evidence at the site identified as Ekron (Tel Miqne) by its excavators suggests that the town was small throughout the ninth and most of the eighth centuries when compared to its predecessor in the Iron I.[55] One should note that the city was largely uninhabited from the early sixth century B.C.E. until the Roman period.[56] Thus, unless it represents an anachronism, the story may have been composed at a time when Ekron had reached the zenith of its growth in the seventh century B.C.E.[57]

---

[54]See further, P. L. Day, *An Adversary in Heaven: Satan in the Hebrew Bible* (HSM 34; Atlanta:Scholars Press, 1988) 151-159; and C. Gordon, *Ugaritic Textbook* (Rome: Pontifical Biblical Institute, 1965) 393.

[55] See S. Gitin, "Ekron of the Philistines: Part II:Olive Oil Suppliers to the World," *BARev* 16 (2, 1990) 34. We shall follow the consensus in the identification of Tel Miqne with Ekron.

[56]S. Gitin, "Ekron of the Philistines: Part II...," *BARev* 16 (2, 1990) 41-42. A. Rofé (*The Prophetical Stories* [Jerusalem: Magnes, 1988] 35-36) adduces linguistic arguments (e.g., the use of אחזיה and אליה instead of the longer forms אחזיהו and אליהו) to date our story in the Second Temple period. However, the longer form אליהו does occur in verses 10, 13, 15 and 17. Moreover, the fact that Ekron was abandoned in the early sixth century makes it unlikely that the author would choose an abandoned city to make a point which presupposes that Ekron was a consultative alternative that should be avoided. Thus, a date prior to the Second Temple period seems best. On other chronological problems in the prophetical stories of Elijah and Elisha, see J. M. Miller and J. H. Hayes, *A History of Ancient Israel and Judah* (Philadelphia: Westminster, 1986) 252-253. None of these chronological problems negates the use of the prophets in the pre-Exilic period as health care consultants.

[57]B. Peckham (*The Composition of the Deuteronomistic History* [HSM 35; Atlanta: Scholars Press, 1985] fig. 7) dates all of 2 Kgs 2

The story follows a familiar pattern that bases the evaluation of kings on their loyalty to Israel's God in DtrH. The story also reflects the importance of the role of the prophet. The story regards as illegitimate a patient's consultation of a foreign deity. It is important to note that it is doubtful that DtrH would have seen as any more favorable the consultation of Baal-zebub (or any other deity) *and* Yahweh. The mere act of consulting a foreign temple is an expression of a sinful doubt of Yahweh's power. Thus, for the author of DtrH joint consultations are probably decried as much as the consultation of Yahweh *and* a foreign temple.

Elijah's protestation (v. 3) concerning Ahaziah's consultation emphasizes that Israel has a God that is available for such consultations. The story also should be viewed within the tradition that emphasizes that the "God of Israel" is as, or more, powerful and useful than any other neighboring deity. Such stories note not only that the God of Israel is better than neighboring deities, but that the land of Israel itself is better because of the favor of Yahweh. Thus, the socio-religious interests of mono-Yahwism are clearly behind the prohibition of going to non-Yahwistic temples.

Ekron may not have been the only temple in Philistia with a role in health care. Although excavations have not yet revealed a temple at Ashkelon, the existence in the 5th c. B.C.E. of a dog cemetery with hundreds of dog skeletons

---

to the post-Exilic Dtr 2. But the archaeological evidence suggests that a better date would be Dtr 1. The story assumes that the reader would be familiar with Ekron, and such would not likely be the case if the story was written during a time when Ekron was an uninhabited ruin. If the author wished to select a city with more didactic import, it is unclear why he would choose a city such as Ekron when other cities closer to Samaria could have illustrated the point.

may indicate the presence of the temple of a healing deity that parallels Gula or Asclepius, at least insofar as the importance of dogs in the cult of healing deities is concerned.[58] If these dogs represent the existence of healing cult, then it might have provided yet one more "illegitimate" option that is not explicitly discussed in the biblical texts.

Since one sees the repeated tendency to maximize options by the patient when this is economically feasible, one would not be surprised that the consultation of foreign temples would be a recurrent practice if therapy consistent with "Yahwism" did not achieve the desired results. One may view this story, therefore, as one that reflects a fear of the competition of other consultative options that might undermine Yahwistic ones.

(2) The רפא

The profession denominated by the Hebrew term רפא does not exhibit uniformity in all the biblical texts. In particular, there is apparently a difference between the group in Genesis 50:2 and the group of the same name elsewhere in the Bible.

(a) Gen 50:2

The רפאים mentioned in this passage are probably different from those to whom the name is applied elsewhere in the Bible. Here they are primarily concerned with

---

[58]On the dog burials at Ashkelon and their possible connections with a healing cult, see L. E. Stager, "Why Were Hundreds of Dogs Buried at Ashkelon?" *BARev* 17 (3, 1991) 27-42.

embalmment of the dead, while elsewhere in the Bible רפא
refers to a group involved in treating live patients. What is
interesting about the passage in Genesis is that the Egyptian
consultants (רפאים) do not seem to be placed in an
unfavorable light. This is particularly significant because
elsewhere in the Bible humans who are labelled רפאים are
viewed unfavorably. Moreover, the רפאים in this story are
principally involved in embalming Jacob, and the process of
embalming was a procedure normally performed in an
Egyptian temple.[59] The Egyptian embalmers were priests
who usually undertook embalmment together with rituals to
gods such as Anubis. The fact that the author was indeed
familiar with the embalming procedures of the Egyptians is
evident in the ascription of some 40 days (Gen 50:3) to the
embalming process, a period sufficiently close to what is
posited by modern scholars.[60] Thus, it would be unlikely
that an author who was familiar with specific aspects of
embalmment would not have known that embalmment
involved rituals in a pagan temple.

　　The notice concerning the embalmment of Jacob, of
course, reflects an effort to portray Jacob as a man of high
stature in Egypt. Needless to say, such procedures and the
use of a "pagan" temple would probably not have been
allowed by a prophet such as Elijah (see above), and one
may say that the story also implies a tolerant attitude towards
foreign temples by the author.

　　However, there is much evidence that DtrH and
most biblical traditions regarded the רפא negatively. This

---

[59]See comments by R. Ghalioungui, *Médicine des Pharaohs*
(Paris:Robert Laffont, 1983) 205.
[60]R. Ghalioungui (*Médicine des Pharaohs*, 105) notes that the process
could take some 66 days.

negativity must be viewed in light of a recurrent, and particularly Deuteronomistic, theme that Yahweh is the only being (human or divine) who can be designated as a genuine רפא. Perhaps,the most succinct expression of this theme is found in Exodus 15:26:

לא אשים עליך כל המחלה אשר שמתי
במצרים כי אני יהוה רפאך

> I shall not inflict upon you any plague which I inflicted upon Egypt, because I, Yahweh, am your healer.

As Childs notes, most recent commentators regard this verse as a Deuteronomistic addition to the main narrative.[61] The theology expressed in that verse is similar to that found in Mesopotamia insofar as it was the "sender/controller" of an illness who was usually the only one who could heal it. In Deuteronomy, in particular, illness was a sure sign that Yahweh was displeased with the patient because health and illness were direct barometers of Yahweh's favor. Yahwistic intermediaries who succesfully pray for the healing of a patient, and who might otherwise have a claim to such a designation, are *never* called רפאים, particularly in DtrH. Such intermediaries always pray that Yahweh heal the patient (e.g., 2 Kgs 20:8, Num. 12:13). Some prophets (e.g., Hosea 11:3) decry the fact that some segments of Israelite society attribute to others healing done by Yahweh.

In summary, most biblical texts outside of Genesis 50:2 regard the term רפא as one which can only be

---

[61]For example, B. Childs, *Exodus* (Philadelphia:Westminster, 1974) 266.

legitimately applied to Yahweh. He is the only רפא, in heaven or on earth. The fact that Yahweh is the only רפא colors the application of the term to humans. As we shall see below, when the term is applied to beings other than Yahweh, it is usually a sarcastic commentary on human therapeutic inefficacy, or on the illegitimacy of the רפא as a healing consultant altogether.

(b) The רפא in Jeremiah

Jeremiah was part of a tradition that viewed Yahweh as the only genuine רפא. Note, for example, Jeremiah 17:14, which the RSV translates as: "Heal me, Oh Yahweh, and I shall be healed" (רפאני יהוה וארפא). The statement is part of a meditation which contrasts trust in Yahweh with trust in humans. Jeremiah 17:5 states: "Cursed is the man who trusts humans" (ארור הגבר אשר יבטח באדם), while Jer 17:7 says: "Blessed is the man who trusts in Yahweh" (ברוך הגבר אשר יבטח ביהוה).[62] In this light, one can see that the theology expressed in this meditation implies that healing is one thing for which Yahweh and his rightful intermediaries, not other professions, should be consulted. Consequently, Jer 17:14 may be translated as: "Treat me, Oh Yahweh, and I shall really be healed."

Jeremiah emphasizes elsewhere that it is Yahweh who will heal. For example, Jeremiah 30:17 says: "I shall restore your health, and I shall heal your wounds" (כי אעלה ארכה לך וממכותיך ארפאך). Similarly, in Jer 33:6

---

[62]On the literary relationship between Jer 17:5-8 and 14-18, see W. Holladay, *Jeremiah* I (Hermeneia; Philadelphia:Fortress, 1986) 504.

one finds: "Indeed, I shall bring restoration and healing"
(הנני מעלה לה ארכה ומרפא). Although these texts refer
to Israel, the socio-political entity, as the patient, it is clear
that these references are part of a theology that regards
Yahweh as the only רפא that should be trusted. In light of
the discussion above, specific references to the human רפא
may be viewed as examples of the type of trust in the human
רפא that has already been labeled as futile because Yahweh
is the only genuine רפא. Note the question in Jeremiah
8:22:

הצרי אין בגלעד

אם רפא אין שם

Is there no 'balm'[63] in Gilead?

Is there no healer there?

Jeremiah formulates a type of rhetorical question for which
he is well known.[64] However, the question may be
interpreted as a sarcastic commentary on the inefficacy of
these healers and medications. But is the inefficacy of these
healers due to the enormity of the problem besetting a patient
as large as Israel, or does the passage imply that a human
רפא is inherently ineffective? If read within the larger
theological context of Dtr and Jeremianic traditions that we
have discussed, then the answer is probably that the human

---

[63]The substance (צרי) translated as "balm" or "balsam" alleviated pain
according to Jer 46:11 and 51:8. The Hebrew word צרי is found in
Genesis 37:25. See further, M. Zohary, *Plants of the Bible*
(Cambridge:Cambridge University Press, 1982) 198-199; and W.
Holladay, *Jeremiah* I (Hermeneia; Philadelphia:Fortress, 1986) 294.

[64]See W. Brueggemann, "Jeremiah's Use of Rhetorical Questions,"
JBL 92 (1973) 358-74.

רפא is inherently ineffective because Yahweh is the only genuine רפא.[65]

This interpretation is corroborated by a similar sarcastic reference to healing and *materia medica* in Jeremiah 46:11:

עלי גלעד וקחי צרי בתולת בת מצרים
לשוא הרביתי רפאות תעלה אין לך

> Go up to Gilead, and procure balsam, Oh virgin, daughter of Egypt, but in vain do you accumulate medications, for there is no (possible) recuperation for you.

The instruction to go to Gilead for treatment is clearly nothing more than a taunt, for the author immediately adds that it is useless to do so. A similar sarcastic instruction to Babylon to seek balsam is found in Jeremiah 51:8-9.

פתאם נפלה בבל ותשבר הילילו עליה
קחו צרי למכאובה אולי תרפא רפאנו את
בבל ולא נרפתה

> Suddenly, Babylon was stricken, and broken. A wail was upon her. Take some balsam, perhaps she might be healed. We treated Babylon, but she was not healed.

---

[65]See also G. Hasel, "Health and Healing in the Old Testament," *Andrews University Seminary Studies* 21 (1983) 191-202.

Again, the instruction to use medication becomes a sort of taunt, and the inefficacy of the treatment is clearly expressed.[66]

The texts above indicate that Jeremiah views the human רפא as inherently ineffective. The reason is that Yahweh is the only genuine רפא, especially when he strikes the patient. Any human beings to whom the term is applied are either ineffective or counterfeits. Since most, or all, illnesses are sent by Yahweh, no individual patient could expect to be healed by a human רפא and his medications. Consequently, this implies that, for Jeremiah, the human רפא is inherently ineffective for most illnesses. The same type of ideology may be reflected in Job's complaint (Job 13:4) that his friends were "useless physicians" (רפאי אלל כלכם). Accordingly, one can infer that the רפא and his techniques were probably not considered to be part of the legitimate Yahwistic consultative system according to Jeremiah and other biblical traditions.

These texts allow some other interesting inferences about health care in ancient Israel. One inference is that Gilead was a center for medicinal resins such as "balsam." Genesis 37:25 and Jer 46:11 indicate that such medicinal resins were exported from Gilead to Egypt. It is likely that the רפאים of Gilead were famous for their knowledge of these medicaments (רפואות). In summary, the cumulative evidence above allows one to characterize the רפאים in Jeremiah as a group of non-Yahwistic health consultants who specialized in *materia medica*.

---

[66]R. Carroll (*Jeremiah* [Philadelphia:Westminster, 1986] 844) also notes the possible satirical tone of the passage.

(c) Asa's consultants (2 Chr 16:12)

The discussion above allows us to place a much discussed reference to the רפא in 2 Chr 16:12 in a better light. The crucial portion of v. 12 reads: "He [Asa] did not consult Yahweh, but only the רפאים" (לא דרש את יהוה כי ברפאים). The attitude towards Asa's use of the consultant called רפא is an example of the negative attitude towards the human רפא. The exact nature of Asa's disease is unclear,[67] and it is not immediately obvious what the specific sin committed by Asa was. Was it that he consulted the רפאים to the total exclusion of Yahweh? Would it have been permissible to consult both Yahweh and the רפאים? Or is the consultation of the רפאים *eo ipso* regarded as an exclusion of Yahweh?

Jacob Myers is representative of those who believe that the sin was that Asa consulted only the רפא, and not Yahweh.[68] He points to Exodus 21:19, Jeremiah 8:22, and Isaiah 38:21 to argue that the רפא was a legitimate option for Israelites. As we have noted, however, Jer 8:22 is a sarcastic commentary that in no way implies legitimacy of the רפא. Isa 38:21 refers to the use of a natural remedy by a Yahwistic prophet (Isaiah), not a רפא. Exod 21:19 (שבתו יתן ורפא ירפא / "He [the attacker] shall compensate him [the victim] for his time, and he [the attacker] shall be thoroughly responsible for his [the victim's] treatment") need not imply more than a general requirement for the attacker to compensate the victim for his

---

[67]H. G. M. Williamson (*1 and 2 Chronicles* [NCBC; Grand Rapids, MI: Eerdmans, 1982] 276-277) has correctly refuted diagnoses such as gangrene on textual, philological and literary grounds.

[68]J. Myers, *II Chronicles* (AB 13; Garden City, New York, 1965) 95.

loss of time and for his medical treatment, and a referral to a specific professional is not necessarily implied. But even if this law had referral to a רפא in mind, we shall show that 2 Chr 16:12 must reflect a different tradition.

First, one must note that the phraseology of v. 12 itself indicates that Chr does not view the רפאים as Yahwistic consultants. Most healers in the Near East were sponsored by a deity, even when they specialized in *materia medica* (cf. *asû*). If the רפא was sponsored by Yahweh, then the consultation of the רפא would surely be reckoned as a consultation of Yahweh. But if the consultation of the רפא was reckoned as a consultation of Yahweh, then it would be impossible to consult only the רפא, and not Yahweh. The latter situation could only exist if the רפא was considered to be non-Yahwistic by Chr. Similarly, since consultation of a נביא is reckoned as a consultation of Yahweh, it would be incongruous to say that one could consult only a נביא, and not Yahweh. Since Chr does not appear to view the רפא as part of the cult of Yahweh, then it is reasonable to assume that Chr saw the רפא as a health consultant sponsored by a pagan deity, and so it would be unlikely that Chr would advocate the joint consultation of the רפא and Yahweh.

Our interpretation is supported by the Chronicler's use of the same vocabulary and grammar (דרש + ב + object) that is used to describe Ahaziah's illegitimate consultation in 2 Kgs 1:2:

2 Chr 16:12	2 Kgs 1:2
דרש....ברפאים	דרש בבעל זבוב

Ahaziah's sin surely does not consist only in the consultation of Baal-zebub to the exclusion of Yahweh, for joint

consultation of Baal-zebub and Yahweh probably would
have been regarded as illegitimate as well. Chr must have
known of this theme in the stories of Kings, and he even
may have modeled the story of Asa upon that of Ahaziah.
Viewed in this light, Chr simply expresses an illegitimate
consultation with laconic language whose implications
would have been obvious to those who were familiar with
similar reprimands applied to other kings (דרשׁ + ב +
"illegitimate" consultant). By using language similar to 2
Kgs 1:2, Chr likewise implies that the mere act of consulting
the רפאים (alone or jointly with Yahweh) was illegitimate
and sinful.[69]

The value of consulting Yahweh through prayer
alone for Chr is reflected in the story of Hezekiah. Unlike
DtrH, which mentions the involvement of Isaiah, Chr
dispenses with the prophet altogether. Instead, the
Chronicler's story implies that prayer from the patient was
sufficient to heal Hezekiah. Again, this would show that
Chr was not one to emphasize the use of both a human and a
divine consultant even when the human consultant was
otherwise viewed as legitimate (as we assume Isaiah would
be). One would expect less sympathy, therefore, for a
person who described himself as a רפא. Thus, even if
Exod 21:19 implied the legitimacy of the רפא, one must
deem Chr as an advocate of a different tradition that viewed
the רפא as an illegitimate consultant.

---

[69]There may also be an ironic motive in the ascription of an
illegitimate healing consultation to Asa, for the latter name may be a
hypocoristic form of "El/Yahweh heals" (*'asa 'el/yahu*). See further J.
D. Fowler, *Theophoric Personal Names in Ancient Hebrew* (Sheffield:
JSOT, 1988) 159.

(d) The רפא in Sirach 38

Sirach 38 is one of the most sustained commentaries on the רפא in ancient Hebrew literature.[70] What is significant about Sirach 38 is that, in contrast to Chronicles and Jeremiah, it contains a lengthy commendation of the value of the רפא. Sirach argues that God had established the profession of the רפא (v. 2), and he advocates the use of both God (presumably direct prayer and petitionary rituals) and the רפא (vss. 9-12). Furthermore, Sirach argued that medicinal herbs were provided with their power directly by God (v. 4).

Sirach exemplifies the view that by the second century B.C.E. the רפא was deemed to be worthy of being a primary, if not the primary, human health care consultant within normative Judaism. The fact that, with the possible exception of devotion to Yahweh, the רפא remained virtually the same type of profession as the one described in Jeremiah is substantiated by the mention of botanical substances in Sirach 38. On the other hand, the lengthy poem also has a promotional color that indicates that the רפא was not yet accepted as the primary human health care consultant by all Jews.[71] This provides further evidence that the profession was not regarded earlier as a universally accepted one within Hebrew religion. In any event, Sirach illustrates that by the second century there was a movement

---

[70]As noted by P. Skehan and A. A. Di Lella (*The Wisdom of Ben Sira* [*AB* 39; Garden City, New York, 1987] 439), the Hebrew word is attested in Manuscript D of the Geniza fragments of Sirach, and the Hebrew word is used elsewhere in Hebrew manuscripts of Sirach (e.g., 10:10).

[71]Note, for example, that *Wisdom of Solomon* 16:12 (ca. 1 c. B.C.E.) denies that herbs have healing power at all.

toward the acceptance of the רפא as the primary human health care consultant within normative Judaism.

(e) The רפא and the *asû*

As we have noted above, the רפא was probably distinguished by his concern with natural remedies. The use of *materia medica* by the רפא leads one to posit the Mesopotamian *asû* as the best analogy on the basis of the limited data available. It may be that it was the expertise in natural plants that has influenced the application of the word to the embalmers of Egypt, even though the latter probably did not specialize in handling "live" patients.   In other words, anyone with a specialized expertise in the use of botanical substances was labeled as a רפא, even though the actual specializations of such individuals may have had a wider range in terms of the types of patients treated.

(3) "Sorcerers"

As previously mentioned, there is evidence that divination of the type seen in Mesopotamia was available in Canaan prior to the formation of Israel, and it undoubtedly persisted throughout the Israelite period. Such divination may have been used in cases of illness. The types of professions denounced in Deut 18:10-11 and elsewhere in the Hebrew Bible also may have provided consultative services in cases of illness, though one can only adduce indirect evidence.

The terms found in Deut 18:10-11 include: the necromancer (דרש אל המתים), the "pit diviner" (שאל

אוב),[72] the sorcerer (ומכשף),[73] and the "fortune teller"
(ומנחש). These renditions are very tentative because not
much other information is available about their practices.
Other professions mentioned in Deut 18:10 are not
understood much at all (e.g., קסמים מעונן).

The fact that these professions are juxtaposed with
the legitimacy of the Yahwistic prophet in Deut 18:15-22
argues that the "illegitimate" consultants may have been used
for services similar to those that should be sought from a
נביא. In particular, Deut 18:14-15 says:

כי הגוים האלה אשר אתה יורש אותם אל
מעננים ואל קסמים ישמעו ואתה לא כן נתן
לך יהוה אלהיך נביא מקרבך מאחיך כמני
יקים לך יהוה אלהיך אליו תשמעון

Indeed, these nations whose land you shall inherit
obey "diviners" and "sorcerers." But Yahweh your
God shall not permit you to do likewise. Yahweh
your God shall establish a prophet like me from
among you, from your brothers. You shall obey
him.

---

[72]On this type of divination, see H. A. Hoffner, "Second Millennium
Antecedents of the Hebrew *'ôb*," *JBL* 86 (1967) 385-401. For a
different etymology of אוב, see J. Lust, "On Wizards and Prophets,"
VTSup 26 (1974) 133-142.

[73]This term is certainly related to the Akkadian *kispu* which usually
denotes a malevolent type of magic. See further, J. Bottero, "Magie
A," *RLA* 7:200-234; Marie-Louise Thomsen, *Zauberdiagnose und
Schwarze Magie in Mesopotamien* (Carsten Niebuhr Institute of
Ancient Near Eastern Studies, 2 Museum Tusculanum, 1987); and T.
Abusch, *Babylonian Witchcraft Literature:Case Studies* (Brown Judaic
Studies 32; Atlanta:Scholars Press, 1987).

These verses may be read as a charter for the Yahwistic
נביא, and they clearly indicate that he alone shall provide
most, or all, of the types of consultations asked of non-
Yahwistic consultants in Canaan. Since illness was included
among the consultative services provided by the נביא, one
may infer that the "illegitimate" consultants were also sought
in cases of illness. This polemic may have more than simply
an ideological base, for these diviners probably derived
economic benefit from such consultations. Thus, the text
may be a witness to a struggle that one sees in many health
care systems in which alternative consultants compete for
clients. As in Israel, many of these competing consultants
are "illegitimized" in some societies by force of law.[74]

c) The consultants in socio-historical perspective

The most distinctive aspect of Israelite health care
relative to Greece and Mesopotamia is that Israel had a
dichotomous system of health care options--legitimate and
illegitimate--which was created by a mono-Yahwistic
ideology, among other factors. The sum of the evidence we
have discussed indicates that ancient Israel probably had
recourse to a variety of health care consultants besides those
regarded as legitimate by the biblical authors. The fact that

---

[74]For modern American examples of competition between "legitimate"
and "illegitimate" consultants which has been resolved by force of law,
see Paul Starr, The Social Transformation of American Medicine (New
York: Basic Books, 1982). For a detailed discussion of the use of law
in the competition between orthodox and unorthodox magical
consultants in England in the 16th and 17th centuries, see Keith
Thomas, Religion and the Decline of Magic (New York:Scribners,
1971). The ultimate definition of "legitimate" belongs to the victor.

biblical authors are so vehement in the denunciation of "illegitimate consultants" reflects the latter's popularity. We can only speculate as to the reasons for the conflict. As mentioned, economics may have played a role in the conflict, though we cannot claim it as the only motive. As in many health care systems, alternative health care consultants not only can have competing economic interests, but also different ideologies on the nature and cause of illness.[75]

The רפא, a specialist in natural remedies, was regarded as illegitimate in most biblical texts, and the prophet was the most widely accepted human health care consultant during the biblical period. The acceptance of the רפא as a legitimate consultant seems to coincide or follow the decline of the prophets early in the Second Temple period. By the time of Sirach (2nd c. B.C.E.), when prophets had ceased to be a viable institution, the רפא seems to be accorded respect denied in Chronicles and Jeremiah.

Since the loss of the prophet meant that the health care system lost its primary consultant, a vacuum may have paved the way for the רפא to achieve legitimate status. Moreover, since the temple was not a petitionary or therapeutic locus in the normative Judaism of the Second Temple period, there was additional reason for allowing the רפא to become "normalized." The theoretical shift would only require that the powers that were formerly attributed to pagan gods[76] in the endeavours of the רפא now be

---

[75]For relatively modern American examples of the role of religious ideology and economics in conflicts between "legitimate" and "alternative" health care consultants, see Robert C. Fuller, *Alternative Medicine and the American Religious Life* (New York: Oxford, 1989).

[76]It is uncertain whether the רפא was connected with the group of beings called the Rephaim, and to what extent any such connection might have contributed to his illegitimate status. The Mesopotamian

attributed to Yahweh. Such a shift is clear in Sirach 38 which argues that the רפא is an agent of God. Since expertise with *materia medica* did not necessarily involve the invocation of pagan deities, the legitimatization of the רפא was not as problematic as that of other consultants (for example, those in Deut 18:10ff) whose work presupposed the invocation of pagan deities.

4. Temple and health in ancient Israel

a) General remarks

There were a number of temples dedicated to Yahweh during the biblical period. Some of these temples are not explicitly named in the biblical texts, though archaeological remains attest to their Yahwistic origins (e.g., Arad).[77] Unfortunately, not many data are available

---

asû was associated with Gula and Damu, who were regarded as divine sponsors or as the divine beings who empowered the profession's treatments. On the Rephaim in general, see W. Beyse, "רפאים," *TWAT* 7:625-639; C. E. L'Heureux, "The Ugaritic and Biblical Rephaim," *HTR* 67 (1974) 265-274; and T. Lewis, *The Cults of the Dead at Ugarit* (Atlanta:Scholars Press, 1989). On the possible connection of the Rephaim with healing, N. Lohfink, "'Ich bin Jahwe, dein Arzt (Ex 15:26) '" *Stuttgarter Bibelstudien* 100 (1981) 13-73.

[77]On the problems associated with interpreting cultic archaeological remains of Yahwistic temples, see A. Biran, ed., *Temples and High Places in Biblical Times* (Proceedings of the Colloquium in Honor of the Centennial of Hebrew Union College-Jewish Institute of Religion, Jerusalem, 14-16 March, 1977; Jerusalem: HUC-JIR, 1981); W. G. Dever, "Material Remains and the Cult in Ancient Israel:An Essay in Archaeological Systematics," in Carol Meyers and M. O'Connor, eds., *The Word of the Lord Shall Go Forth:Essays in Honor of David Noel Freedman* (Winona Lake, Indiana:Eisenbrauns, 1983) 571-587; J. S.

concerning the actual role, if any, of these temples in the health care system of ancient Israel. We shall first attempt to describe the role of the best known temple(s) reflected in the biblical text without reference to their historicity. We shall subsequently offer a discussion of the extent to which the situation depicted in these biblical texts corresponded to actual socio-historical conditions.

(1) Purity in the Priestly Code

(a) General comments

The relationship between the role of the temple in the health care system and Israelite ideas concerning purity and illness is a widely attested one in the biblical texts, but the relationship is not without complications. The most salient complication is the definition of purity itself.[78] For the sake

---

Holladay, "Religion in Israel and Judah under the Monarchy: An Explicitly Archaeological Approach," in P. D. Miller, P. D. Hanson and S. Dean McBride, eds., *Ancient Israelite Religion* (Philadelphia:Fortress, 1987) 315-335; Y. Shiloh, "Sanctuaries and Cult Elements in Palestine," in F. M. Cross, ed., *Symposia Celebrating the Seventy Fifth Anniversary of the Founding of the American Schools for Oriental Research (1900-1975)* (Cambridge, MA:ASOR, 1979) 147-158.

[78]For general discussions of purity, see J. Neusner, *The Idea of Purity in Ancient Judaism* (SJLA 1; Leiden, Brill, 1973); Tikva Frymer-Kensky, "Pollution, Purification, and Purgation in Biblical Israel," in Carol Meyers and M. O'Connor, eds., *The Word of the Lord Shall Go Forth:Essays in Honor of David Noel Freedman* (Winona Lake, Indiana:Eisenbrauns, 1983) 399-414; Hannah K. Harrington, *The Impurity Systems of Qumran and the Rabbis: Biblical Foundations* (Atlanta: Scholars Press, 1993); David P. Wright, *The Disposal of Impurity*; John G. Gammie, *Holiness in Israel* (Philadelphia:Fortress,

of simplicity, we shall concentrate first on the most coherent description of purity in the Hebrew Bible, a description found in Leviticus.

There is a scholarly majority which assigns Leviticus to the Priestly tradition. In the concluding sections of this chapter, we shall note how the debates surrounding the relationship of the Holiness Code (Lev 17-26) to the rest of Leviticus limit how specific we can be in our reconstruction of the health care system.[79] But, for the moment, we shall use the rubric P to designate texts on which there is a broad agreement in their assignment to that source.[80] We shall focus on this corpus of priestly texts to guide our biblical comparisons. In particular, we shall compare other biblical descriptions of purity when we treat passages that speak of the role of the temple in the health care system.

There are a number of scholars who view P as a pre-Exilic product.[81] While we shall follow the majority by

---

1989); and H. Eilberg-Schwartz, *The Savage in Judaism* (Bloomington:Indiana University, 1990).

[79]See, for example, the discussion of the relationship of the Holiness Code (H) to the rest of Leviticus by J. Milgrom (*Leviticus 1-16* [New York: Doubleday, 1991]), and especially his review (pp. 13-35) of the theory expounded by Israel Knohl ("The Priestly Torah versus the Holiness School: Sabbath and the Festivals," *HUCA* 58 [1987] 65-117) that H is the redactor of P.

[80]For a critique of Milgrom's recent commentary of Leviticus, and on whether we should still use the terms "priestly code" or "priestly source," see Rolf Rendtorff, "Two Kinds of P? Some Reflections on the Occasion of the Publishing of Jacob Milgrom's Commentary on Leviticus 1-16," *JSOT* 60 (1993) 75-81. See also, J. Milgrom, "Response to Rolf Rendtorff," *JSOT* 60 (1993) 83-85.

[81]One recent example is Israel Knohl ("The Priestly Torah," 65-117). According to Knohl, H, which for him developed between the time of Hezekiah and the early Persian Period, is the redactor of P. The latter dates no later than the middle of the eighth century B.C.E. See also,

opting, for the moment, to view the priestly texts as ones written in the post-Exilic period, our reconstruction of the health care system is not inconsistent with the composition of P in the pre-Exilic period. In fact, our reconstruction of the history of the role of the temple in P's health care system is sufficiently broad to accommodate dates from the late eighth century B.C.E. to the post-Exilic period. What is important is that it is in the post-Exilic period where one finds the most evidence for the actual application of the ideology of P, albeit not necessarily in a consistent manner.

In its most general sense, one may characterize purity in the Priestly traditions as *the state of being that renders persons, places, or things as acceptable to participate in the cult and to maintain the presence of the deity.* A fundamental principle of purity is expressed in Leviticus 19:2: "You shall be holy for I the Lord your God am holy." Those things that were deemed acceptable (pure) were usually designated in P by the word טהר.[82] The antonym was טמא,[83] and it designated all those things that were not fit to participate in the cult.

The fundamental principles that separate "pure" and "impure" have been a matter of debate. P. Henninger, for instance, argues that transitional periods are inherently impure, and such periods include birth, initiation, puberty,

---

Y. Kaufmann, *The Religion of Israel* [tr. M. Greenberg; Chicago:U. of Chicago, 1960] 175-200; and A. Hurvitz, *A Linguistic Study of the Relationship of The Priestly Source and the Book of Ezekiel* (Paris: J. Gabalda, 1982).

[82]For a full treatment of the word, see H. Ringgren, "טהר..." *TDOT* 5:287-296.

[83]For a full treatment of the word, see G. André, "טמא..." *TDOT* 5:330-342.

marriage, and death.[84] However, the biblical texts do not designate marriage or puberty as impure states, and so this scheme has not been well accepted by scholarship. M. Douglas proposed that "wholeness" was the fundamental criterion, and so, for example, bodily discharges are impure because they are viewed as a diminution of "wholeness."[85] Though this theory does have some validity, it does not explain why the level of "impurity" affecting a given feature (e.g., postparturition) varies with, among other things, the gender of the child (see further below).

Mary Douglas[86] also developed a schema that has been used by Bruce Malina,[87] John Pilch[88] and other New Testament scholars to speak about purity and "leprosy." Douglas' schema is based on two basic societal measures called Group and Grid. As John Pilch describes it, Group refers to the degree of societal pressure at work on a given social unit to conform to societal norms. At one extreme, Strong Group indicates high pressure to conform along with strong corporate identity. Weak Group indicates a weak pressure to conform along with a pliable definition of group identity. According to Pilch,

---

[84]P. Henninger, "Pureté et impureté: l'histoire de religions," *DBSup* 9 (1979) 399-430.

[85]M. Douglas, *Purity and Danger: An Analysis of of the Concepts of Pollution and Taboo* (London:Routledge and Kegan Paul, 1966).

[86]Mary Douglas, *Natural Symbols: An Exploration in Cosmology* (New York: Vintage, 1973).

[87]Bruce Malina, *Christian Origins and Cultural Anthropology: Practical Models for Biblical Interpretation* (Atlanta: John Knox, 1986).

[88]John J. Pilch, "Biblical Leprosy and Body Symbolism," *BTB* 11 (4, 1981) 108-113.

> Grid: refers to the degree of assent normally given to
> the symbol system--the classifications, patterns of
> perception and evaluation--through which the society
> enables its members to bring order and intelligibility
> to their experiences.[89]

High Grid indicates a high degree of congruence between the individual's experiences and societal norms. Low Grid indicates a low degree of congruence between an individual's experiences and societal patterns of perception and evaluation. These measures are then divided into a matrix with four quadrants: 1) Weak Group, High Grid 2) Strong Group, High Grid, 3) Weak Group, Low Grid, and 4) Strong Group, Low Grid.

According to Pilch "Biblical leprosy turns our attention to strong group because that's the nature of biblical societies."[90] The rules of purity in Leviticus, according to Pilch, derive from a society that may be described as Strong Group/High Grid. These societies view the body as tightly controlled and a symbol of life.

Although such typologies are useful in some instances, they assume too much of the data. For example, Israelite society was not monolithic, and so to say that a strong group is "the nature of biblical societies" is misleading. It is true that Leviticus shows a great concern for social conformity, but that is not all that will determine rules of purity. Socioeconomic interests clearly play a role in what is classified as pure and impure. It is no accident that laws requiring that only the best of the flock be brought to the temple for sacrifice in effect demanded the allocation

---

[89]Pilch, "Biblical Leprosy and Body Symbolism," 110.
[90]Pilch, "Biblical Leprosy and Body Symbolism," 109.

of the best animal resources (cattle, sheep and goats) for the priestly establishment. The best animal resources were classified as "pure" while less desirable species were classified as "impure."[91]

In addition, the temple establishment did not always believe or follow its own rules of purity, something evident in the many passages that attack the lack of observance on the part of certain temple personnel (Ezek 44:10; Neh. 9:4-9). Priestly groups that regarded themselves as pure were regarded as impure by other priestly groups (cf. 1 Kings 12:31). There were questions about what constituted "purity." (cf. Hag 2:14). Thus, the language of purity may reflect true beliefs as well as rationales or apologetic strategies used to promote the allocation of power and the best resources for particular social groups, regardless of their place within or outside of power structures. Similarly, how much a state is able or willing to care for the ill may also determine the classification of the ill with the idiom of purity. In sum, the Group/Grid approach may be useful in some instances, but it is too simple to address the dynamics of "purity" in Israelite society.

A widely accepted criterion concerning the definition of purity in P has been proposed by J. Milgrom.[92] He views the fundamental criteria as ones which involve the dichotomy of life and death. The grade of purity, or impurity, forms a

---

[91]For a study of socio-economic factors in animal classifications, see M. Harris, *The Sacred Cow and the Abominable Pig* (New York, 1985).

[92]See, for example, J. Milgrom, "Rationale for Cultic Law: The Case of Impurity," *Semeia* 45 (1989) 103-9. We agree with Milgrom and D. Wright (*The Disposal of Impurity*) that, although most of the laws of purity may have originated from a belief in demons in some manner, these laws have been "de-demonized" by the Priestly Code.

continuum that is proportional to the proximity to each pole of the dichotomy. Since Yahweh represents the ultimate in "life," anything that is akin to "death" is regarded as impurity. Illness is a state that is closer to "death" than to "life," and, therefore, a sick person is more impure than a healthy one. Illnesses such as צרעת produce states in patients (e.g., decaying flesh) that are most akin to corpses in the view of many biblical texts, and so these patients are regarded as extremely impure. In Numbers 12:12, for example, one finds a direct analogy between being afflicted with צרעת and being dead. As we shall see, many psalms also use death imagery to portray an illness. Some illnesses are depicted as posing the danger of contagion that can spread the impurity to the community and temple to the point that Yahweh may leave the community.[93]

Perhaps the best model that accounts for the difficulty of using one criterion of purity is proposed by H. Eilberg-Schwartz.[94] He views the fundamental ideology as one in which a variety of codes interact to yield the purity laws found in the Bible. Such codes may be viewed as oppositions such as: life/death, men/women, control/lack of control. So, for example, the fact that the period of postparturition impurity for the birth of a daughter lasts twice as long as it does for the birth of a son does not necessarily reflect only a code based on the opposition between life and death. Instead, this law of impurity is influenced by a code that saw women as inherently more impure than males

---

[93]See J. Milgrom, "Israel's Sanctuary: The Priestly 'Picture of Dorian Gray'" *RB* 83 (1976) 62-72.

[94]H. Eilberg-Schwartz, *The Savage in Judaism* (Bloomington: Indiana University Press, 1990) 177-216.

because the laws of purity were also an expression of power and status in the society.

In summary, one single Ur-principle, if it ever existed, that will encompass all notions of purity in ancient Israel will probably not be found. It is just as probable that there were a number of criteria from the beginning which underwent and evolution and were not uniform throughout Israel. J. Gammie, for example, has recently attempted to show how different traditions (priestly, wisdom, prophetic) viewed purity.[95] Insofar as illness in P is concerned, we regard the theories of Milgrom and Eilberg-Schwartz as the most useful, but we have added our own refinements. Our approach argues that the laws of purity show intimate interrelationships among socio-economic features that are not simply related to fears of contagion. We shall provide further discussion below on the relationship among illness, purity, and socio-economic factors.

(b) Site and plan of the Temple of Jerusalem

The temple was perhaps the most important "object" that was to be maintained free from impurity. Commenting on the importance of purity in P, J. Neusner says:

> All sources of impurity according to that code produced a single practical result: one must not enter the Temple.[96]

We shall concentrate our study on any structure designated as a Yahwistic shrine. In particular, we shall be

---

[95]J. Gammie, *Holiness in Israel* (Minneapolis:Fortress, 1989).
[96]J. Neusner, *The Idea of Purity in Ancient Judaism*, 118.

concerned with the structure attributed to Solomon, and considered the most important temple of Yahweh in Israel by the biblical texts.[97] Although the exact plan of Solomon's temple still eludes us, it is generally agreed that the temple building was a tri-partite structure. If we assume that a royal cubit equals 21 inches, the temple building would be approximately 122 feet long, 35 feet wide, and 35 feet high.[98]   As noted by J. M. Miller and J. H. Hayes, the structure was not made to accommodate large crowds.[99]   As we shall see below, the size of the temple affects its use as a therapeutic locus.

Biblical terminology regarding the temple complex is not always clear, but it is necessary to provide some broad categories which are relevant for the study of access of the ill to the temple. In the priestly descriptions of the temple, the word היכל was used to describe the sanctuary proper.[100] Usually only healthy Aaronite priests were permitted inside in P (cf. Num 18:7ff). Another term, בית, denoted the larger temple buildings which did permit the presence of non-Aaronite priests, but בית may also be used for the entire temple complex (including the courtyard) in some

---

[97]See J. Milgrom, "Israel's Sanctuary: The Priestly 'Picture of Dorian Gray'" *RB* 83 (1976) 62-72. For a treatment of the organization of the temple, see M. Haran, *Temples and Temple Service in Ancient Israel* (Oxford:Clarendon, 1978).

[98]Following J. M. Miller and J. H. Hayes, *A History of Ancient Israel and Judah* (Philadelphia: Westminster, 1986) 202.

[99]J. M. Miller and J. H. Hayes, *A History of Ancient Israel and Judah* (Philadelphia: Westminster, 1986) 202.

[100]For a fuller treatment, see M. Ottosson, "היכל," *TDOT* 3:382-388.

passages.[101] Finally, there was a courtyard (חצר) which surrounded the sanctuary (cf. 1 Kgs 8:64).[102] This area generally permitted the presence of healthy Israelites (Lev 3:2, 8:3).[103]

One of Julius Wellhausen's enduring contributions to biblical studies was that he synthesized the evidence that showed that there was a historical evolution in the degree of restriction imposed on non-Aaronite priests.[104] In Joshua 9:27, for example, foreigners (e.g., the Gibeonites) were allowed to minister at the altar. The evolution of access is reflected in the parallel stories of restoration of king Joash after Athaliah's usurpation in 2 Kgs 11 and 2 Chr 23:1ff. The version in Kings supposes that foreigners were employed as legitimate guards in the temple, while the version in 2 Chr is careful to specify that only "priests and levites" were allowed to enter the "house."[105] The shift

---

[101]In 2 Kgs 21:4, for example, Manasseh builds altars in the "House of God." Since altars require an open space, the passage shows that בית must refer to areas outside of the shrine proper, whether in the courtyard area or on the roof.

[102]We follow J. Milgrom (*Studies in Levitical Terminology* I [Berkeley:U. of California Press, 1970] 23 n. 78) in viewing the term מקדש as one which applies to the sacred precincts and its contents, of which the tabernacle/temple was only one component. The most cogent passages are Num 10:21 and 1 Chr 28:10.

[103]See further M. Haran, *Temples and Temple Service in Ancient Israel* (Oxford: Clarendon, 1978) 175ff.

[104]J. Wellhausen, *Prolegomena to the History of Israel* (Gloucester: Peter Smith, 1983 [Trans. and Repr. of 1883 German edition] especially 152-167. For a recent discussion of Ezekiel 40-48, see J. D. Levenson, *Theology of the Program of Restoration: Ezekiel 40-48* (HSM 10; Atlanta: Scholars Press, 1986 [Repr. of 1976 ed.])

[105]We differ with Milgrom (*Studies in Levitical Terminology* I [Berkeley:U. of California Press, 1970] 13f) who argues that the word

away from using foreigners to guard the temple is discussed in Ezekiel 44:6ff.[106] Milgrom argues that Ezekiel's innovations were intended, in part, "to rid the sacrificial court of laymen."[107] For our purposes, the most significant feature of the priestly regulations discussed above is that, under normal circumstances, the temple/tabernacle in the Priestly materials allowed the presence of healthy laypersons in the courtyard, but not in the sanctuary building.[108] While priests who had physical deformities apparently were permitted in the courtyard (cf. Lev 21:22-23), P explicitly did not allow the presence of many types of illnesses among laypersons within any portion of the temple or courtyard, and we shall provide further details below.

בית in 2 Chr 23:6 must refer to the sanctuary area, not the sanctuary building. One reason for our conclusion is that the interpretation of בית as "sanctuary area" in the second half of the verse would yield a situation which allowed only priests and Levites into the sanctuary area. But this contradicts verse 5 which states that the people of Israel were allowed inside the enclosure (= sanctuary area), a situation which accords with P. The most natural contrast in access in 2 Chr 23:5-6, therefore, is one which permits the people of Israel access only into the sanctuary area, and only priests and levites access to the sanctuary building itself. The fact that 2 Chronicles 29:16 seems to allow only the priests to enter the sanctuary building, and the Levites access only to the court, may reflect customs pertaining to different editions of the Chronicler's work posited by F. M. Cross ("A Reconstruction of the Judean Restoration," *Int* 29 [1975] 187-203).

[106]For the view that Ez 44:6-16 represents a restoration, not an innovation, see R. K. Duke, "Punishment or Restoration? Another Look at the Levites of Ezekiel 44:6-16," *JSOT* 40 (1988) 61-81.

[107]J. Milgrom, *Studies in Levitical Terminology* I (Berkeley:U. of California Press, 1970) 85 n. 316.

[108]See discussion by J. Milgrom, *Studies in Levitical Terminology* I, 13f.

Recent anthropological studies clearly show that demarcations of space in many cultures often correlate not simply with fears of contagion but also with a system of symbols that expresses status and power in terms of differential access to physical space. In fact, power and status are often expressed in demarcations of space in institutions ranging from households to nation-states. The insights from such studies have been applied most recently by J. Z. Smith to the Israelite temple.[109] We shall discuss more fully the implications of these insights below.

(2) Purity and Illness in P

(a) "Leprosy" (צרעת)

According to P, there are a large variety of phenomena that render persons, places and things impure, and many illnesses were among these. In Leviticus it is clear that "leprosy" was regarded as an impurity that excluded one from the cult. In this regard, Leviticus is consistent with Mesopotamian sentiments about skin diseases such as *saḫaršubbû*. "Leprosy" and other impurities were excluded from the temple according to P (e.g., Lev 12:4, 13:46, and 15:31).

There is now a consensus that צרעת is not the modern disease denominated as leprosy and known also as Hansen's Disease, nor is it the disease(s) denominated by

---

[109]J. Z. Smith, *To Take Place:Toward Theory in Ritual* (Chicago:U. of Chicago, 1987); see also, P. P. Jenson, *Graded Holiness: A Key to the Priestly Conception of the World* (Sheffield: JSOT, 1992).

the word λεπρα (*lepra*) in Greek.[110] In fact, צרעת is probably a word that refers to a wide range of conditions which result in an abnormal disfigurement or discoloration of surfaces---including human skin.[111]

The confusion among a number of pathological entities (or complex of entities) with Hebrew צרעת by many modern translators probably began with the use of the Greek word *lepra* to translate the Hebrew word. The Greek word, however, designated a wide range of diseases which had scales as part of their configuration (e.g., something akin to, or identical with, the modern condition classified as "psoriasis").[112]

Another stage in the confusion was advanced by G. H. Armauer Hansen, a Norwegian physician. In 1874 he described an organism (*Mycobacterium leprae*) that he had

---

[110]Some of the representatives of this consensus include: J. Zias, "Lust and Leprosy:Confusion or Correlation?" *BASOR* 275 (1989) 27-31; E.V. Hulse, "The Nature of Biblical 'Leprosy' and the Use of Alternative Medical Terms in Modern Translations of the Bible," *PEQ* 107 (1975) 87-105; J. Wilkinson, "Leprosy and Leviticus:The Problem of Description and Identification," *Scottish Journal of Theology* 30 (1977) 153-69; *idem*, "Leprosy and Leviticus: A Problem of Semantics and Translation," *Scottish Journal of Theology* 31 (1978) 153-166.

[111]As J. Preuss (*Biblical and Talmudic Medicine*, 326 n. 10) notes, Maimonides (*Hilcoth Tzaraath* 16:10) may also have regarded the biblical term as a collective designation for a wide variety of illnesses.

[112]My discussion on the history of use of the word *leprosy* is indebted to E.V. Hulse, "The Nature of Biblical 'Leprosy'..." *PEQ* 107 (1975) 87-105; J. Wilkinson, "Leprosy and Leviticus:A Problem of Semantics and Translation," *Scottish Journal of Theology* 31 (1978) 153-166; *idem*, "Leprosy and Leviticus: The Problem of Description and Identification," *Scottish Journal of Theology* 30 (1977) 153-69; and J. Lowe, "Comments on the History of Leprosy," *Leprosy Review* 9 (1955) 9 and 25.

discovered in 1864, and that produces a mildly infectious disease which came to be known as Hansen's disease. This disease was identical with at least some of the conditions denominated as "leprosy" in Medieval times. The name of the bacterium implies that the condition caused by the microorganism was the same as some of the conditions described by the Greek word *lepra*, and Hansen himself thought that the condition that he described in modern patients was identical with the condition(s) described in Leviticus. Julius Preuss, whom we have already discussed in the Introduction, was one of the writers on biblical medicine that also identified Hansen's disease with צרעת, though he was not dogmatic about the identification.[113]

In any event, a wide range of evidence (philological, historical, and paleo-osteological) indicates that biblical צרעת is not to be identified exclusively with Hansen's disease (if it is to be identified with the latter at all). As Hulse notes, Hansen's disease is "active mainly in the skin, the mucous membrane of the nose, the lymph nodes, and the peripheral nerves."[114] R. G. Cochrane notes that, in contrast to the conditions described in Leviticus, the lesions of modern leprosy are never white, and that modern leprosy of the scalp is quite rare.[115] J. Zias, among others, doubts seriously if Hansen's disease even existed at the time

---

[113]J. Preuss (*Biblical and Talmudic Medicine*, 325-26) comments: "The interpretation that *tzaraath* is leprosy is at best a diagnosis of probability. Indeed it shares this lot with a large number of names of illnesses in antiquity."

[114]Hulse, "The Nature of Biblical 'Leprosy'..." 87.

[115]R. G. Cochrane, *Biblical Leprosy: A Suggested Interpretation* (2nd ed.; London:The Tyndale Press, 1963) 14.

Leviticus was written.[116] Some corroboration of this non-existence of Hansen's disease is provided by the fact that no skeletons of the biblical age show any signs of leprosy. Although this is an argument *ex silentio*, this silence is significant in light of the brilliant work of V. Møller-Christensen who used large quantities of skeletons to document the changes in bones that can be produced by Hansen's disease.[117] Zias notes that no indisputable cases of Hansen's disease have been identified in skeletal material in Israel prior to the 5th c. C.E.,[118] and S. G. Browne notes that not a single case has been found in the entire Fertile Crescent.[119]

The fact is that צרעת probably designates a wide range of conditions that may have subsumed Hansen's disease (if such a disease existed in Israel in the biblical period) but was certainly not limited to this condition. The wide range of conditions subsumed under צרעת is quite evident even in Leviticus. Not only humans, but inanimate objects could be struck with צרעת. This alone eliminates identification with Hansen's disease. As we shall discuss in more detail below, Leviticus also states that not all cases of צרעת required the same amount of quarantine periods.

---

[116]J. Zias, "Lust and Leprosy, 27; *idem*, "Leprosy in the Byzantine Monasteries of the Judean Desert," *Koroth* 9 (1-2, 1985) 242.

[117]V. Møller-Christensen, *Bone Changes in Leprosy* (Copenhagen, 1961).

[118]J. Zias, "Leprosy in the Byzantine Monasteries of the Judean Desert," *Koroth* 9 (1-2, 1985) 242.

[119]S. G. Browne, "Some Aspects of the History of Leprosy:The Leprosy of Yesterday," *Proceedings of the Royal Society of Medicine*, 68 (1975) 501-504; *idem*, "Leprosy in the Bible," in B. Palmer, ed., *Medicine and the Bible* (Exeter: Paternoster, 1986) 101-125.

What is significant about צרעת for our purposes is that it did encompass so many conditions. Almost any disease that exhibited chronic dermatological changes probably would have been designated, or suspected of being, צרעת. Among the conditions that, if they existed in that period, might have been included under צרעת are diseases that modern science has designated as:[120]

Hansen's disease
lupus erythematosus
nutritional deficiencies which
        result in dermatological changes (e.g., pellagra)
psoriasis
smallpox
skin cancer
vitiligo

The sociological implications of this wide range of conditions regarded as impure were probably enormous. The story in 2 Chr 26:16-21 of Uzziah's bout with instant צערת indicates, at least for the author, that the exclusion from the temple of those afflicted with צערת even included kings. In the beginning of the story, one sees a healthy Uzziah (or at least one with no צערת) inside of the temple itself. He is performing tasks that were not permitted to non-priests. Thereupon he is told to exit the temple area (v. 19: המקדש מן צא). But almost immediately Uzziah is struck with "leprosy", and he then is told to exit the temple with even

---

[120]For a detailed discussion of skin diseases, see T. Kwan and M. C. Mihm, "The Skin" in S. L. Robbins and R. S. Cotran, eds., *Pathologic Basis of Disease* (New York:Saunders, 1979) 1417-1461.

greater urgency (v. 20: ויבהלוהו משם). The story ends
with the following notice in verse 21:

ויהי עזיהו המלך מצרע עד יום מותו
וישב בית החפשית מצרע כי נגזר
מבית יהוה

So king Uzziah remained a "leper" until the day of his
death, and consequently he lived in a "special abode."
(Because he was) a "leper," he was certainly excluded
from the temple of Yahweh.

Insofar as the role of the temple is concerned, it is obvious
that the wide range of conditions probably subsumed under
צרעת meant that patients with a wide range of illnesses
would not be able to use the temple as a petitionary or
therapeutic locus under the ideals of the P. We shall discuss
further below the historical and chronological relationship of
these regulations in P with those of other biblical traditions.

(b) Uro-genital illnesses

One may also infer that any illnesses involving the
abnormal visible secretion of bodily fluids which issued
from the genitalia would have been excluded from the
temple. All abnormal visible secretions from the male and
female genitalia were designated with an appropriate form of
the word זב (זוב). The Priestly regulations in Numbers
5:2 clearly state:

צו את בני ישראל וישלחו מן מחנה
כל צרוע וכל זב וכל טמא לנפש

> Command the people of Israel that they may expel
> from the camp every "leper," and everyone with
> "abnormal genital secretions" and everyone who is
> contaminated with matters of life [and death].

Insofar as our subject is concerned, the most significant aspect of this injunction is the exclusion of those with זב. As we have stated, the term encompasses fluids produced not only by men, but also by women (cf. Lev 15:19).

If fluids which result from a variety of sexually transmitted diseases are subsumed under the term זב, then the Priestly ideology would exclude the temple as a petitionary or therapeutic locus for patients suffering from diseases which are classified by modern medicine as: gonorrhea, herpes, and other non-sexual infections of the uro-genital tract that produce abnormal secretions.[121] This would contrast with the Asclepieia, which, judging from a number of texts and figurines of votive penises, did allow the use of the temple as petitionary and therapeutic loci for sexually transmitted diseases.

One should also note that postparturition brought an initial period of intense impurity that lasted 7 days for a woman who bore a son, and 14 days for one who bore a daughter (Lev 12:1-5). Following this period is a second one that lasts 33 days for the birth of a male and 66 days for the birth of a female. Leviticus 12:4 is explicit in stating that:

ואל מקדש לא תבא
עד מלאות ימי טהרה

---

[121] Some Rabbinic authorities attempted to distinguish semen from abnormal discharges by counting as abnormal those discharges which issued from the flaccid penis (e.g., *Tosefta Zabim*, 2:4).

> She shall not enter the sanctuary
> until her purification period is complete.

In light of the fact that the period covered by these laws is
one in which the medical dangers of postparturition are at
their height, the law constitutes a *de facto* exclusion of the
temple as a petitionary or therapeutic locus for women who
suffer such complications during that period.

That the "leper" is categorized under טמא is clear
from Leviticus 13:15 which says of the person who bears
some of the indications of "leprosy": "He is impure,
(because) it is 'leprosy'" (טמא הוא צערת הוא).
Accordingly, the "leper" is certainly prohibited from entering
the temple.

(c) Other conditions

i) Formal prohibitions. There are indications that
access to the temple was denied to those who suffered
diseases other than צערת or זב. The blind for example,
seem to be excluded in at least one tradition. The word עור
refers to blindness. Modern societies recognize degrees of
blindness, as did the Talmud.[122] But עור apparently
refers to total blindness in Deut 28:29: "You shall grope in
daylight, as the blind person gropes in darkness."(והיית
ממשש בצהרים כאשר ימשש העור באפלה). Deut
28:28-29 also views blindness as one of the curses which
befalls those who break the covenant.

The word פסח seems to apply to a condition that
renders one unable to use the legs (and/or feet). Proverbs

---

[122]See discussion by J. Preuss, *Biblical and Talmudic Medicine*, 270ff.

26:7 describes the legs of a person with פסח as dangling uselessly (דליו שקים פסח). The most famous story concerning this condition is that of Mephibosheth in 2 Sam 9:3-13. It is clear that פסח is synonymous with the phrase נכה רגלים (injured in the legs) in the same narrative (2 Sam 9:3). The condition could afflict one or both legs as implied by the phrase פסח שתי רגליו (v. 3: "disabled in both legs"). In the case of Mephibosheth it was not a birth defect, but the result of an injury sustained while an infant (cf. 2 Sam 4:4). Mephibosheth's impairment was so severe that he could not saddle an ass by himself (2 Sam 19:26), and he was apparently unable to secure a livelihood. David brought him into his household for life (2 Sam 9:9ff).

Evidence for the exclusion of the blind and the lame from the temple may be found in a curious note in 2 Sam 5:8:

על כן יאמרו עור ופסח לא

יבוא אל הבית

> Because of this it is said "the blind
> and the lame shall not enter into the
> temple."

This note appears to be a secondary addition to an episode in which David had been taunted with the Jebusite threat that the blind and the lame would repel his attack on "the stronghold of Zion."[123] However, the note is significant for at least two reasons. First, it suggests that, no matter what

---

[123] See further, P. K. McCarter, *II Samuel* (*AB* 9; Garden City, NY: Doubleday, 1984) 140.

the precise origin of the custom described in its content, there was a tradition that forbade entry of the lame and blind into the temple precincts. As we have seen, the word בית may be used for the holy shrine or for the larger building. But access to the shrine itself was generally denied to healthy laypersons, and, therefore, the tradition in 2 Sam 5:8 would be superfluous unless it referred to the temple sanctuary in its largest sense.

Second, while the blind and the lame were not allowed to serve as priests according to Lev 21:18, such priests were apparently not barred from the courtyard. If the regulation reflected in 2 Sam 5:8 is contemporaneous with those of Lev 21:18, then there appears to be a double-standard. Blind and lame priests may be allowed in the temple, but laypersons with the same conditions were not. As we shall argue below, socio-economic reasons, and not simply fear of contagion from the blind the and lame, may best account for this disparity in the treatment of priests and laypersons with the same illnesses.

ii) Self-censorship. As we have noted, most typical patients assume that impurity or a transgression (moral or cultic) is the reason that God has punished them with illness. If patients assume that they are impure, then they might *eo ipso* consider themselves ineligible to visit the temple until after the healing has confirmed God's forgiveness. The practical consequences of this theology for the role of the temple are twofold and complementary for a patient following the Priestly regulations:

1. The patient is ineligible to enter the temple because illness has rendered him/her impure; and

2. The patient assumes that a transgression which produces
   impurity has led God to impose illness in the first place,
   and such impurity is assumed to remain for the duration
   of the illness and/or until the nature of the transgression
   is discovered.

In other words, the impurity of illness may dovetail with the
impurity which may have caused Yahweh to strike the
patient, and this renders the patient doubly-impure and
ineligible to enter the temple until God confirms such
impurity is forgiven or expelled. These assumptions by the
patient may amount to a sort of "self-censorship" in which
the patient refrains from going to the temple for fear of
contaminating it. Women who followed the postparturition
purification schedule of Leviticus 12:1ff, for example, might
stop themselves from going to the temple (rather than being
stopped by the priest directly).

(d) The actuality of the P regulations

To what extent was the ideology of P actually
implemented? According to 2 Chr 23:19, the priestly
regulations concerning impurity were enforced by the
placement of guards whose task it was to prohibit access to
the temple to those who were impure:

ויעמד השוערים על שערי בית יהוה ולא יבא
טמא לכל דבר

And he stationed the gate-keepers upon the gates of
the temple of Yahweh so that no one who was
impure in any manner might enter.

The practice of guarding the temple probably originated in the pre-Exilic period. The Deuteronomist speaks of foreign guards in the temple, while the Chronicler speaks of only Levites and priests as guards. However, the original tasks of these guards may have been primarily intended to safeguard the temple against robbery or vandalism.[124] P, therefore, may have added guarding against impurity to previous duties for these guards.

Nehemiah 6:10-11 indicates that entering the temple was forbidden even if it was meant to save one's life. In that passage Shemaiah attempts to persuade Nehemiah to enter into the temple in order to hide from those who were attempting to kill him. Nehemiah, however, refuses to hide in the temple. His answer is:

ומי כמוני אשר יבוא
אל ההיכל וחי לא אבוא

Shall someone like myself enter the temple,
in order to live? I certainly shall not enter.

---

[124]As noted by H. Güterbock ("The Hittite Temple According to Written Sources," in *Le Temple et le Culte* [XXth Recontre assyriologique internationale; Nederlands Historisch-Archeologisch Institut:Leiden, 1975] 131), Hittite temples had guards ($^{lú}GI\check{S}.\check{S}UKUR$ = "man of the spear" and $^{lú}NI.DU_8$ = "gate keeper") in the middle of the second millennium B.C.E., and it appears that their function was to provide protection from robbery or vandalism. For a study of the relationship between Israelite and Hittite temple-guardian customs, see J. Milgrom, *Studies in Levitical Terminology* I, 50-59. Note that some Asclepieia also had guards despite the fact that they had very lax laws of purity. The fact that the Deuteronomist allowed foreigners as guards also indicates that purity originally was not their foremost duty.

Perhaps Nehemiah's answer adds to the suggestion made on other grounds that he may have been a eunuch who would certainly be excluded from the temple according to the laws in Leviticus 21:20, which looks unfavorably upon those with mutilated organs.[125] In any event, the story seems to assume that at least some of the laws in P were supposed to be enforced during the time of Nehemiah.

Indirect evidence for the vitality of these regulations may be found in some extra-biblical texts that expressed a desire to extend the laws of illnesses in P to unprecedented levels. For example, the following types of patients were expressly forbidden to enter the sanctuary city according to the Temple Scroll:[126]

The blind in 11QT 45:12-13

בול איש עור לוא יבואו לה
בול ימיהמה ולוא יטמאו
את העיר אשר אני שוכן בתוכה

All blind persons shall not enter into it for
their entire life, so that they might not defile
the city within which I dwell.

---

[125]See comments by J. Myers, *Ezra-Nehemiah* (*AB* 14; Garden City, New York, 1965) 139.

[126]Following the edition of Y. Yadin, מגילת המקדש (Jerusalem, 1977) II:136-137. Among the most important studies of this aspect of the Temple Scroll are: L. H. Schiffman, "Exclusion from the Sanctuary and the City of the Sanctuary in the Temple Scroll," *HAR* 9 (1985) 301-320; J. Milgrom, "'Sabbath' and 'Temple City' in the Temple Scroll," *BASOR* 232 (1978) 25-27; *idem*, "Studies in the Temple Scroll," *JBL* 97 (4, 1978) 501-23.

Those afflicted with צרעת in 11QT 45:17-18

וכול צרוע ומנוגע לוא יבואו לה
עד אשר יטהרו
ובאשר יטהר והקריב

Any 'leper,' or afflicted (person) shall not enter it
until they are purified.
Once he is purified, he shall offer....

Both of these types of patients are excluded from the temple
on the basis of biblical precedents. The exclusion of "lepers"
from the "city" (העיר) is easily derivable from
commandments in P that exclude the "leper" from the camp.
However, the exclusion of the blind from the city for their
entire life carries biblical laws to unprecedented levels. The
"leper," on the other hand, may re-enter the temple after he
has recovered from his illness, and undertaken the
appropriate purification rituals.

Josephus (*Antiquities* 3: 261-4) says the following
concerning Moses' regulations:

> Ἀπήλασε δὲ τῆς πόλεως καὶ τοὺς λέπρα τὰ
> σώματα κακωθέντας καὶ τοὺς περὶ τὴν γονὴν
> ῥεομένους. καὶ τὰς γυναῖκας δ᾽ αἷς ἡ τῶν
> κατὰ φύσιν ἔκκρισις ἐπίοι μετέστησε πρὸς
> ἡμέραν ἑβδόμην.[127]

---

[127]Note that Josephus' terminology (τῆς πόλεως) is more consistent
with the terminology employed by the Temple Scroll (העיר) than with
that of Leviticus which mentions exclusion from the camp.

He banished from the city alike those whose body
was afflicted with "leprosy" and (abnormal) genital
secretions. Also women when beset by their natural
flow he quarantined until the seventh day.

This comment is part of a larger discourse which ends by
noting that Moses' laws were still observed during his time,
at least by some (cf. *Antiquities* 3:320ff).

There is extra-biblical epigraphic evidence that the
ideology of P was an actuality during the time of Herod's
temple. As E. Bickerman notes, Herod's temple had a
warning inscription that may have been based on the
regulations of P. It reads:[128]

μηθένα ἀλλογενῆ εἰσπορεύσθαι ἐντὸς τοῦ
περὶ τὸ ἱερὸν τρυφάκτου καὶ περιβόλου.
Ὃs δ᾿ ἂν ληφθῆ ἑαυτῶι αἴτιos ἔσται διὰ τὸ
ἐξακολουθεῖν θάνατον

No foreigner may enter within the balustrade of the
temple and the compound. Whoever is apprehended,
shall be deemed responsible for his own subsequent
death.

Ezekiel 44:7 clearly expresses the idea that uncircumcised
foreigners are not welcome in the ideal temple, and it was
apparently taken seriously by Agrippa I.[129] This ideology
would, of course, exclude non-Israelite patients of all types

---

[128]E. J. Bickerman, "The Warning Inscriptions of Herod's Temple,"
JQR 37 (1947) 388.
[129]See further, J. M. Baumgarten, "Exclusions from the
Temple:Proselytes and Agrippa I," *JJS* 33 (1982) 215-225.

who were not circumcised. The inscription in Herod's temple indicates that there was an effort to implement this ideology hundreds of years after similar biblical laws were enunciated.

In summary, the Priestly medical theology did not permit many types of illnesses to be present in the temple. Moreover, this system advocated, and probably instituted, the physical means to enforce these regulations. While there is much evidence that the temple did not always function according to the ideals envisioned in P (e.g., Ezek 8 and Neh 13), yet the vitality of these regulations was acknowledged hundreds of years after their initial formulation, and this suggests that the regulations were actually implemented at some points. Patients who subscribed to the medical theology of P may also have exercised various forms of self-restraint in visiting the temple while ill because illness was often assumed to be a consequence of impurity. Under such an ideology the temple area would not likely function as a direct petitionary or therapeutic locus. However, it is clear that the ideology of P encouraged the use of the temple as a thanksgiving locus after an illness.

b) The role of the temple in the health care system

One should not conclude from the discussion above that the Priestly texts excluded all the main functions of a temple within the health care system. The view of the temple in the Priestly traditions also was neither universal nor without historical development, and this allows one to paint a more complex portrayal of the role of the temple in the health care system of ancient Israel. We shall examine the three main functions of temples (petitionary, therapeutic, and thanksgiving) which we have discussed in conjunction with other temples in the Near East in order to assess the role(s) of the Temple of Jerusalem and other Israelite sanctuaries in the health system of ancient Israel.

(1) Petitionary function/ Infertility in 1 Samuel 1

The petitionary function of a Yahwistic shrine in the case of illness is reflected in the story of Hannah's petition for fertility at the shrine of Shiloh in 1 Sam 1. However, the story bears a number of literary problems that affect our ability to judge the extent to which it represents an actual socio-historical situation in ancient Israel. Diverse theories have been offered concerning the unity, date and motives of the story.

(a) Literary critical issues in 1 Sam 1

The genre of 1 Sam 1 is best described as a birth story. In its present state it is the birth story of Samuel, though I. Hylander and other scholars have attempted to make a case that it originally referred to Saul.[130] Although

---

[130] I. Hylander, *Die literarische Samuel-Saul-Komplex (1. Sam. 1-15) traditionsgeschichtlich untersucht* (Uppsala: Almqvist & Wiksell, 1932). For other studies of the Samuel narratives, see Michael Fishbane, "1 Samuel 3: Historical Narrative and Narrative Poetics," in K. R. R. Gros Louis and J. Ackerman, eds., *Literary Interpretations of Biblical Narratives* (2 vols.; Nashville: Abingdon, 1982) vol. 2: 191-203; Moshe Garsiel, *The First Book of Samuel: A Literary Study of Comparative Structures, Analogies, and Parallels* (Jerusalem: Rubin

the original character in the birth story may be Saul, our
main interest is in the depiction of the shrine of Shiloh.   The
shrine of Shiloh is the setting for the story, and Eli's
ministry at the shrine also forms a stable element. Although
Dus believes that verses 12-28 were part of an originally
different narrative in which Eli announces the birth of the
child, he agrees that 1 Sam 1 is a relatively coherent literary
account.[131]   Even though Walters has recently argued for the
treatment of the Hebrew and Greek versions as separate
stories,[132] both versions are consistent in their depiction of
Hannah's purpose in visiting the shrine at Shiloh.

For our purposes, Hannah's visit is crucial because it
depicts the shrine of Shiloh as a petitionary locus for an
infertile woman. It is not clear where she was within the
shrine, but her petition was placed "before Yahweh" (1:12:
לפני יהוה). Though one cannot be dogmatic, the petition
may have been uttered before the ark which was housed at
Shiloh. She must have been close to Eli, for, according to
the story, he could see her lips move. Eli was sitting in a
chair near the door of the shrine.

The legitimacy of the petitionary function for the
shrine of Shiloh within the story is corroborated by the fact
that such a function needs no explanation or justification.
The use of the temple in this manner seems to be a natural
and customary practice. It is one which is legitimated in the
text by the very fact that Hannah's petition was answered.

Mass, 1990); R. Polzin, *Samuel and the Deuteronomist* (San
Francisco: Harper, 1990).

[131]J. Dus, "Die Geburtslegende Samuel I Sam. 1: Eine
traditionsgeschichtliche Untersuchung zu 1 Sam. 1-3," *RSO* 43 (1969)
163-94.

[132]S. D. Walters, "Hannah and Anna:The Greek and Hebrew Texts of 1
Samuel 1," *JBL* 107 (3, 1988) 385-412.

We shall attempt to draw a more coherent picture below of the role of the shrine of Shiloh in the health care system.

The extent to which one can draw a coherent picture of the role of the shrine of Shiloh from various references in 1 Sam 1-3 depends, in part, on the literary coherence of those chapters. P. K. McCarter argues that while chapters 1-7 were formed from composite elements, their present state may be seen as a unit deriving from the prophetic history layer of DtrH.[133] The coherence of 1 Sam 1-3 is specifically supported by R. K. Gnuse, who states: "1 Samuel 1-3 is a late literary creation, perhaps brought into existence by the hand of the Deuteronomist."[134] The central theme, according to Gnuse, is the condemnation of the house of Eli. Even P. D. Miller and J. J. M. Roberts, who argue against John Willis' view of a unified narrative stretching from 1 Sam 1-7, see a relatively coherent depiction of Shiloh's cultus under Eli in 1 Sam 1-3.[135]

We agree that 1 Samuel 1-3 has resulted from various traditions about different persons, and has mixed different genres such as a birth story (1 Sam 1:1-28), a poem (2:1-10), a judgment speech by an anonymous prophet (2:27-36), and a dream experience of Samuel (3:1-4:1a). We also agree that the anti-Elide tendency of some sections

---

[133]K. McCarter, *1 Samuel* (*AB* 8; Garden City, New York: Doubleday) 19.

[134]R. K. Gnuse, *The Dream Theophany of Samuel* (Lanham, MD: U. Press of America, 1984) 202.

[135]For example, P. D. Miller and J. J. M. Roberts, *The Hand of the Lord: A Reassessment of the "Ark Narrative of 1 Samuel* [Baltimore: Johns Hopkins, 1977] 20) note that, in 1 Sam 1-4, "The role of Eli is consistently given as *kwhn*, 'priest'..." For the argument that 1 Sam 1-7 is a unified narrative, see John Willis, "An Anti-Elide Narrative Tradition form a Prophetic Circle at the Ramah Sanctuary," *JBL* 90 (1971) 288-308.

may have exaggerated the role of Samuel in the first 3
chapters in order to contrast him with the Elides. But we
follow the scholars cited above in seeing a relatively unified
depiction of Shiloh's shrine and cultus in 1 Samuel 1-3.

In particular, the depiction of the shrine as an
institution that operated at variance with P remains
consistent. For example, except for the mention of the "tent
of the meeting" in 2:22,[136] 1 Sam 1-3 consistently assumes
that the shrine of Shiloh is a permanent temple.[137]

1 Sam 1:9	1 Sam 3:3	1 Sam 3:15
מזוזת היכל יהוה	בהיכל יהוה	דלתות בית יהוה

The legitimate cultic practices of the shrine of Shiloh are also
consistently depicted as different from those of the ideal
shrine (tabernacle or temple) of the well known regulations
in P and D. For example, in 1 Sam 2:13-14 the
author/redactor describes as proper a priestly custom of
inserting a fork at random in a pot in order to secure the
rightful share of a sacrifice. This is quite different from the
regulations in Deut 18:3 which reserve for the priest "the
shoulder, and the two cheeks, and the stomach" of each
sacrificial animal (ox or sheep). It is this perversion of the
custom in 1 Sam 2:13-14 which is the reason for the
punishment of the Elides.

Similarly, the Nazirite vow in 1 Sam 1 is quite
different from the one in Numbers 6, which is generally

---

[136]F. M. Cross suggests that this is an archaic fragment (*CMHE*, 243
n. 101). The LXX does not attest it, and neither does 4Q Sam[a]. This
portion of the verse, however, was known to Josephus (Ant. 5.339) and
to LXX[L].

[137] See also comments by Schley (*Shiloh*, 193.)

assigned to P. In 1 Sam it appears to be a life-long dedication, while in Numbers 6 it is a temporary state. Samuel's status at the shrine is also incompatible with regulations in P that allow only the Aaronite priests to serve as priests, and only Levites as servants.

In summary, the form of the Nazirite vow in I Sam 1, the consistent depiction of the shrine as permanent temple in 1 Sam 1-3, and the modes of priestly remuneration in 1 Sam 2:14, all form a coherent depiction of a shrine and cultus that is at variance with P and other portions of the biblical traditions. Moreover, such features are not regarded as improper by these chapters. For these reasons we shall view the practices relating to health care in 1 Sam 1-3 as part of a relatively coherent tradition that differed from P.

(b) Infertility as an illness

We cannot claim on the basis of 1 Sam 1 that all types of illnesses were allowed in the shrine of Shiloh, but one can conclude that infertility was regarded as an illness in 1 Sam 1 and elsewhere in the Bible. Illness, we have mentioned previously, "comprises all deviations from an ideal of individual fulfilment, the physiognomy of which is to a large extent culturally determined."[138] One may classify as an illness any culture's categorization of deviations from a normal life which are linked with the malfunction of normal bodily processes. With this in mind, one can demonstrate that infertility was categorized as an illness in ancient Israel.

The first piece of evidence is that Hanna's infertility is linked with the malfunction of a part of her anatomy--

---

[138]K. van der Toorn, *Sin and Sanction in Israel and Mesopotamia* (Aasen/Maasricht:Van Gorcum, 1985) 67.

namely, her womb. The MT specifically notes in verse 5 that
"Yahweh had closed her womb" (ויהוה סגר רחמה). This
linkage between infertility and the malfunction of the womb
is also made in Genesis 20:18, and this physical linkage
would be within the confines of an illness (and a "disease")
even in modern society.

Within Israelite society such a condition was
certainly one which assigned the patient a biologically and
socially dysfunctional role. In fact, Hannah seems depressed
by her condition, and she is treated as an inferior by the rival
wife. Infertility is a condition which Hannah sought
desperately to reverse. Further indication that infertility was
regarded as an illness in ancient Israel is the fact that the verb
רפא is used to describe the reversal of the condition under
the agency of God in Genesis 20:17. This verb, of course, is
the principal one used in describing the healing of illnesses.

There are some health-related features in the story
which also are seen in Mesopotamia. One is that infertility,
as an illness, is viewed as being under the direct control of a
"sender/controller," though it may not always be viewed as
a punishment (certainly, not in the case of Hannah). The
story, therefore, exhibits the type of medical theology,
discussed in the chapter on Mesopotamia, which entreats the
"sender/controller" of an illness. In Israel, of course, there
was only one "sender/controller" within mono-Yahwism.

There are other observations that impinge on this
particular depiction of the shrine as a petitionary locus. One
is that the petitionary procedure depicted in the story does
not seem to require the priest. In fact, Eli's role seems to be
peripheral in the petitioning process portrayed in the story.
Hannah, for example, has been coming for years for the
same purpose, and Eli does not seem to be aware of her
problem.

In the particular occasion portrayed in 1 Samuel, Eli's ignorance of her condition also implies that prerequisite rituals that might have divulged Hannah's condition to the priest were not part of the petitionary process. If a pre-petitionary ritual process that involved the priest at the shrine were required, it is difficult to understand how an author could have evaded such a process within his plot without arousing the objections of his readers. In any event, the *modus operandi* at the shrine of Shiloh contrasts markedly with the procedures at Asclepieia and the temples of Gula where priests or other personnel are expected to help the patient with petitionary and/or therapeutic rituals. Though we would expect that Hannah's vow to give up her son to Yahweh would eventually involve some discussions with the priest of the shrine, she does not seem to use the priest as an intermediary, her prayer to Yahweh being direct (vv. 10-11). Indeed, no special techniques or rituals are recorded. Eli intrudes into her activities only when he becomes curious about the dramatic mode of petitioning used by Hannah.[139]

The value of Shiloh as a petitionary locus may have been enhanced by the presence of the Ark (the place where Yahweh was most likely to be found or entreated), and by the oracular tradition which has been ascribed to the shrine of Shiloh by some scholars.[140] Biblical texts provide a number of examples of the oracular use of the Ark (e.g., 1 Sam 14:18), the ephod (cf. 1 Sam 23:9-12), and the Urim

---

[139]We acknowledge that the theme of Eli's ignorance may have literary and didactic motivations within 1 Sam 1-3. Eli is criticized for being unaware, for example, of his son's activities despite the fact that those activities would have been noisy. However, the story still does not depict Hannah as seeking out the priest or asking him for any sort of ritual at all.

[140]For example, J. Blenkinsopp (*A History of Prophecy...*, 63).

and Thummim.[141] We are uncertain of the extent to which such oracular devices were used in health-related divination at Shiloh or anywhere else. Such oracular devices were used by priests (1 Sam 23:9-12, 30:7-8), but most of the examples of their use involve political and military oracles (e.g., I Sam 14:36, 41-42). In any case, the fact that oracles could be sought from a priest only adds to the notion that oracles regarding illness prognoses could also have been sought from priests at shrines if the ill (or their proxy) were allowed to enter them.

In sum, the story of Hannah's petition at Shiloh indicates that in her case it was the locus (i.e., the place where Yahweh manifested his presence) that was the key, and not so much the therapeutic or divinatory techniques of the personnel that administered the locus. Nonetheless, the divinatory techniques at such shrines may have been used in other cases.

(c) The allowance of illness in the shrine

Since infertility was an illness, one can conclude that the story of Hannah ascribes a petitionary function to the shrine of Shiloh in the case of at least one type of illness--infertility. If the shrine of Shiloh is depicted as coherently in 1 Samuel 1-3 as we have affirmed, then one can also observe that the shrine allowed the presence of another illness--notably, blindness. In particular, 1 Sam 3:2 affirms that Eli became blind (ועיניו החלו כהות לא יוכל לראות). This is repeated in 1 Sam 4:15 (ולא יבל לראות). This, of

---

[141]See further, K. van der Toorn and C. Houtman, "David and the Ark," *JBL* 113 (2, 1994) 209-231; and E. Robertson, "The Urim and Tummim:What Were They?" *VT* 14 (1964) 67-74.

course, is at variance with Leviticus 21:18, which stipulates that the blind may not serve as priests in the sanctuary (לֹא יִקְרַב אִישׁ עִוֵּר). Eli was never explicitly excluded from service as a priest, nor is there any indication that his blindness constituted the type of inappropriate behavior that caused the downfall of his dynasty.

We cannot claim that the allowance of the blind in the shrine signified that the shrine of Shiloh was used as a petitionary locus for the blind. But the fact that it did allow the blind within the shrine signifies that it could have functioned in such a manner, whereas the same cannot be said of a shrine under the medical theology of P. The apparent legitimacy of an active blind priest at the shrine of Shiloh is yet another instance of a consistent depiction of Shiloh as a shrine that had a level of access for the sick (and healthy personnel) which was beyond the allowances of P. If this is so, then one may at least claim the possibility that the shrine of Shiloh may have served as a petitionary locus for other types of illnesses excluded by P. We shall discuss in more detail in the Excursus some of the problems in establishing the historical accuracy of 1 Sam 1-3.

(d) Summary of the role of the shrine of Shiloh

As the Excursus (below pp. 398-404) will make clear, one cannot claim that the functions depicted in 1 Sam 1-3 belong to the historical shrine of Shiloh. It is difficult to decide if there was a permanent temple at Shiloh or if the shrine of Shiloh continued to exist until the time of the Assyrian captivity. Insofar as the role of the temple in health care is concerned, the final result of the analysis is this: There probably existed in ancient Israel a Yahwistic tradition, probably pre-Exilic in origin, which regarded as legitimate (1) the use of the temple as a petitionary locus for an illness such as infertility, and (2) the presence of active blind priests within the temple cult. The fact that the last situation is at variance with the traditions of P allows the inference that the role of Yahwistic temples in the health care system underwent historical development and/or was not uniform throughout Israel in the biblical periods. The health care practices at Shiloh probably reflect an early tradition relative to P, though they may have continued (e.g., at "illegitimate" Yahwistic shrines) even after the regulations in P were enunciated in their present form.

The fact that it was regarded as legitimate for the Yahwistic temple (at least by some authors, and during some imprecise period) to bear the role depicted in 1 Sam 1-3 seems to be supported by the fact that the practices did not require justification or explanation in the stories. The behavior of Hannah is legitimized by the fact that Yahweh answered her prayer at the shrine. Even if the narratives are anti-Elide in motivation, it is clear that the presence of a blind priest was not deemed to be part of the disobedience of proper cultic regulations that brought the downfall of his dynasty.

One ought not to be puzzled by the fact that different temples in ancient Israel had traditions that differed in regards to a number of issues, including their role within the health care system. Yahwistic temples existed in Transjordan and Arad, among other places.[142] One need not argue that these traditions concerning the cult of Shiloh were only "pre-Deuteronomic," for they could very well reflect traditions

---

[142]For a discussion of such shrines, see W. G. Dever, "Material Remains and the Cult in Ancient Israel:An Essay in Archaeological Systematics," 571-587; Y. Shiloh, "Sanctuaries and Cult Elements in Palestine," 147-158.

that continued into the time of the Deuteronomistic author.[143] We shall provide further discussion of the date of the Priestly medical theology below.

(2) Therapeutic function

Even though it is not abundant, there is evidence that the temple served as a therapeutic locus, even if only for a limited period of time.

(a) The bronze serpent

The therapeutic function of the temple of Jerusalem may be reflected in the notice in 2 Kgs 18:4 concerning the presence of the bronze serpent (נחש הנחשת) in the temple prior to its expulsion by Hezekiah.[144] Already in 1940 J. Pedersen had made the following comment:

---

[143]McCarter, *1 Samuel*, 83.

[144]It is true that 2 Kgs 18:4 does not explicitly place the bronze serpent in the temple of Jerusalem, but there is strong evidence in the text itself that it was in a temple. First, the offering of incense to the bronze serpent would make any locus where the ritual is undertaken a *de facto* cultic locus (in effect, a temple). Moreover, many of the bronze serpents found in the ANE have been in or near temples. Second, the fact that, without further locational specifications, the text mentions the destruction of the bronze serpent with the destruction of Ashera (which was often explicitly placed in the temple of Yahweh [e.g., 2 Kgs 23:5]), may indicate that both of these objects were in such a prominent place that their location needed no further specification. Such a prominent place would most likely be the temple of Jerusalem itself. Third, the fact that the bronze serpent was made by Moses renders it likely that a main temple was the place to keep such a venerable object (cf. the rod of Aaron in Num 17:10). J. Milgrom

Up to the time of Hezekiah there was a special cult
for any one who sought to be healed in the royal
temple of Jerusalem.[145]

Pedersen, however, does not provide a detailed argument for
his conclusion, and most scholars have ignored it.[146]
Doubts concerning the antiquity of the bronze serpent
traditions were expressed by H. H. Rowley.[147] However,
there are three strong lines of evidence that can be developed
to argue that the bronze serpent probably was being used in
therapeutic rituals in the Jerusalem temple prior to its
expulsion by Hezekiah. Some of this evidence has come to
light after Pedersen's comments.

The first piece of evidence is that the biblical tradition
concerning the origin of the bronze serpent is explicit in
affirming that the purpose of the bronze serpent was
therapeutic, at least in the case of snake bites. In Numbers
21 Moses makes the bronze serpent (v. 8: נחש הנחשת) as
part of a therapeutic ritual for snake bites. It is useful to
review briefly the history and function of bronze serpents

(*Numbers* [JPS Commentary; New York, 1990] 459-60]) also notes
that the שרפים in Isaiah 6:4 may be part of the tradition of serpentine
creatures participating in the cult of the temple of Jerusalem.

[145] J. Pedersen, *Israel:Its Life and Culture*, III-IV (Copenhagen:Korch,
1940) 452.

[146] K. Joines (*Serpent Symbolism in the Old Testament* [Haddonfield,
New Jersey: Haddonfield House, 1974] 95), for instance, relegates
Pedersen's comments to a footnote.

[147] H. H. Rowley ("Zadok and Nehushtan," *JBL* 58 [2, 1939] 133)
says: "Had this symbol [the Bronze Serpent] come down from the
Mosaic age, we should have expected to hear of it in the intervening
period."

found in ancient Near Eastern temples in order to understand
and place the episode in a sound comparative perspective.

i) **In non-Israelite contexts.** One of the most
complete surveys of the use of the bronze serpent is that of
Karen Joines.[148] In the following table, we collect some of
the occurrences of metallic serpents, many of which are
found in probable sacral areas.

Place	Stratum	Quantity	Date (B.C.E.)
Megiddo[149]	X	2	MB IIC
	VIIIB	1	LB
Gezer[150]	"High Place"	1	LB?
Hazor[151]	IB/Area H	2	LB

---

[148]*Serpent Symbolism,* which is based on the more detailed
dissertation, "The Serpent in the Old Testament" (Dissertation,
Southern Baptist Theological Seminary, Louisville, Kentucky, 1966).

[149]G. Loud, *Megiddo* II:Plates (Chicago:U. of Chicago, 1948) 240:1.
Though the stratigraphy is unclear, a temple (2048) was a few feet away
in Stratum IX. The serpent in Stratum VIIIB was found in the floor of
Room 3187 in Square K6 (Area AA).

[150]R. A. Stewart Macalister (*The Excavation of Gezer* [London:John
Murray, 1912] II, p. 399, Figure 488) stated: "In the pavement inside
the northern enclosure was found a large collection of fragments of the
grey cyma-shaped bowls with wishbone handles of Cypriot origin. In
the middle of this pile of potsherds was a small bronze model of a
serpent. The serpent was about 9 cm. long and evidently represents a
cobra." However, the stratigraphy and the reported dimensions of the
serpent are not certain.

[151]The serpent was found in locus 2174 of stratum IB (14th c.
B.C.E.), and was about 5 inches long. See Y. Yadin et al., Hazor III-

Shechem[152]	LB/Field V?	2	LB?
Timna[153]		1	LB
Tell Mevorakh[154]		1	LB
Lachish[155]		1	LB?
Babylon[156]	Esagila	8	559-556

IV:PLates (Jerusalem:Magnes Press, 1961) Plate CCCXXXIX:5-6; *idem*, "The Fourth Season of Excavations at Hazor, " *BA* 22 (1959) 5-6. Yadin believes that the temple near the place where the serpent was found was dedicated to Hadad.

[152]G. Ernest Wright, "The Second Campaign at Tell Balatah (Shechem)" *BASOR* (Dec. 1957) 11-28.

[153]B. Rothenberg, *Timna*, especially pages 152, 173 and plates XIX-XX. The serpent was about 12 cm. in length, and it was the only reported "votive" found in the temple.

[154]E. Stern (*Excavations at Tell Mevorakh (Qedem* 18; Jerusalem:Israel Exploration Society, [1984] II, p. 22 and plate 31:1) says (p. 22): "The figurine is made of bronze. The snake has a twisted body and gives the impression of a lifelike creature. The head is badly eroded, but the marking of the eyes can still be distinguished. If the figurine was originally coated with some other precious metal, none of it has been preserved. It was found in pieces in locus 185 on the surface of the platform of the stratum X temple." The serpent was about 20 cm. in length.

[155]An unpublished metal snake was reported to me by Gabriel Barkay in the area of the Summit Temple at Lachish (personal communication, February, 1990).

[156]See A. Deimel, "Die Schlange bei den Babyloniern," *Orientalia* XIV (1924) 49-57.

After the study of K. Joines, bronze serpents were reported at Pergamum (1st c. C.E.).[157] Although not all metal serpents have been found in clearly sacred areas, the data above show that, contrary to Rowley's opinion, the use of metallic serpents in temples was an ancient and persistent phenomenon that spanned at least three millennia.[158]

Although it is difficult to argue that all the depictions of bronze serpents in the ancient Near East had a therapeutic function, the link between bronze serpents and a therapeutic function is certainly well supported by a number of lines of evidence. The best case is perhaps Asclepius, who could assume the form of a snake in order to heal. Serpents were recommended for their medicinal value, and, as we have mentioned, bronze serpents have been found in the Asclepieion at Pergamum.

In 1974 Joines argued: "The motif of repelling serpents with the representation of a serpent was extremely common in ancient Egypt, but apparently was almost entirely absent in Mesopotamia-Palestine."[159] But the link of

---

[157]See O. Ziegenaus and G. de Luca, *Altertümer von Pergamon*, XI, 1 (1968) p. 169 and Tafel 61 no. 465.

[158]Some of the 17 serpents found at Tepe Gawra (strata VII-V) may date as early as the late fourth millennium B.C.E. according to E. A. Speiser, *Excavations at Tepe Gawra I:Levels I-VIII* (Philadelphia:U. of Pennsylvania Press, 1935) 111-112. However, Seton Lloyd (*The Archeaology of Mesopotamia* [Rev. ed.; London: Thames and Hudson, 1984) 66) dates level VII at Tepe Gawra no earlier than about 2800 B.C.E. Speiser does not characterize the metal as "bronze," but as "copper," even though he admits that it is an alloy of tin and copper. He speculates on a chthonian function for the snakes. Speiser (p. 112) notes that the locus in Stratum VI, which furnished 12 of the objects, "was in no way whatever a religious center," though "Stratum V was dominated by a shrine."

[159]Joines, *Serpent Symbolism*, 91.

serpents with therapeutic functions is, in fact, well attested to in Ugarit and Mesopotamia. For example, *KTU* 1.100 and 1.107 contain lengthy rituals against snake bite.[160] Levine and de Tarragon have linked these anti-snake incantations with scenes depicting serpents on a goblet from 'Ain Samia (2200-2000 B.C.E).[161] Even if the scene on the cup cannot be interpreted in the manner suggested by Levine and de Tarragon, the textual evidence speaks for the existence of "anti-snake" rituals in Syria-Palestine.

Joines' study also does not consider Mesopotamian namburbi rituals against serpents.[162] Although not always explicit, the namburbi rituals frequently did involve the use of figurines that represented various animals, including serpents, that were to be repelled.[163] The practice of repelling maladies with figurines which represent them probably undergirds the practice described in 1 Sam 5, where the Philistines make figurines of gold as part of the ritual which they hope will remove the plague. Rather than

---

[160]B.A. Levine and J-M. de Tarragon, "'Shapshu Cries Out in Heaven:' Dealing with Snake-Bites at Ugarit (*KTU* 1.100, 1.107)," *RB* 95 (4, 1988) 481-518; C. H. Bowman and R. B. Coote, "A Narrative Incantation for Snake Bite," *UF* 12 (1980) 135-139; P. Bordreuil, "Venin de printemps, venin foudroyant," *UF* 15 (1983) 299-300; and I. Kottsieper, "*KTU* 1.100--Versuch einer Deutung," *UF* 16 (1984) 97-110.

[161]See B. Shantur and Y. Labadi, "Tomb 204 at 'Ain-Samia," *IEJ* 21 (1971) 73-77; Z. Yeivin, "A Silver Cup from Tomb 204a at 'Ain-Samiya," *ibid* 78-81; Y. Yadin, "A Note on the Scenes Depicted on the 'Ain-Samiya Cup," *ibid* 82-85.

[162]For example, R. Caplice, *The Akkadian Namburbi Texts:An Introduction* (Los Angeles:Undena, 1974) 18.

[163]*Ibid*, Texts 5 (frog) and 7 (a dog). For namburbis involving serpent figurines, see R. Caplice,"Namburbi Texts in the British Museum," *Or* 34 (1965) 32-34.

drawing Joines' contrast between Egypt and Mesopotamia, therefore, one should now stress the continuity in the ancient Near Eastern traditions that used figurines to repel the animal (or forces which those animals incarnate) represented by those figurines.

ii) Israelite usage. The best known narrative concerning the therapeutic use of the bronze serpent is found in Numbers 21:4-9. The occurrence there of the word עם, the hiphil of עלה, and the hithpael of פלל have all been used to assign the story to J or E (or JE).[164] The story emphasizes the obedience of Moses. It is worthwhile to review its use of the bronze serpent from the perspective of our study. The serpent forms part of a familiar story of rebellion and dissafection in the desert,[165] and the structure of the story may be schematized as follows:

A. Complaint of the people against Moses and Yahweh;
B. Yahweh sends snakes as punishment;
C. Expression of repentance and request for help;
D. Moses intercedes;
E. Yahweh instructs Moses to make the bronze serpent and provides a ritual;
F. The ritual heals (i.e., removes the punishment).

There are some short namburbi texts that share some of the elements in the relative sequence seen in the biblical

---

164 See P. Budd (*Numbers* [WBC 5, 1984] 232-33), who assigns it to J; M. Noth (*Numbers* [London: SCM, 1968] 156) assigns it to E.
165G. W. Coats, *Rebellion in the Wilderness* (Nashville:Abingdon, 1968); and S. J. DeVries, "The Origin of the Murmuring Tradition," *JBL* 87 (1968) 51-58.

episode. A namburbi may begin with a description of the problem (e.g., snakes, dogs, etc.) which is followed by a prescription addressed by the deity to the consultant. This prescription often includes the manufacture of a figurine of the animal to be repelled. It may end with a notice assuring a positive result for the ritual.

The biblical episode also has a description of the problem, it contains a ritual prescribed by the deity to the consultant (Moses),[166] and it includes the making of a figurine of the animal to be repelled. It also ends with a notice of the ritual's efficacy. While there are sufficient dissimilarities to discourage the claim that a namburbi format has been directly adopted by the author(s) of the biblical episode, the similarities argue for related Near Eastern traditions which use figurines of the animals to be repelled, and a tradition which has instructions provided by the god to the intermediary/ consultant on behalf of the patient.

Although many namburbi rituals invoke gods, there was no contradiction in invoking the gods and also attributing an instrumental value to the figurine. The figurine did not exclude or minimize the powers of the gods. The episode in Numbers, therefore, also may be viewed as operating within a similar conceptual scheme, here invoking Yahweh and acknowledging the efficacy of a material magical instrument in the operation (cf. the use of the Ark in war, and Aaron's Rod).

---

[166]B. Levine (*In the Presence of the Lord*, 86-87) draws a slightly different Mesopotamian parallel to the transmission of a prescription from a god to an intermediary. He sees a parallel in cases where Marduk acts on behalf of a patient, and receives prescriptions from Ea. Although this involves the principle of intermediaries who receive instructions from a deity, the closest analogy would be one that depicts a divine being providing instructions to a *human* consultant.

What is unclear is the supposed operational magic of the ritual which rendered the therapy efficacious. Although the use of the bronze serpent in Numbers 21 may be viewed as part of a tradition that used the figurine of the animal to be repelled, it is also important to note that there are some differences between it and the Mesopotamian namburbi rituals. The namburbi rituals usually destroyed the figurine or disposed of it in a manner that was supposed to parallel the magical disposal of (the evil of) the real animal. In the case of Numbers 21, there is no hint of the destruction or disposal of the snake figurine. The namburbis also can become quite complicated in their use of large varieties of ingredients for the rituals, but this complexity seems to be lacking in the Hebrew ritual.

In the case of Numbers 21, the ritual seems to consist of gazing upon the serpent. However, the expression נבט אל sometimes may signify more than the act of visual perception. The term may denote reverence, respect, or adoration. In this regard, compare the Song of Jonah when his brush with death provokes the following concern (Jonah 2:4: "How shall I ever gaze upon your holy temple again." (אך אוסיף להביט אל היכל קדשך). In 1 Sam 16:7 the verb is used to urge the Israelites not to focus on the physical stature of Saul, and the context clearly fits the idea of "respect," and not merely visual perception. Even more decisive is the use of the expression in Psalm 119:6, which may be rendered: "I shall not be ashamed when I observe (or obey) all your commandments" (אז לא אבוש בהביטי אל כל מצותיך). Similarly, the use of נבט אל in Numbers 21:9 cannot exclude the meaning of "reverencing, respecting" etc. Indeed, the therapeutic value of the act described by נבט אל הנחש נחשת may indicate that the reverencing or the providing of due respect to the bronze serpent is what is demanded of the patient. Such an interpretation would also be useful in explaining the value of the bronze serpent in the Israelite cultus. The story supports the notion that the bronze serpent was not an idol, but a Yahwistic instrument worthy of legitimate reverence (as were the ephod, ark, and other "relics"). Facing and acknowledging it, therefore, had therapeutic efficacy.

The foregoing examination emphasizes that serpent figurines had a long tradition in the ancient Near East. The bronze serpent in Numbers 21 may be part of a Near Eastern tradition in which a likeness of the animal that was to be repelled was manufactured. However, metal serpents are not as easily destroyed as the ones in namburbi rituals, and, as we mentioned, the Hebrew example was not destroyed in a healing ritual. Likewise, the serpents found in the temples in our table do not seem to have been destroyed in a ritual.

So perhaps the best analogy for the Israelite object may be the metal serpents found at the Asclepieion. As we have mentioned, a bronze serpent at the Asclepieion at Pergamum, which was clearly a therapeutic locus. It is uncertain, of course, whether the function of bronze serpents was the same in all the temples of the ancient Near East. Nevertheless, it does not seem likely that the therapeutic use of bronze serpents in Greece and Israel reflects some independent development in each culture. Perhaps there was a common Near Eastern tradition that ascribed therapeutic value to metallic serpents. The temples at Tell Mevorakh, Timna, Jerusalem, and elsewhere may have been part of such a tradition. Of course, one cannot exclude the possibility that some serpent figurines were associated only with healing infertility.[167] But, as is the case with Asclepieia, metallic serpents may have been used at places that offered a wide variety of therapeutic rituals.

The last point is particularly important because 2 Kings 18:4 indicates that the bronze serpent was not simply an ancient relic being stored at the temple. The text clearly states that Nehuštan was being used in rituals while it was housed in the temple, and this constitutes yet another piece of evidence for the use of the bronze serpent as a therapeutic device within the temple. The passage says:

כי עד הימים ההמה היו בני ישראל
מקטרים לו ויקרא לו נחשת

> Because even until that time the sons of Israel were
> offering incense to it, and it was called Nehuštan.

According to M. Haran, the use of the piel stem of קטר suggests a cereal-offering, not an incense offering.[168] But whether it was incense or a cereal offering, the rituals seems to have been more elaborate than simply "looking at" or "reverencing" the serpent. These rituals may indicate that the bronze serpent was not merely an instrument of Yahweh in 2 Kgs 18:4, but that it was regarded as a deity itself. Even if Nehuštan was not regarded as a deity, the rituals associated with it were apparently disturbing to the biblical author. While the purpose of the rituals is not explicit, it would be

---

[167]For the connections of serpents with fertility cults, see M. Haran, *Encyclopedia Miqra'it* 5:826-27.

[168]M. Haran, *Temples and Temple Service in Ancient Israel* (Oxford:Clarendon, 1978) 233-34. D. Edelman ("The Meaning of *qiṭṭēr*," *VT* 35 [1985] 395-404) proposes that the piel stem of קטר is best rendered as "to burn the food offerings."

reasonable to assume, in light of the therapeutic value ascribed to the bronze serpent in Numbers and elsewhere, that such rituals were therapeutic.

Pedersen suggested that the bronze serpent may have been part of the temple from the beginning, and the ancient nature of the tradition in 2 Kgs 18:4 is expressed in the text itself, even if the composition of the text dates to the post-Exilic period.[169] First, it links the serpent with Moses who, by the time of Hezekiah, was regarded as an ancient hero. If the tradition were not ancient, then it seems odd that the author would note its antiquity when novelty could have served as better grounds for expulsion (i.e., the claim that the bronze serpent was an illegitimate innovation). Indeed, the mention of the ancient tradition regarding the serpent would have been of little value to one who advocated its expulsion. On comparative grounds, the antiquity of the serpent certainly would be consistent with the antiquity of its association with temples in the ancient Near East.

In summary, the foregoing evidence indicates that it is reasonable to suggest tentatively, as did Pedersen, that the bronze serpent in the Temple of Jerusalem was used in therapeutic rituals. Furthermore, one may suggest that the use of the bronze serpent in therapeutic rituals represents a

---

[169]B. Peckham (*The Composition of the Deuteronomistic History* [HSM 35; Atlanta: Scholars Press, 1985] fig. 7) dates all of 2 Kgs 18 to the post-Exilic Dtr 2. But there is good evidence which suggests that 2 Kgs 18 should be assigned to Dtr 1. For example, Peckham assigns 2 Kgs 18:5 and 2 Kgs 23:25 to Dtr 2. But 2 Kgs 18:5 says that there was no king *before* and *after* who was as righteous as Hezekiah, and it would be difficult to see how the same writer could also say the same of Josiah, a successor of Hezekiah, in 2 Kgs 23:25. A better solution would be to assign 2 Kgs 18:4 to Dtr 1, and 2 Kgs 23:25 to Dtr 2.

continuation (or resumption) of an ancient tradition. The
temple of Jerusalem, therefore, may have preserved and
justified such traditions until the time that Hezekiah decided
to discontinue them. We shall discuss possible reasons for
Hezekiah's actions below.

(b) The Prayer of Solomon: 1 Kgs 8

i) General comments. Another indication of the
role of the temple in the health care system comes from the
Prayer of Solomon. On a general level, the passage states
that God shall answer from heaven the prayer of anyone
who extends his hands towards the temple of Jerusalem.
The relevant portion (1 Kgs 8:37-39), which bears
identifiable Deuteronomic phraseology,[170] reads as follows:

רעב כי יהיה בארץ...כל נגע כל מחלה כל
תפלה   כל תחנה אשר תהיה לכל האדם לכל
עמך ישראל   אשר ידעון איש נגע לבבו
ופרש כפיו אל הבית   הזה ואתה תשמע השמים
מכון שבתך

If there be a famine in the nation...or a plague, or an
illness then any prayer and request which any man
among your people, Israel, [might make] when he
learns of the inner affliction, and when he spreads his

---

[170]For example: בל עמך ישראל (Deut 21:8). For other examples of
Deuteronomistic phraseology in 1 Kings 8 and other passages, see M.
Weinfeld, *Deuteronomy and the Deuteronomistic School* (Oxford:
Clarendon, 1972), especially 320-358.

hands toward this Temple, you shall hear in Heaven,
the (true) place of your residence.

The passage raises some questions relevant to illness
and health care. What is the function of the extended hands
in the prayer? Is it a symbolic gesture, or is it part of a
magical procedure? The best view considers such gestures
as ones which include both symbolic and magical efficacy.
The symbolic aspect expresses devotion to a particular deity
or sacred object, including pagan deities (cf. Ps 44:21).
Psalm 28 speaks of spreading the hands toward the temple
by a suppliant who may be ill. More specifically, v. 2
speaks of directing the hands towards the innermost sanctum
of the shrine (בנשאי ידי אל דביר קדשך). Although
the word פרש is not used in Exodus 17:8-16, the passage
makes a direct correlation between Moses' lifted arm(s)
(ידו) and the success of the battle against the Amalekites.

The gesture of stretched or uplifted hands is also
depicted in stelae and other types of objects in many places
in the Near East. One example from a Late Bronze cultic
place at Hazor, for example, bears two uplifted hands
pointing toward a crescent moon and what appears to be a
solar disk.[171] Other examples show persons stretching their
hands while genuflecting before a king.[172] In light of the

---

[171]See Y. Yadin, "Symbols of Deities at Zinjirli, Carthage, and
Hazor," in J. A. Sanders, ed., *Near Eastern Archaeology in the
Twentieth Century: Essays in Honor or Nelson Glueck* (New York:
Doubleday, 1970) 200-231. For a recent discussion, see S. Schroer, *In
Israel Gab es Bilder* (Göttingen: Vandehoeck & Ruprecht, 1987) 309-
310.

[172]For a general discussion, see O. Keel, *The Symbolism of the
Biblical World* (New York: Crossroad, 1978) 308-323.

foregoing, it may be best to state that the symbolic act of reverencing the deity by pointing one's hands toward him (or his temple) was believed to prompt the deity to act favorably towards the suppliant. Thus, both symbolism and magical efficacy were integrated by the gesture.

ii) Literary critical issues. Before we can provide some suggestions concerning the significance of the passage for the health care system, we must comment on the debate concerning the literary structure and date of the passage. At its most general level, the passage is part of a larger prayer in 1 Kgs 8. As noted by J. Levenson, there are at least 3 separate speeches (12-13, 15-21, and 23-53).[173]

The unit of most relevance to our inquiry is 1 Kgs 8:23-53 which is classified as the "third speech" by J. Levenson.[174] The section's unity has been defended by J. Gamper[175] and J. Levenson[176] against the formidable arguments of A. Jepsen who sees 31-43 as a different unit from 44-53.[177] We believe that the arguments of Levenson and Gamper for the unity of 31-53 are cogent. In particular, Levenson notes that, with the exception of 2 Chr 6:20, which is dependent on 1 Kgs 8, a relatively rare phrase ("that your eyes may be opened"/ להיות עינך פתחות)

---

[173]J. Levenson, "From Temple to Synagogue:1 Kgs 8," in J. D. Levenson and B. Halpern, eds., *Traditions in Transformations:Turning Points in Bibical Faith* (Winona Lake, Indiana: Eisenbrauns, 1981) 154.

[174]J. Levenson, "From Temple to Synagogue:1 Kgs 8," 154.

[175]J. Gamper, "Die Heilsgeschichtliche Bedeutung des Salomonischen Tempelweihegebets," *ZKT* 85 (1963) 55-61.

[176]J. Levenson, "From Temple to Synagogue:1 Kgs 8," 155f.

[177]A. Jepsen, *Die Quellen des Königsbuches* (Halle: Max Niemeyer, 1953) 15-17.

occurs in that precise form only in verses 29 and 52.[178]
Following C. F. Keil, Levenson also notes that 1 Kgs 8:23-
53 follows the model of Deut 28:15-68 and Leviticus 26:14-
45.

To these arguments, we may add the results of the
work of Avigdor Hurowitz who has argued that the Prayer
of Solomon is part of a larger pattern found in the accounts
of kings who build temples in Mesopotamia and Ugarit.[179]
This pattern is delineated as follows:

Theme	1 Kgs
I. Divine command	5:15-19
II. Relation of command	---------
III. Preparations	5:20-30
IV. Construction and Description	6-7
V. Dedication	8:1-11, 62-66
VI. Blessing	8:12-61
VII. Revelation	9:1-9
VIII. Blessing and curses	9:3-9

Similar patterns have been ascribed by Hurowitz to the
account of the building of the Tabernacle in Exodus 25ff,
and the account found in Samsu-iluna's Bilingual Inscription
B. We agree that such a pattern is apparently followed in 1
Kgs. Thus, the comparative work of Hurowitz would view
1 Kgs 8:23-52 as part of a well-known unitary theme that
occurs in this type of temple dedication.

---

[178]J. Levenson, "From Temple to Synagogue:1 Kgs 8," 156.
[179]A. Hurowitz, "The Priestly Account of Building the Tabernacle,"
JAOS 105 (1, 1985) 21-30; *Idem, I Have Built You and Exalted House*
(Sheffield: JSOT, 1992) 109ff.

Another significant question revolves around the date of the composition. Two main hypotheses have been proposed. One advocated by Friedman, among others, argues that the passage (or specifically, vv. 46-53) is pre-Exilic.[180] The main evidence is that it speaks of the temple as though it were still standing. However, the fact that detailed regulations can be proposed for temples that are not in existence during the author's lifetime (e.g., Ezekiel's temple) does not make Friedman's argument a decisive one.

The other date, advocated by J. Levenson, is that the passage is Exilic.[181] We believe that this is the most probable date, but not for all the reasons cited by Levenson. The main argument for this date, assuming the unity of 1 Kgs 8:23-53, is the emphasis on captivity and exile in verses 46-50.[182]

Another crucial issue in dating the passage is the allowance of foreigners in the temple. In the case of foreigners who come from afar (v. 41: הנכרי אשר לא מעמך ישראל הוא ובא מארץ רחוקה), the Prayer of Solomon clearly encourages them to pray at the temple locus (v. 42: ובא והתפלל אל הבית הזה), and states that God shall listen to them (v. 43: אתה תשמע). Levenson adduces,

---

[180]R. E. Friedman, *The Exile and Biblical Narrative* (HSM 22; Chico:Calif.:Scholars Press, 1981) 21.

[181] The date correlates with F. M. Cross' Dtr 2. B. Peckham, (*The Composition of the Deuteronomistic History* [HSM 35; Atlanta:Scholars Press, 1985] figure 7) assigns all of chapter 8 to Dtr 2.

[182]Another possible indication of a post-Exilic date which was not cited by Levenson is the use of פרש ידים, which M. Gruber (*Nonverbal Communication in the Ancient Near East* [Rome:Biblical Institute Press, 1980] II. 43) regards as post-Exilic, in contrast to the predominantly pre-Exilic expression פרש כפים.

among other passages, (Third) Isaiah 56:6-8, to show that
the use of the temple as a "House of Prayer," and
particularly for all nations, is a uniquely Exilic theme.

But, the idea that all nations would or should come to
the temple is not necessarily post-Exilic. The exclusion of
foreigners is certainly against the ideology of P, which most
scholars regard as a post-Exilic composition. Ezekiel 44:7
clearly expresses the idea that uncircumcised foreigners
(בני נכר...וערלי בשר) are not welcome in the temple.[183]
Herod's inscription likewise does not encourage foreigners
to come into the temple late into the Second Temple period.
But, foreigners were clearly allowed in the temple in the pre-
Exilic period. These tensions between those who saw the
temple as a place for all nations and those who would not
admit foreigners may reflect the struggle in the early post-
Exilic era between the hierocrats and the visionaries that has
been described by P. Hanson.[184]

iii) The Prayer in socio-religious context.

For our purposes, the most significant aspect of the
Prayer of Solomon is that it does not encourage the use of
the temple as a direct petitionary or therapeutic locus for the
ill.   Note, for example, that it encourages general prayer at
the temple locus on the part of the king and the people in vv.
29-31. It encourages people to come to the temple locus to
pray if they have been defeated in war (v. 33). As we have
mentioned, vv. 41-42 encourage foreigners who come from

---

[183]On the status of the גר, see J. Levenson, *Theology of the Program
of Restoration: Ezekiel 40-48* (HSM 10; Atlanta: Scholars Press, 1986
[Repr. of 1976 ed.])123-125.

[184]For a recent statement, see P.D. Hanson, *The People Called* (San
Francisco:Harper and Row, 1986) 253ff.

afar to pray at the temple locus, and v. 43 states that God shall listen to them.

Since the Prayer encourages people on three separate occasions to come to the temple, one would expect it to do so in the case of illness. But it does not do so. Instead, the patients are told to extend their hands toward the temple to receive healing. Since the author is careful to provide explicit instructions for suppliants who are living in distant lands (e.g., 44 and 48), it is not likely that the reason for the distinct instructions to the ill is that they necessarily are living as captives in foreign lands or in exile. The Prayer assumes that such instructions would be used by all patients, whether in exile or in Israel.

It appears, therefore, that the instructions for the ill represent a distinction between the ill and the healthy. One could argue that this distinction in the Prayer presupposes laws of purity similar to those in P. But since many sick persons would live near the temple, and since foreigners are encouraged to come into the temple, purity laws may only provide part of the answer. We propose that the Prayer addresses the inconvenience of using the temple as a petitionary locus in the case of illness under a centralized cultic system.

Since the Prayer represents a major speech within DtrH, then one may at least suggest the possibility that centralization, which is a major policity of DtrH, could have played a role in the instructions for the sick found in the Prayer. The idea of a central Yahwistic temple that serves even foreigners certainly permeates the Prayer. It is not necessary that centralization be systematically applied in reality for such concerns to be addressed because concepts may be worked out in theory even if the theory has not been applied (e.g., Ezekiel's visionary temple). If the author advocates the centralization of worship at the temple of Jerusalem, then the passage may seek to address concerns that would have been precipitated by such a policy.

In particular, if outlying shrines are eliminated, even if only in theory, then this would also eliminate any shrines that might serve as petitionary (or even therapeutic) loci for the ill. The ill, furthermore, might not have the physical mobility to come to the central shrine in Jerusalem even if they were welcome there. An advocate of centralization, therefore, might attempt to mitigate the elimination of outlying shrines by proposing that simply praying toward the temple in Jerusalem is sufficient to receive healing.

Our hypothesis is supported by Deuteronomic passages which explicitly acknowledge that distance could be a problem within a centralized cultic system. For example, Deut 12:21-22 has explicit provisions for those who live far from the temple:

כי ירחק ממך המקום אשר יבחר יהוה
אלהיך לשום שמו שם וזבחת מקרבך
ומצאנך אשר נתן יהוה לך באשר
צויתך ואכלת בשעריך בכל אות נפשך

> If the place which Yahweh your God has chosen
> to establish his name there is too far from you,
> then you may slaughter any of your flock which
> Yahweh has given you, as I have commanded
> you, and may eat as much as you desire within
> your towns.

Note that these provisions are meant for those who live within Israel, not in foreign lands.

A related scenario may be linked with the historical developments described during the reign of Hezekiah in 2 Kgs 18:4. As we have mentioned, Hezekiah expelled a device that was probably connected with therapy, and that may have reflected the therapeutic function of the temple. The expulsion of Nehuštan, therefore, may have been accompanied by an effort to emphasize that coming to the temple was not necessary to receive healing. Rather, the author might emphasize that simply praying towards the temple was sufficient. Instead of praying with one's gaze toward the bronze serpent, one should pray toward the temple to achieve the same results. The temple becomes a "long distance" therapeutic device in itself without being a therapeutic locus.

The elimination or diminution of the direct petitionary and therapeutic functions of the temple may also be accompanied by a story that exemplifies the proper procedures in illness--this is the story of Hezekiah's illness. As we have mentioned, that story clearly shows that Hezekiah did not use the temple as a petitionary or therapeutic locus, though the narrative itself reports his intent to use it as a thanksgiving locus *after* he was healed (2 Kgs 20: 5).

In summary, we have attempted to show that the Prayer of Solomon distinguishes between the ill and the healthy insofar as the role of the temple is concerned. This distinction should be viewed within the context of the Deuteronomic program for the temple. Unlike healthy Israelites and even foreigners, the ill were not encouraged to use the temple as a petitionary (or, implicitly, a therapeutic) locus because physical mobility may have been viewed as an obvious problem for the ill in a centralized cultic system. Instead, patients are encouraged to use the temple as a "long-distance" petitionary/therapeutic device. Although the Prayer of Solomon may be assigned to Dtr 2, we submit that the ideology concerning the use of the temple by the ill could date from the pre-Exilic period, and particularly as a result of efforts to centralize the cult under Hezekiah and Josiah. We shall provide further comments below on the relationship between the centralization and the role of the temple in the health care system.

Centralization and the "normative" Yahwistic use of the temple, however, probably were not achieved in actuality in some periods. If the temple of Arad, assuming it was mono-Yahwistic, was functional throughout Josiah's reign, then it might indicate that centralization was indeed not realized, at least in the ideal form of Deuteronomy.[185] And even if there were only one temple, the latter still might not function in the manner idealized by the Deuteronomist. For example, Ezekiel 8 and Nehemiah 13 note the illicit use of the temple locus, and DtrH is replete with instances where the temple was being used illicitly (cf. 2 Kings 23). Such "illegitimate" practices may reflect the resilience of Canaanite temple traditions which probably did permit the use of the temple for petitionary rituals and therapeutic rituals (cf. the Bronze serpent tradition and the temple of Ekron), particularly in the case of infertility.

(3) Thanksgiving function

The thanksgiving function of the temple is attested to in a number of psalms and in other biblical books. As

---

[185]For a general discussion of temple of Arad, see Z. Herzog, M. Aharoni, and A. Rainey, "Arad: An Ancient Israelite Fortress with a Temple to Yahweh," *BARev* 13 (2, 1987) 16-35.

Seybold notes, a number of biblical passages demonstrate that it was either customary or obligatory for a patient to present himself at the temple after an illness.[186] In Leviticus 13-14, for example, the person afflicted with צרעת was to go to the temple after recovery to undergo certain purification rituals and to make offerings. The same applies to persons suffering from זב. It is probable, therefore, that such regulations also provided an opportunity to thank the deity for the healing of those conditions. It is uncertain, however, how many different types of illnesses would have been subsumed under similar customs, but persons were encouraged to bring thank offerings to the temple for a variety of blessings, and healing would certainly be among them.

As we have noted, the story of Hezekiah's illness provides a clear indication of the thanksgiving function of the temple. In 2 Kgs 20, Hezekiah prays that he might go up to the temple after his recovery. In Isa 38:9 Hezekiah sings a psalm after he was healed. This psalm was probably set in the temple, and verse 20 indicates the suitability of the temple for songs that express gratitude (ונגנותי ננגן כל ימי חיינו על בית יהוה יהוה להושיעני).

Since this psalm in Isaiah 38:10-20 is explicitly linked with healing, it is useful to describe its salient features in order to help identify other psalms that might serve a similar purpose. The psalm begins with a description of the health crisis which the patient suffered. This health crisis is depicted as a journey into the underworld, something, as we shall see, that is typical of many psalms depicting illnesses. Another important feature is the animal imagery of the

---

[186]K. Seybold, *Das Gebet des Kranken im Alten Testament* (Stuttgart: W. Kohlhammer, 1973) especially 169ff.

psalm. The patient feels him/herself attacked by an animal
such as a lion (v. 13) and cries like a bird for help (v. 14).
The plea for healing assumes the form of a rational argument
to persuade God to heal the patient. For example, the patient
argues that it is in God's interest to heal him because failure
to do so would be tantamount to a triumph of Sheol over
God, and it would leave one less person to praise the deity
(vv. 18-19). The psalm ends with a reference to singing in
the temple (v. 20).

K. Seybold has attempted to identify other
"Heilungspsalmen" which may have been recited at the
temple after an illness.[187] One of these is Psalm 30, and
verse 2 clearly indicates the connection with illness: "Oh
Yahweh, my God, I cried unto you, and you have healed
me" (יהוה אלהי שועתי אליך ותרפאני). As in
Hezekiah's psalm, the patient describes his health crisis as a
journey into the underworld (cf. vv. 3 and 9), and as an
attack by enemies (v. 1), but in this case human ones. The
patient also attempts to persuade the deity of the latter's self-
interest in overcoming death and in preserving those who
will praise his name, presumably in the temple. Although
the place of recitation is not explicit in the text, it is probable
that, like other psalms of thanksgiving, it was set in the
temple. Even though the introductory note is often of little
historical value, it also links the psalm with the temple.

Psalm 41 may also be a thanksgiving psalm, though
its interpretation as a pure lament is also possible. Verse 12
appears to describe a favorable outcome to the health crisis
described in the preceding verses. The reference to enemies
does not appear to be a metaphor for the illness itself, but
one which refers to the actual social consequences of the

---

[187]K. Seybold, *Das Gebet des Kranken*, especially 169ff.

patient's illness. As in the Mesopotamian poem *Ludlul*, the patient complains that illness is often an opportunity for the healthy to condemn the patient. The psalm also links the patient's illness with a sin against God (v. 4). Note that the patient's place seems to be in the home bound to a sickbed (vv. 3 and 8), and no hint that one should go to the temple for therapy is enunciated.

Other psalms which do give thanks for a healing may have been recited at the temple, but such a setting is not as clear as in the cases above. Psalm 103:3, for example, cites healing from illness as one of the many saving acts of God. Psalm 32 mentions being struck by the hand of God, and subsequently restored.

Although there is textual evidence (e.g., the story of Hannah) that vows related to healing were part of Yahweh's cult, currently there are no objects which may be linked explicitly to vows associated with healing in Yahweh's cult. In view of the importance of vows in the petitionary and thanksgiving aspects of the cults of Asclepius and Gula, it is reasonable to assume that material objects were also part of petitionary and thanskgiving strategies of patients within Yahwism.

In summary, the thanksgiving function of the temple is probably the most certain and constant of all the temple functions related to illness which we have discussed. It is supported by narratives, priestly regulations, as well as some psalms. As we shall argue below, P probably was decisive in establishing the superiority of this function at the expense of the petitionary and therapeutic ones in the health care system.

(4) The temple as the headquarters of the guardians of purity

The ideas of purity in P prevented the use of the temple as a petitionary or therapeutic locus for the patient, but P did promote the thanksgiving function. However, according to P, the temple did have an additional role in the health care system, and this was as the headquarters for the "guardians" of purity. The priestly establishment was charged with judging whether persons had, among other things, illnesses which required exclusion from the temple and the community. Although no mention of therapy is found, the priest in Lev 13-14 was a health care consultant insofar as he was probably consulted to judge the seriousness of certain illnesses, particularly צרעת and זב. Yet such judgments were always intended to see if the person was fit to enter the temple or to live in the "healthy" community. It is in this sense that J. P. Trusen's conception of the Levites as "Polizeiärtze" has some merit.[188]

The role of the priest as a health care consultant for צרעת is clear in Leviticus 13-14. The role of the priest was to examine the afflicted, and to declare him "clean" or "unclean." As D. Wright notes,[189] the regulations in Leviticus 13 outline four [190] different cases and quarantine

---

[188]*Krankheiten der alten Hebräer*, 8.

[189]D. Wright, *The Disposal of Impurity*, 211ff. See also J. Milgrom, *Leviticus 1-16*, 768-826.

[190]Not all scholars agree as to how many cases are actually delineated. K. Seybold and U. B. Mueller (*Sickness and Healing* [Nashville: Abingdon, 1978] 72-73) argue that a total of seven cases are involved. In addition to those cited by Wright, Seybold and Mueller cite the following cases: a) verses 9-17 b) 38, 39; c) 40-44. However, Seybold and Mueller concede that verses 9-17 may simply constitute an elaboration of the case in 2-8; They also concede that verses 38 and 39

periods encompassed by the word צרעת. One group of
cases is discussed in Lev 13:18-23 and 24-28, and has a
single quarantine period with no laundering at its
termination. These cases may be schematized as follows:[191]

Leviticus 13:18-23

Initial inspection >	QP >	2nd Insp./Rec.
If white eruption	7 days	If healed, the
or a reddish-white		patient is
בהרת		declared clean;
has developed after		If condition
a boil(שחין) has healed		worsens patient is
		declared a "leper"

Leviticus 13:24-28

Initial inspection >	QP >	2nd Insp./Rec.
1)If reddish-white or	7 days	If no spreading,
white בהרת		patient is pure/
which is not deeper		If spreading,
than the skin		it is "leprosy"
develops		
out of a burn;		
2) If no white hair		
in the suspected area		

---

should not be classified as צרעת. Verses 40-44 may be seen as a
different case or as a further elaboration of the cases dealing with the
body. In any event, the variety of cases demonstrates that no single
modern medical classification can be employed.

[191]The following symbols and abbreviations are used in our scheme:
Insp. = Inspection results; Rec.= recommendation; QP = quarantine
period; > = sequence of events.

The second group of cases is described in 2-8 (with perhaps further elaboration in 9-17) and 29-37, and has two consecutive quarantine periods, the last of which is punctuated by laundering the clothing of the patient. These cases may be schematized as follows:

Leviticus 13:2-8

Initial inspection >	QP	>	2nd Insp.	> QP >	3rd Insp.
1) If white בהרת	7 days		If no spreading	7 days	If no spreading,
not deeper than					patient is
the skin;					declared
2) If no white hair					"clean"
in the afflicted area.					and launders.

Leviticus 13:29-37

Initial inspection >	QP	>	2nd Insp.	> QP >	3rd Insp.
1) If נתק on the	7 days		If no spreading;	7 days	If no spreading,
scalp or chin which			if no discolored		patient declared
is not deeper than			hair in the		clean,
the skin;			area in question,		patient
2) If no black hair			patient shaves		launders his
in unafflicted areas					clothing

The procedures outlined above constitute a type of "flowchart" which determined the conclusions that the priests reached. If the patient was regarded as "leprous," then the instructions are as follows (v. 46):

1) The patient is to shout out "Impure, Impure" (טמא טמא);
2) The patient shall live alone (בדד ישב);

3) The patient shall live outside the camp community
(מחוץ המחנה מושבו);
4) Regulations apply as long as the patient is afflicted
(כל ימי אשר הנגע בו).

In case of human patients (objects could also be afflicted) the patients went (or were brought) to the priest for inspection. It seems probable that these patients went to the temple, though this is not explicit in the regulations. A patient was apparently excluded from the temple and the community only after the priest confirmed that the affliction was צרעת or something that would render the patient sufficiently impure to be excluded from the temple and the community. As we have mentioned, guards were posted in the gates to prevent the entry of impure persons into the temple area.

As a health care consultant, the priest does have some similarities with the Mesopotamian *āšipu*. Like the *āšipu*, the priest seeks to discover signs of the *qāt DN* (נגע) through a direct inspection of the patient's bodily symptoms. As we mentioned in the previous chapter, sometimes signs of the *qāt DN* in Mesopotamia were sought at the temple, and so this would render the shrine in P a sort of petitionary locus. However, there are a number of significant differences between the work of the *āšipu* and the work of the priest in Leviticus. The Israelite priest in Leviticus seeks the signs of the *qāt DN* not for therapeutic purposes, but to exclude the patient from the community. Indeed, the procedures outlined in the Leviticus 13-15 suggest that the priests were wholly concerned with preserving the purity of the community, not with the comfort or therapy of the patient. The patient does not come to the priest for therapy, nor is therapy mentioned. The only concern reflected in the regulations is whether the patient is pure or impure. Once the patient is declared impure, there are no therapeutic procedures suggested, and Lev 13:46 indicates that the patient is beyond therapy. Once impurity is confirmed, the patient is directed to live alone and outside the community.

In general, the peripheral role of the priest in therapeutic consultation is evident in the absence of any such connections in the Hebrew Bible. This is an argument *ex silentio*, but there are reasons why this silence is significant. First, all biblical referrals for consultation in which there is an opportunity to mention the priest or the temple never do so. We have seen, for example, that the referral (2 Kings 5:3) for leprosy by the slave-girl in the story of Naaman is to a prophet, not a priest.

On the other hand, many passages that refer to the role of the priest or temple in the health care system involve the post-therapeutic process (e.g., purification and thanksgiving rituals). All of the references to the priest in the health care system involve a role as a "purity inspector," or as a "post-therapeutic consultant," and not a therapist *per se*. Leviticus 13:46, in particular, is cogent evidence that the interaction between the priest and the "leper" ends with the final declaration of a "leper's" impurity. The "leper" is excluded from the camp, and he is not referred to any further therapy. This is not the case in the stories involving prophets where "lepers" are encouraged to contact these consultants for therapy.

On the other hand, it is possible to argue that the purification process itself constituted a type of therapy. However, this would not be therapy for the bodily illness itself. Purification rituals may be regarded as a type of social therapy which restores the patient to the "healthy community." In effect, the purification rituals are a public confirmation that the patient is indeed healed, and able to undertake his/her normal social role.

It should also be noted that the priesthood in Leviticus does not always restrict inspections to the temple gates. In the case of houses which were suspected of צרעת (Lev 14), the priest goes to the suspected house. This aspect may represent a significant expansion of the priestly establishment into non-temple venues. The main concern is the purity not only of the temple, but of the dwellings of the inhabitants. Yet, this concern is tied to the belief that the impure dwelling could confer impurity upon the inhabitant that might be brought into the temple. We may note that the priest is here concerned with purity of the community, not therapy for individuals. These house inspections may also represent a continuation or adoption of a Mesopotamian tradition which brought the health care consultant to the home for problems dealing with house fungus.[192]

There are a number of social inferences that may be made if the regulations in Leviticus 13-15 were implemented faithfully. One is that a large population would probably overtax a single or a few priests, something that would lead to a division of labor in order to manage inspections. This increase in labor would be especially taxing if the priests had to go out to inspect homes. Lev 13:2 hints that one priest alone would probably not be able to manage all the inspections (Aaron, the priest, or one of his sons, the priests). Thus, 2 Chron 29:34 mentions other situations (sacrifices) which required more personnel because, according to the author, the priests were few (רק הבהנים היו למעט ולא יבלו להפשיט את בל העלות).

---

[192]See Sam Meier, "House Fungus:Mesopotamia and Israel," *RB* 96 (1989) 184-92.

Since צרעת probably encompassed a wide variety of dermatological disorders, one may infer that significant proportions of "impure persons" may have been produced by such regulations. There are biblical texts that suggest that afflicted individuals probably had to resort to forming their own communties and modes of livelihood in order to survive. Note, for example, the band of four "lepers" who seem to scout the countryside for food (2 Kgs 7:3). Although we are not certain that all the regulations in P are reflected in that particular story,[193] one would expect to find these lepers outside the community if P (cf. Lev 13:46) were followed. In the late Second Temple period one finds a band of ten lepers who call on Jesus to help them (Luke 17:11-18). It is clear that the author of Luke alludes to the laws in Leviticus.   In effect, the regulations of P promoted the development of a new demographic group.

(5) The temple in eschatological views of illness

There are a number of views concerning illness and health care in the vision of the future of some biblical authors. We shall restrict ourselves to a brief discussion of how these visions affect the role of the temple within the "eschatological" community.

---

[193]The story is assigned to the post-Exilic period (Dtr 2) by B. Peckham (*The Composition of the Deuteronomistic History*, fig. 7), though it may preserve a pre-Exilic tradition. If the story presupposes the laws of P, then an ironical interpretation is quite suitable: The "outsiders" were living much better than the "insiders" during that famine. "Leprosy," of course, existed prior to P.

Isaiah 35:5-6 indicates that some, if not all, illnesses shall be eliminated when the Divine Warrior returns from victory in the future.[194]

אז תפקחנה עיני עורים ואזני חרשים
תפתחנה אז ירלג באיל פסח ותרן לשון אלם

At that time the eyes of the blind shall be opened and
the ears of the deaf shall hear; the lame shall leap like
rams, and the tongue of the speechless shall sing.

Note that some of these illnesses (lameness and blindness) are ones which other traditions (e.g., 2 Sam 5:8) would exclude from the temple.

Isaiah 65:20 promises that children shall not die a few days after birth, and Isaiah 65:24 promises that Yahweh shall answer before he is called for help. Isaiah 33:24 promises that in the future no one shall need to say: "I am sick" (ובל יאמר שבן חליתי). These visions logically imply that the temple shall not have a petitionary or therapeutic role in the health care system of the future because none will be needed. An eternal thanksgiving function, however, is indicated. The occasion for the thanksgiving is that all of Israel (land, society, and individuals) has, in effect, been healed forever.[195]

---

[194]The passage is assigned by P. D. Hanson (*The Dawn of Apocalyptic* [2nd ed.; Philadelphia:Fortress, 1979] 313) to a disciple of Second Isaiah or to the late phase of the career of Second Isaiah.

[195]For further discussion of the theme of healing in eschatology, see L. Greenspoon, "The Origin of the Idea of Resurrection," in B. Halpern and J. D. Levenson, eds., *Traditions in Transformation: Turning Points in Biblical Faith* (Winona Lake, Indiana: Eisenbrauns, 1981) 247-321. On the relationship between healing and the view of the temple as a

But not all of the visions of the future temple are the
same. Remarkably, Ezekiel 47:12 attributes a possible
therapeutic function to the future temple and its garden.

ועל הנחל יעלה על שפתו מזה ומזה כל
עץ מאכל לא יבול עלהו ולא יתם
פריו לחדשיו יבכר כי מימיו מן המקדש
המה יוצאים והיו פריו למאכל ועלהו לתרופה

By the river on both banks shall grow every type of
tree fit for food. Their leaves shall not wither, and its
fruit shall never cease. Every month it shall renew its
fruit, for its waters spring from the temple itself; And
its fruit shall be fit to eat, and its leaves (shall serve
as) medicine.

The passage evokes visions of the Garden of Eden as well as
the waters in Psalm 1. Assuming that the plants may be used
for the purposes which the author attributes to them (food
and medicine), it is remarkable that he envisions the temple
and its garden as a place where persons might go to receive
healing. This description of the garden is also reminiscent of
the description of the temple of Ninisina called the *Eunamtila*
("House of the plant of life").[196]

These visions of the future may be viewed as a
commentary on the past relationship of illness and the role of
the temple. Under P, which has a strong affinity with
Ezekiel, the ill did not have access to the temple itself, as we

---

cosmic center, see J. D. Levenson, *Theology of the Program of
Restoration: Ezekiel 40-48* (HSM 10; Atlanta: Scholars Press, 1986
[Repr. of 1976 ed.] 11-13.
[196]See D. Frayne, *RIME* E.4.2.13.22, l. 12, and *RIME* 4, p. 244.

have seen, because illness was associated with impurity. Equally important is that Israelite society was helpless in curing most serious diseases such as blindness or severe musculo-skeletal defects that were excluded from the temple in some traditions. Even if the priests wished to cure such patients so that they could partake in the temple cult, all consultants were unable to do so. Thus, P has detailed regulations that declare persons fit or unfit to enter the temple, but P does not provide any therapeutic advice because realistically there was not much anyone could do in certain cases. If the biblical text is any indication, it does not appear that P was interested in therapy even for illnesses that might have been cured or ameliorated by priests in Mesopotamia and Greece. In some ways P is more realistic about the incurability of some illnesses than the theologians of cult of Gula or Asclepius (and we shall discuss this aspect of these systems in our concluding chapter).

The visions of the future in Isaiah and Ezekiel see a time when it will be unnecessary to exclude any Israelite from the temple because of illness. Illness shall become irrelevant in the theological system. Illnesses that could not be cured in the past shall be cured because all of Israel shall evince genuine repentance. Instead of simply excluding from the temple those who cannot be cured, there will finally be the means to cure formerly incurable illnesses that produced impurity (and exclusion from the cult).

(6) Job as a commentary on his health care system

Job has often been seen as an essay on theodicy, and this is certainly justified.[197] Insofar as illness and health care are concerned, Job is also a magnificent essay on a question to which we have alluded in our comments on the Deuteronomistic medical theology. Briefly the question is: To what extent does the deity use, and have the right to use, illness as an instrument? Job's answer is best appreciated in comparative perspective. We shall not claim to provide a thorough exegesis of Job, and we shall only mention some points of departure that may be examined from the perspective of our study.

As we noted, Deuteronomy restricts the use of illness by Yahweh to the enforcement of covenants whose stipulations are fully disclosed to the patient. Deuteronomy denies that illness is an arbitrary instrument of Yahweh. Since the conditions for a healthy life are so clear, a patient need only recall what the transgression was in order to find the cause of his/her illness. In contrast, Mesopotamian medical theology assumes that illness is an instrument of divine policy for any and all matters which the gods may decide is in their interest, and such matters need not always be disclosed to the patient.

Job does not question whether God should use illness as a barometer of good and bad behavior. Job questions why it is that he, a righteous man, should be ill. Thus, the author of Job certainly shows awareness of the etiology of health expressed in Deuteronomy even if he might not be directly familiar with that work.

---

[197]For a detailed discussion of such interpretations, see M. Pope, *Job* (AB 15; Garden City, NY: 1986) LXXIII-LXXXIV.

As D. N. Freedman notes, it is a cardinal premise of the book that Job (1:1) was indeed a righteous man.[198] Indeed, the reality is that Job is righteous *and* ill, and this precipitates a case of cognitive dissonance. So the issue becomes whether Yahweh may use illness as an instrument for purposes which are his own private affair. In this case, Yahweh's motive was a wager made with the heavenly being known as Satan, who seems to be regarded as a legitimate member of Yahweh's council. Satan suggests that Job is righteous because he has been given everything he wants. Satan's first challenges Yahweh to take away everything that Job values, and wagers that Job will curse Yahweh for this loss (Job 1:11-12). However, even after the loss of his possessions and children, Job did not curse Yahweh. Finally, in Job 2:4-6, Satan challenges Yahweh to take the last valuable thing that Job has, his health. Yahweh accepts the wager, telling Satan: "Behold, he is in your power, only spare his life" (Job 2:7).

The rest of the book is devoted to Job's search for the reason for his suffering. Yet, Job never receives a direct answer. Instead, Yahweh protests that he need not disclose anything to human beings. For example, in Chapters 40-41 Yahweh enumerates a host of items about which Job has no knowledge. In particular, Yahweh speaks of Behemoth (40:15-24) and Leviathan (41), creatures which, for reasons undisclosed to human beings, have been endowed with all of the physical might in the world, forming a stark contrast to Job's sick state. Yahweh complains that Job cannot judge Yahweh (40:8), because the patient does not have all the information necessary to make a judgment. In Job 42:3 the

---

[198]D. N. Freedman, "Is it Possible to Understand the Book of Job?" *Bible Review* 4 (2, 1988) 26.

patient acknowledges that he does not know everything about the workings of Yahweh.

Job receives a new understanding of righteousness, and this understanding involves the maintenance of faith in Yahweh even if the patient does not understand all the purposes of the deity. The use of an illness as an instrument to test the faith of a patient, is justified, even if such tests are the result of a wager. But such tests cannot always be disclosed to the patient for obvious reasons. In fact, the book shows that Yahweh was proven right in his wager with Satan; Job did not curse Yahweh even after he lost everything of value.

So, in contrast to Deuteronomy, illness in Job is a divine instrument whose purposes, though not arbitrary, are not always disclosed to the patient. Deuteronomy has argued that the etiology is always clear (righteousness = health/ unrighteousness = illness). Job is more realistic because he argues that illness does not have an etiology that is always understandable by a patient. The link between illness and unrighteousness, in particular, is not clear at all. Moreover, Job affirms that the best human support mechanism for the patient is not a medical profession or a temple. The best human health care is not judgmental. The best human health care is psychological[199]---namely, the support and encouragement of friends and family.

---

[199]For a reading of Job from a Freudian perspective, see D. Bakan, *Disease, Pain, and Sacrifice* (Boston:Beacon Press, 1968) 95-128.

(7) Temple and illness at Qumran

Although we shall not attempt to make a detailed study of illness and health care in the Qumran community, there are some observations that are important for our purposes. Perhaps the most significant feature of the Qumran health care system is that the Qumran community exemplifies a theology that is not strictly monotheistic. It was a dualistic system in which the "Spirit of Wickedness" could, at least temporarily, cause illness of its own volition, and sometimes contrary to the wishes of Yahweh. Although the Qumran community seems to have followed some principles concerning "leprosy" which are delineated by Leviticus, various Qumranic texts add an etiology that is not found in Leviticus. For example, the Damascus Document says that leprosy is caused by the evil spirits which act on their own volition.[200] This is idea is different from that in biblical texts (e.g.,1 Sam 16), where spirits can cause illness at the direct command of Yahweh. In effect, illness and the patient are demonized in the Qumran texts.

As noted by F. M. Cross, the Qumran community was, at least in part, a priestly party.[201] The Qumran community, however, had more severe forms of exclusion than P. Note, for example, that patients with the following

---

[200]J. T. Milik, "Fragment d'une source du Psautier, et fragments des Jubilees, du Document de Damas, d'un Phylactère dans la Grotte 4 de Qumran," *RB* 73 (1966) 105-06. Comments on the ideas about "leprosy" at Qumran, see Emanuel Toff (Tov), "A Commentary on 4Q D^a 1, Col. XVII or 'The Wiles of the Wicked Spirit'" (Harvard Divinity School Seminar Papers XIII, March 25, 1968); and Joseph M. Baumgarten, "The 4Q Zadokite Fragments on Skin Disease," *JJS* 41 (1990) 153-65.

[201]F. M. Cross, *CMHE*, 332.

types of illnesses were not to be admitted into the community in 1QSa II:4-9:[202]

מנוגע בבשרו נכאה רגלים או ידים פסח
או עור חרש או אלם איש זקן כושל ...

Dermatological disease(s), injured feet or hands,
lameness and blindness, deaf and muteness, doddering
old men.

Similarly, as we have seen, the Temple Scroll would go beyond the biblical texts insofar as the exclusion of the sick from the ideal sanctuary and the city.[203]

We have argued that purity laws usually do have social components. The medical theology of the Qumranites becomes more understandable if one considers the socio-economic situation of the sect. It is a sect which probably cannot afford or does not wish to become a repository for the ill and the aged in the society. In view of its small size and location in a harsh desert environment, the Qumran sect probably could afford to sustain the ill even less than the temple establishment of Jerusalem (assuming the latter wished to do so). The belief in an imminent eschatological war might also prompt the community to admit into its ranks only the most phsycially fit persons available. The Qumran sect, thus, can be characterized as quite minimalist in its

---

[202]Following the edition of E. Lohse, *Die Texte aus Qumran: Hebräisch und Deutsch* (Munich:Kösel, 1971) 50.
[203]See also *CD* xi:18-xii:6.

approach to the community's investment in illness and health care.[204]

(8) The temple in P in socio-historical perspective

Insofar as illness and health care are concerned, we have argued that during much of the pre-Exilic period the temple probably could have had a petitionary role for a wide variety of illnesses. This is reflected in Hannah's use of the shrine of Shiloh as a petitionary locus for infertility and in the existence of relatively lax laws of purity evident in some portions of 1 Sam 1-3 and other early traditions of the Bible (e.g., the use of foreign guards, and the presence of blind priests). The involvement of priests in divination and the provision of oracles (cf. Urim and Thummim) may also have added to the value of shrines as petitionary loci in the pre-Exilic period.

The therapeutic role of the temple is reflected in the presence of the bronze serpent and in the prayer of Solomon. The link of the bronze serpent with Moses even by its

---

[204]J. Charlesworth ("4Q Therapeia (43.437): Cryptic Notes on the Medical Rounds of Omriel, A New Text and Translation," in H. C. Kee, *Medicine, Miracle and Magic in New Testament Times* [Cambridge:Cambridge University Press, 1986] 128-134) has recently argued that a text from Qumran labeled as 4Q Therapeia, and dated to the first century C.E., is an actual medical document. J. Naveh ("A Medical Document or a Writing Exercise? The So-called 4Q Therapeia," *IEJ* 36 (1986) 52-57), however, argues cogently that the text was a meaningless exercise and does not constitute any type of medical writing at all. Charlesworth ("A Misunderstood Recently Published Dead Sea Scroll (4QM 130)," *Explorations* 1 [2, 1987] 2) subsequently renounced his original position. We may add that the contempt for illness by the Qumran community makes it questionable that they would invest time in skilled medical endeavours.

detractors suggests that the therapeutic function of the object (and the temple locus) was regarded as legitimate and Yahwistic at some points in Israel's history. One cannot be certain how long the temple had a therapeutic role, but the biblical texts cite the elimination of the bronze serpent during Hezekiah's reign. However, it is possible that the temple had a recurrent therapeutic ("illegitimate" or "legitimate") function because the temple was often used for functions which were not approved by the canonical biblical texts. The Prayer of Solomon, however, describes the temple as a "long distance" therapeutic device which operates in a manner similar to that of the bronze serpent (i.e., it brings healing to those who face it and stretch their hands towards it.)

Although the main locus of health care was probably in the home, the temple may have been a viable petitionary or therapeutic locus prior to the full implementation of P. Indirect evidence for the existence of these functions comes from P itself. The very fact that P commands people not to come to the temple when they are ill suggests that people might have done so in prior times, for one usually does not prohibit a behavior which has never been practiced. Furthermore, Israelites certainly knew that temples were used as petitionary and/or therapeutic loci in some pagan societies (e.g., the temple at Ekron),[205] and the biblical texts themselves attest to the fact that Israelites were prone to follow pagan cultic practices.

The thanksgiving function of the temple after an illness is probably the most common and least problematic of

---

[205]We may also assume that biblical authors had knowledge of the therapeutic function of some Egyptian temples, and of Asclepieia during most of the Second Temple period.

the functions that we have outlined, even if strict laws of purity were enforced during the pre-Exilic period. P, moreover, promoted the thanksgiving function of the temple after an illness. The thanksgiving function probably remained vigorous throughout the entire history of Yahwistic shrines, and it was a significant source of income for the temple.

By the time that the laws in P were implemented, the petitionary and therapeutic functions of the temple were, for most practical purposes, eliminated. The wide range of conditions encompassed by צרעת alone would have excluded a wide range of patients. However, the thanksgiving function was enjoined upon former patients in great detail. What socio-historical developments might have led to the formulation of the laws concerning illness and health care in P? We only shall provide a number of brief tentative answers, which are admittedly hypothetical at points, in the hopes of constructing a reasonable explanatory model that may be tested by further research.

We begin by noting the physical limitations involved in centralization (as an idea or as an actuality) of the cult in Israel during the eighth and seventh centuries.[206] Instead of many shrines distributed throughout Israel to serve the needs of the population, centralization proposed that one temple

---

[206]Since our thesis focuses on the effects of centralization, we shall not provide a full discussion of the causes of centralization. One of the most attractive hypotheses is that of J. Milgrom ("Hezekiah's Sacrifices at the Dedication Services of the Purified Temple:2 Chr 29:21-24," in Ann Kort and Scott Morschauser, eds., *Biblical and Related Studies Presented to Samuel Iwry* [Winona Lake, Indiana:Eisenbrauns, 1985]) who argues that the Assyrian devastation of the north may have prompted Hezekiah to make new efforts to unite all of Israel, and centralization of the cult was part of the plan.

should serve the entire population. In effect, this elimination of outlying shrines under centralization promised a vast reduction of "cultic floor space" and a vast increase in potential users (i.e., all of Israel) for the remaining shrine. Since the central shrine did not expand to meet the increase potential demand, simple arithmetic indicates that physical limits could have been a real problem, even as increased population now being served at the shrine would mean increased revenues for it. Just this dual situation is indicated by 2 Chron 29:34. As we have noted, it states that the temple establishment needed extra help during Hezekiah's reign because the priests were not able to manage the large numbers of sacrifices coming to the temple (רק הבהנים היו למעט ולא יבלו להפשיט את בל העלות). The Chronicler places this note immediately after the description of Hezekiah's reforms.

One must also note that during the eighth and seventh centuries the Assyrian devastation of the north may have brought streams of refugees to Jerusalem. In the time of David Jerusalem probably had been a small administrative and cultic center, not a population center.[207] In regard to Jerusalem, M. Broshi notes that:

> one can claim with certainty that around 700 B.C.E.
> the city had expanded to three to four times its former
> size. This growth cannot be explained by natural

---

[207]L. Stager ("The Archaeology of the Family in Ancient Israel," *BASOR* 260 [1985] 25) estimates that no more than 1000 inhabitants occupied Jerusalem in David's time.

population increase or by normal economic growth.[208]

In particular, Broshi argues that the city grew from 44 dunams in David's time to 500-600 dunams around 700 B.C.E. The population, which he estimates at 6,000-7,000 in the eighth century, grew to some 24,000 around 700 B.C.E.[209] Broshi attributes this expansion to the influx of dispossessed refugess from the north. Even if Broshi's numbers are overstated, even a smaller increase in population would burden a single temple that had not grown to meet an increased demand.

Accordingly, we suggest that the establishment of a single temple for increasing number of users was probably a significant factor in the limitation of access to the temple. We suggest that one obvious solution to this limitation was to select a type of user that could be eliminated, and we hypothesize that the ill were the most vulnerable to elimination. One need only note that the Prayer of Solomon encouraged a variety of users to come to the temple, including foreigners, but made a distinction in the case of the ill. Perhaps such a restriction began simply by encouraging the ill to use the temple as a "long distance" therapeutic device akin to the bronze serpent that had been destroyed.

The Prayer of Solomon also reflects a feature of the deity which may have contributed to the decreasing value of the temple as a petitionary locus. Whereas some segments of Israelite religion probably conceived of Yahweh as a deity

---

[208]M. Broshi, "The Expansion of Jerusalem in the Reigns of Hezekiah and Manasseh," *IEJ* 24 (1974) 22; and N. Avigad, "Jerusalem and the Jewish Quarter of the Old City," *IEJ* 25 (1975) 260-261.
[209] Broshi, "The Expansion..." 23-24.

who favored particular loci (e.g., the tent of meeting, the ark, Sinai), the theology of the Deuteronomist and P indicates that Yahweh did not restrict himself to the temple. This contrasts, as we have seen, with the case of Asclepius, where the localization of the god at the temple increased its petitionary and therapeutic value because, if one wanted to contact the deity, one would tend to go the place where the god was most likely to be localized.

Non-temple Yahwistic prophets were probably the main legitimate health care consultants in the pre-Exilic period. At least in the biblical texts, these prophets promoted themselves as consultants for virtually any health problem, and their power resided in their special relationship with the deity whom they could contact from virtually any location.

But physical limitations in sacred space and the virtual omnipresence of Yahweh were not the only factors which led to the Priestly regulations concerning illness. The exclusion of the ill included some socio-political factors that were intimately linked to the laws of purity. As noted by a number of scholars, the laws of purity in P had, among other elements, a strong socio-political motive.[210] They were clearly used to express status differences, particularly in the wake of the Exile. As argued by P. D. Hanson, the Exile precipitated a conflict between the hierocrats who came back from Babylon and the group which had remained in Israel.[211] The hierocrats wanted to limit access to the temple, and they largely succeeded.

A wide variety of anthropological studies have observed that the control of physical space is indeed a

---

[210]See most recently, H. Eilberg-Schwartz, *The Savage in Judaism*, 177-216.

[211]P. D. Hanson, *The People Called*, 253ff.

frequent vehicle for expressing differences in power, status, and prestige in human societies.[212] That the temple is no exception to this observation is demonstrated by the fact that gradations in access to the temple were directly linked to status differences assigned by the hierocratic establishment which controlled the temple. The expression of power through the control of space may have begun when the Temple bureaucracy was instituted early in the history of the Temple.[213] In effect, the temple functioned as a symbolic system that expressed status differences in terms of access to physical space.[214] The highest status in the society was reserved for the deity himself, and he reserved the temple (and the Holy of Holies, in particular) as his special place. The degree of purity correlated with the degree of access to the deity's special place. Access to the deity's special place correlated with the degree of status assigned by the group (the priests) that controlled (or attempted to control) the temple and the society.

At the top of Israelite society in the post-Exilic period stood healthy Aaronite (or Zadokite) priests who assigned

---

[212]See, for example, J. Z. Smith, *To Take Place:Toward Theory in Ritual* (Chicago:U. of Chicago, 1987); C. Geertz, *Negara:The Theater State in Nineteenth Century Bali* (Princeton, 1980); *idem*, "The Doctrine of Graded Spirituality," in *Islam Observed:Religious Developments in Morocco and Indonesia* (New Haven:Yale U. Press, 1968) 36-38. L. Dumont, *Homo Hierarchicus:The Caste System and Its Implications* (2nd ed.; Chicago:U. of Chicago, 1980).

[213]On the early bureaucracy of the Israelite kingdom and temple, see T. Mettinger, *Solomonic State Officials:A Study of Civil Government Officials of the Israelite Monarchy* (Lund: CWK Gleerup, 1971).

[214]For explorations of the temple as an expression of status, see J. Levenson, *Theology of the Program of Restoration: Ezekiel 40-48* (HSM 10; Atlanta: Scholars Press, 1986 [Repr. of 1976 ed.] 119ff); and J. Z. Smith, *To Take Place*, 60ff.

the degrees of purity, controlled the temple, and allowed themselves access to the inside of the temple building. Next in status came the Levites who in the wake of the Exile became temple servants who were not allowed into the temple building itself. Below the Levites and other temple servants in status were healthy Israelites who were allowed only into the courtyard. Although the king or the "prince" (*nasî*) may have been above the priests in pre-Exilic society, in the post-Exilic period he was either an (impotent) equal to the priests or intermediate in status between the priests and the laity.[215] One clear status difference among healthy laypersons was between male and females. Women did have a lesser status in the society. This lesser status was expressed by, among other things, the longer period of impurity which followed the birth of a female compared to the birth of a male.

The differences in the purity of males and females are not solely grounded by P in a greater fear of contagion from female infants than for male infants. Instead, one sees here a clear case in which social status was the principal determinant in the degree of purity assigned by the priestly class (and the society) to females compared to males. As noted by H. Eilberg-Schwartz, there are always factors other than the simple fear of contagion which lead to the assignment of impurity and lesser status.[216]

What factors other than fear of contagion would have led the assignment of lesser status and access for the ill? One additional factor may be found in the link between status

---

[215]On the status of the *nasî*, see J. Levenson, *Theology of the Program of Restoration: Ezekiel 40-48* ; and J. Z. Smith, *To Take Place*, 61-62.

[216] H. Eilberg-Schwartz, *The Savage in Judaism*, 177-216.

and economic productivity in P. The economic function of the temple was an important one throughout the ancient Near East. That economic contributions to the temple were important is revealed by the extensive laws concerning offerings which clearly functioned as *de facto* economic contributions to the temple.[217] One of the main arguments of the hierocratic party for building the temple in the early post-Exilic era was that the temple would guarantee an increase in agricultural production (Haggai 1). Agricultural offerings, in turn, were a main source of income for the temple.

Further evidence of the concern of the temple establishment with economic revenue comes from the fact that opponents of the temple used the temple's requirement of wealth (in the form of animals etc.) as a reason for complaint (e.g., Isaiah 1:11ff). Certain narratives (e.g., Eli's sons in 1 Sam 2) also indicate the tendency of certain shrines to increase income by illicit means.

Is there a relationship between the purity assigned to a person and his/her economic worth in Priestly Code? Even a cursory examination reveals that there was such a relationship. The relationship among purity, status, economic worth, and exclusion from the temple may even be expressed in quantitative terms using data from P. These relationships become clear if we begin with Leviticus 27:1-8, which discusses the "special vow of persons to the Lord." Such vows could include "donating" a child to the temple of

---

[217]For a study of the economic value of the offerings in Israel, see G. Anderson, *Sacrifices and Offerings in Ancient Israel:Studies in their Social and Political Importance* (HSM 41; Atlanta:Scholars Press, 1987). For the ancient Near East, as a whole, see E. Lipinski, ed., *State and Temple Economy in the Ancient Near East* (2 volumes; Leuven: Departement Oriëntalistiek, 1979).

Yahweh (e.g., Samuel in 1 Sam 1:11). However, money could be paid in exchange for actually giving a person as a vow. Leviticus 27:1-8, enumerates the worth of such exchanges, and so the worth of different persons in strict monetary terms. If one compares the economic worth of male and female infants in Lev 27:6 (1 month to 5 years of age)[218] with the degree of impurity and days of exclusion from the temple which such infants impart to the mother, one obtains the following correlation:

	Monetary worth (Lev 27:6)	Number of days of temple exclusion incurred by the mother (Lev 12:4-5)
Male	5 shekels	7 + 33 days
Female	3 shekels	14 + 66 days

We see an inverse relationship between economic worth and the degree of impurity caused to the mother by each gender (and consequent length of exclusion from the temple caused to the mother). So at least in these cases the length of exclusion from the temple "caused" by a person is related to the economic worth of the person, and to the degree of purity assigned. Even if this correlation does not prove a necessary causal relationship between the variables, it does show the intimate manner in which economic worth and the degree of purity could be correlated on a wider scale in P. At the very least, one may express this relationship as: socio-

---

[218]This group was chosen because its age range is nearest to the ages of infants discussed in Lev 12:2-5.

economic worth $\approx$ degree of impurity $\approx$ degree of exclusion
from the temple.[219]

Other types of productivity were also important. The
fertility of a human being, for example, was important to the
Priestly writers. The spilling of semen was probably
regarded as "impurity" because it was a waste of a most
productive substance. A menstruating woman may have
been assigned a "sick" role, not only because of the loss of
blood, but because she was not (re)productive.[220] Infertility
is not physically dangerous, but an infertile woman is
unproductive insofar as the society is concerned. Her lack
of productivity means the death of the "family." Clearly, her
lack of productivity, not imminent physical danger, is mainly
responsible for her assignment to a sick and inferior role.
Note that the test for an adulterous woman in Numbers 5:28
makes a direct link between being pure and being fertile:

ואם לא נטמאה האשה וטהרה
היא ונקתה ונזרעה זרע

But if the woman has not defiled herself and is clean,
then she shall be free and shall conceive children.

In view of the foregoing observations concerning the
intimate relationship between socio-economic worth and the
assignment of the degrees of purity, it may be that the lowest

---

[219] $\approx$ is related to.

[220] See similar comments by H. Eilberg-Schwartz, *The Savage in
Judaism*, 183. For a cross-cultural study of menstrual customs, see T.
Buckley and Alma Gottlieb, *Blood Magic:The Anthropology of
Menstruation* (Berkeley: U. of California, 1988).

status in the society was assigned to those who were least productive to the socio-economic system--namely, the chronically ill. The idea that they could contaminate others and the temple itself simply added to the notion that they were a burden, and a "danger." This is especially the case insofar as patients who had severe and visible manifestations of illness. Gradations in the ability to make contributions were explicit in P (Lev 5:7ff). However, the ill were not simply the least able to contribute; they were also "a burden" in other ways that made them even more vulnerable to exclusion.

Evidence that exclusion from the temple was correlated with socio-economic productivity may be seen in the types of patients that were "singled out" for the most extreme exclusion by P and other biblical traditions. These types include those with "long-term disabilities"-- the blind, the lame, and the "leper." Note also that when the Qumranic sect adds another category to be excluded, it excludes only those aged men who were not physically fit and, therefore, unable to contribute to the sect. When the temple did admit a surplus of possibly economically disadvantaged individuals it admitted those who could make an economic contribution. For example, the Nearim (נערים), who might have been drawn from a surplus population of economically disadvantaged individuals, could provide an economic contribution in the form of labor.[221] The chronically ill (blind, lame, "lepers"), of course, were the least able to

---

[221] See further, L. Stager, "The Archaeology of the Family in Ancient Israel," *BASOR* 260 [1985] 1-35; J. MacDonald, "The Status and Role of the *Na'ar* in Israelite Society," *JNES* 35 (1976) 147-70. The same may be said of the Nethinim, on which see J. M. Baumgarten, "The Exclusion of 'Netinim' and Proselytes in 4Q Florilegium," *RevQ* 8 (1972) 87-96.

(blind, lame, "lepers"), of course, were the least able to provide an economic contribution to the temple or to the society.

Although the fear of contagion from "lepers" may have been regarded as a real "danger" in P, the exclusion of illnesses such as lameness and blindness cannot be explained by the fear of contagion alone. If blindness and lameness were thought to be inherently "impure" and dangerous to the temple, for example, then why are blind and lame priests not excluded from the temple? Leviticus 21:18 only excludes the blind and lame priest from officiating at sacrifices, but not from being present at the temple. Why are the blind and the lame not considered "dangerous" in Asclepieia? Indeed, the many violations (e.g., Uzziah in 2 Chr 26) of the purity laws of P or Dtr in ancient Israel indicate, at the very least, that not everyone was convinced of the real danger of contagion, or that the definition of "contagion" was far from being uniform. It is possible, in fact, that the fear of contagion sometimes functioned as little more than a rhetorical instrument by which opposing groups in ancient Israel (and elsewhere in the ancient Near East) sought to justify their maintenance of, or quest for, power. The opposing or unwanted group is thus defined as "impure" in some manner, even if the definition of "purity" or "contagion" is not clear to everyone.[222]

---

[222]Some modern examples of rhetorical instruments that might have functioned like the rhetoric of "purity" in ancient Israel abound in modern America, and are expressed in such rubrics as "real American," "true Christian," and "liberal." While some of these rubrics purport to describe a real phenomenon, it is clear that often they are effective precisely because they are so ambiguous. For a recent review of views of rhetoric as ideological instruments, see S. E. Shapiro, "Rhetoric as

In any event, the limits of physical space under a centralized system, the economic burden represented by the ill, the use of the temple to express status differences, and any "danger" posed by the sick, may have converged to render the direct petitionary and therapeutic functions of the temple as the least attractive and/or the least necessary to the temple establishment. The thanksgiving function, however, would be the most attractive in a system that promoted the accumulation of offerings at a single temple. The promotion of the thanksgiving function at the expense of the petitionary and therapeutic functions had the added advantage of circumventing the dangers of any "contagion."

Most societies have mechanisms (conscious and unconscious) to manage problems posed by socioeconomically "burdensome" populations. Solutions could include increased taxation for the support of the chronically ill, institutionalization,[223] exile, or infanticide.[224] P tends toward the realist pole in its illness etiology and prognosis, and toward the minimalist pole in its view of the responsibility of state institutions toward the ill. P certainly shares with Deuteronomy the notion that good deeds maintain good health, but P also concedes that often there was nothing that could cure chronic illnesses such as צרעת or blindness. Its response was to minimize the burden of the ill by excluding them altogether from the temple and/or the

---

[223]On institutionalization as a mechanism to manage "burdensome" populations, see M. Foucault, *The Birth of The Clinic* (New York:Vintage, 1973).

[224]On the social reasons for infanticide, see G. Hausfater, and S. Hardy, eds., *Infanticide: Comparative and Evolutionary Perspectives* (New York: A. De Gruyter, 1984); and L. E. Stager and S. R. Wolf, "Child Sacrifice at Carthage: Religious Rite or Population Control?" *BARev* 10 (1984) 30-51.

community. P had only minimal provisions which prohibited the cursing of the deaf or the placement of obstacles in the path of the blind (Lev 19:14). One may also speculate that such regulations may have been designed to unburden overpopulated cities of the most burdensome social classes. Only in a future age would illness become irrelevant because formerly incurable illnesses would be eliminated by the waters of the temple itself (Ezek 47:12).

The response of communities which had even less means to support the ill (e.g., Qumran) was to promote even more extreme forms of exclusion for the ill. Unlike P, however, the Qumranic notion that patients are possessed by the spirit of wickedness condemns patients to exclusion even in the future. The addition of the notion of predestination resulted in a sort of permanent caste system for the chronically ill.

In DtrH, in contrast, there was no illness too serious for treatment in the present. Leprosy, and even death, could be conquered if one found a good Yahwistic consultant and followed Yahweh's prescriptions. So Dtr was, in some ways, more utopian than P or Qumran. In Dtr illness followed a systematic order whose components were fully disclosed to the patient. Dtr regarded illness as an instrument of the deity only insofar as it was used to enforce covenants whose stipulations were fully disclosed to the patient. In contrast, one finds a more realistic approach in Job who argues that the deity does use, and has the right to use, illness for purposes that are not always disclosed to the patient. A righteous person is one who trusts that the deity is good without asking for a full disclosure of the divine motives that rule the universe.

Our reconstruction is not affected by the relationship of P to H. We only argue that the regulations in those

Our reconstruction is not affected by the relationship of P to H. We only argue that the regulations in those sources (whether they were originally independent or not) became sufficiently unified by the early post-Exilic period to legitimize the exclusion of the conditions described in the corresponding sections of Leviticus. For example, the case of Uzziah in Chronicles, which is generally dated to the post-Exilic period, presupposes that the laws of Leviticus concerning "leprosy" should be observed. By the Second Temple period the Temple Scroll can view as legitimate the exclusion from the temple (and from Jerusalem) of patients with "impure" conditions mentioned in all sections of Leviticus.

Likewise, our reconstruction allows a broad range for the dates of the implementation of these laws. Our reconstruction argues that access for the sick at temples was generally greater prior to centralization. Thus, we have no objection to the theory that the regulations in P (or H) might have crystallized by the late eighth century B.C.E. In fact, our theory concerning Hezekiah's centralization would be quite consistent with such a date for P or H. We also argue that the allowance of the petitionary and therapeutic functions of the temple for fertility and perhaps other illnesses precedes the formulation of P and H because such functions can be traced to the pre-Israelite period (e.g., bronze serpent traditions in temples, fertility figurines in pre-Israelite shrines).

Nonetheless, such archaic petitionary and therapeutic functions could have continued even after the completion of P and H. Thus, even if P was formulated prior to Hezekiah, the biblical texts themselves suggest that prior to the reign of that king the temple at Jerusalem was the site of a healing cult associated with the bronze serpent. We have already

may have had a petitionary and therapeutic function for illness throughout most of the biblical period. We assume that the thanksgiving function was constant in most shrines in Israel throughout the biblical period. Indeed, the thanksgiving function of the temple after an illness is never assailed in any biblical text.

The implementation of the regulations in P was probably a reality in at least some periods. The social impact of this implementation would have been enormous because large classes of patients would have been forced to leave the "normal" community. The formation of large populations of "sick outcasts" may eventually constitute a political or social threat to the "normal community." The Hebrew Bible does not provide much indication of this potential threat. However, the New Testament indicates that it was these populations of outcasts that appear to have been the focus of Jesus and his disciples in the development of a dissident Jewish sect which became known as Christianity.[225] The healing activities of Jesus and his disciples may be viewed as a critique of the traditional Priestly health care system.[226] In effect, the regulations in Leviticus promoted the development

---

[225]For similar observations, see H. Eilberg-Schwartz, *The Savage in Judaism*, 202.

[226]For a critique of the notion that healing played a prominent role in early Christianity, see Gary B. Ferngren, "Early Christianity as a Religion of Healing," *Bulletin of the History of Medicine* 66 (1, 1992) 1-15. Ferngren attempts, unsuccessfully in our opinion, to show that stories of healing miracles were intended mainly to authenticate the divine authority of Jesus and his disciples. Aside from such authentication, Christianity had no inherent interest in healing. However, as we have mentioned, authentication of divine authority is a constant element in cults (e.g., Asclepius cult) which focused on healing.

of a significant demographic group of which early Christianity took advantage.

C. SYNTHESIS

In contrast to the health care systems in Greece and Mesopotamia, that in Israel presents a dichotomous set of consultative options--legitimate and illegitimate. This distinction is intimately linked with the monolatrous theological system of Israel, and with the fact that Yahweh was not solely concerned with healing. Social, religious, and political boundaries were important, and consultants who were outside of those boundaries were not legitimate for a Yahwistic patient.

The most important consultant in health care was the person designated as the prophet. The biblical texts promote him extensively as virtually the sole legitimate human consultant within Israel. This consultant constantly struggled to be acknowledged as the legitimate consultant in the face of numerous "illegitimate" consultants who existed in ancient Israel.   According to various narratives in DtrH, women were often charged with the care of the ill within the home, and women often seem to have been entrusted with the search for health care consultation outside the home whenever home care was not efficacious. One of the main "illegitimate" consultants during most of the biblical period was the רפא, a profession akin to the *asû* of Mesopotamia. However, the demise of the prophetic office early in the post-Exilic period left a vacuum in health care consultation that was eventually resolved by the legitimization of the רפא.

The analysis of the health care functions of the temple also reveals a significant difference relative to the functions of temples of Asclepius and Gula. In Mesopotamia the temple of Gula was a resource center that stored and distributed information and paraphernalia to the health consultants. It also had a thanksgiving function, and perhaps petitionary and therapeutic functions on a limited scale. In Greece, the Asclepieion was a locus which definitely had petitionary, therapeutic, and thanksgiving functions for patients. Most Asclepieia may also have been a repositories of medical information and a resource centers for healing consultants. At the very least, the typical Asclepieion probably disseminated medical information to patients. Such resource functions, however, were probably secondary to its function as a direct therapeutic center.

Prior to the development of the idea of centralization in the late eighth century B.C.E., Israelite shrines, including the temple in Jerusalem, may have had petitionary, therapeutic, and thanksgiving functions. By the time that P's regulations were imposed, however, only the thanksgiving function seems prominent. We have no objection to the theory that P's regulations may have begun in the late pre-Exilic period, or that they may have been associated with the reforms of Hezekiah. In any event, P is the best preserved source on the role of the temple in the health care system, and it became the "official" statement through most of the Second Temple period. For this reason, it serves as the basis of our synthesis. The promotion in P of the thanksgiving function at the expense of the petitionary and therapeutic functions can be explained by the following factors in the socio-religious framework.

1. A centralized cultic system in which one temple was established to serve a relatively large population. This centralization resulted in a reduction of "sacred floor space" which may have led to the restriction of access to the temple.

2. The development of a priestly hierarchy in which power and status in the society were expressed in terms of control over physical space, and sacred space in particular. The priestly establishment viewed status as directly proportional to its physical access to the most sacred locus within the community. Those with the lowest social status had the least access to the temple, and the ill were in the lower social strata.

3. A hierarchical social system that relegated the least socio-economically productive members of society to the lowest status. While materialist aspects of Israel's culture were not the only important factors, socio-economic productivity, status, and purity were intimately linked. The least productive members of society were the chronically ill. The ill also presented other burdens such as contagion. As the members of the lowest social status, the chronically ill bore the highest measure of exclusion from the temple (and often the healthy community altogether). Exclusion of the ill reached extreme proportions in the ideology expressed in the Temple Scroll, where some patients were denied access to the city of Jerusalem itself.

4. A temple establishment which followed a realist approach to the etiology and prognosis of illnesses, and a minimalist approach to the state's responsibility in health care. Patients were either excluded from the temple and community or entrusted to non-temple health care consultants. Conversely,

the temple chose to promote and/or preserve the most economically advantageous function for the (former) patient--namely, the thanksgiving function.

5. A monolatrous theology. The belief in one god was a principal ingredient in creating a dichotomous system of options ("legitimate" and "illegitimate") for the patient. Monolatry also facilitated the development of a bureaucracy (particularly the priesthood) which could control access to this single deity. In polytheistic systems many temple bureacracies provided different "legitimate" options for patients if one deity or temple did not produce the desired results.

Another significant aspect of the theology of P (and DtrH) is that Yahweh had (or came to have) a large range of efficacy. While earlier traditions may have emphasized the value of going to the temple to petition for healing in some cases, various historical developments worked to de-emphasize the localization of the deity at the temple.

This configuration of factors represents a tentative proposal, and we shall offer a further discussion which relates the role of the temple in all three of our case studies (Greece, Mesopotamia, and Israel) in our final synthesis and conclusion.

EXCURSUS

The historicity of the Eli/Shiloh traditions

Our literary analysis of 1 Sam 1-3 attempted to show that that narrative contained a coherent depiction of health practices which differed from P. In this Excursis we shall attempt briefly to review how questions concerning the historicity and date of the shrine at Shiloh affect our reconstruction of the history of Israel's health care system.

The type of shrine of Shiloh

There is no certainity about the type of shrine that existed at Shiloh. There are two basic positions, one of which views the shrine as the tent,[227] while the other sees the presence of a genuine temple.[228] It is important to note that, regardless of whether the shrine was a tent or a permanent structure, most scholars and biblical references affirm the presence of the ark in that sanctuary prior to its capture by the Philistines (1 Sam 4:1-11).

The scholarly positions are consonant with the fact that there are two distinct biblical traditions concerning the

---

[227]For example, M. Haran ("Shiloh and Jerusalem:The Origin of the Priestly Tradition in the Pentateuch," *JBL* 81 [1962] 14-24); F. M. Cross, "The Priestly Tabernacle in the Light of Recent Research," in T. G. Madsen, ed., *The Temple in Antiquity* (Provo, Utah:Brigham Young University, 1984) 91-105.

[228]For example, R. de Vaux, *Ancient Israel: Its LIfe and Institutions* (London:Darton, Longman and Todd, 1961) 304. The views had been propounded by, among others, K. H. Graf (*De templo Silonensi commentatio ad illustrandum locum Iud. xviii 30,31* [1855] 2-8) in the 18th c.

nature of the shrine at Shiloh. One tradition views the shrine as a permanent temple (notably, 1 Sam 1-3), and the other, exemplified in 1 Sam 2:22 and Psalm 78:60-72, views the shrine as a tent. The latter position also is supported by the notice in 2 Sam 7:6 which states that Yahweh had only dwelt in a tent prior to Solomon's Temple. In the Mishnah Zebahim 14.6, one finds both traditions combined. Insofar as our purpose is concerned, it does not matter much if the shrine at Shiloh was a tent or a temple; either may have a petitionary function. What is important is that our brief inquiry shows that there was a consistent tradition which affirmed the existence of a shrine at Shiloh.

As we mentioned, 1 Samuel 1-3 consistently depicts the shrine as a temple. Some of the scholars that cite the antiquity of the tent traditions cite the value of archaic poetry. For example, F. M. Cross cites the archaic poetic references (Ps. 78:60, and perhaps 1 Sam 2:22) to the tabernacle at Shiloh as more reliable than the prose counterparts which mention a temple.[229] Cross is followed by Schley.[230] The latter also suggests that the reference to the shrine of Shiloh as a permanent temple may be a retrojection based on the Jerusalemite structure known in the First Temple period.

Even if the shrine of Shiloh was a tent, we may note that it would not be unexpected to find a Yahwistic permanent temple at Shiloh prior to the construction of the Jerusalem temple. Such buildings would be a continuation of a long tradition in Canaan. According to Finkelstein, the presence of objects such as "cultic stands, votive bowls, and a bull-shaped zoomorphic vessel" indicate that a shrine was

---

[229]F. M. Cross, "The Priestly Tabernacle in the Light of Recent Research," 91-105.
[230]D. G. Schley, *Shiloh*, 5ff.

present as early as the MB IIC period in a summit in Shiloh's northern or northwestern sector.[231]

The date of the shrine at Shiloh.

The debates surrounding the date of the destruction of Shiloh also prevent us from rendering too precise a historical reconstruction of the role of Shiloh's sanctuary in the Israelite health care system. The biblical texts do not explicitly mention the destruction of the sanctuary at the time of the capture of the Ark (1 Sam 4-6). Following Holm-Nielsen and other scholars, D. G. Schley has recently argued that Shiloh and its sanctuary continued until the devastation of the North by the Assyrians.[232] Albright and other scholars contend that Shiloh was destroyed by the Philistines in the Iron I period.[233] I. Finkelstein, who recently has undertaken major excavations at Shiloh, observes:

---

[231] I. Finkelstein, "Excavations at Shiloh 1981-84:Preliminary Report," *TA* 12 (1985) 163.

[232] D. G. Schley, *Shiloh:A Biblical Tradtion and History* (Sheffield: JSOT, 1989) 76-80.

[233] See W. F. Albright, "The Danish Excavations at Shiloh," *BASOR* 9 (1923) 11-11; *idem*, "The Danish Excavations at Seilun--A Correction," *PEFQS* 59 (1927) 157-58); *idem*, "Shiloh," *BASOR* 48 (1932) 14-15.

> Shiloh in the Iron II was a small and insignificant
> village, in which no evidence of destruction has ever
> been discovered.[234]

Finkelstein also observed the following concerning a building complex (312) which he dated to the Iron I.

> The building complex was destroyed in a fierce con-
> flagration. Burnt floors were found throughout.[235]

This leads him to conclude that Shiloh was probably destroyed by the Philistines, and not during the Assyrian conquest.

Part of the chronological problems of Shiloh also revolve around the dates assigned to collared rim jars, which often are considered "type-fossils" of Israelite settlements in the Iron I period.[236] Finkelstein and many other archaeologists argue that collared rim jars were used primarily in the Iron I period (1200-1000 B.C.E.). Schley, representing a minority position, argues that collared rim jars cannot be used to date the destruction of Shiloh because these vessels are also found in Iron II strata (e.g., Stratum VII at Tell Mevorakh). But while collared rim jars at Tell Mevorakh do occur in an Iron IIA stratum (1000-925 B.C.E.), most archaeologists would dispute Schley's apparent attempt to extend such occurrences to the Iron IIB

---

[234] I. Finkelstein, *The Archaeology of the Israelite Settlement* (Jerusalem: Israel Exploration Society, 1988) 232; *idem*, "Shiloh 1981-84..." *TA* 12 (1985) 174.

[235] Finkelstein, *The Archaeology of the Israelite Settlement*, 225.

[236] For a recent study of the collared rim jar, see D. L. Esse, "The Collared Pithos at Megiddo: Ceramic Distribution and Ethnicity," *JNES* 51 (2, 1992) 81-103.

period (925-722 B.C.E.) in Israel, the end of which is marked by the Assyrian conquest.[237]

Schley also argues that Judges 18:30-31 definitely place Shiloh's demise during the Assyrian conquest. But although Judges 18:30 does speak of the existence of the priesthood of Jonathan and his sons at Dan "until the day of the captivity of the land," Judges 18:31 does not explicitly speak of the existence of the shrine of Shiloh until the Assyrian captivity. Although Schley's reading of Judges 18:30-31 may be correct, it is not certain whether the biblical author is synchronizing the Assyrian captivity in 18:30 with the demise of the shrine at Shiloh in 18:31. The statement in Jeremiah 7:14 need not be interpreted as a destruction of Shiloh in the eighth century B.C.E. because Jeremiah might have had the destruction by the Philistines in mind.[238] The fact that the ark's reappearance was linked with Kiriath-Jearim (cf. 1 Sam 6:21 and Ps 132:6), not Shiloh, also corroborates the conclusion that, for biblical authors, Shiloh was destroyed by the Philistines.

Priesthood

One final issue is the nature of the priesthood of Shiloh. F. M. Cross has been a leading proponent of a Mushite priesthood at Shiloh.[239] Cross notes that the gloss in 2:22 adopts an anti-Mushite theme seen in Num 25.[240]

---

[237]For example, L. E. Stager ("Shemer's Estate," *BASOR* 277-78 [1990] 102-103) argues that the demise of the collared rim jar should be dated somewhere between the eleventh and ninth centuries B.C.E.

[238]See J. Day, "The Destruction of the Shiloh Sanctuary in Jeremiah vii 12, 14," *VTSupp* 30 (1979) 87-94.

[239]F. M. Cross, *CMHE*, 207ff.

[240]Cross, *CMHE*, 203

Schley has recently revived arguments for an Aaronite priesthood.[241] We have already mentioned that, as depicted in I Sam 1-3, the cultus at Shiloh had many differences from P.

Summary

The fact that 1 Samuel 1-3 does depict a health care approach that is different from P is evidence that such a difference is probably genuine. If Samuel 1-3 is accurate in depicting health care practices at Shiloh, then we may claim that such practices were in place prior to the Assyrian conquest. Indeed, regardless of the chronological issues discussed above, no major scholar dates the destruction of Shiloh later than the Assyrian conquest. On the other hand, scholars who advocate a pre-Exilic date for P and/or H (e.g., Knohl and Milgrom) may date either of those sources earlier than the Assyrian conquest.[242]

Nonetheless, if one argues that early Yahwism arose out of a Canaanite matrix, then the petitionary function of a shrine in the case of infertility would not be unexpected even in the earliest stages of Israel's religious life, and, for that matter, even during the entire biblical period. The role of Canaanite temples in fertility cults in the Late Bronze Age is well documented archaeologically.[243] The vitality of fertility cults around Jerusalem, the capital of Yahwism, in the pre-Exilic period is attested to by the large number of nude

---

[241]D. G. Schley, *Shiloh*, 139ff.

[242]Milgrom (*Leviticus 1-16*, 28), for example, places the date "not later than the middle of the eighth century (ca. 750 B.C.E.).

[243]See comments by W. G. Dever, "Material Remains and the Cult in Ancient Israel:An Essay in Archaeological Systematics," *The Word of the Lord Shall Go Forth*, 578-79.

female figurines found in the Jerusalem area.[244] Thus, one could argue that the petitionary function of the shrine, as depicted in 1 Sam 1, represents one unsurprising continuity with the pre-Israelite fertility cults of Canaan. Accordingly, the depiction of Shiloh's health practices in 1 Sam 1-3 would not be inconsistent with those of Israelite shrines that existed prior to P or H. As we have reiterated, such ancient practices could, and probably did, continue at "illegitimate" Yahwistic shrines even after the formulation of P and/or H.

---

[244]See T. A. Holland, "A Study of Palestinian Iron Age Baked Clay Figurines, with Special Reference to Jerusalem:Cave 1," *Levant* 9 (1977) 121-155; and Abdel-Jalil 'Amr, "Ten Human Clay Figurines from Jerusalem," *Levant* 20 (1988) 185-196.

System of consultation options reported in the biblical texts
(The options are not necessarily contemporaneous)

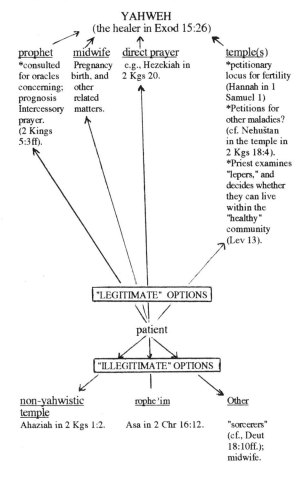

YAHWEH
(the healer in Exod 15:26)

prophet	midwife	direct prayer	temple(s)
*consulted for oracles concerning; prognosis Intercessory prayer. (2 Kings 5:3ff).	Pregnancy birth, and other related matters.	e.g., Hezekiah in 2 Kgs 20.	*petitionary locus for fertility (Hannah in 1 Samuel 1) *Petitions for other maladies? (cf. Nehuštan in the temple in 2 Kgs 18:4). *Priest examines "lepers," and decides whether they can live within the "healthy" community (Lev 13).

"LEGITIMATE" OPTIONS

patient

"ILLEGITIMATE" OPTIONS

non-yahwistic temple	rophe'im	Other
Ahaziah in 2 Kgs 1:2.	Asa in 2 Chr 16:12.	"sorcerers" (cf., Deut 18:10ff.); midwife.

patient   > = option(s) patient may select
consultant > Yahweh = option facilitates access to Yahweh
Midwives probably could be legitimate or illegitimate

CONCLUSION

We have examined the role of the temple in the health care systems of three areas--Greece, Mesopotamia and Israel. Each society has a temple with a configuration of functions that is unique and yet overlaps in some features with the role of the temple in the other cultures. The role of the temple must be studied in light of the health care system. Our focus on the three main possible functions of a temple of a healing deity--petitionary, therapeutic, and thanksgiving-- has helped to explore the socio-religious framework that led each society to develop the role of the temple in its health care system. Sometimes we found unexpected functions (e.g., resource center for health care consultants in Mesopotamia). We found that some temples did emphasize one or more functions in contrast to the others. The temple in the Priestly Code, for instance, emphasized the thanksgiving function of the temple.

We may summarize the functional analysis of the temples of the respective deities in Greece, Mesopotamia and Israel as follows:[1]

---

[1]Our abbreviations and symbols are as follows: P = Priestly Code; RC = Resource center as explained in Chapter 2; st = short term; X = presence of the function at the head of the column; ? = questionable presence of the function.

	Petitionary	Therapeutic	Thanksgiving	Other
Mesopotamia	X	Xst	X	RC
Israel (P)	?		X	
Greece	X	X	X	

Insofar as the utopian and realist conceptions of illness etiology and prognosis are concerned, the picture is slightly more complicated. The Asclepieion, at least in part of its pre-Roman stage, may be characterized as the most utopian of all the temples that we have studied. All illnesses were capable of being cured, and there was a prescription for every ailment. The specialization of Asclepius in healing was so intense that discovering the etiology of an illness mattered very little, and then only insofar as it promoted the value of Asclepius' cures. We may characterize the role of the state in the Asclepius cult as one which tends toward the maximalist pole in state responsibility in the health care system. Various city governments cooperated to build Asclepieia, and the city provided the salary of some of the priests. In effect, the city states helped to provide therapeutic loci, personnel, and other amenities for patients. Some cities also paid non-temple physicians.

The medical theology of Mesopotamia is probably the most realistic of all the cultures that we have studied. Illness could be due to a host of causes, sometimes contradictory, that were not always understood by the patient. Some causes were regular (e.g., breach of covenants), but the myriads of gods were metaphors for the inexplicability of illness. The response to this inexplicability in Mesopotamia is a therapeutic strategy that can be quite labor-intensive--a maximalist approach that seeks to address all the possible causes of illness.

The Mesopotamian health care system tended toward the maximalist pole in its view of the state responsibility in the health care system, though not as much as the Greek system. Mesopotamian temples were sponsored and maintained by the state/king. The state provided, if only as an ideal, a legal apparatus that regulated health care consultants. This included prices for medical services, penalties for malpractice, and the long-term care of the ill in the society. However, the ill were also seen as a burden in some ways. The state obligated individual households for the care of the chronically ill, and the temples were not large-scale infirmaries.

Israelite medical theology was not monolithic. One finds a very utopian concept of illness etiology and prognosis in Deuteronomy 28. All illnesses come from unrighteousness, and righteousness produces health. This simple equation was reiterated in Deuteronomistic narratives and laws. All illnesses, including death, were curable if the patient obeyed the legitimate health care consultant. In effect, the narratives in DtrH functioned to advertise this explanatory model of illness and health care to the patients (readers/listeners). In Job one finds a more realistic approach to illness etiology and prognosis. According to Job, Yahweh is not arbitrary, but he may use illness as an instrument for reasons unknown to the patient.

The role of the state in P may be described as minimalist. The medical theology of P may be described as realist relative to DtrH because P acknowledged that some illnesses were not curable by the priests or any other consultant. The state did help to build the temple that functioned as a thanksgiving locus. However, the evidence that we have at present indicates that the state saw the chronically ill as a socio-economic burden. In particular, a central temple serving the entire population placed the ill in the lowest socio-economic status, and excluded them from the temple and the community.

What explains the different configurations that we have seen in the role of the temple and in the views concerning etiology, prognosis and state responsibility in the health care system? To answer this question, we may also ask the following related questions.

1. Are there common factors that explain common roles and functions for the temple among the cultures in question?

2. Are there specific factors that are decisive in differentiating the roles of temples in the societies in question?

Among the most important common factors governing the value of the temple locus is the geographical range of the deity. Both Mesopotamia and Israel (e.g., in P) had deities with a large range of efficacy. The temple locus, therefore, was not always the only place to contact the deity. In contrast, the value of the temple locus in the Asclepius cult often is directly linked to the fact the Asclepius does not have a wide range of efficacy. The range of the god and the value of a petitionary/therapeutic locus are directly related. However, as we have mentioned, this tension between localization and omnipresence may be a dynamic one. Many modern Catholics may acknowledge that God is omnipresent, and yet believe that Lourdes has a special therapeutic value.

Specialization was another important factor that explains contrasts in the role of the temple in our case studies. Asclepius was the most specialized, and this is certainly related to the importance of his cult. It was this high degree of specialization that rendered the Asclepius cult accessible and acceptable to the widest variety of clients. among the temples that we have studied. Gula specialized in healing, but not as much as Asclepius. Her cult, therefore, never could become the only divine therapeutic option for the ill. Yahweh was the least specialized among the three deities in our study, but monolatry prevented the wide array of "legitimate" divine options one sees in Mesopotamia.

Monolatry is probably responsible for the development of a dichotomous system of options in Israel. This dichotomous system is not seen in any other health care system that we have studied. Since there was only one deity that sent illnesses, only one deity was necessary for consultation. Since there was only one legitimate deity, it was only logical that other deities were seen as "illegitimate." As mentioned above, monolatry also neutralized the wide array of other legitimate divine options that might have been developed because Yahweh did not specialize in healing to the degree that Asclepius did.

Although more research is needed, we suspect that monolatry is also a primary factor in the relative simplicity of therapeutic rituals seen in Israel. In Mesopotamia there does appear to be a relationship between the complexity of rituals and the number of divine beings that must be contacted, expelled, or entreated. For instance, the length and complexity of the Mesopotamian ritual against malaria that we have studied was directly related to the number of deities mentioned in the ritual. However, one cannot claim that there was a *necessary* connection between the complexity of healing rituals and polytheism. Healing rituals performed by Jesus, for example, seem quite simple, even though they assume a large variety of demons as causes. Nonetheless, one may speculate that polytheistic theological systems do have a higher potential for developing complex rituals than do monolatrous systems.

A factor that might affect the access of the ill to the temple is bureaucratization. The more developed the bureaucracy the more important the control of space seems to become in many cultures. Space may be used to indicate differences in social status and rank. Both Israel and Mesopotamia developed highly stratified priestly hierarchies that used space to symbolize status. In the early Asclepieia, the priestly hierarchy was not highly developed, and the priesthood was not always hereditary. As we have mentioned, Pausanias and other classical authors indicate that Asclepieia were intended to be the home to both suppliants and temple personnel. Such was not the case in Israel or Mesopotamia, where temples were primarily home of the priestly bureaucracy.

Both Israel and Mesopotamia evaluated access to the temple, in part, on the basis of socio-economic productivity. We have suggested that this type of evaluation was an important factor in the relegation of the chronically ill to the least amount of access to the temple. The link between access and socio-economic status is probably most evident in Israel where the specific demarcations of access proposed by the priestly hierarchy correlated closely with socio-economic status. The Asclepieion was least interested in correlating access with socio-economic status or productivity, though one cannot claim that some shrines may not have made such a link in some periods. As we have mentioned above, this situation in Greece is related, in part, to a conscious choice to manage a socio-economically burdensome population (the ill) by providing funds for their care in the form of a temple.

Our anthropological approach also shows that purity is not solely related to fears of contagion. Purity is also an assignment of status, and purity often reflects the status of a person in a society. One must be aware of who is assigning and outlining the rules of purity in a society. In Israel and Mesopotamia the priestly bureaucracy defined purity in such a manner that the ill were not allowed to participate in the cult or use the temple for most petitionary or therapeutic rituals. Such regulations, in turn, were related, in part, to the views of these bureaucracies regarding the responsibility of the state in the health care system. It is certainly true that one cannot establish a temple with a direct therapeutic or petitionary function if the patients are too impure to enter the temple.

Our study shows that a feature common to two of the major cults that we have examined also deserves more detailed attention than we have provided. This common feature is the role of the dog in the cults of Gula and Asclepius. The dog (as Anubis) also acts in concert with Isis, an Egyptian goddess who had healing as a major part of her repertory. In Lydney Park, England there was a Romano-Celtic cult center of Nodens, a Celtic god. This cult center served as a sanatorium, and it reached its zenith in the fourth century. C.E. Seven bronze dogs were buried in the floor of the temple.[2] The fifth c. B.C.E. dog burials at

---

[2]See Ralph Jackson, *Doctors and Diseases in the Roman Empire* (U. of Oklahoma, Norman, OK: 1988) 166-169. The temple was excavated by R. E. M. and T. V. Wheeler, *Report on the Excavation of the Prehistoric, Roman, and post-Roman Site in Lydney Park, Gloucestershire* (Oxford:Clarendon, 1932). The report was not available to me at the time of this writing.

Ashkelon may also be connected with the cult of a healing deity.[3]

The reason for such a widespread role of dogs in the cults of healing gods and goddesses is unclear. The theory that the dog assumed an important role in healing cults because of its tendency to lick wounds deserves further research.[4] The actions of the dogs in this manner are mentioned in classical sources.

However, healing rituals in Mesopotamia do not seem to involve licking by dogs whenever dogs are involved. It appears, therefore, that one must search for a more fundamental common motive. One hypothesis that might be pursued is that the dog was viewed as a "helper/defender" of humans. In Mesopotamia, in particular, the dog was viewed as a defender against the attacks of illnesses that were often visualized as attacking wild animals. For example, we mentioned that Gula and dogs appear in a number of incantations against the lion-headed Lamaštu-demons, which were notorious for their attacks on babies.[5] So, for example, just as dogs were used to attack lions in actual hunts,[6] dogs perhaps were deemed to possess the power to hunt and defend against lion-headed illness demons. The use of dogs to defend human beings might

---

[3]See L. E. Stager, "Why Were Hundreds of Dogs Buried at Ashkelon?" *BARev* 17 (3, 1991) 27-42.

[4]The theory is espoused by I. Fuhr ("Der Hund als Begleiter der Göttin Gula und anderer Heilgottheiten," *IB* I, 135-145) and L. Stager ("Why Were Hundreds of Dogs Buried at Ashkelon?" 39).

[5]For examples, see W. Farber, *Schlaf, Kindchen, Schlaf: Mesopotamische Baby-Beschwörungen und -Rituale*, 69 and 103-105.

[6]For examples in the Near East of the use of dogs against lions, see H. Frankfort, *The Art and Architecture of the Ancient Orient* (4th ed.; Chicago: U. of Chicago, 1970) figure 269.

explain why dog figurines were used as apotropaic devices placed around the neck, temples, doorways, etc.

On the other hand, dogs themselves could attack human beings. We have discussed numerous rituals against dogs or the evil caused by dogs. Amulets against lion-headed Lamaštu-demons sometimes depict dogs suckling at the breast of these entities.[7] Thus, perhaps we have a phenomenon akin that of Rešep and other beings who can both heal and hurt human beings. The patient's request in *RTA* 71:6 that Ninkarak halt her attacking dogs may reflect the view that she could both hurt and heal the patient depending on whether she commanded her dogs to attack, or retract their attack from, a patient.[8]

Although the Asclepius cult did not view illnesses as wild animals, the dog as "helper of humans" also would be compared to the work of the master "physician" (Asclepius), whose task it is to help humans. We have already mentioned that, according to Aelianus, the dog was honored as "a truly faithful guard and inferior to none of the sacristans in watchfulness."[9] No other animal was viewed as such an "all-around helper." The socio-historical developments that can explain the wide distribution of dogs in healing cults are undoubtedly more complex, and will only be explained more adequately when a sustained and systematic study of dogs within the societies in question is completed.

In the Introduction to our study we mentioned the main conclusions expounded by Seybold and Mueller in

---

[7]W. Farber, "Tamarisken-Fibeln-Skolopender," in Rochberg-Halton, ed., *Language, Literature and History*, 85-105.

[8]See our Chapter II.C.1 for the text and discussion.

[9]*De Natura Animalium*, VII, 13 = T. 731: φύλαξ πιστὸς καὶ τῶν νεωκόρων οὐδενὸς τὴν ἐπιμέλειαν.

their study of illness and health care in the biblical traditions. Seybold and Mueller were representatives of the critical approach to illness and health care who did not consider the advances in medical anthropology. We can now evaluate those conclusions with more confidence to see if our medical anthropological approach has changed any of them.

As we have noted, Seybold is responsible for the section dealing with the Hebrew Bible and ancient Israel (Mueller focused on the New Testament), and so we shall refer mainly to his analysis. The first of Seybold's main conclusions stated that, in contrast to other Near Eastern cultures, the Israelite patient had 1) no aids worth mentioning, 2) no physicians in the real sense, and 3) no knowledge of medicine. Seybold's second conclusion stated that the Israelite patient had "*no* really recognized or tolerated healing procedures or *practices*, including no ritualistic incantations or exorcism-related manipulations." In effect, Seybold implies that Israel had virtually no "real" health care on a human level.

We believe that our study has shown that such conclusions are overly superficial, especially in light of medical anthropology. First, Seybold's use of "physicians in the real sense" is a product of a modern Western bias. Seybold apparently assumes that "secular physicians" are the only "real" consultants in a health care system. Seybold clearly does not regard prophets as "real" health care consultants. We have seen that if physicians are defined as a group of healing specialists who use only non-supernatural assumptions, then Mesopotamia also did not have physicians, and neither did most of the neighboring cultures. The conclusion that Israel had no knowledge of "medicine" is also quite superficial. We have shown that the Bible was familiar with *materia medica* and medical procedures.

Seybold fails to see that Israel had a dichotomous system of options, and so his statement that Israel had "no really recognized or tolerated healing procedures or practices" is most misleading. Israel had recognized and tolerated healing procedures, and we have seen specific descriptions of such procedures in the work of the prophets. We have demonstrated that prophets, prayer, the temple in certain traditions, "self-medication," and household care were all legitimate options in the Israelite health care system and deserve to be viewed as part of "tolerated healing procedures and practices" just as much as a modern physician is part of our tolerated practice.

Seybold also would have benefited from differentiating the degree of state responsibility in health care from health care itself. Seybold's conclusion that the Israelite patient had no aids or healing procedures is primarily based on the Priestly Code. However, we have shown that the Priestly Code represented the state's view of health care in certain periods only, and not the entire health care system. Moreover, one must acknowledge the socio-historical developments that preceded the Priestly Code.

Seybold's third conclusion concerning the variety of therapeutic options ("a sick person in ancient Israel was limited") does have some merit. The Israelite patient did have less options than the other cultures that we have studied. Many options were declared "illegitimate." On the other hand, sources such as the Priestly Code represent an "official" religion, and one must acknowledge that many, if not most, Israelites probably did use "illegitimate" consultation options, including pagan temples, in many periods. The vehement denunciations of "illegitimate" options are in themselves eloquent testimony of the tendency to use those options by Israelite patients. It should also be

noted that monolatry would require less options than
Mesopotamia, and such a diminished requirement may not
necessarily be perceived as a restriction if the one option was
deemed as "superior" by the Israelite patient. If a single god
is believed to do the work that requires a multiplicity of gods
elsewhere, then monolatry may not seem restrictive. From a
modern scientific perspective, however, a single divine
option was probably as inefficient as multiple ones, insofar
as none of them would probably cure serious illnesses.

Seybold's fourth conclusion seems to lack
coherence, and merits full repetition:

> The sick person in Israel had undisturbed,
> unconditional access to only one path--at least
> according to the Old Testament--if he wanted to
> comprehend his illness religiously; namely to turn to
> his God in supplication and prayer.[10]

Seybold seems to regard as unique Israel's "religious"
understanding of illness because it involved turning to God
in supplication and prayer. However, unless "religion" is
defined in some idiosyncratic manner by Seybold, the
recourse to God in supplication and prayer is expected to be
an essential characteristic of any patient's efforts "to
comprehend his illness religiously." Prayer to a god or
goddess is a constant component of all the health care
systems that we have studied.

In regard to Seybold's conclusions, therefore, we
may claim that the use of medical anthropology does make a
significant contribution to our understanding of ancient
health care systems. Perhaps the most important contribution

---

[10]K. Seybold and U. B. Mueller, *Sickness and Healing*, 35.

is that it has helped us to become aware of the variety of consultation options that were available in ancient health care systems. Because Seybold sees the modern Western model of a physician as the only source of "real" health care, he has overlooked the fact that Israel also had a variety of consultation options. Seybold also did not explore a variety of socio-economic factors that helped to explain the role of the temple in the health care systems of particular societies.

It is probably natural to ask which health care system was best. We have mentioned in our Introduction that R. K. Harrison, J. P. Trusen, and other scholars studied illnesses in ancient Israel to show that its health care was superior to that of other cultures. But the question of which health care system was best is quite complicated. From a strictly scientific standpoint, the data that might tell us about longevity or rates of mortality in each health care system are not available. For example, one might be tempted to say that the Asclepieion was best because it welcomed the sick without much restriction. However, the Asclepieion may have contributed to the spread of many diseases that might have been checked by isolating patients. Thus, from a modern epidemiological standpoint, the Asclepieion may not have been the best type of health care to offer. A psychologist, however, might be attracted to the acceptance of the sick person without the exclusivism seen in P. Any efforts to answer such questions must outline clear criteria and develop new typologies in order to provide even the most general answers. Moreover, such efforts would also have to confront Western scientific biases that might affect a sound evaluation of the therapeutic efficacy of health practices in other cultures.[11] This is beyond our scope.

In summary, medical anthropology is helpful insofar as it encourages us to explain the socio-religious framework that led to, and interacted with, the system of health care that a society devised for its members. The socio-religious framework forms a web whose primary features are intimately interlinked. There are many features of ancient health care that we have left unexplored, and we only hope that the results attained here serve as an encouragement for other researchers to pursue and test our interdisciplinary approach to ancient health care systems.

---

[11]For a discussion of the role of cultural biases in evaluating therapeutic efficacy, see Arthur Kleinman and B. Good, eds., *Culture and Depression* (Berkeley: U. of California Press, 1985).

ILLUSTRATIONS

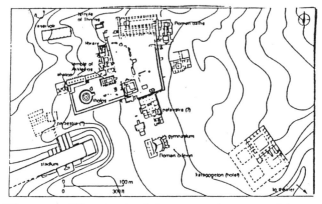

Figure 1. The Asclepieion complex at Epidauros. The basic construction of the temple, Tholos and Abaton can be dated to the 4th century B.C.E., but most of the other buildings date to the Roman period.

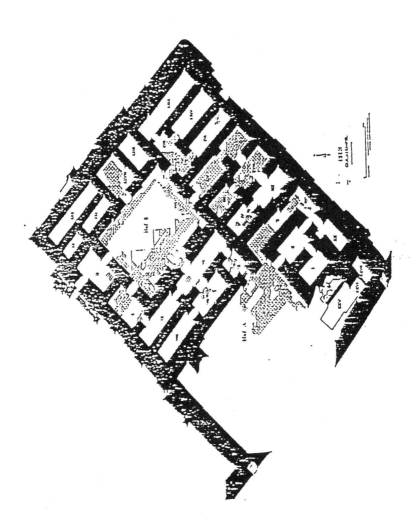

Figure 2. Plan of the temple of Gula at Isin.

IB 314

Figure 3. Terracotta relief (possibly OB period) of a woman breastfeeding a child and what appears to be a basket beside her.

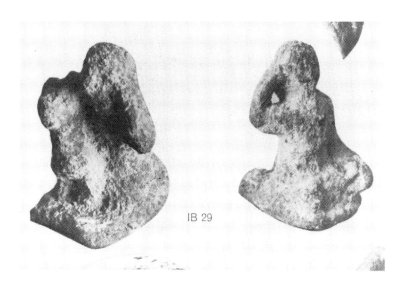

Figure 4. Part of a group of metallic figurines, perhaps from the early first millennium BCE, which may depict suppliants of Gula at Isin.

IB 29

Figure 5. A possible depiction of a suppliant of Gula from Isin.

BIBLIOGRAPHY

Selected list of items cited, consulted, or provided as further reference for the reader.

Aberbach, D. *Surviving Trauma: Loss and Literature.* New Haven: Yale, 1989.

Abusch, T. *Babylonian Witchcraft Literature:Case Studies.* Brown Judaic Studies 32; Atlanta:Scholars Press, 1987.

Acheson, P. H., D. Hewitt, C. Westropp and M. N. McIntyre. "Some Effects of Adverse Environmental Circumstances on Skeletal Development," *AJPA* 14 (1953) 375.

Ackerknecht, E. H. "On Collecting Data Concerning Primitive Medicine," *AA* 47 (1945) 427-432.

_____. *A Short History of Medicine.* Baltimore: Johns Hopkins, 1982.

Aleshire, Sara B. *The Athenian Asklepieion: The People, their Dedications, and the Inventories.* Amsterdam: J. C. Gieben, 1989.

Angel, J. "Osteoporosis: Thalassemia?" *AJPA* 22 (1964) 369-374.

_____. "Ecology and Population in the Eastern Mediterranean," *World Archaeology* 4 (1972) 88-105.

Angel, J. and S. Bisel. "Health and Stress in an Early Bronze Age Population," Pages 12-30 in J. V. Canby et al., eds. (see below).

Baines, John. *Fecundity Figures.* Oak Park, Ill: Bolchazy-Carducci, 1986.

Bakan, David. *Disease, Pain and Sacrifice: Toward a Psychology of Suffering.* Beacon Press: Boston, 1968.

Barkun, M. *Disaster and the Millennium.* New Haven: Yale, 1974.

Barnett, R. D. "Sirens and Rephaim," Pages 112-120 in J. V. Canby et al., eds. (see below).

Baumgarten, Joseph M. "Exclusions from the Temple:Proselytes and Agrippa I," *JJS* 33 (1982) 215-225.

_____ . "The 4Q Zadokite Fragments on Skin Disease," *JJS* 41 (1990) 153-65.

Beard, M. and J. North. *Pagan Priests: Religion and Power in the Ancient World.* Ithaca:Cornell, 1988.

Behn, Pedro C. "The Use of Opium in the Bronze Age in the Eastern Mediterranean," *listy filologicke* 109 (4, 1986) 193-97.

Biggs, R. D. "Medicine in Ancient Mesopotamia," *History of Science* 8 (1969) 94-105.

_____ . "Medizin A," *RLA* 7 (1990) 623-629.

Black, F. L. "Measles Endemicity in Insular Populations: Critical Community Size and Its Evolutionary Implications," *Journal of Theoretical Biology* 11 (1966] 207-11.

Bleeker, C. J. "The Religion of Ancient Egypt," Pages 40-114 in C. J. Bleeker and G. Widengren, eds., *Historia Religionum: Handbook for the History of Religions,* Vol. 1. Leiden: Brill, 1969.

Blondheim, S. H. "The First Recorded Epidemic of Pneumonic Plague: The Bible, I Sam. VI," *Bulletin of the History of Medicine* 29 (1955) 254-55.

Bonanno, Anthony. *Archaeology and Fertility Cult in the Ancient Mediterranean.* Papers Presented at the First International Conference on Archaeology of the Ancient Mediterranean, The University of Malta, 2-5 September, 1985. Amsterdam: Grüner, 1986.

Bottéro, Jean. *Mesopotamia: Writing, Reasoning, and the Gods.* Trans. by Z. Bahrani and M. Van de Mieroop; Chicago: U. of Chicago, 1992.

Bowman, C. H. and R. B. Coote. "A Narrative Incantation for Snake Bite," *UF* 12 (1980) 135-40.

Bramwell, A. *Ecology in the 20th Century: A History.* New Haven: Yale, 1989.

Brinkman, J. A. *Materials and Studies for Kassite History.* Volume I; Chicago:U. of Chicago, 1976.

Brothwell, D.R. "The Paleopathology of Early-Middle Bronze Age Remains from Jericho," In K. M. Kenyon, ed. *Jericho* 2 (London, 1965) 685-93.

_____. "The Real History of Syphillis," *Science Journal* 6 (1970) 27-33.

_____. *Digging up Bones.* Cornell: Ithaca, 1981.

Brothwell, D. R. and B. A. Chiarelli. *Population Biology of the Ancient Egyptians.* London, 1973.

Brothwell, D. R. and A. T. Sandison. *Diseases in Antiquity.* Springfield, Illinois, 1967.

Browne, E. G. *Arabian Medicine.* Lahore: Hijra International Press, 1921.

Browne, S. G. "Leprosy in the Bible," in B. Palmer, ed., *Medicine and the Bible* (Exeter: Paternoster, 1986) 101-125

Burde, C. *Hetitische medizinische Texte.* *StBoT* 19; Wiesbaden, Otto Harrasowitz, 1974.

Burns, Chester R. "Traditions of Health in Western Culture," *Second Opinion* 2 (1986)120-136.

Busvine, J. *Insects, Hygiene and History.* London: Athlone, 1976.

Canby, J. V., E. Porada, E. Ridgeway et al., eds. *Ancient Anatolia: Aspects of Change and Cultural Development: Essays in Honor of Machteld J. Mellink.* Madison: University of Wisconsin, 1986.

Caplice, R. *The Akkadian Namburbi Texts: An Introduction.* Los Angeles: Undena, 1974.

Cartwright, Frederick F. *Disease and History.* London, 1972.

Cass, Victoria, "Female Healers in the Ming and the Lodge of Ritual and Ceremony," *JAOS* 106 (1, 1986) 233-40.

Cavigneaux, A. "Texte und Fragmente aus Warka," *BaM* 10 (1979) 111- 117.

Chase, Debra. "*ina šitkuki napišti*: Starvation (KWASHIORKOR-MARASMUS) in Atra-Hasis," *JCS* 39 (1987) 241-246.

Civil, M. "Prescriptions médicales sumériennes," *RA* 54 (1960) 57-72.

Cockburn, Aidan and Eve. *Mummies, Disease and Ancient Cultures.* Cambridge: Cambridge U. Press, 1984.

Cohen, Mark N. *Health and the Rise of Civilization.* New Haven: Yale, 1989.

Conrad, Lawrence I. "The Biblical Tradition of the Plague of the Philistines," *JAOS* 104 (2, 1984) 281-87.

Cooper, J. S. "Structure, Humor, and Satire in the Poor Man of Nippur," *JCS* 27 (1975) 163-174.

Crain, J. B. "Human Paleopathology: A Bibliographic List," *Papers of the Sacramento Anthropological Society* 12 (1971).

Crosby, A. W. *Ecological Imperialism: The Biological Expansion of Europe, 900-1900.* Cambridge: Cambridge University Press, 1986.

Cross, F. M. *Canaanite Myth and Hebrew Epic.* Cambridge, Mass.:Harvard, 1973.

Crossan, John Dominic. *The Historial Jesus: The Life of a Mediterranean Jewish Peasant.* San Francisco: Harper and Row, 1991.

Crump, J. A. "Trephining in the South Seas," *Journal of the Royal Anthropological Institute* 31 (1901) 167-72.

Dandamayev, M. A. "About Life Expectancy in Babylonia in the First Millennium B.C.," *Mesopotamia* 8 (1980) 183-186.

Darby, W. J., P. Ghalioungui and L. Grivetti. *Food: The Gift of Osiris.* London:Academic Press, 1977.

Davies, M. L. "Levitical Leprosy: Uncleanness and the Psyche," *ExpTim* 99 (1988) 136-39.

de Moore, J. C. "An Incantation against Infertility," *UF* 12 (1980) 305-10.

Desse, Jean. "Analysis of Bones from Tell el-'Oueili Lower Levels (Obeid 0, 1, 2, 3), 1983 Campaign," *Sumer* 44 (1985-86; published 1987) 123-25.

de Vaux, Roland. *Ancient Israel: Its Life and Institutions.* London: Dartman, Longman and Todd, 1961.

Dever, Wiliam G. "Material Remains and the Cult in Ancient Israel:An Essay in Archaeological Systematics," in Carol Meyers and M. O'Connor, eds., *The Word of the Lord Shall Go Forth: Essays in Honor of David Noel Freedman.* Winona Lake, Indiana: Eisenbrauns, 1983, 578-79.

_____ . "The Contribution of Archaeology for the Study of Canaanite and Early Israelite Religion," in P. D. Miller, P. D. Hanson, and S. D. McBride, eds, *Ancient Israelite Religion.* Philadelphia: Fortress, 1987, 209-247.

Dietrich, M. and O. Loretz. "Ein ug. Fruchtbarkeitsritus (KTU 1.16 III 1-11)," *UF* 10 (1978) 424-25.

_____ . "Kerets Krankheit und Amtsunfähigkeit," *UF* 17 (1986) 123-128.

Dion, P. E. "Medical Personnel in the Ancient Near East," *ARAM* 1.2 (1989) 206-16.

Dolan, J. P. and W. N. Adams-Smith. *Health and Society: A Documentary History of Medicine.* New York: The Seabury Press, 1978.

Dols, Michael W. *The Black Death in the Middle East.* Princeton, 1977.

Donceel, R. et R. Lebrun, eds. *Archéologie et religions de l'Anatolie Ancienne:Mélanges en l'honneur du professeur Paul Naster.* Louvain, 1984.

Douglas, M. *Purity and Danger.* London: Boston and Henley, 1970.

_____ . *Natural Symbols: An Exploration in Cosmology.* New York: Vintage, 1973.

Durand, J. M. "Maladies et médecins," in *Archives épistolaires de Mari* I/1. Paris: Éditions Recherche sur les Civilisations, 1988, 543-584.

Ebeling, E. "Keilschrifttafeln medizinische Inhalts," *Archiv für Geschichte der Medizin* 13 (1921) 1-42, 129-44.

Ebstein, W. *Die Medizin im Alten Testament.* Ruprecht: Leipzig, 1901.

Edel, E. *Ägyptische Arzte und ägyptische Medizin am hethitisches Königshof.* Göttingen: Hubert, 1976.

Edelstein, L. and E. Edelstein, *Asclepius.* Baltimore: The Johns Hopkins University Press, 1945.

Edgar, I. I. *The Origins of the Healing Art: A Psycho-Evolutionary Approach to the History of Medicine.* New York: Philosophical Library, 1978.

Eilberg-Schwartz, H. *The Savage in Judaism:An Anthropology of Israelite Religion and Ancient Judaism.* Bloomington:Indiana University Press, 1990.

Eisenberg, L and Arthur Kleinman, eds. *The Relevance of Social Science for Medicine.* Boston: D. Reidel, 1978.

Elkadi, Ahmed. "Health and Healing in the Qur an," *American Journal of Islamic Social Science* 2 (2, 1985) 291-296.

Ellison, R. "Diet in Mesopotamia: The Evidence of the Barley Ration Texts (c. 3000 to 1400 B.CE)," *Iraq* 43 (1981) 35-45.

_____. "Some Thoughts on the Diet of Mesopotamia from c. 3000- 600 B.C.E.," *Iraq* 45 (1983) 146-150.

Engelhardt, H. T. "The Social Meanings of Illness," *Second Opinion* 1 (1986) 27-39.

Evans-Pritchard, E. E. *Witchcraft, Oracles and Magic among the Azande.* Oxford: Clarendon, 1937.

Farber, W. *Schlaf, Kindchen, Schlaf:Mesopotamische Baby-Beschwörungen und -Rituale.* Mesopotamian Civilizations 2; Winona Lake, Indiana:Eisenbrauns, 1989.

Favazza, Armando R., and O. Oman. *Anthropological and Cross Cultural Themes in Mental Health: An Annotated Bibliography 1925-1974.* University of Missouri Studies, vol. 65; Columbia: U. of Missouri Press, 1977.

Feldman, David M. *Health and Medicine in the Jewish Tradition.* New York: Crossroad, 1986.

Fensham, F. C. "Widow, Orphan and the Poor in Ancient Near East Legal and Wisdom Literature," *JNES* 21 (1962) 129-39.

Ferngren, Gary B. "Early Christianity as a Religion of Healing," *Bulletin of the History of Medicine* 66 (1, 1992) 1-15.

Fortes, M. *Oedipus and Job in West African Religion.* Cambridge: Cambridge U. Press, 1959.

Foster, George M. "Disease Etiologies in Non-Western Medical Systems,"*AA* 78 (1976) 773-782.

_____ . and B.G. Anderson. *Medical Anthropology.* New York: John Wiley & Sons, 1978.

Foucault, M. *The Birth of The Clinic.* New York:Vintage, 1973.

Fox, M. V., ed. *Temple in Society.* Winona Lake: Eisenbrauns, 1988.

Frankenberg, R. and J. Leeson. "Disease, Illness and Sickness: Social Aspects of the Choice of Healer in a Lusaka Suburb," Pages 223-58 in J. B. Loudon, ed. (see below).

Geller, M. J. *Forerunners to Udug-hul: Sumerian Exorcistic Incantations.* Freiburger Altorientalische Studien 12; Stuttgart:Franz Steiner, 1985.

Gesler, Wilbert M. *The Cultural Geography of Health Care.* Pittsburgh: U. of Pittsburgh, 1991.

Ghalioungui, P. *The House of Life: Magic and Medical Science in Ancient Egypt.* Amsterdam: B. M. Israel, 1973.

_____ . and Z. El-Dawakhly. *Health and Healing in Ancient Egypt.* Cairo: Dar el-Maaref, 1965.

Giles, M. "The Human and Animal Remains: The Crania," in O. Tufnell, *Lachish IV: The Bronze Age, Text.* Oxford: Oxford University, 1958, 318-33.

Gluckman, M. *Custom and Conflict in Africa.* Oxford: Basil Blackwell, 1955.

Goetze, A. "Mesopotamian Laws and the Historian," *JAOS* 69 (1949) 115-20.

Goffman, E. *Stigma.* Englewood Cliffs, N.J.: Prentice-Hall, 1963.

Goltz, D. *Studien zur altorientalischen und griechischen Heilkunde.* Wiesbaden: Otto Harrassowitz, 1974.

Gottdiener, M. *The Social Production of Urban Space.* Austin: U. of Texas, 1985.

Gottlieb, Alma. *Blood Magic: The Anthropology of Menstruation.* Berkeley: U. of California, 1988.

Grapow, H. *Grundriss der Medizin der alten Ägypter.* 9 volumes; Berlin: Akademie Verlag, 1954-73.

Gray, Bradford H. *The Profit Motive and Patient Care: The Changing Accountability of Doctors and Hospitals.* Cambridge, Mass., Harvard, 1991.

Greenberg, M. "The Biblical Concept of Asylum," *JBL* 78 (1959) 125-132.

Greenblat, R. B. *Search the Scriptures: Modern Medicine and Biblical Personages.* Philadelphia and Toronto: J. B. Lippincott, 1977.

Greenfield, J. C. "*Adi baltu*--Care for the Elderly and its Rewards,"*AfO* Beiheft 19 (1982) 309-316.

Grmek, M. D. *Diseases in the Ancient Greek World.* Baltimore: Johns Hopkins, 1989.

Grollig, Francis X. , and H. B. Haley. *Medical Anthropology.* The Hague: Mouton, 1976.

Gurney, O. R. *Literary and Miscellaneous Texts in the Ashmolean Museum.* Oxford:Clarendon, 1989.

_____ . "The Tale of the Poor Man of Nippur," *Anatolian Studies* 6 (1956) 154-64.

Güterbock, H. G. "Authority and Law in the Hittite Kingdom," *JAOS Suppl.* 17 (1954) 16-24.

Hackett, C. J. *Diagnostic Criteria of Syphilis, Yaws and Treponarid (Treponematosis) and of some other Diseases in Dry Bones for use in Osteoarchaeology.* Berlin: Springer, 1976.

Hägg, R. and Nanno Marinatos, eds., *Sanctuaries and Cults in the Aegean Bronze Age.* Svenska Institutet I Athen: Stockholm, 1981.

Hahn, Robert A., and A. Kleinman. "Belief as Pathogen, Belief as Medicine; 'Voodoo Death' and the Placebo Phenomenon in Anthropological Perspective," *Medical Anthropology Qaurterly* 14 (4, 1983) 3, 16-19.

Hallo, W. "The Royal Correspondence of Larsa: A Sumerian Prototype for the Prayer of Hezekiah?" *AOAT* 25 (1976) 209-224

Hanson, P.D. *The People Called: The Growth of Community in the Bible.* San Francisco: Harper and Row, 1986.

_____ . *The Dawn of Apocalyptic: The Historical and Sociological Roots of Jewish Apocalyptic Eschatology.* 2nd ed.; Philadelphia: Fortress, 1979.

Haran, M. *Temples and Temple Service in Ancient Israel.* Oxford: Clarendon, 1978.

Harrington, Hannah K. *The Impurity Systems of Qumran and the Rabbis: Biblical Foundations.* Atlanta: Scholars Press, 1993.

Harris, J. E. and E. F. Wente. *An X-Ray Atlas of the Royal Mummies.* Chicago: U. of Chicago Press, 1980.

Harris, J. Gordon. *Biblical Perspectives on Aging: God and the Elderly.* Philadelphia: Fortress, 1987.

Harris, M. *The Sacred Cow and the Abominable Pig.* New York, 1985.

Harrison, R. K. "Medicine," *IDB*, 331-332.

Hart, Gerald D. ed. *Disease in Ancient Man.* Toronto: Clarke Irwin, 1983.

Hasel, G. "Health and Healing in the Old Testament," *Andrews University Seminary Studies* 21 (1983) 191-202.

Healy, J. F. "*MLKM/RPUM* and the *KISPUM*," *UF* 10 (1978) 89-92.

Heath, D.B., and A. M. Cooper. *Alcohol Use and World Cultures: A Comprehensive Bibliography of Anthropological Sources.* Toronto: Toronto Addiction Research Foundation, 1981.

Heinrich, E. *Die Tempel und Heiligtumer im Alten Mesopotamien.* 2 volumes; Berlin: De Gruyter, 1982.

Hellman, C.G. *Culture, Health and Illness: An Introduction for Health Professionals.* Littleton, Mass.:PSG Publishing Co., 1984.

Hempel, J. "Ich bin der Herr, dein Arzt (Ex. 15,26)" *ThLZ* 82 (1957) 809-26.

_____. *Heilung als Symbol und Wirklichkeit im biblischen Schriftum.* Göttingen: Kenner, 1965.

Henschen, F. *The History of Diseases.* London: Helm, 1966.

Herrero, Pablo. *La thérapeutique mésopotamienne.* Paris: Editions Recherche sur les civilisations, 1984.

Hill, Carole E. *Training Manual in Medical Anthropology.* Washington, D.C.:American Anthropological Association, and the Society for Applied Anthropology; no. 18; 1985.

Hölbl, Günther. "Egyptian Fertility Magic within Phoenician and Punic Culture," in A. Bonanno, ed., *Archaeology and Fertility Cult in the Ancient Mediterranean.* Amsterdam: Grüner, 1986, 113-124.

Holden, Lyn. *Forms of Deformity.* Sheffield: JSOT, 1991.

Houtart, F., ed. "Religion, Health and Healing: Sociological Perspectives," *Social Compass* 34 (4, 1987) 315-548.

Hrouda, B. et al., eds. *Isin-Išān Baḥrīyāt I: Die Ergebnisse der Ausgrabungen 1973-1974.* München:Bayerische Akademie der Wissenschaften, 1977.

_____. *Isin-Išān Baḥrīyāt II: Die Ergebnisse der Ausgrabungen 1975-1978.* München:Bayerische Akademie der Wissenschaften, 1981.

_____. *Isin-Išān Baḥrīyāt Die Ergebnisse der Ausgrabungen 1983-1984.* München:Bayerische Akademie der Wissenschaften, 1987.

_____. *Isin-Išān Baḥrīyāt IV: Die Ergebnisse der Ausgrabungen 1986-1989.* München: Bayerische Akademie der Wissenschaften, 1992.

Hudson, R. P. *Disease and Its Control: The Shaping of Modern Thought.* Westport, Conn.:Greenwood, 1983.

Hulse, E.V. "The Nature of Biblical 'Leprosy' and the Use of Alternative Medical Terms in Modern Translations of the Bible," *PEQ* 107 (1975) 87-105.

Humbert, P. "Maladie et médicine dans l'Ancien Testament," *Revue d'histoire et de philosophie reliegieuses* 44 (1964) 1-29.

Hussey, M. I. "Anatomical Nomenclature in an Akkadian Omen Text," *JCS* 2 (1949) 21-29.

Hutter, Manfred. "Der legitime Platz der Magie in den Religionen des Alten Orients," *Grenzgebiete des Wissenschaft* 36 (1987) 315-28.

Ivanovsky, A. "Physical Modifications of the Population of Russia under Famine," *AJPA* 6 (1923) 331-53.

Jackson, B. S. *Essays in Jewish and Comparative Legal History. Studies in Judaism in Late Antiquity* 10; Leiden: Brill.

Jaco, E.G., ed. *Patients, Physicians and Illness.* New York: Free Press 1979.

Jacobovitz, I. *Jewish Medical Ethics.* New York: Bloch, 1967.

Jacq, C. *Egyptian Magic.* Bolchazy-Carducci: Oak Park, Ill., 1985.

Jansens, P. A. *Palaeopathology: Diseases and Injuries of Pre-historic Man.* London: Baker, 1970.

Jarcho, S. ed. *Human Palaeopathology.* New Haven: Yale, 1966.

Jayne, W. A. *The Healing Gods of Ancient Civilizations.* New Haven: Yale, 1925.

Jelliffe, E.F. and D. B. Jelliffe, *Adverse Effects of Foods.* New York: Plenum Press, 1982.

Jonckheere, F. *Une maladie égyptienne. L'Hematurie parasitaire.* Uitgaven van de Egyptologische Stichting Koningin Elizabeth, 1944.

Katz, Solomon H. and M. M. Voigt. "Bread and Beer: The Early Use of Cereals in the Human Diet," *Expedition* 28 (2, 1986) 23-34.

Kee, H. C. *Medicine, Miracle and Magic in New Testament Times.* Cambridge: Cambridge U. Press, 1986.

Kinnier Wilson, "An Introduction to Babylonian Psychiatry," *A S* 16: 289-298.

———. "Leprosy in Ancient Mesopotamia," *R A* 60 (1966) 48-58.

———. "Gleanings from the Iraq Medical Journals," *JNES* 27 (1968) 243-247.

———. "Medicine in the Land and Times of the Old Testament," in T. Ishida, ed., *Studies in the Period of David and Solomon.* Winona Lake: Eisenbrauns, 1982, 337-375.

Kleinman, Arthur. *Patients and Healers in the Context of Culture: Explorations of the Borderland Between Anthropology, Medicine and Psychiatry.* Berkeley: University of California Press, 1980.

———. *The Illness Narratives.* New York: Basic Books, 1988.

———, and B. Good, eds. *Culture and Depression.* Berkeley: U. of California Press, 1985.

Köcher, F. *Die babylonisch-assyrische Medizin in Texten und Untersuchungen.* 4 volumes; Berlin:De Gruyter, 1963-80.

Koelbing, H. M. *Arzt und Patient in der Antike Welt.* Zürich und München:Artemis, 1977.

Kuntz, Stephen J. *Disease Change and the Role of Medicine.* Berkeley: U. of California Press, 1983.

Labat, R. *Traité akkadien de diagnostics and prognostics medicaux* Leiden: Brill, 1951.

———. *La médicine babylonienne.* Paris: Université de Paris, 1953.

Lambert, W. G. "*Dingir.šà.dib.ba* Incantations," *JNES* 33 (1974) 267-322.

Lebrun, R. *Hymnes et priéres hittites.* Louvain: CDHR, 1980.

Levenson, J. *Theology of the Program of Restoration: Ezekiel 40-48.* HSM 10; Atlanta: Scholars Press, 1986.

Levin, S. *Adam's Rib:Essays in Biblical Medicine.* Los Altos, Calif.: Geron X, Inc., 1979.

_____ . "The Judgment of Solomon: Legal and Medical [1 Kgs 3:16-28]," *Judaism* 32 (1983) 463-65.

_____ . "The Sickness of Sodom," *Judaism* 35 (3, 1986) 281-283.

Levine, B.A. and J-M. de Tarragon, "'Shapshu Cries Out in Heaven:' Dealing with Snake-Bites at Ugarit (KTU 1.100, 1.107)," *RB* 95 (4, 1988) 481-518.

Lintott, Andrew. *Violence, Civil Strife, and Revolution in the Classical City.* London: Croom Helm, 1982.

Lipinski, E., ed., *State and Temple Economy in the Ancient Near East.* 2 volumes; Leuven: Departement Oriëntalistiek, 1979.

Livingstone, A. "The Isin 'Dog House' Revisited," *JCS* 40 (1, 1988) 54-60.

Lods, A. "Les idées des Israélites sur la maladie, ses causes et ses rémedes," *BZAW* 41 (1925) 181-93.

Loudon, J. B., ed. *Social Anthropology and Medicine.* New York: Academic Press, 1976.

Macarthur, W. P. "The Occurrence of the Rat in Early Europe: The Plague of the Philistines (I Sam., 5,6)," *Transcriptions of the Royal Asiatic Society of Tropical Medicine and Hygiene,* XLVI (1952) 209-12, 464.

Madsen, G. ed., *The Temple in Antiquity.* Provo, Utah: Brigham Young University, 1984.

Majno, G. *The Healing Hand.* Cambridge, Mass.: Harvard U. Press, 1975.

Malina, Bruce. *Christian Origins and Cultural Anthropology: Practical Models for Biblical Interpretation.* Atlanta: John Knox, 1986.

Manchester, K. *The Archaeology of Disease.* Bradford, 1983.

Manniche, L. *An Ancient Egyptian Herbal.* Austin: U. of Texas, 1989.

Margueron, Jean. *A propos des temples de Syrie du Nord.* Paris: Geuthner, 1985.

_____ . "Sanctuaires sémitiques," *Supplement au Dictionnaire de la Bible*. Tome onzieme; Paris: Letouzey & ANE, 1991, 1104-1257.

Martinez, R. M. "Epidemic Disease, Ecology, and Culture in the Ancient Near East," in *ANETS* 8 (1990) 413-457.

Matossian, M. K. *Poisons of the Past: Molds, Epidemics and History.* New Haven: Yale, 1989.

Mayer, W. *Untersuchungen zur Formensprache der babylonischen Gebetbeschwörungen.* Rome: Biblical Institute Press, 1976.

McNeill, W. H. *Plagues and Peoples.* New York: Doubleday, 1976.

Merillees, R. S. "Opium Trade in the Bronze Age Levant," *Antiquity* 36 (1962) 287-304.

Middleton, J. *Magic, Witchcraft and Curing.* Austin: U. of Texas, 1976.

Milgrom, J. *Studies in Levitical Terminology* I. Berkeley: U. of California Press, 1970.

_____ . "Israel's Sanctuary: The Priestly 'Picture of Dorian Gray'" *RB* 83 (1976) 62-72.

_____ . "'Sabbath' and 'Temple City' in the Temple Scroll," *BASOR* 232 (1978) 25-27.

_____ . "Studies in the Temple Scroll," *JBL* 97 (4, 1978) 501-23.

_____ . *Leviticus 1-16.* New York: Doubleday, 1991.

Minnis, Paul E. *Social Adaptation to Food Stress: A Preshistoric Southwestern Example.* Chicago: U. of Chicago, 1980.

Møller-Christensen, V. *Bone Changes in Leprosy.* Copenhagen, 1961.

Molleson, Theya. "The Eloquent Bones of Abu Hureyra," *Scientific American* 271 (August, 1994) 70-75.

Morse, D., D. R. Brothwell and P. J. Ucko. "Tuberculosis in Ancient Egypt," *American Review of Respiratory Diseases* 90 (1964) 524-541.

Mumcuoglu, K. Y. and J. Zias. "How the Ancients Deloused Themselves," *BARev* 15 (6, 1989) 66-69.

Münch, G. N. "Die *Zaraath* (Lepra) der hebräischen Bibel," *Dermatologische Studien* 16 (1893) 135-64.

Murdock, George P. *Theories of Illness: A World Survey.* Pittsburgh: U. of Pittsburgh Press, 1970.

Neufeld, E. "Hygiene Conditions in Ancient Israel (Iron Age)," *BA* 34 (2, 1971) 42-66.

_____ . "The Earliest Document of a Case of Contagious Disease in Mesopotamia (Mari Tablet X 129)," *JANES* 18 (1986) 53-66.

Neustatter, Otto. "When Did the Identification of the Philistine Plague (I Samuel 5 and 6) as Bubonic Plague Originate?" *Bulletin of the History of Medicine,* XI (1942) 36-47.

Nielsen, O. V. *The Nubian Skeleton through 4000 Years.* Copenhagen, 1970.

Oliver, Paul. *Dwellings: The House across the World.* Austin: U. of Texas, 1987.

Olson, C., ed. *The Book of the Goddess, Past and Present.* New York: Crossroad, 1983.

Oppenheim, A. L. "On the Observation of the Pulse in Mesopotamian Medicine," *Or* 21 (1962) 27-33.

_____ . *Ancient Mesopotamia: Portrait of a Dead Civilization.* Chicago: University of Chicago, 1964.

Ortíz de Montellano, Bernard. *Aztec Medicine, Health, and Nutrition.* New Brunswick, N.J.: Rutgers U. Press, 1991.

Palmer, B., ed. *Medicine and the Bible.* Exeter: Paternoster Press, 1986.

Parker, R. *Miasma: Pollution and Purification in Early Greek Religion.* New York: Oxford, 1983.

Parry, Donald W., Stephen D. Ricks and John W. Welch, *A Bibliography on Temples of the Ancient Near East and the Mediterranean World.* Lewiston, New York: E. Mellen, 1991.

Pedersen, O. *Archives and Libraries in the City of Assur.* 2 volumes; Uppsala: Almqvist & Wiksell, 1985 and 1986.

Pilch, J. J. "Biblical Leprosy and Body Symbolism," *BTB* 11 (4, 1981) 108-113.

_____ . "The Health Care System in Matthew: A Social Science Analysis," *BTB* 16 (3, 1986) 281- 283.

_____ . "Healing in Mark: A Social Science Analysis," *BTB* 15 (4, 1985) 142-150.

Popham, R. E. "Trepanation as a Rational Procedure in Primitive Surgery," *University of Toronto Medical Journal* 31 (1954) 204-11.

Preuss, J. *Biblical and Talmudic Medicine*. Trans. of *Biblisch-talmudische Medizin* [Berlin, 1911] by F. Rosner. Brooklyn, N.Y.: Hebrew Publishing Co., 1977.

Price, R. M. "Illness Theodicies in the New Testament," *Social Analysis* 47 (2, 1986) 309-315.

Price, T. Douglas, ed. *The Chemistry of Prehistoric Human Bone*. Cambridge: Cambridge University Press, 1989.

Proceedings of the Second International Symposium on Medicine in Bible and Talmud, Jerusalem, December 18-20, 1984. Leiden: Brill, 1985.

Radt, Wolfgang. *Pergamon: Geschichte und Bauten, funde und Erforschung einer antiken Metropole*. Cologne: Du Mont, 1988.

Requena, A. "Evidencia de Tuberculosis en la America Precolombiana," *Acta Venezolana* 1 (1946) 1-20.

Remus, H. *Pagan-Christian Conflict over Miracle in the Second Century*. Cambridge, Mass.: Philadelphia Patristic Foundation 1983.

Renfrew, Jane M. "Fruits from Ancient Iraq: The Paleoethnobotanical Finds," *Bulletin of Sumerian Agriculture* 3 (1987) 157-61.

Ritter, E. "Magical Expert = (*Ašipu*) and Physician (= *Asû*): Notes on Complementary Professions in Babylonian Medicine," in H. G. Güterbock and T. Jacobsen, eds., *Studies in Honor of*

Benno Landsberger on his 75th Birthday, April 21, 1965. AS 16; Chicago: U. of Chicago, 1965, 299-321.

Robbins, S. L. and R. S. Cotran. *The Pathologic Basis of Disease.* Philadelphia: Saunders, 1979.

Robertson, E. "The Urim and Tummim; What were They?" *VT* 14 (1964) 67-74.

Roebuck, Carl. *Corinth XIV: The Asklepieion and Lerna.* Princeton: The American School of Classical Studies at Athens, 1951.

Römer,W. H. Ph. "Einige Beobachtungen zur Göttin Nini(n)sina auf Grund von Quellen der Ur-III Zeit und der Altbabylonischen Periode, " in M. Dietrich and W. Röllig, eds., *lišān-mithurti-Festschrift W. von Soden.* AOAT 1; Kevelaer/Neukirchen Vluyn, 1969, pp. 279-305.

Rosner, F. *Medicine in the Bible and in the Talmud: Selections from the Classical Jewish Sources.* New York: Ktav, 1977.

Rotberg, R. I. and T. K. Rabb. *Hunger and History.* Cambridge: Cambridge University Press, 1983.

Rouse, I. *Migrations in Prehistory.* New Haven: Yale, 1986.

Rouse, W. H. D. *Greek Votive Offerings.* Cambridge: Cambridge University Press, 1902.

Salama, N. and A. Hilmy. "An Ancient Egyptian Skull and a Mandible Showing Cysts," *British Dental Journal* 90 (1951) 17-18.

Sallares, Robert. *The Ecology of the Ancient Greek World.* Ithaca: Cornell, 1991.

Sasson, J. "Circumcision in the Ancient Near East," *JBL* 85 (1966) 473-6.

Sawyer, J. F. A. "A Note on the Etymology of *ṣaraʿat*," *VT* 26 (1976) 241-45.

Scarry, E. *The Body in Pain: The Making and Unmaking of the World.* Oxford:Clarendon, 1985.

Schiffman, L. H. "Exclusion from the Sanctuary and the City of the Sanctuary in the Temple Scroll," *HAR* 9 (1985) 301-320.

Schmid, E. *Atlas of Animal Bones for Prehistorians, Archaeologists and Quaternary Geologists.* Amsterdam: Elsevier, 1972.

Schwabe, C. W. *Cattle, Priests and Progress in Medicine.* Minneapolis: U. of Minnesota Press, 1978.

Scurlock, Jo Ann. "Magical Means of Dealing with Ghosts in Ancient Mesopotamia," Ph.D. Dissertation, University of Chicago, 1987.

Seybold, K. *Das Gebet des Kranken im Alten Testament.* Stuttgart: Kohlhammer, 1973 .

_____ , and U. B. Mueller. *Sickness and Healing.* Trans. D. W. Stott; Nashville: Abingdon, 1978.

Shapiro, S. E. "Rhetoric as Ideology Critique: The Gadamer-Habermas Debate Reinvented," *JAAR* 62 (1, 1994) 123-150.

Shatzmiller, J. "Doctors and Medical Practice in Germany around the Year 1200:The Evidence of the *Sefer Hasidim*," *JJS* 33 (1982) 583-93.

Short, A. R. *The Bible and Modern Medicine.* London: Paternoster Press, 1953.

Siegel, S. C. "History of Asthma Death from Antiquity," *Journal of Allergy and Clinical Immunology* 80 (1987) 458-62.

Sigerist, Henry E. *A History of Medicine.* Oxford: Clarendon, 1987.

Sigrist, M. "On the Bite of a Dog," in J. H. Marks and R. M. Good, *Love and Death in the Ancient Near East: Essays in Honor of Marvin H. Pope.* Guilford, CT: Four Quarters, 1987, 85-88.

Sillen, Andrew. "Dietary Reconstruction and Near Eastern Archaeology," *Expedition* 28 (2, 1986) 16-22.

_____ , and Patricia Smith. "Weaning Patterns are Reflected in Strontium-Calcium Ratios of Juvenile Skeletons," *Journal of Archaeological Science* 11 (1984) 237-45.

Simons, R. C. and H. P. Pardes, eds. *Understanding Human Behavior in Health and Illness.* Baltimore: Williams and Wilkins, 1977.

Smith, J. Z. *To Take Place:Toward Theory in Ritual.* Chicago: U. of Chicago, 1987.

Smith, Patricia. "The Physical Characteristics and Biological Affinities of the MB I Skeletal Remains from Jebel Qa'aqir," *BASOR* 245 (1982) 65-73.

_____. "Evolutionary Trends in Pre-Agricultural Populations," *Rivista di Antropologia* LXVI Suppl. (1988) 281-94.

_____, and B. Peretz. "Hypoplasia and Health Status: A Comparison of two Lifestyles," *Human Evolution* 1 (6, 1986) 535-544.

_____, R. A. Bloom, and J. Berkowitz. "Diachronic Trends in Humeral Cortical Thickness of Near Eastern Populations," *Journal of Human Evolution* 13 (1984) 603-611.

Snell, D. "Plagues and Peoples in Mesopotamia," *JANES* 14 (1982) 89-96.

Snijders, L.A. "The Meaning of זר in the Old Testament," *OTS* 10 (1954) 1-154.

Sognnaes, R. F. "Histological Evidence of Developmental Lesions in Teeth Originating from Paleolithic, Pre-historic and Ancient Times," *American Journal of Pathology* 32 (1956) 547-77.

Sollberger, E. "Two Kassite Votive Inscriptions," *JAOS* 88 (1968) 192-193.

Speiser, E. "Authority and Law in Mesopotamia," *JAOS Suppl.* 17 (1954) 8-15.

Stager, L. E. "The Archaeology of the Family in Ancient Israel," *BASOR* 260 (1985) 1-35.

Steinbock, R. T. *Paleopathological Diagnosis and Interpretation of Bone Diseases in Ancient Human Populations.* New York, 1976.

Stewart, T. D. "Stone Age Skull Surgery: A General Review with Emphasis on the New World," *Smithsonian Institution Annual Report for 1957* (1958) 469-91.

_____. "The Effects of Pathology on Skeletal Populations," *AJPA* 30 (1969) 443-50.

Stol, M. *Epilepsy in Babylonia.* Broomall, PA: Styx, 1993.

Struckmann, R. *Important Medical Centers in Antiquity: Epidaurus and Corinth*. Athens: Editions Kasas, 1979.

Sullivan, L. E. ed., *Healing and Restoring Health and Medicine in the World's Religious Traditions*. New York:Macmillan, 1989.

Sussman, Max. "Sickness and Disease," *The Anchor Bible Dictionary* New York: Doubleday, 1992; 6:6-15.

Szpunar, C. B., J. B. Lambert, and J. E. Buikstra. "Analysis of Excavated Bone by Atomic Absorption," *AJPA* 48 (1978) 199-202.

Tabor, D. "Babylonian Lecanomancy: An Ancient Text on the Spreading of Oil on Water," *Journal of Colloid and Interface Science* 75 (1, 1980) 240-45.

Taylor, P. E. *Border Healing Woman*. Austin: U. of Texas, 1981.

Thomsen, Marie-Louise. *Zauberdiagnose und Schwarze Magie in Mesopotamien*. Carsten Niebuhr Institute of Ancient Near Eastern Studies, 2; Copenhagen: Museum Tusculanum, 1987.

Thompson, R. C. *Assyrian Medical Texts*. Oxford: Clarendon, 1923.

Tomlinson, R. A. *Greek Sanctuaries*. New York: St. Martin's Press, 1976.

Trusen, J. P. *Sitten, Gebräuche und Krankheiten der alten Hebräer*. Breslau: Wilh. Gottl. Korn., 1973.

Turner, Harold W. *From Temple to Meeting House*. The Hague: Mouton, 1979.

Vaillant, G. E. *The Natural History of Alcoholism: Causes, Patterns and Paths to Recovery*. Cambridge, Mass.: Harvard, 1983.

van der Toorn, K. *Sin and Sanction in Israel and Mesopotamia*. Assen/Maastricht: Van Gorcum, 1985.

_____ , and C. Houtman, "David and the Ark," *JBL* 113 (2, 1994) 209-231.

van Verk, G. N. *Some Statistical Procedures for the Investigation of Prehistoric Human Skeletal Material*. Groningen: Rijksuniversiteit, 1970.

Vernant, J. et al. "Symptômes, signes, écritures en Mésopotamie ancienne," *Divination et Rationalité* (1974) 70-196.

Waldron, H. A. , A. Mackie and A. Townshend. "The Lead Content of some Romano-British Bones," *Archaeometry* 8 (1976) 221-227.

Wallace, J. D. *Diseases of Exotic Animals*. Philadelphia: Saunders, 1983.

Walton, A. *The Cult of Asklepios*. Ithaca: Cornell University Press, 1894.

Watty, W. W. "Man and Healing: A Biblical and Theological View," *Point* 10 (2, 1981) 147-60.

Wells, C. *Bones, Bodies and Disease*. London: Thames & Hudson, 1964.

Westermann, C. "Heilung und Heil in der Gemeinde aus der Sicht des Alten Testament," *WzM* 27 (1975) 1-12.

White, G., D. J. Bradley and A. U. White. *Drawers of Water: Domestic Water Use in East Africa*. Chicago: U. of Chicago, 1984.

White, W. "Diagnostic Principles of Assyrian Medical Texts," Paper presented at the International Congress of Orientalists, U. of Michigan, Ann Arbor, August 16, 1967 (1967) .

_____ . "An Assyrian Physician's *Vade Mecum*," *Clio Medica* 4 (1969) 159-71.

Wild, R. A. *Water in the Cultic Worship of Isis and Serapis*. Leiden:Brill, 1981.

Wilkinson, J. "Leprosy and Leviticus:A Problem of Semantics and Translation," *Scottish Journal of Theology* 31 (1978) 153-166.

_____ . "Leprosy and Leviticus:The Problem of Description and Identification,"*Scottish Journal of Theology* 30 (1977) 153-69.

Wiseman, D. J. "Medicine in the Old Testament World," Pages 13-42 in B. Palmer, ed., *Medicine and the Bible*. Exeter: Paternoster Press, 1986.

Witty, Robert G. *Divine Healing*. Nashville: Broadman, 1989.

World Health Organization. *Expert Committee on Leprosy Technical Report Series 71*; Geneva, 1953.

Zias, Joseph. "Three Trephinated Skulls from Jericho," *BASOR* 246 (1982) 55-58.

_____ . "Death and Disease in Ancient Israel," *BA* 54 (3, 1991) 146-59.

Ziegenaus, O. and G. de Luca, *Das Asklepieion* 1-2; *Altertümer von Pergamon* XI; Berlin: De Gruyter, 1968-75.

Zivanovic, Srboljub. *Ancient Diseases: The Elements of Palaeopathology*. Trans. by L. F. Edwards; New York: Pica, 1982.

INDICES

GREEK

Aelianus

De Natura Animalium

Fragmenta

Aristides

Oratio(nes)

Aristophanes

Plutus

Corinth Inscriptions

Diocles

Hypotyposeis

Epidauros Stele (T. 423)

QUMRAN

1QSa II:4-9   376
11QTemple 45   323-24

SUMERIAN

Forerunners to Udug-hul (Geller, 1985)
24-25:93-94   106

Kurigalzu D   115n

**Nazi-maruttaš
inscription**, Sollberger,
JAOS (1968)
ll. 1, 14-25   205-06

OECT
5, 8   111

RIME
E4 1.7.2001: 3   106
E4 1.10.6   103
E4 2.13.22:3   107

SRT
6   104, 223
7   104, 223

TCL
5   169

UGARITIC

KTU
1.16 V 10   239
1.16 VI 1-14   240
1.100   342
1.107   342

B. TERMS

Akkadian

arua, 176
asû, 106, 109,128, 142-72
ašipu, 106, 110, 128, 142-72
bārû, 110, 168-72
qāt DN, 130-37
saḫaršubbû, 129, 311
šangû, 125-27, 212, 215
su'alu, 146n

Greek

εὐχή, 57